THE CONSEQUENCES
OF
THE COVENANT

SUPPLEMENTS
TO
NOVUM TESTAMENTUM

VOLUME XX

LEIDEN
E. J. BRILL
1970

THE CONSEQUENCES
OF
THE COVENANT

BY

GEORGE WESLEY BUCHANAN

LEIDEN
E. J. BRILL
1970

To
MORTON SMITH
Scholar, Teacher, Friend

TABLE OF CONTENTS

PREFACE

This book is the result of a very practical way of thinking that is most obvious when studying the meanings of words. In order to learn, for instance, whether an expression has a literal or metaphorical meaning, the literature related to Christian origins is studied with an effort to visualize the events in their own geographical and cultural situations. The concepts thought to be the most important have been examined with the assumption that the author was able to communicate clearly to people of his day, using very ordinary expressions with ordinary meanings. This does not always prove to be the case, but it is the place where study begins. *E.g.*, a principality would be expected, first of all, to be the territory ruled by a prince and a kingdom, the country governed by a king. Life and death are first thought to describe conditions related to breathing and pulse rate, and walking, to locomotion on foot. In many cases, the text makes very good sense when understood in its most elementary meaning, but in order to appreciate even its simple meaning, it is necessary to know many everyday practices and customs related to community living, hospitality, war, politics, economics, labor, and family life. This type of study deals with topography, natural resources, natural boundaries, and other practical considerations necessary for national existence, security, and well being.

Sometimes simple meanings do not make sense. From a literal point of view, for instance, corpses cannot bury corpses; people cannot be born twice; and hills do not leap for joy. It is at that point that as many related expressions as possible must be studied to learn precisely what the metaphorical meaning of the term must be. This is learned by comparing contexts and looking for possible non-literal meanings that make sense used as analogies for the literal meaning. If, for example, the term "harvesting" were used metaphorically to describe gathering spoils after victory in war, a knowledge of farming practices in the Ancient Near East would be important for appreciating the analogy. If "walking" were used to mean observance of the law, then an acquaintance with the nomadic nature of the Near Eastern patriarchs would be necessary to visualize the reason for transferring the meaning of daily loco-

motion on foot to daily observance of the law. The book is not
limited to the meanings of words, but the manner of learning word-
meanings illustrates the approach that is generally made in dealing
with historical problems.

Because the faith of ancient Israelites and their later Samaritan,
Jewish, and Christian posterity was very closely related to land,
politics, law, literature, community living, and worship; and because
life's meaning was interpreted in relationship to God's covenant
with his people Israel; this study will show various consequences
of the covenant on the history, politics, faith, and ethical behavior
of the chosen people from the beginning of the OT record until
NT times. The consequences seen will be presented in two basic
areas: The first topic will deal with the relationship of the covenant
to the Land of Palestine,[1] the community called to be a nation,
and its consequent activities in relationship to other nations. The
second area involves the law related to the covenant and its
consequences in liturgical practices, the formation of sects, and
common sectarian practices. This area in its origin is more closely
related to the diaspora than to the promised land.

Although these chapters do not pretend to show all of the
consequences of the covenant, the range of subject matter is quite
broad. Different chapters could be studied as units without reading
all of the rest of the book. The reason this is possible is that the
book represents an early stage in a projected study that some time
in the distant future would expand each chapter into a separate
volume. Time will tell whether the larger project will ever be
completed or not, but in the meantime, the present survey will
expose one stage in an attempt to understand the practical bases
upon which later Judaism and Christianity have been established.
Scholarly reactions to this book may help correct, clarify, and
direct further research in this area. Those devoted to abstractions
and metaphysics may not enjoy a book dealing with the small
everyday details with which this study is concerned, but others who
understand better objects they can visualize may find here some
answers to practical questions they have previously asked. They
may also find unanswered questions which they, themselves, can
answer adequately. Whenever either discovery is made, the book

---

[1] Palestine is not a biblical name for the promised land, but it is used to
distinguish it from modern Israel, whose boundaries vary but not in exactly the
same directions in which the boundaries of Canaan were originally extended.

will have fulfilled its purpose, which is intended to stimulate analysis more than to confirm well known views. After customs and doctrines are understood in context, the task of relating them to twentieth century faith and ethics is still to be done, but that will not be attempted here.

Interest in biblical research has been stimulated and guided by several scholars at Drew University, Hebrew Union College, and Hebrew University, but the two professors who have had the most influence on my research and writing are Dr. William Reuben Farmer and Dr. Morton Smith, both of whom were on the faculty of the graduate school at Drew University while I was engaged in graduate studies there. Both have continued to encourage and criticize my research in helpful ways, and both are scholars whose personal friendship has meant much to me. Prof. Farmer's greatest influence in this book is reflected in the first two chapters, relating faith to politics and history. Prof. Smith's influence is reflected in every chapter, and it is to him that this book is dedicated. It was he who stimulated me to study languages extensively and to seek to master the vast amount of extra-canonical literature necessary for understanding the meaning of the scriptural text. Without his motivation and guidance I could never have recognized the problems analyzed here.

Several scholars have read parts of this book in some stage. Except for chapter 3, Professors Farmer and Smith read the whole manuscript in the first draft and made many helpful suggestions for improvement. In Israel Prof. David Flusser read the entire book and was very helpful in many ways during the year we were together. Rav. Z. W. Gotthold read chapters 1, 2, and 4; Dr. Hans Kosmala read chapters 5-8; and Dr. Shemuel Safrai read chapters 5 and 6. All of these spent a great deal of time discussing various Jewish customs with me. For their kindness and scholarly helpfulness I am very grateful. Much of the material they discussed with me has been extensively rewritten. and for any mistokes which it now contains, I only am responsible.

Jewish studies at Hebrew Union College were undertaken with the aid of fellowships provided by the Louis J. and Mary E. Horowitz Foundation and the S. H. Scheuer Foundation. Mr. Scheuer's kindness extended beyond the provision of a fellowship and provided further financial aid necessary to remove other obstacles to research. Archaeological studies in Jordan in the summer of 1957 were accomplished with the aid of a grant from the Bollingen Foundation. Research on geography and topography in Syria, Lebanon, Jordan, and Israel was done with the aid of a grant from the American Association of Theological Schools during the summer of 1966. The academic year, 1966-67, was spent in Israel, studying and rewriting this book with the aid of a Hebrew Union College Biblical and Archaeological School fellowship. I appreciate all of this support very much.

The list of colleagues, students, professors, and other friends to whom I am indebted in various ways is too long to list but not too long to remember. I hope all of them who read this book will realize their contribution and my appreciation for their friendship.

Wm. B. Eerdmans Publishing Co. has granted permission to use material originally prepared for an article, "Essenes," for the new edition of *The International Standard Bible Encyclopedia*. *Revue de Qumran* has permitted me to use again material that appeared in "The Role of Purity in the Structure of the Essene Sect," *Revue de Qumran* 4 (1963), 397-406. Material from these articles was used here in chapter 7, "Covenantal Sectarianism," and will be noted in the footnotes there. The same is true for chapter 2, "The Kingdom of God," which has brought up to date material previously published in the introduction to the reprinting of R. H. Charles, *Eschatology: The Doctrine of a Future Life in Israel, Judaism and Christianity* (New York: Schocken Books, c1963), i-xxx. Schocken Books, Inc. has granted permission for this use. A part of chapter I was condensed for prior publication as an essay, "Sabbatical Eschatology," for *Christian News from Israel*, 18 (1967), 49-55, with the understanding that it would later appear also in this book. I am grateful to all of these companies for their generosity.

September 1, 1968

ABBREVIATIONS

Adv. Haer.	Irenaeus, *Against Heresies*
Adv. Marc.	Tertullian, *Against Marcion*
Ant.	Josephus, *Antiquities of the Jews*
Apoc. Mos.	Apocalypse of Moses
Apos. Cons.	Apostolic Constitutions
ATR	*Anglican Theological Review*
BA	*Biblical Archaeologist*
BASOR	*Bulletin of the American Schools of Oriental Research*
BJ	Josephus, *Wars of the Jews*
BK	Baba Kama
BS	*Bibliotheca Sacra*
Cat.	Cyril of Jerusalem, *Catecheses*
Cant. R.	Song of Solomon Rabba
CBQ	*Catholic Biblical Quarterly*
CDC	Damascus Document (Zadokite Document)
CH	*Canones Hippoliti*
Clem. Hom.	Clementine Homilies
Clem. Rec.	Clementine Recognitions
Conf.	Philo, *De Confusione Linguarum*
Congr.	Philo, *De Congressu Quaerendae Eriditionis Gratia*
Decal.	Philo, *De Decalogo*
De Fuga	Philo, *De Fuga et Inventione*
Deus	Philo, *Quod Deus sit Immutabilis*
EB	*Encyclopaedia Britannica*
Ebr.	Philo, *De Ebrietate*
ECO	Egyptian Church Order
Ep. Barn.	Epistle of Barnabas
ETL	*Ephemerides Theologicae Lovanienses*
Haer.	Epiphanius, *Heresies*
HE	Eusebius, *The Ecclesiastical History*
HTR	*Harvard Theological Review*
HUCA	*Hebrew Union College Annual*
Hyp.	Philo, *Hypothetica*
ICC	*International Critical Commentary*
IEJ	*Israel Exploration Journal*
1Q, 4Q, *et al.*	Caves 1, 4, *et al.* of Qumran
1QM	Cave 1, War Scroll
JBK	Jerusalem Talmud, Baba Kama
JBik.	Jerusalem Talmud, Bikkurim
JBL	*Journal of Biblical Literature*
JE	*Jewish Encyclopedia*
JJS	*Journal of Jewish Studies*
JNES	*Journal of Near Eastern Studies*
JQR	*Jewish Quarterly Review*
JSS	*Journal of Semitic Studies*
JTaan.	Jerusalem Talmud, Taanith
LA	*Liber Annus*
Leg.	Philo, *De Legatione ad Gaium*

Leg. All.	Philo, *Legum Allegoria*
Mid. Ps.	Midrash on Psalms
Mig.	Philo, *De Migratione Abrahami*
MPG	Migne, *Patrologia Graeca*
Nat. Hist.	Pliny, *Natural History*
Nov.	*Novum Testamentum*
NT	New Testament
NTS	*New Testament Studies*
Num. R.	Numbers Rabba
Op.	Philo, *De Opificio Mundi*
OS	*Oudtestamentische Studien*
OT	Old Testament
Ox. Pap.	Oxyrhynchus Papyris
PEQ	*Palestine Exploration Quarterly*
PR	Pesikta Rabbati
PRE	Pesikta de Rabbi Eliezer
PRK	Pesikta de Rav Kahana
Praem.	Philo, *De Praemiis et Poenis*
Prob.	Philo, *Quod Omnis Probus Liber Sit*
RH	Rosh Ha-Shanah
RQ	*Revue de Qumran*
RSR	*Recherches de Science Religieuse*
San.	Sanhedrin
SO	Sibylline Oracles
Spec.	Philo, *De Specialibus Legibus*
ST	*Studia Theologica*
Targ. Isa.	Targum on Isaiah
TDNT	The Theological Dictionary of the New Testament
T. Gad	Testament of Gad in the Testaments of the Twelve Patriarchs
TL	*Theologische Literaturzeitung*
TWNT	Theologisches Wörterbuch zum Neuen Testament
UJE	*The Universal Jewish Encyclopedia*
ZDPV	*Zeitschrift des deutschen Palästina Vereins*
ZNTW	*Zeitschrift für die Neutestamentliche Wissenschaft*

CHAPTER ONE

THE THEOLOGY OF CONQUEST

INTRODUCTION

The God of armies.—The consequences of Israel's covenant with
the Lord were extensive. The agreement was that the Lord would
be Israel's God, and Israel, in turn, would be the Lord's people.
Being the Lord's people meant understanding God's nature,
learning his will, and following his commandments. Israel believed,
on the one hand, that God was just, and on the other hand, that
he had chosen Israel as his special people. This meant that God
was obligated by the covenant to direct international affairs so
that other nations would deserve more punishment than Israel
and allow Israel to become the greatest of all peoples. There could
be no side-stepping the demands of justice; therefore Israel would
have to suffer for all her sins as did the nations of the world, but
the punishment would come at such times and in such ways as
would chasten Israel but not destroy her. On the other hand, the
nations would be punished in such ways and at such times as
would be most expedient for Israel. Like other nations of antiquity,
Israel believed that the nation's deity won the nation's wars.[1]
For Israel, Jehovah [2] was the God who directed the affairs and
destiny of his chosen people. He was the God of armies [3] who
decisively disclosed his character and intention at the Reed Sea
when he delivered his chosen people from the hand of Pharaoh
and set them free to return to the land which he had promised

---

[1] Herodotus described military victories which he attributed to divine
intervention: The storm from Pelion destroyed many of Xerxes' ships to
equalize the forces between the Persians and Greeks (VIII. 12-13). Also
when a great ebb tide lured the Persians to leave their boats and reach Pallene
on swampy ground, they were less than halfway to shore, when a mammoth
flood tide drowned them or left them helpless for the soldiers of Pallene to
slay. This was the work of the god, Poseidon, whose temple the Persians
had profaned (VIII. 129).

[2] Jehovah will be the pronunciation used here. See Appendix I for its
justification.

[3] One of the first to call attention to holy war theology (the active aspect
of conquest theology) in Israel was G. von Rad, *Der Heilige Krieg im alten
Israel* (Zürich, 1951).

them as an inheritance by a covenant previously made with their father Abraham.[1]

The God of armies required two different types of ethics of his chosen people: 1) When they had sinned, they had to suffer until their sins had been atoned; and 2) After they had been freed from sin, they were sometimes obligated to take up arms against the enemy. Then the Lord would strengthen their hand in battle so that they would be victorious. Whenever Israel's position was unfavorable, she was faced with the question: should she fight or suffer? Sometimes she chose one course of action and sometimes the other. Both had been successful. The exodus from Egypt, the conquest of Palestine,[2] and the Maccabean revolt were testimonies for the success of activistic ethics;[3] and the exodus from Babylon proved the value of suffering passively.[4] Although these were often intermingled, the survey here will show first the active ethics in force and then the passive ethics.

ACTIVISTIC ETHICS

The theology of holy war.—Warfare for Israel was a religious practice, undertaken at God's command. If Israelites were free from sin, they could attack with confidence any nation with only a small, poorly armed troop, because the Lord went forth with them to battle. He it was who won the victory for them.[5] Careful rules were given for the way to attack a city, dispose of the spoil, and maintain Israel's purity.[6] Military camps were maintained according to purity rules so that the Lord could be present with his armies. This meant that latrines were placed two thousand cubits from camp, and children who were not yet responsible for their toilet habits were not allowed in camp. Males who had not been cleansed from seminal discharges were not admitted into

---

[1] Gen 12:1-3; 15:1-6, 18-19.

[2] Here used to mean the promised land. It is not a biblical name but the name "Israel" might be confused with modern Israel whose borders are different.

[3] Although victory was preceded by slavery, hardship, and the slaughtering of the infant males before the exodus and persecution before the Maccabean revolt.

[4] But not without the use of diplomacy and influence to help the Persians, on the one hand, and sabotage the Babylonians, on the other. They understood before the event the effect of Cyrus' victory on the Jews in Babylonia.

[5] Dt. 20 : 1-4.

[6] Dt. 20 : 5-18; 21 : 10-14.

camp. Those who were blind, crippled, blemished, or more than ordinarily susceptible to defilement could not accompany the warriors into battle. All soldiers had to be perfect in spirit and body.[1] Priests had specific roles in war, but they did not go into battle to become defiled with the dead or with unclean blood, because the priests were holy (קדושים).[2] Soldiers were reminded before battle that it was God who walked with them into war, together with his military angels (צבאות מלאכים) and army of spirits (צבא רוחיו). God would deliver them and give them the victory.[3] Battle prayers recounted God's victorious acts in war when the people trusted him.[4] After battle soldiers sang the hymn of return, and the next morning washed their garments from the blood of guilty corpses.[5]

Theology in action.—After the required amount of suffering, Moses led the Israelites from Egypt at night, in a well-planned undercover movement. Because advance preparations had been made, there was an adequate supply of unleavened bread that would not spoil. All had eaten a good meal just before they left, and they acquired as much Egyptian wealth as possible. They left at night while the Egyptians were distracted by their own sufferings.[6] The Hebrews left Egypt as armies (צבאותיכם) [7] equipped for battle (חמשים).[8] The Lord's presence was indicated by a continually burning fire whose smoke was visible from a distance as a pillar

---

[1] 1QM 7 : 2-7; Dt. 23 : 10-15; Num. 35 : 1-5.

[2] 1QM 7 : 9-9 : 9; 15 : 4-10; 18 : 6-9.

[3] 1QM 10 : 3-12; 12 : 1-9; 17 : 6-9.

[4] 1QM 11 : 1-12.

[5] 1QM 14 : 2-3.

[6] Ex. 11 : 1-9; 12 : 8-39; Rabbi Tanḥuma said that the three days of darkness were for the Egyptians only. For the Hebrews it was light. It happened just before the exodus to provide for the Hebrews access to the houses of the Egyptians so that Israelites could know where the wealth of Egypt was and ask to "borrow" it (*Bo'*, 20a-20b).

[7] Ex. 12 : 17. צבאות was used as an ascription of the Lord (יהוה) 297 times in the OT. It was employed only in five passages (Ex. 12 : 4; Dt. 20 : 9; I Kgs. 2 : 5; Ps. 68 : 13; and Jer. 3 : 19) in the entire OT that do not describe Jehovah. Of these instances, Ex. 12 : 41 told about the Hebrews leaving Egypt with Moses, and might possibly be rendered "multitudes," but they were armed for battle (13 : 18). The other examples refer to troops or armies. The Akkadian *ṣabu* means "soldier," R. Labat, *Manuel d'Epigraphie Accadienne* (Paris, 1952), 179.

[8] Ex. 13 : 18. Jos., *Contra Apion* 2 : 17 said Moses was the general of an army.

of cloud during the day and whose flame was easily seen as a pillar of fire at night. [1] Egyptians pursued, but the forces of nature worked against them as the Lord directed, so they were drowned in the sea, while Israel escaped securely on the east side of the

---

[1] Ex. 13 : 21-22. The burning fire was taken from Egypt with the Israelites as a "pillar of cloud by day and a pillar of fire by night" (Ex. 13 : 21-22; 14 : 19-24; Neh. 9 : 12). In the wilderness, Israelites worshipped when Moses went into the tent of meeting and they saw a pillar of cloud (i.e. smoke). Then the Lord promised Moses that his "presence" would go with Israel and give the people "rest" (Ex. 33 : 7-14; cf. Num. 12 : 4-8; 14 : 14). When the ark of the Lord was brought into the city of David and set inside the tent provided for it, sacrifices and burnt offerings were placed before the Lord (Il Sam. 16-19). This happened after the Lord had given David "rest" from all his enemies (II Sam. 7 : 1). After the temple was built, Solomon's prayer confessed that heaven and the highest heaven could not contain the Lord, but he prayed that the Lord would pay attention day and night to the "house" where the Lord's name was to dwell (I Kgs. 8 : 27-29). From then on, so long as the temple was functioning, there was kept a fire on the altar day and night for continual burnt offerings and other offerings. The pillar of fire and cloud continued to signify the presence of the Lord. As the Lord appeared to Moses in a thick cloud on Mt. Sinai (Ex. 19 : 1-25) or in the tent of meeting (Ex. 33 : 7-14; Num. 12 : 4-8), so he appeared to the prophet Isaiah in the temple which was filled with smoke (Isa. 6 : 4) when there were burning coals on the altar (Isa 6:6), and again to Ezekiel in a great cloud and flashing fire (Ezek 1:4, 26-27) apparently in the temple. In Isaiah's dream of a restored Jerusalem, he promised that the Lord would create a cloud by day and smoke and the shining of a flaming fire at night over Mt. Zion and her assemblies (Isa 4:5). The rabbis held that when the temple was not functioning God's presence did not cease being with his people. The Shekinah went with them (Mekilta, *Pisha* 14 : 85-106) into captivity and returned with them. It would be with them even after the fall of Jerusalem in 70 A.D. (14 : 1-5-111). When the temple did not exist to keep the pillar of cloud and fire over Mt. Zion, then the congregation was itself evidence of the Lord's presence; wherever ten persons assembled in a meeting, the Shekinah was with them. Rabbis found scriptural justification for fewer than ten: for three, two, and even one person was enough to claim the divine presence (Mekilta, *Bahodesh* 11 : 42-52). It was against this background that Jesus promised that wherever two or three were gathered in his name, he would be in their midst (Mt. 18 : 20). But the idea that God's presence was evident wherever the congregation was did not negate the belief that the congregation at best was gathered in the temple. Even though it was not permitted to kindle a fire on the Sabbath, it was permitted to kindle a fire in the temple when the temple was standing, so that sacrifices might be offered continually and so that there might always be a pillar of cloud by day and a pillar of fire by night (Mekilta, *Shabbata* 2 : 34-54). In some Jewish temples and some Christian churches the large altar where the animals were roasted no longer exists, but lights are kept burning over the altar in the front of the building where the altar of incense used to be. These are only slight memorials of the huge bonfires that formerly filled the temple with smoke. But it is still intended to call attention to the real presence.

Reed Sea.[1] The poet described the Lord as a Man of War (יהוה איש
מלחמה),[2] who controlled the forces of nature,[3] performed miracles,[4] and redeemed his people so that they could return to the
promised land.[5] In similar acts of valor and faith, Joshua captured
Jericho,[6] Gideon conquered the camp of the Midianites with three
hundred men,[7] and Jonathan with his armor bearer overthrew a
garrison.[8] When Israel was hard pressed and without arms, the
soldiers of Deborah and Barak ventured to fight against the
mighty Sisera in the Valley of Jezreel.[9] The victory seemed
certain for Israel's enemies, but the Lord intervened:

"From heaven fought the stars,
   from their courses they fought against Sisera.
The river Kishon swept them away." [10]

As the rising tide at the Reed Sea, so the deluge in the Valley of
Jezreel swallowed up Israel's enemies. In the end even Sisera was
slain.[11] The poem concluded:

"Thus may all your enemies be destroyed, Jehovah!
   but those who love him like the rising of the sun in its might." [12]

When David fought to gain and expand his kingdom, he regularly
consulted Jehovah, either directly,[13] or through a priest.[14] His two
priests were Abiathar and Zadok,[15] but at the death of David,

---

[1] Ex. 14 : 23-31.
[2] Ex. 15 : 3.
[3] Ex. 15 : 10-12.
[4] Ex. 15 : 11.
[5] Ex. 15 : 16-18.
[6] Josh. 6.
[7] Judges 7.
[8] I Sam. 14 : 1-15.
[9] Judges 5 : 1-22.
[10] Judges 5 : 20-21. J. Bloch, *On the Apocalyptic in Judaism*, *JQR* Monograph, no. II (Philadelphia, 1952), 9, noted the similarity between cosmic
upheavals in such OT passages as Isa. 13 : 5-13, but said, "*Unlike* [italics
mine] later apocalyptic writings, early apocalypses evidently dealt not with
the end of the world, but with the end of a period." The relationship Bloch
has shown in his book between apocalyptic literature and nationalism
denies his conclusion that they are different. He has evidently accepted this
from secondary sources without question. Yet, he acknowledged that Jewish
eschatological teachings have their roots in Jewish heritage (57-58).
[11] Judges 5 : 24-30.
[12] Judges 5 : 13.
[13] I Sam. 22 : 4-5.
[14] I Sam. 22 : 6-14; 30 : 7-10.
[15] II Sam. 15 : 24-29, 35; 17 : 15; 19 : 11; 20 : 25; I Chron. 15 : 11; 18 : 16.

Abiathar promoted Adonijah as the new king,[1] whereas Zadok and Nathan supported Solomon.[2] After Solomon became king, it was natural for Zadok and his successors to have the choice positions among the priests of the kingdom. The memory of their priestly status in the time of Solomon continued until NT times when the members of the sect who followed the Damascus Document called themselves the sons of Zadok. Religion and politics were closely related.

The wages of sin.—The God of armies fought the battles of Israel, but victory was not automatic. Sinlessness and faith were requirements for the people if they were to win. Although the Lord was prepared to give them the Land of Canaan, the Israelites doubted that they could take it by their own strength, so they spied out the land, and the Lord swore that all the doubters would perish in the wilderness, leaving only Joshua and Caleb of that generation to enter the land.[3] Moses was also included in the curse.[4] In the wilderness the Lord provided manna, quails, and water,[5] but the people tempted (נסתם) the Lord by their unbelief.[6] Sinfulness did not cease with the wilderness. When they were defeated at the battle of Ai, it was concluded that there was sin in their ranks. Not until the sin had been purged,[7] would Joshua attempt again to take Ai.[8] Saul's failure to establish a dynasty to succeed him was attributed to carelessness about holy war rules [9] and failure to wait dependently for the priest before going into battle.[10] When Ahaz was threatened by the combined forces of Damascus and Ephraim, Isaiah assured him that he would not need to fear if he only had faith and was not upset.[11] This counsel did not advocate war, but it was based on conquest theology. It was

---

[1] I Kgs. 1 : 7-8, 25.

[2] I Kgs. 1 : 7-8, 26-27, 38-48.

[3] Dt. 1 : 19-40.

[4] Dt. 1 : 37; 3 : 23-26. Another explanation for Moses' death before entrance into the land was that he volunteered to accept the sins of the people upon himself if the Lord would only atone for his people (Ex. 32 : 30-34; Num. 14 : 13-35).

[5] Ex. 16 : 1-17 : 7.

[6] Ex. 17 : 7.

[7] Josh. 7 : 11-26.

[8] Josh. 8 : 1-29.

[9] I Sam. 15 : 1-31.

[10] I Sam. 13 : 2-15.

[11] Isa. 7 : 1-16.

God who won Israel's battles, not Assyria.[1] Ahaz did not heed Isaiah's counsel, but instead paid Tiglath-Pileser to capture Damascus and carry off the inhabitants.[2] The price was high, however, since Ahaz was forced to submit to Assyria for that favor.[3] It was only a matter of time after that until Assyria also captured Samaria.[4] The historian explained the fate of the Israelites as the result of their sin against their God who brought them out of the Land of Egypt.[5] Because of Israel's sin,[6] Amos said the day of the Lord would be for them a day of darkness and not light.[7] The Lord would take Israel into exile,[8] leaving only a small remnant.[9] The Lord who brought his people up from Egypt [10] would also punish them if they continued to sin. Israel's only hope was to return, seek the Lord, seek good, and turn away from evil.[11]

In agreement with Amos, Hosea threatened that Israelites would be taken captive into Assyria where they would have to eat food not permitted by dietary laws [12] because they had played the harlot and defiled themselves [13] by worshipping Baals,[14] sacrificing on high places,[15] and worshipping idols.[16] They trusted kings who were not from David's line [17] and worshipped in temples that were not in Jerusalem.[18] They trusted alliances with lovers, namely Assyria and Egypt.[19] Because of her international commitments, Israel would be taken captive,[20] but Judaeans would be delivered without the aid of foreign military powers.[21] One of the

---

[1] Isa. 7 : 17-20.
[2] II Kgs. 17 : 1-6.
[3] II Kgs. 16:10-20.
[4] II Kgs. 17:1-6.
[5] II Kgs. 17 : 1-13.
[6] Amos 2 : 6-12; 3 : 10-12; 6 : 3-6.
[7] Amos 5 : 18-20.
[8] Amos 5 : 27; 6 : 7.
[9] Amos 3 : 12; 5 : 15.
[10] Amos 4:10; 5:14.
[11] Amos 5 : 5, 6, 14, 15.
[12] Hosea 9 : 3.
[13] Hosea 4 : 10; 5 : 3; 6 : 10; 9 : 1-2, 9.
[14] Hosea 2 : 8-13; 9 : 10; 13 : 1.
[15] Hosea 4 : 7-14; 8 : 11; 10 : 7-9.
[16] Hosea 4 : 17; 8 : 3-6; 10 : 5-6; 11 : 2; 13 : 2-3; 14 : 8.
[17] Hosea 8 : 4; 10 : 7.
[18] Hosea 8 : 5.
[19] Hosea 7 : 11; 8 : 9-10; 12 : 1.
[20] Hosea 3 : 1-4; 8 : 13.
[21] Hosea 1 : 7; 11 : 12.

greatest concerns of this pro-Judaic prophet was that Israel's sins
might influence Judah so that she too would require punishment.[1]

Isaiah said Israel fell because of her sins,[2] but he warned Judah
that Zion was also noted for its sin [3] and could therefore expect
similar treatment.[4] Jeremiah agreed that Judah would fall, but
not because of her lack of military fortifications. It was because of
her sin. She had forsaken the Lord, worshipped idols and Baals,
played the harlot, and become defiled.[5] Therefore the enemy from
the North would not only plunder Jerusalem,[6] but also burn the
temple.[7] Those who thought the temple was indestructible had
forgotten that Shiloh was destroyed.[8] Such confidence was naïveté;
now the people of Judah would be taken into exile.[9] This was not
the work of Nebuchadnezzer but of Jehovah.[10] The covenanters
could not resist the Lord's certain justice. He was sure to chasten
his people [11] in just measure.[12] This justice, Jeremiah calculated,
would be measured in terms of indebtedness, slavery, and release.
This is the basis of all later eschatology and will here be given
separate attention, not only as Jeremiah began with it, but as it
influenced later Jewish and Christian literature.[13] For convenience
it will be called "sabbatical eschatology." [14]

---

[1] Hosea 4 : 15; 5 : 5. W. R. Harper, *ICC Hosea* (Edinburgh, c1905),
202-203, believed Hosea was written in the North, but he listed the following
earlier scholars who believed Hosea was Judaean: H. Ewald, *Die Propheten
des Alten Bundes* (1840; 2d ed., 1867; trans. as *Commentary on the Prophets
of the OT* [1875-81], I, 210-214); Jahn, *Einleitung*, II.i. § 94; R. Kittel,
History of the Hebrews (Eng. trs. by J. Taylor, 1875-76), II, 310 f; Knobel,
Prophetismus der Hebräer (1837), II, 155, anm. 5; Maurer, *Commentarius
grammaticus historicus criticus in Prophetas Minores* (1840); *Observat. in
Hoseam*; H. P. Smith, *OT Hist.*, 221 ff., and Wünsche, *Der Prophet Hosea
Übersetzt und erklärt, mit Benutzung der Targumim der jüdischen Ausleger
Raschi Aben Ezra und David Kimchi* (1868), vi-vii.

[2] Isa. 9 : 8-10 : 8; 28 : 1-4.   [3] Isa. 1 : 21-26; 3 : 1-8.

[4] Isa. 3 : 18-4 : 6; 5 : 1-7; 10 : 11; 22 : 1-14.   [5] Jer. 2 : 1-3 : 10.

[6] Jer. 1 : 13-19; 4 : 5-10; 5 : 14-17; 6 : 1-12, 22-30.

[7] Jer. 7 : 1-34; 8 : 18-9 : 26; 22 : 1-30; 32 : 24-44; 34 : 1-7, 17-22; 37 : 6-
10; 38 : 17-23.

[8] Jer. 7 : 4-15; 26 : 4-9.   [9] Jer. 26:18; 13:18-19.

[10] Jer. 5 : 15; 25; 6 : 1-2, 6; 9 : 7-11, 25-26; 16 : 5-16; 19 : 14-15; 21 : 3-6;
25 : 28-29; 40 : 9.

[11] His servant Jacob, Jer. 46 : 27.   [12] Jer. 30 : 11; 46 : 27-28.

[13] For the significance of the sabbath in Near Eastern culture, see J. and
H. Lewy, "The Origin of the Week and the Oldest West Asiatic Calendar,"
HUCA 17 (1942-43), 1-152a. See also R. North, *Sociology of the Biblical
Jubilee* (Rome, 1954).

[14] The basic message of "Sabbatical Eschatology," appeared in an article
by that name in *Christian News in Israel*, 1967.

Sabbatical Eschatology

Sabbatical rules.—An ancient covenanter who loaned money to a fellow Israelite received no interest. The ultimate protection he had for his investment was the right to force the debtor who could not repay in cash to work for him at half wages until the debt had been cancelled. [1] Every sabbatical year, however, creditors were required to release their debtors even if the debt had not been paid.[2] Every forty-nine years marked a jubilee when the trumpet was sounded and not only were debtor-slaves set free but family property that had been sold for financial need was restored to the families of original Israelite owners.[3] These rules insured freedom for covenanters and preservation of their property within the community, whatever their fortune. This concept of justice was later transferred to national terms.

The national debt.—When Israel sinned she was expected to be treated like a covenanter in debt. If she failed to observe sabbath years, then the Lord would enforce the required obligations of rest for the land by removing the people to a foreign country for the number of sabbath years she had overlooked.[4] Jeremiah said that because Israelites did not really let their brothers go on years of release, the Lord would give them a new type of "freedom"— freedom to the sword, pestilence, and famine.[5] Like the individual debtor that could not repay, Israel would be sent into slavery until she had paid double for all her sins.[6] Jeremiah may have predicted that the exiles would return on the seventh year rather than the seventieth, because he bought a field, confident that the captivity would be over within his lifetime.[7] When the expected time passed the exiles may have adjusted their expectation for

---

[1] Dt. 15 : 12-13, 18. He might be released earlier if some relative paid his debt, thus becoming his "redeemer" (גואל) (Lev. 25 : 48-54). In this context the Lord was considered a Redeemer when he paid Israel's debt and restored her to the land. See Jer. 50 : 34 and Ps. 119 : 54.

[2] *Ibid.*

[3] Lev. 25 : 8-10.

[4] Lev. 26 : 27-35, 43-45. R. Eliezer of Modiᶜim said that if Israel kept the Sabbath, the Lord would give her the Land of Israel, the future world, the new world, the kingdom of the house of David, the priesthood, and the Levites (Mekilta, *Vayassaᶜ* 5 : 66-73).

[5] Jer. 34 : 13-20.

[6] Dt. 15 : 18; Jer. 16 : 18.

[7] Jer. 25 : 11-12; 29 : 10-11; 32 : 6-15.

the jubilee year. Although Zerubbabel's return was about forty-nine years, [1] it was exactly seventy years from 587 to 516 B.C. when the temple was completed. It was probably in anticipation of that event or just after it that Jeremiah's number was changed to ten sabbath years to agree with the facts, but the correction was made on Jeremiah's sabbatical logic. The Chronicler accepted the seventy year prophecy and also the sabbatical threat given in Leviticus as Jeremiah's.[2] Zechariah reported a complaint from the people after seventy years had elapsed, because Jeremiah's promise had not been fulfilled.[3] In Babylon II Isaiah foresaw deliverance just ahead. Jews had already paid double for all their sins so the time was ripe to proclaim release (דרור) to the captives.[4] He reasoned that, if release was granted, the term of servitude at half wages had been completed. They had paid double for all their sins.[5]

The national jubilee.—An Isaianic apocalypse anticipated a trumpet blast, as at jubilee, when exiles from Assyria and Egypt would return to Jerusalem.[6] The prophecy was not fulfilled, but after the Maccabean victory, some careful student of scripture who believed this was the real fulfillment of Jeremiah's prophecy, was not perplexed by the delay. He noticed that instead of seventy years about seven times seventy years had elapsed since the captivity. With only slight adjustments the scheme worked out perfectly: seven weeks of years were spent in Babylon,[7] sixty-two weeks of years intervened from the return until a certain covenant was made: $62 + 7 = 69$—only one more week of years until there would be seventy weeks of years—time for the tenth jubilee! One-half week of years later the temple was defiled and sacrifice

---

[1] The first attempt about 538 B.C. was thwarted. J. Klausner, *The Messianic Idea in Israel*, tr. W. F. Stinespring (New York, 1955), 93, erroneously conjectured that "seventy years" meant one generation. He noted that the exile itself was not longer than forty-nine years, but saw no relationship to a jubilee.

[2] II Chron. 36 : 20-21. See also Lev. 26 : 27-35, 43-45.

[3] Zech. 7 : 4-5.

[4] Isa. 40 : 2; 61 : 7.

[5] Dt. 15 : 18; Jer. 16 : 18; Isa. 40 : 1.

[6] Isa. 27 : 13.

[7] From 587 to 538 B.C. when Cyrus decreed that the Jews could return to Jerusalem was exactly 49 years. The fact that the plans were interrupted did not effect Daniel's dating.

stopped.[1] Before the second half week of years was over the temple had been cleansed.[2] The end that Daniel "predicted" was the end of the foreign control of the temple and the land. According to his interpretation of the Torah and Jeremiah, this was the national jubilee when the promised land was restored to its "original" owners, the seed of Abraham. With the Maccabean victory, freedom was proclaimed throughout the land; the land had rest.[3] The Book of Jubilees and Pseudo-Jonathan narrated the history of Israel from creation until the "anticipated" entrance into the promised land so that it would occur on the jubilee of jubilee years. The Assumption of Moses, *mutatis mutandis*, followed the same pattern of eschatology.[4] Zechariah announced that Israel's enemies would be overthrown and her king enter in procession when the Lord sounded the trumpet, when he set the captives free, and when he restored them double, as at jubilee.[5]

Later eschatology.—After Daniel, II Isaiah, and Jeremiah had been accepted as sacred scripture, later Jews and Christians who understood themselves to be in captivity looked forward to a release in the same terms as those prophets. Some fragments in cave II near Qumran disclosed the anticipation of a jubilee that would come at the end of days for the captives (לאח]רית הימים על שבויים), the sons of light, who belonged to the lot of the heritage of Melchizedek (מנחלת מלכי צדק ;גו[רל מל[כי]צדק). Melchizedek was

---

[1] Dan. 9 : 24-27.

[2] Dan. 7 : 25; 8 : 14; 9 : 27; 12 : 7.

[3] Once Daniel is considered *vaticinium ex eventu*, then the Son of Man who would lead the saints of the Most High when both he and they would receive power, honor, and the kingdom (Dan. 7 : 13-28) three and a half years after the temple was defiled (Dan. 8 : 14; 12 : 11) would probably have been Judah the Maccabee. Although the whole kingdom had not been "given" by that time, the divine lot seemed already cast, and the temple had been cleansed and rededicated. Instead of the Maccabees, as some interpret, those who provided "a little help" (Dan. 11 : 34) may have been the Romans, whose commander put an end to the insolence of Antiochus Epiphanes (Dan. 11 : 18; Livy 45 : 1-6), who were called "Kittim" (in Vulgate "Romani" Dan. 11 : 30) whose ships came against Antiochus.

[4] I Mac. 1 : 45-54; 4 : 54. Note also that the Book of Daniel "predicted" no messiah, son of David. That would have been a normal expectation before the Maccabean rebellion, but not after the Hasmonean dynasty had been established. Klausner, *Op. cit.*, 232, upheld the usual view that Daniel was written just before the Maccabean revolt. For the details of counting years for these books, see E. Weisenberg, "The Jubilee of Jubilees," *RQ* 3 (1961), 3-40.

[5] Zech. 9 : 1-14.

expected to come to proclaim release to them (וקרא להמה דרר)
and atonement for their sins. This was to be in the year of the last
jubilee (בשנת היובל האחׄרׄוׄן). It was the appointed time of favor
for Melchizedek (שנת רצון למלכי צדק).[1] At that time God would
judge his people and chasten those who showed favoritism to the
wicked that belonged to the lot of Belial. When Melchizedek arose
he would exact vengeance against them on the day of vengeance
in the last days.[2] This would come as a fulfillment of the prophecy
of II Isaiah who foresaw one proclaiming good news and announcing
peace to Zion.[3] The herald of good news was not only the figure,
Melchizedek, but he was also one who had been anointed by the
spirit (המבשר הוׄא מׄשיח הרוׄח).[4]

The message of these small fragments ties together messianic
and eschatological expectations with the figure, Melchizedek, good
news for Zion, release for captives, forgiveness of sins, and peace
—all in the year of the last jubilee. Rabbis said that in the last
jubilee (ביובל האחרון) the son of David would come.[5] This is clearly
national sabbatical eschatology.

IV Ezra said that when the Lord visited the earth, the trumpet
blast would sound and the present age would pass away.[6] Another
prophet foretold a trumpet blast (ܟܒܝ ܗܘܡ ܟܡܐܝܟ), proclaiming

---

[1] Y. Yadin's transcription. The fragments (11Q Melch.) were called to
my attention by Prof. D. Flusser. See his "Melchizedek and the Son of Man,"
Christian News from Israel (April, 1966), 22-29. First published by A.S.
Van der Woude, "Melchizedek als himmlische Erlösergestalt in den neugefundenen eschatologischen Midrashim aus Qumran Höhle XI," *OS* 14 (1965),
354-373. J. A. Fitzmyer, "Further Light on Melchizedek from Qumran
Cave 11," *JBL*, 86 (1967), 29, mentioned that the last jubilee was also
the tenth, meaning the end of the 490 years of Daniel's interpretation.

[2] Van der Woude filled in the lacuna thus: יום הׄהרגה אׄשר ... . But
this statement precedes a quotation from Isa. 52 : 7 and a second from Isa.
61 : 1. II Isaiah's term was נקם (52 : 9) or יום נקם (Isa. 61 : 2). Fitzmeyer,
Op. cit., 39, also objected to Van der Woude's restoration, but offered no
alternative.

[3] Quotation from Isa. 52 : 7.

[4] Yadin's reading, rejected by Fitzmyer who accepted Van der Woude's
initial restoration (p. 40). See Flusser, *Op. cit.*, 29. This is probably from Isa.
61 : 1. Isa. 61 was itself composed in reflection of Lev. 25. The author of
these fragments properly related the two texts. M. was probably a priestly
figure or an Elijah. He was called righteous priest in Suk. 52b, but here he
behaved like a king. Klausner, *Op. cit.*, 515, notes that many anti-Christian
passages in the Talmud say M. was not the Messiah.

[5] San. 97b.

[6] IV Ezra 6 : 23.

in Jerusalem God's visitation of mercy. As a fulfillment of II
Isaiah's prophecy, exiles would be gathered to Jerusalem, and
natural obstacles removed for their return.[1] Rabbis said the Lord
would forgive Israel's debts (חוביגו) on the seventh month, which
is *Tishri*, at the blast of the *shofar*, and just as the Holy One
blessed be He has had mercy (מרחם) on Israel in this age at the
blast of the *shofar*, "also in the future I will have mercy on you
through the *shofar* (על ידי שופר) and bring your redeemed ones
near (ומקרב גאולתכם)." Scriptural proof for this is from Joel 2 : 1:

"Blow the *shofar* in Zion!
Make a noise on my holy mountain!
All those who dwell in the land will tremble,
for the day of Jehovah is coming." [2]

In the Eighteen Benedictions the Lord is urged to "sound the
great trumpet of our freedom and raise the banner to gather in
our exiles."[3] Paul spoke of inheriting the Kingdom of God when
the last trumpet was sounded and the dead would be raised.[4] The
seer who composed the Book of Revelation expected oppression to
end in three and a half years,[5] forty-two months,[6] or one thousand
two hundred and sixty days.[7] When the seventh angel sounded
the trumpet, the kingdoms of the world would become the Kingdom
of the Lord and of his Messiah.[8] The author of Hebrews understood
the entrance into the promised land in terms of a sabbath rest,[9]
just as the Lord promised Moses that his "presence" would go
with Israel and give the people "rest"[10] and promised David that
he would establish the throne of his kingdom forever and give
David "rest" from all his enemies.[11] Those who asked Jesus when
the end of the age would come probably wondered how long they
had been in bondage and when the captivity would end. When
would the jubilee year arrive?[12] Expressions like "the end of the

---

[1] Ps. of Sol. 11 : 1-9; Isa. 43 : 6-7; 60 : 3-5; see also Isa 40 : 4; 42 : 15.
[2] *PR* 40(172a) *Behodesh Hashebiʿi.*
[3] O. Holtzmann, "Berakot," *Die Mischna* (Giessen, 1912), 16, 20.
[4] I Cor. 15 : 51-52; I Thes. 4 : 16.
[5] Rev. 12 : 14.
[6] Rev. 11 : 2; 13 : 5.
[7] Rev. 11 : 3; 12 : 6.
[8] Rev. 11 : 15.
[9] Heb. 3 : 11, 18; 4 : 1, 3, 5, 10, 11.
[10] Ex. 33 : 7-14; cf. Num. 12 : 4-8; 14 : 14, 23; Josh. 1 : 13.
[11] II Sam. 7 : 11-13.
[12] Mt. 24 : 3; also Mt. 13 : 39-40, 49; 28 : 20.

age" or "the end of days" refer to the end of the period of enslavement before the jubilee. One of the covenanters said, "And the
sign *Nun* (= 50, the jubilee year) is for the opening of his mercies
of the age for the beginnings of seasons (feasts) in every time that
will be . . . a season of harvest in summer and a feast of sowing
for the season of foliage; feasts of years for their sabbaths, and at
the beginning of their sabbaths for the feast of release (i.e. jubilee)."[1]
Rabbis spoke of the "week" (שבוע) during which the son of David
would come, listing the events that must happen in the six steps
prior to the seventh (שביעית).[2] R. Joseph said many "sevenths"
had passed and the son of David had not come.[3] Based on
Ps. 90 : 4, R. Eliezer said a "day" of the Messiah was a thousand
years.[4] R. Kattina said the "age" would last six thousand years
and then one thousand years would be desolate, just as for a week
of years the seventh lies dormant.[5] Elijah said to Rab Judah, the
brother of Salla the saint, "The age (העולם) is not less than eighty-
five jubilees, and in the last jubilee the son of David comes."[6]

---

[1] 1QS 10 : 3-4, 7-8. It has already been shown that the expression, באחרית
הימים, and its equivalents in Aramaic and Greek, did not refer to the
end of time and history or the cosmos ("Eschatology and the 'End of Days,' "
JNES XX [1961], 188-193). It is now clear that it refers to the end of the
"enslavement" period before "jubilee release" or "sabbath rest." Klausner,
Op. cit., 114-115, 192, 272-273, mistakenly thought the expression "end of
days" referred to the remote future, beyond the political perspective. The
expression did not mean either near or far, but the end of the then existing
evil age, whenever that was expected to happen. M. Black, "The Gospel and
the Scrolls," *Studia Evangelica*, ed. K. Aland and others (Berlin, 1964), 575,
said, "So far as Qumran eschatology is concerned it seems to be fairly generally assumed that the Qumran sectarians shared the general eschatological
outlook of the NT period. Their eschatology was of the apocalyptic order.
But the view that it was dominated by the belief in the imminent end of the
world and its destruction by fire does not seem to me to be very convincingly
borne out by the evidence."

[2] San. 97a.

[3] *Ibid.*

[4] Mid. Ps. 90 : 17. This is the basis for the millennial expectations of
Rev. 20 : 2-7; Eusebius, *HE* VIII. xxiv. 1-3; and elsewhere. Non-sabbatical
periods were based on such factors as the gestation period before a birth,
e.g. Yoma 10a; Rom. 8 : 20-23 or the length of time spent in Egypt.

[5] San. 97a; see also the Life of Adam and Eve 10 : 3-4; Ep. Barn. 15 : 3-5,
8-9; Enoch 91 : 12-17; 93 : 1-10. For an examination of Barnabas' eschatology in relationship to international and interfaith affairs, see S. Lowy,
"The Confutation of Judaism in the Epistle of Barnabas," *JJS* 11 (1960),
28-32. For an analysis of Samaritan eschatology in relation to the Day of
Atonement, the Day of Vengeance, and the beginning of The World Sabbath,
see J. Bowman, "Early Samaritan Eschatology," *JJS* 6 (1955), 63-72.

[6] San. 97a.

R. Jonathan was impatient with the rabbis' attempts to calculate the time of the release: "Let despair come upon the bones of those who calculate the end. For they used to say, 'Since time for the end has come and again he did not come, he will never come—but wait for him'!" [1] R. Nathan said all calculations proved false. Contrary to expectations, "the first kingdom [Maccabean] lasted seventy years, the second [Herodian], fifty-two, and the kingdom of Bar Kozibah [only] two and a half years." [2]

Historical events required Zionistic Jews to reorganize time tables considerably, and they frequently became discouraged, but they continued to calculate. They transferred years to tens of years, days to thousands of years, days to years, or sabbaths to jubilees, but the basis of their reckoning was the justice of the sabbath year and jubilee, when they were promised "rest" or "release" and the land was to be restored to its "original" owners. This insight relates eschatology closely to history and ages to periods of history.

Ages, generations, and jubilees.—Rabbis said Noah, Moses, Mordecai, and Job all saw three "ages" (עולמות): For Noah, there was the period before the flood, the flood, and the restoration; for Moses, there was the time when Israel was enforced into slavery in Egypt, the term of slavery, and the redemption; for Mordecai, the time before enslavement by Haman, the time of the decree, and Israel's redemption; for Job, the initial period of perfection, his torture, and healing. All these "ages" refer to different changes of fortune within the lifetime of people on earth. They were of unspecified length, but whenever the fortune of an Israelite or Israel changed, a "new age" began.[3] R. Joshua interpreted "from generation to generation" to mean from "life in this age" to "life in the age to come." [4] A generation was roughly fifty years, so a generation was reckoned as a jubilee of years which was sometimes considered the length of time necessary to endure in this age

---

[1] San. 97b

[2] *Ibid.*

[3] Tanḥuma, *Vayeshev*, 90b.

[4] Ps. 72 : 5; Mekilta, *Amalek* 2 : 186-188; Mekilta de R. Shimon ben Yohai, *Beshalaḥ* 17 : 15, 5-10. Further reason for considering an age to be a jubilee is that *dôr* is similar in form and context to the Akkadian *dâru* which Lewys, *Op. cit.*, 91-96, identified with the Hebrew *dôr*. A *dâru* was a fifty year period. R. North, *Op. cit.*, 62-85, related *dôr* to the Nuzi *andurâru* which meant "release," and which Gordon equated with the *derôr* of Lev. 25 and *šudûtu*, which also meant "release."

before the Lord would release his people to return to their land. That
an age was sometimes thought of as a jubilee period is confirmed by
the assertion that "a slave of an age" (עבד עולם) was to serve as long
as his master lived (עולמו של אדן; i.e. a generation). [1] He was also
committed to the year of jubilee. [2] "Rabbi said, 'Come and see that
there is no age (עולם) except fifty years. "And he shall serve him
for the age" (לעולם)—until the jubilee year. How is that ? When the
jubilee arrives (הגיע) he goes free. If his master dies he goes free.' " [3]

The rabbinic definition of an "age" as fifty years makes sense
in certain contexts—enough to consider expressions like "the age
to come" in terms of time and history. Expressions like "from age
to age" can be understood to mean "from generation to generation," [4]
or "from jubilee to jubilee." [5] The recurring flattery in Daniel,
"O King, live for ages!" [6] is just as realistic in context meaning
"O King, live for generations!" as an invocation for eternal life.
Either interpretation is hyperbolic. God who endures for "ages"
sets up a kingdom that will stand for "ages." [7] The kingdom of
the age was to rule "generation and generation." [8] An unending
succession of generations or jubilees was temporally everlasting.
A dynasty that endured from age to age was one that had not
been deposed or failed to produce a male heir to the throne.

The ages were related to one another temporally and in continuity.
One age began when the previous age ended, just as one day
follows the day before. Thus the age of Esau-Edom-Rome had to
end before the age of Jacob-Israel could begin. [9] Ages, like human
beings or fruit, became "ripe" [10] or "grew old" [11] before they passed
away and came to an end. [12]

---

[1] Literally "for the age of his master." JKid. 59d. R. Hayim Galipapa,
fourteenth century Spanish rabbi, also said an עולם meant one jubilee (See
Ikkarim, IV. 42, 10-11).

[2] Mekilta, *Nezikin,* 2 : 83, 86-89; Jos., *Ant.* IV. viii.28.

[3] Ex. 21 : 6; Mekilta, *Nezikin* 2 : 88-90.

[4] Mekilta, *Amalek* 2 : 186-188.

[5] I Chron. 16 : 36; 29 : 10; Neh. 9 : 5; Ps. 90 : 2; 106 : 48; Jer. 7 : 7;
25 : 5; Dan. 2 : 20.

[6] Dan. 2 : 4; 3 : 9; 5 : 10; 6 : 7, 22.

[7] Dan. 2 : 44; 6 : 27.

[8] Dan. 3 : 33; 5 : 31.

[9] IV Ezra 6 : 7-10.

[10] II Bar. 70 : 3.

[11] IV Ezra. 14 : 10-11, 16.

[12] IV Ezra 6 : 20; 11 : 44; 12 : 25; II Bar. 4 : 11; II Cor. 5 : 17. Many
years ago, P. Volz, *Die Eschatologie der jüdischen Gemeinde in neutestament-*

Those who calculated the end were apocalyptists who tried to learn how old the age was or how close they were to the "end of days" after which the messianic age would follow in time sequence, rather than parallel it in some metaphysically different essence.

The laws for observance of jubilee that are now preserved in the Torah prompted an Isaianic eschatologist to anticipate the release of the Assyrian and Egyptian captives to return to Jerusalem at the sound of the trumpet on jubilee. Jeremiah further interpreted the Lord's dealing with his indebted people the way a creditor dealt with his brother who owed him money. This interpretation was accepted, varied, and reinterpreted by Ezekiel, II Isaiah, Zechariah, the Chronicler, and Daniel, and still further reapplied in relationship to hopes of nationalistic deliverances through NT and post NT times both by Jews and Christians. This is the biblical basis for all Jewish and Christian eschatology.[1] When biblical eschatology is seen in terms of sabbaths and jubilees, the distinction between the eschatology of the prophets and apocalypses vanishes and the composition of Daniel seems clearly to have been written after the saints of the Most High had received the kingdom, i.e. some time after Judas Maccabeus. Biblical eschatology is then more closely related to politics and military conquest than has formerly been thought. Sabbatical eschatology

---

lichen Zeitalter (Tübingen, 1934), 142-143, listed many of the references to periods considered as bases for calculation of the end, but he noted no relationship between these figures, most of which were multiples of seven, and the theology related to the sabbath year or jubilee.

The continuance of "sabbatical eschatology" is reflected in O. Cullmann, *Christ and Time*, tr. F. V. Filson (Philadelphia, 1950), who has insisted that "all Christian theology in its innermost essence is Biblical history" (p. 23). *Aion*, he said, referred to a duration of time (pp. 39, 62). Time is not abstract but deals with temporal space that can be fulfilled in history (pp. 54, 109) and take place precisely on earth (p. 142). Although he did not see the relationship of eschatology to the sabbath, he correctly understood eschatology in terms of space, time, and history. The "ages" (αἰῶνας) which God made (Heb. 1 : 2) may have referred to temporal periods rather than "worlds." So S. G. Sowers, *The Hermeneutics of Philo and Hebrews* (Zürich, c1965), 92-93.

[1] This statement assumes under the title "sabbatical eschatology" all temporal periods that belong to the same type of deliverance even though the period be based on some other number than a sabbath or jubilee. For instance, a forty year period comparable to the forty years in the wilderness or four hundred years compared to the captivity in Egypt still anticipates a political, military deliverance related to the acquisition of the promised land in time and should be related to biblical eschatology. It might even be called "sabbatical eschatology" for convenience.

is more closely related to temporal and historical concepts than some modern types of eschatology. Whatever philosophical notions become accepted as eschatology, early biblical eschatologists who expected the son of David, the age to come, the end, the rest, or the year of release, thought these periods and events would take place on earth, in time that could be measured by days, weeks, and years. This knowledge will be important for understanding the meaning of the Kingdom of God to be considered in Chapter II, but before that it will be necessary to consider the role of passive ethics in Israel's governmental policies. Passive ethics were employed only when Israel was in captivity where she was sentenced to suffer until her debt had been paid or the jubilee arrived.

PASSIVE ETHICS

Eschatology and ethics.—Just as the exodus from Egypt was the focal point around which activistic holy war theology was centered, so the exodus from Babylon was the famous testing ground for the effectiveness of passive suffering. Together with Jeremiah's sabbatical eschatology was his doctrine of passive suffering. This was not a new theology, opposed to war in principle, but it took into account God's unfailing justice. When the people were righteous, they could fight any enemy with only small, poorly armed troops and expect to win, but in Jeremiah's time Israel had committed so many sins that her treasury of merits was overdrawn. She had such a heavy debt of sin against her account that she was unable to repay it by ordinary offerings and penances. She had to be sold into slavery before she could start all over again. This was not her first experience in "bankruptcy," however. Before the Israelites in Egypt were delivered, they suffered at the hand of Pharaoh.[1] Two reasons were given for Israel's delay in possessing the land: One was that Abraham's seed had to wait until the iniquity of the Amorites was complete so that the Lord could justly punish them.[2] The other was that the Lord punished them for their lack of faith at the boundary of the promised land. They were forced to wander in the wilderness for forty years until the sinful generation had died and its posterity could be admitted into the land.[3]

---

[1] Ex. 1 : 8-9 : 42.
[2] Gen. 15 : 16.
[3] Dt. 1 : 19-40.

Isaiah urged kings not to rush into war, but rather to wait and be confident.[1] This was not because Isaiah was opposed to war, but because he believed in the theology of conquest. God's people should trust in the Lord and not in Egypt and her horses.[2] If they were faithful they could still expect the God of armies to destroy the enemy nations of Israel and defend his chosen people.[3] Isaiah, like Amos and Hosea, had warned his nation of its sinfulness and the punishment that would inevitably follow, but his reason for urging passivity was not the same as Jeremiah's. Jeremiah did not think that Israel's quietness and confidence would protect her against Nebuchadnezzar. He urged the people to accept the yoke of the king of Babylon so that they could receive the punishment necessary to balance the books. He believed the people had broken the covenant; they were uncircumcised of heart; they had not trusted in Jehovah. Therefore Jehovah's hand was against them, and it was Jehovah rather than Nebuchadnezzar whose work would accomplish this destruction in Judah.[4] This punishment did not mean that the God of armies had broken his promise to give the land to the children of Abraham. Justice was required, but as soon as the terms were fulfilled, Jeremiah promised that Judah and the northern tribes would all be reestablished with Jerusalem as the capital.[5] So influential was Jeremiah on the Jews taken into Babylon that his teachings were reiterated there by Ezekiel and, just before the restoration, again by II Isaiah. Before the captivity, Jeremiah's threats were not well received, but after the punishment was over, the same theology was proclaimed by II Isaiah as good news.

Promise and fulfillment.—II Isaiah declared that the term of of service Jeremiah promised was over. The Lord's servant Jacob had paid double for all his sins, so now the Lord would comfort his people.[6] As Jeremiah promised, Zion would be the mountain

---

[1] Isa. 7 : 4; 30 : 16.

[2] Isa. 30 : 7; 31 : 1; 36 : 6-7.

[3] Isa. 10 : 12-27; 13 : 1-15 : 9; 17 : 1-3; 19 : 1-21 : 16; 23 : 1-18; 25 : 10-12; 34 : 1-17; 39 : 1-8.

[4] Jer. 5 : 15, 25; 6 : 1-2, 6; 9 : 7-11, 25-26; 16 : 5-16; 19 : 14-15; 21 : 3-6; 25 : 28-29; 40 : 9.

[5] Jer. 31 : 1-9; 33 : 1-18; 50 : 4-7, 17-20; 51 : 5, 10; Isa. 40 : 2, 9; 41 : 27; 44 : 26-28; 49 : 5-6; 51 : 17; 52 : 1-2, 9; 62 : 1, 6-7; 64 : 10, 18, 19; 66 : 10-13, 20.

[6] Jer. 30 : 11; 46 : 27-28; 16 : 18; 25 : 11-12; 29 : 10-11; 31 : 13; Isa. 40 : 1-2; 41 : 8-16; 42 : 1-4, 18-25; 44 : 1-5; 45 : 1-4; 49 : 13; 51 : 3, 12; 52 : 9; 53 : 1-12; 57 : 18; 61 : 2; 66 : 13.

from which good news could be heralded.[1] The highway Jeremiah promised was redescribed with miraculous expansions,[2] and his confidence that even the blind, lame, and pregnant could return was reemphasized.[3] As Jeremiah said, all twelve tribes would be restored [4] with the capital at Jerusalem. Jehovah would make a new covenant with his people,[5] restore confidence in David,[6] and reestablish Levitical purity.[7] The temple vessels would be returned [8] and voices of joy would again be heard in the streets of Jerusalem.[9] The enemies Jeremiah promised that the Lord would stir up against Babylon from the North[10] turned out to be the troops of Cyrus, whom II Isaiah classed as the one coming both from the East[11] and from the North.[12] II Isaiah affirmed again Jeremiah's belief that Israel's God who would keep covenant with his people was the Creator of the world and therefore controlled men and nations. For him all the nations were like a drop from a bucket.[13] In agreement with Jeremiah,[14] II Isaiah said the exodus from Babylon would be greater than the exodus from Egypt [15] since from Babylon they would not have to leave in haste. The Lord would go before them and be their rear guard, just as the pillar of fire and cloud went either before or behind the Israelites when they left Egypt.[16] Like Jeremiah, II Isaiah believed that Jehovah was the God of armies,[17] a Man of war,[18] who would punish his enemies [19] on the day of vengeance.[20] Neither prophet advised

---

[1] Jer. 31 : 12; Isa. 40 : 9; 41 : 27; 42 : 10-11; 52 : 7-10.

[2] Jer. 31 : 21; Isa. 35 : 8-10; 40 : 3-5; 49 : 9-13.

[3] Jer. 31 : 8; Isa. 35 : 3-6; 42 : 16-19; 49 : 14-26.

[4] Jer. 31 : 1-9; 33 : 1-18; 50 : 4-7, 17-20; 51 : 5, 10; Isa. 49 : 5-6. See also *PRK* 16 : 8.

[5] Jer. 31 : 31-35; Isa. 42 : 6; 49 : 8; 54 : 10; 55 : 3; 56 : 4-6; 61 : 8-9.

[6] Jer. 33 : 17; Isa. 55 : 3.

[7] Jer. 33 : 17; Isa. 35 : 8; 52 : 11.

[8] Jer. 27 : 19-22; Isa. 52 : 11.

[9] Jer. 33 : 10-11; Isa. 35 : 10; 51 : 11.

[10] Jer. 50 : 8-10.   [11] Isa. 41 : 2-4.

[12] Isa. 41 : 25-28; cf. 48 : 14-19.

[13] Jer. 51 : 15-19; 27 : 5-7; Isa. 40 : 12-31; 41 : 1-4, 25-28; 43 : 1-7; 44 : 24-45 : 25; 46 : 11; 65 : 17-25.

[14] Jer. 23 : 7-8.   [15] Isa. 43 : 15-21.   [16] Isa. 52:12.

[17] Isa. 44 : 6; 45 : 12-13; 47 : 4; 48 : 2; 51 : 15; 54 : 5.

[18] Isa. 42 : 13.

[19] Isa. 47 : 4. Enoch 9 : 6-7 is the admonition to suffer so that the Lord would avenge Jewish blood. Enoch 10 : 1-10 is the promise of national miracles such as those reported in Judges 5 to gain victory for Israel over her enemies.

[20] Jer. 25 : 15-38; 30 : 14-17; 46 : 1-51 : 64; Isa. 63 : 4.

Israelites to engage in combat with their enemies. Their duty was to suffer until they atoned for the sins of Israel; then, without lifting a little finger, Israelites would be led back into the promised land. The Lord of armies would take complete charge by creating international involvements whereby the Persian king, Cyrus, would overthrow the Lord's enemies as successfully as the Lord previously overthrew the Egyptians at the Red Sea or Sisera at the Valley of Jezreel. Only this time the covenanted people would be restored to the promised land without a battle.

When the Jews returned to Jerusalem, conditions were not so glorious as Jeremiah and II Isaiah expected. The twelve tribes were not unified; the size of the land was not so great as they hoped. The temple was still in ruins. The first settlers became discouraged. When, under the leadership of Nehemiah, the walls were finally rebuilt and government established, there was no hesitation to use arms; it was necessary to keep the program going.[1] But the success of the venture involved more diplomacy than warfare. The influence of Nehemiah with the king of Persia provided Nehemiah with authority, documents, and supplies that minimized his problems.[2] Nehemiah's administrative skills reduced his need for arms, but the theology that required passivity in Babylon was not opposed to military force to conquer the land. It was all conquest theology with the same goals for the captives in Egypt as for the captives in Babylon. The practical behavior required by Gideon was different from the ethics advocated by Jeremiah, but the purpose of establishing a righteous people of God on the land promised to Abraham's seed was the same for both. Since both the exodus from Egypt and the exodus from Babylon had been successful, later generations were faced with the question: how should Israel act in the face of oppression? Should the people gird themselves for battle, confident that the Lord of armies would overthrow their enemies? Should she wait in confidence as Isaiah recommended? Or should the people suffer in silence until their sins were atoned and the enemy's sins accumulated so that the Lord would take vengeance against Israel's adversaries and reward the covenanters with the land freed from enemy control? These alternatives had advocates in later generations of Jews who had not complete possession of the kingdom.

---

[1] Neh. 4 : 9-20.
[2] Neh. 1 : 1-2 : 10.

Continuation of Active Resistance

Conquest and captivity.—After the successful return of the Jews
to Palestine, the ethics that mostly dominated the nation's conduct
was the pacifistic ethics of the Babylonian captivity. But under
Syrian rule, Jewish ethics changed. After the Roman forces turned
Antiochus Epiphanes back from his attempt to annex Egypt to
his kingdom,[1] he entered Jerusalem, plundered and defiled the
temple, took the city, and established a citadel near the temple.[2]
From then on Antiochus tried by force to root out the religious
practices that made Jews obstinately opposed to control by other
nations.[3] Finally Mattathias, the priest, and his five sons responded
by leading an active guerilla war against the Syrians. The pro-
Hasmonean historian of these events undoubtedly overglorified
his heroes, but his basic emphasis of a religious motivation for
the resistance was correct. The zeal of the Hasmoneans was compared to the zeal of their forefather, Phineas, who took the law in
his own hands and killed Zimri when he became liberal in his
relationships toward the Gentiles.[4] The zealous Jews battled
successfully until they controlled and cleansed the temple,[5] just
three years after Antiochus had defiled it.[6] That was well within
the period of three and a half years "prophesied" by Daniel.[7]
During these struggles, Mattathias ordered Jews to fight in defense
on the Sabbath Day so that they could defeat the Gentiles and
regain the land, making it possible then to keep all of the law.[8]
The war continued vigorously until, during the rule of Simon
(144-143 B.C.), the tax imposed by the Syrians was removed and
the nation was free from foreign rule.[9] The land promised to

---

[1] Livy 45 : 12; I Mac. 1 : 20; Dan. 11 : 30.
[2] I Mac. 1 : 21-36.
[3] I Mac. 1 : 41-63.
[4] I Mac. 2 : 26; Num. 25 : 6-8.
[5] I Mac. 2:27-4:61.
[6] I Mac. 4 : 54.
[7] Dan. 8 : 13-14; 9 : 27; 12 : 7, 11-12. Wellhausen was not the only scholar
to wonder why Baruch was excluded from the canon and Daniel not (F.C.
Burkitt, *Jewish and Christian Apocalypses* [London, 1914], 9). The probable
reason was that Daniel's "prophecy" concerning the restoration was thought
to have been fulfilled, whereas Baruch was used to fan the flames of the war
of 66-70 A.D. and/or 132-135 A.D.—both of which were unsuccessful and
the prophecies, therefore, considered false.
[8] I Mac. 2 : 39-41.
[9] I Mac. 13 : 36-42.

Abraham's seed was finally in their possession. As with the original conquest of Canaan, the Lord proved himself to be the God of armies who could win Israel's battles against overwhelming odds, strengthening the arm that took up the sword in Jehovah's name. This victory revived activistic holy war theology which continued to be strong in NT times. The Hasmonean dynasty, however, that had led the successful conquest, soon became involved in civil strife which allowed the kingdom to slip from their hands. Some Jews welcomed the Roman opposition of Popilius,[1] and also Pompey into Jerusalem to oppose Aristobulus.[2] After he had taken Jerusalem, over the dead bodies of those who did not welcome him, Pompey entered the temple as Antiochus had done more than a hundred years earlier, but he did not plunder its goods. Instead he ordered it cleansed and appointed John Hyrcanus II as high priest.[3] The situation was not quite as bad as it had been prior to the Maccabean Revolt, but Hyrcanus II soon let the political control fall into the hands of Antipater and his son, Herod the Great, who were friends of Rome. The whole change was shocking. A Roman general had entered the holy of holies and lived! Furthermore, he left the impression that Rome could invade other prohibited areas whenever she wanted. After Hyrcanus II's deposition by his nephew, during the Parthian invasion, Herod reconquered the country with Roman help, and ruled it for more than thirty years to Rome's satisfaction. After his death in 4 B.C. Judah and Samaria were entrusted to Herod's son, Archaelaus, who ruled for ten years until Rome confiscated his property, sent him into exile, and appointed procurators over the land. At that time Rome also levied a tax to be paid directly to Rome.[4] This meant that the last semblance of freedom gained by the Maccabeans had been lost, and Palestine was again under subjection to a foreign power.

Ashes to ashes.—Although Herod succeeded in suppressing the Jews, his entire reign was marked with the necessity for protecting himself from them. Hasmoneans were a constant threat. Any leader from that family was able to raise enough popular resistance

---

[1] Livy 45 : 12.
[2] *Ant.* XIV (58-63).
[3] *Ant.* XIV (69-73).
[4] *Ant.* XVII (342-355); *BJ* II (117-118).

to challenge Herod's kingdom if given a chance. There was also other resistance, like the two scholars of high respect who encouraged their disciples to cut down the Roman eagle over the large gate in Jerusalem. This action was based on their understanding of the law and received the ready support of their students. When caught in broad daylight, teachers and students were brought before Herod where they confessed their deed and willingness to die for the laws of their fathers, since they were sure that those who died defending the laws would be raised to eternal life. After hearing this, Herod had the men executed in various ways depending on the extent of their involvement.[1] After Herod's death, latent rebellion became active. Jews came to feasts to organize revolts against Rome and were slaughtered in the temple area.[2] Military leaders arose thick and fast: Judas of Galilee, son of the Hezekiah who fought against the Romans in the beginning of Herod's reign;[3] Simon in Peraea;[4] and Athrongaeus[5]—all were actively engaged in military rebellion against Rome. Before Archelaus' leadership in Palestine had been approved, Romans had to quell these uprisings, crucifying about two thousand,[6] some of whom were of royal blood.[7] After attempting to rule his territory for ten years, Archelaus was exiled, and Rome ruled Palestine directly. This was the beginning of the pro-consulate of Quirinius in Syria (6-7 A.D.). At that time Judas of Galilee led a revolt against Rome, holding that paying tribute to Caesar was against the law that forbade them to have any king but Jehovah.[8] From then until the destruction of Jerusalem, in 70 A.D., there was much unrest in Palestine as pious Jews sought to throw off the yoke of Rome so that they might enforce the laws of the covenant. At the national feasts, Jews came hoping there would be a messiah who could lead them victoriously in battle against the Romans. Palm branches and citrus branches were nationalistic emblems for the Jews, just as the color green and the clover leaf were Ireland's emblems of resistance against England at a later period. Knowing

---

[1] *BJ* I (647-655).
[2] *BJ* II (10-13, 30, 45-54); Lk. 13 : 1-5.
[3] *BJ* II (56).
[4] *BJ* II (57-59).
[5] *BJ* II (60-65).
[6] *BJ* II (75).
[7] *BJ* II (78).
[8] *BJ* II (117-118).

that feasts were occasions for insurrection, Romans regularly kept a military guard on hand to maintain control.[1] Sometimes there were mass slaughters, such as the conflict in the temple area after Herod's reign [2] or the later occasion when Pilate mixed the blood of Galileans with their sacrifices.[3] Sometimes during the panic situations, Jews trampled over each other and killed one another in their attempts to escape through the narrow crowded streets.[4] Those who were wise stayed on the roof tops where they could move without obstruction from the top of one flat roof to the other and thus escape to the mountains.[5] During the seventh decade, when Roman procurators became more oppressive to the Jews, the Roman government itself was threatened with seemingly incurable civil strife. These factors prompted the Jews to need deliverance more and to believe more firmly that the time had come when God would restore his kingdom. During the seventh decade, the following emperors ruled: Nero to 68 A.D., Galba, 68-69, Otho, 69, Vitellius, 69, and finally Vespasian, 69-70 A.D. In addition to the guerilla warfare carried on throughout the country by the zealots, sicarii mingled with crowds at feasts with daggers concealed in their clothing to kill as many Romans or Roman collaborators as they could.[6] Groups gathered in the wilderness to see signs of deliverance like those seen before Joshua's conquest of Canaan.[7] An Egyptian prophet led thirty thousand from the desert to the Mount of Olives and promised to overthrow the Roman garrison. He failed, but his methodology indicated the strong religious motivation for the insurrection.[8] There were enough of these abortive movements for Christians to be warned against false prophets who showed great signs and promised that their leader would be in the wilderness.[9]

An important reason for the Maccabean victory over Syria two centuries earlier was the unstable condition of the Syrian government. From the time the temple was defiled until taxation was

---

[1] *BJ* II (223-224).
[2] *BJ* II (10-13, 30, 45-54).
[3] Lk. 13 : 1-5.
[4] *BJ* II (226-227; 325-329).
[5] Mt. 24 : 16-17.
[6] *BJ* II (252-257).
[7] *BJ* II (258-260; *Ant.* XX (97).
[8] *BJ* II (261-263).
[9] Mt. 24 : 24-26.

removed there were seven Syrian kings. Sometimes when it seemed that the Syrians had the Jewish guerillas in a spot where they would have to surrender, civil strife made it necessary for the general in charge to take his troops back to Syria while the Jews gained still further control over the land. Rome's situation during the seventh decade was very much the same as Syria's had been years before. The city of Rome burned during the reign of Nero, leveling many districts of the city.[1] During one year alone (69 A.D.), there were three emperors who were either killed or committed suicide, and a fourth was crowned emperor. These signs told the Jews that the God of armies was acting in their behalf to overthrow the Romans just as he had defeated the Egyptians, Philistines, and Syrians. Therefore, they expected the Lord to bless their military efforts against Rome.

When Vespasian had taken every fortress in Palestine except Herodium, Masada, Machaerus, and the capital city, he gathered his troops against the walls of Jerusalem.[2] At the strategic moment, Vespasian halted his attack to watch the results of the civil strife in Rome.[3] His cessation of conflict in Jerusalem happened about three years after the war had begun—almost the length of time prophesied by Daniel! This seeming fulfillment encouraged the Jews. They probably remembered other deliverances, such as the time Lysias returned to Syria because Philip was trying to take over the government there.[4] Earlier, Hezekiah prayed for deliverance from the Assyrians that surrounded Jerusalem, after which the angel of the Lord slew a hundred and eighty-five thousand Assyrians in one night, forcing the king to return to Nineveh.[5] When Vespasian halted his attack, Rome was in critical condition. Not only was civil war rampant in the city, but during the conflict the Capitoline temple was burned.[6] Tacitus said that this was the saddest and most shameful crime that had ever happened to Rome, so the Romans feared the divine punishment they would receive.[7] The city of Rome was engaged in battle at three different quarters of the city.[8] Romans mourned the destruction of their

---

[1] Tacitus, *Annals*, XV. xv, xxxviii, xli.
[2] *BJ* IV (545-555).   [3] *BJ* IV (585-604).
[4] I Mac. 6 : 28-63.   [5] II Kgs. 19 : 1-36.
[6] *BJ* IV (645-649); Tacitus, *Histories*, III.71.
[7] Tacitus, *Histories*, III.72.
[8] *BJ* IV (650).

Capitol, but Jews who called Rome the great harlot, the beast, and the enemy God was destined to destroy, rejoiced in the belief that God was then declaring his hand. So "when the city was divided into three parts, and the cities of the nations fell,[1] and Babylon the great was remembered before God so as to give her the cup of the wine of his wrath," [2] then the kings of the earth, the merchants, and the mighty ones who had engaged in business ("committed adultery") with Rome lamented when they saw the smoke of her burning.[3] But zealous Jews cried, "Rejoice over her, Heaven! Also saints, apostles, and prophets, because God has decreed his judgment upon her." [4] They expected Rome to burn until it was destroyed completely and Palestine was liberated, so they shouted, "Hallelujah! Her smoke goes up forever and ever!" [5] When the Jews had been similarly oppressed by Antiochus Epiphanes, Daniel "prophesied" that the fourth beast (Syria) would be judged guilty and the kingdom given to the Son of Man and the saints of the Most High.[6] This was to take place in three and a half years.[7] Since Daniel's "prophecy" had been fulfilled by the establishment of the Maccabean kingdom, Jewish prophets expected a similar restoration to take place during the war of 66-70 A.D. and within the same length of time.[8] Assured the times and the signs were right and that God would give them the victory, Jews quarreled about which revolutionary leader would become the anointed king of the new kingdom.[9]

---

[1] R. H. Charles, *ICC Revelation* (New York, 1920), II, 52, insisted that the city referred to was Rome, but he bracketed the section dealing with the division of the city into three parts as a later addition. But it makes good sense as it is, either taken to be Rome or Jerusalem, because both were divided into three parts at the same time that Vespasian went to Rome and left Jerusalem's three factions to weaken themselves by internal conflict while he was gone. Rev. 16 : 19 may refer to the events in three localities: 1) When "the great city [of Jerusalem] was divided into three parts," 2) "and the cities of the nations fell" (many other cities, see Tacitus, *Histories*, I.ii), and 3) "and Babylon [Rome] was remembered before God to give to her *the cup of the wine of the wrath* (Jer. 32 : 15 LXX) of his anger."

[2] Rev. 16 : 19.   [3] Rev. 18 : 9-12.

[4] Rev. 18 : 20.

[5] Rev. 19 : 3; see also 14 : 11; 17 : 16; 18 : 8-9, 17-18.

[6] Dan. 7 : 1-28.

[7] Dan. 7 : 25; 9 : 27; 12 : 7, 11-13.

[8] Rev. 11 : 1-3; 12 : 6, 14; 13 : 5; see also 22 : 7, 10, 12, 20.

[9] There were also instances in which military terminology was spiritualized and continued in religious usage. See Wis. Sol. 5 : 15-33; Lk. 35 : 38; Rom. 13 : 11-14; Eph. 5 : 6-18; 6 : 10-16; I Thes. 5 : 4-8; I Peter 1 : 13-14.

Jerusalem, like Rome,[1] was divided into three camps: 1) the supporters of John; 2) Eleazar's followers; and 3) those loyal to Simon.[2] Ignoring the Roman threat, John and Simon burned the supplies of grain and provisions in Jerusalem.[3] But after Vespasian had stabilized the Roman government, Titus continued the siege against Jerusalem.[4] By then the city was considerably weakened and the Jews soon forced to conditions of famine.[5] One woman cooked and ate her own son.[6] But in spite of these conditions, Jews held out until the Romans invaded the temple. True to their religious heritage, they believed that when Romans entered the temple God would give victory to his chosen people.[7] It was when the abomination of desolation· occurred and the sanctuary was trampled under foot [8] that the tide would turn and restoration begin.[9] Josephus said that some interpreted scripture to promise that when the temple was defiled, a Jewish king would rule the whole Roman world.[10] When the temple began to burn, Jews were enervated and none attempted to stop the flames. Instead they battled harder, expecting a divine miracle at any moment,[11] but when the flames reached the sanctuary, Jews lost all thought of self-preservation since the object of their defense was perishing.[12] Priests stayed and burned with the temple.[13] Those who survived the fire refused to accept Titus' pledge but only asked permission to retire to the wilderness.[14] Once the temple had been destroyed, the only place they knew to begin again without a temple was the desert where their fathers had wandered before the conquest of Canaan. It took three more years for Rome to conquer Herodium, Machaerus, and Masada. When they finally invaded the fortress of Masada, they found the men, women, and children dead. They

---

[1] Note also Rev. 16 : 19.
[2] *BJ* V (1-38).
[3] *BJ* V (23-24).
[4] *BJ* IV (656-658).
[5] *BJ* V (426-428, 571).
[6] *BJ* VI (201-213); Tacitus, *Histories* V.xii. Cf. also II Kgs. 6 : 28-29; Lam. 2 : 20; II Bar. 62 : 1.
[7] *BJ* VI (73-74).
[8] Dan. 8 : 13-14.
[9] See Mt. 24 : 15-28.
[10] *BJ* VI (310-312).
[11] *BJ* VI (233-235).
[12] *BJ* VI (253).
[13] *BJ* VI (278-280).
[14] *BJ* VI (351).

had killed one another and themselves rather than die at the hand of the uncircumcised.[1] Even after Judaea had been captured, war continued in the diaspora: in Egypt [2] Onias' temple was kept closed so that Jews could not use it again for a fortress; [3] in Cyrene a certain Jonathan was burned alive for promising to show his followers signs from Heaven in the wilderness.[4] Vespasian executed anyone he found of Davidic descent to root out the hope on which Jews relied.[5] Some of Titus' counsellors believed that the Jews would always rebel so long as the temple stood.[6] Although Josephus attributed the war to some exceptional, irresponsible Jews, he refuted the leaders by explaining their misunderstanding of the scripture, because he knew this was basic to the whole concept of Jewish war.

Dust to dust.—II Baruch and IV Ezra reflect the disappointment, lamentation, and soul searching reexamination Jews experienced after the fall of Jerusalem. They thought their theology was right, but they must not have read the signs correctly. Apocalyptists still anticipated the fall of Rome and the reestablishment of the kingdom. The "ages" of history were compared to the births of Esau and Jacob. Jacob (Israel) had hold of Esau's (Rome's) heel from the beginning. The end of the first age, then, would occur at the point of Esau's heel,[7] and the second age would begin with Jacob's hand.[8] Box said that Esau and Jacob symbolized the present evil age and the future incorruptible age.[9] This is correct, but more was implied than Box observed. In Rabbinic literature Esau and Edom regularly meant Rome, and the "ages" involved would have followed in temporal sequence on this earth. Therefore, the end of the age of Esau meant the end of Roman power and the beginning of the new age in which Israel would rule the civilized

---

[1] *BJ* VII (320-398).

[2] *BJ* VII (400-419).

[3] *BJ* VII (420-436).

[4] *BJ* VII (437-450).

[5] So Eusebius, *HE* 3 : 12, 19-20, 32.

[6] *BJ* VI (238-240).

[7] IV Ezra 6 : 7-10. See also IV Ezra 3 : 16-17; J. Bloch, *Op. cit.*, related the heel of Esau in IV Ezra with the עקבות משיח (Ps. 89 : 52) used in *PRE* 32. See further Gen. R. 63.

[8] IV Ezra 6 : 8-10.

[9] B. E. Box, "IV Ezra," *Apocrypha and Pseudepigrapha of the OT*, ed. R. H. Charles (Oxford, c1913), II, 575.

world. The analogy was apt and also accurate in the initial stage, since Israel had been related to Rome from the time Rome moved to the position of being the strongest political force of the Mediterranean world.[1]

In the "Eagle Vision," the eagle (Rome) was confronted by a voice like a lion (Lion of Judah) who accused the eagle of being the fourth beast to rule the world before the kingdom of the saints of the Most High was established. Therefore the eagle's oppressive rule was a sign of hope for the saints.[2] It was the last nation to oppress the Jews. In the time of that fourth kingdom, there would arise many contentions (like those of the seventh decade, A.D.) during which the fourth beast would be in danger of falling, but it would be restored again, and continue for the short reigns of eight more kings.[3] After that the "lion"—the Messiah of the seed of David—would rebuke the eagle and destroy it.[4] Jews of NT times expected God's kingdom (regnum) to appear when Israel's enemies would be punished and Israel would be happy, riding upon the neck of the eagle (aquilae). From her exalted position on Mt. Zion, Israel would look down and rejoice to see her enemies in her garbage heap of Gehenna.[5] The Lord had not forgotten the Jews forever.[6] The fall of Jerusalem was part of his plan before destroying Rome and reestablishing the kingdom.

From the end of Nero's reign (68 A.D.) until Hadrian's reign (117-136 A.D.) there were eight emperors. Hadrian was the ninth whom the apocalyptist believed would be Rome's last emperor before the chosen people would be given the whole Roman world.

The authors of these apocalypses had further activistic support. Simon Bar Cochba led a revolt against Rome that lasted for three years (132-135 A.D.). He was endorsed as the Messiah by Rabbi

---

[1] Much later, R. Naḥman said, "All the time that the light of the wicked Esau shines in the world, the light of Jacob is not diffused: when wicked Esau's light is covered, Jacob's light will be spread abroad" (PRK 5 : 14, 2-6). Reflecting on the terms רוממה and צר in Isa. 43 : 5, R. Kahana said that whenever the scripture read צור, it meant the city of Tyre, but whenever it read צר, "oppress," it meant wicked Rome (7 : 11, 1-2). R. Samuel bar Nahman spoke of the time "the two ages kissed each other," this age and the age to come (PRK, Appendix II, 453).

[2] IV Ezra 11 : 37-46.
[3] IV Ezra 12 : 18-21.
[4] IV Ezra 12 : 22-33.
[5] Assump. Mos. 10 : 1-10.
[6] IV Ezra 12 : 39-48.

Akiba who died as a martyr during the revolt. Throughout this period Christians and Jews were in opposition to one another [1] even though both were being martyred by the same Roman government for the same reasons and were sustained in their faith by the same kind of conquest theology. After the final suppression of Bar Cochba,[2] the Christian leader, Marcion, took a direct stand against Jewish militaristic theology. He held that Jesus revealed a God who offered salvation to all nations that had never been known before Jesus. He was different from the God who proposed to restore the Jewish state. The difference between the two Gods was as great as that between justice and goodness, law and gospel, Judaism and Christianity.[3] Marcion was a prominent leader in Asia Minor, but when he left Pauline territory for Rome, he was excommunicated in 144 A.D. by the Christians there who still sympathized with the theology which had led to two bitter defeats for the Jews in war against Rome. After Bar Cochba's defeat, activistic theology was suppressed but not stifled. The two wars had taught Christians and Jews that, for the time at least, passive ethics were required of the chosen people.[4]

CONTINUATION OF PASSIVE ETHICS

Meritorious suffering.—The historical reports of the events from the Maccabees to Bar Cochba were so badly stained with blood drawn from active resistance that the ethics of the Babylonian captivity seemed almost to have been forgotten, but pacifists continued, nonetheless. Together with the account of a victorious war was the report of the pious Jews who submissively accepted

---

[1] See Tacitus, *Fragments of Histories*: Ber 28b-29a; G. Holtzmann, "Berakot," *Op. cit.*, I, 16; also L. Finkelstein, "Development of the Amidah," *JQR* (n.s.), 16 (1925/26), 1-43; 127-170; Justin, *Dial. cum Trypho*, 16 : 4; Epiphanius, *Haer.* 29 : 9; Jerome, *On Isaiah* 5 : 18; 49 : 7 and 52 : 4; Ignatius, *To the Philadelphians* VI; Justin Martyr, *First Apology*, 31.

[2] Spelled כוזבא in JTaan. 68d 4, and כוסבא in the scrolls from Murabbaʿat; βαρχωχεβας by Justin and χωχεβας by Eusebius. See also JBer. 14b and Lam. R. II.2 4. For discussions of the Bar Cochba Revolt, see Dio Cassius, Roman History, 69; J. A. Fitzmyer, "The Bar Cochba Period," *The Bible in Current Catholic Thought*, ed. J. L. McKenzie (New York, c1962), 133-168; and L. E. Toombs, "Barcosiba and Qumran," *NTS* 4 (1956-57), 65-71.

[3] Tertullian, *Adv. Marc.* VI.

[4] For an account of the pacifistic adjustment of Jews to existence in Rome while Jews waited for God to act after Bar Cochba, see N.N. Glatzer, "The Attitude Toward Rome in Third-Century Judaism," *Politische Ordnung und menschliche Existenz* (München, 1962), 243-257.

death rather than break the Sabbath Day by fighting.[1] The Maccabees decreed that this should not be continued,[2] so historians mention it no more. It is not likely that they suddenly ceased to be, but it is true that they did not capture much attention during the war. Later when Pilate threatened to have his soldiers kill mobs of Jews who gathered at Caesarea to persuade him to remove the standards from Jerusalem, they fell to the ground and bared their necks to be killed rather than transgress the law. The reaction was so astonishing that Pilate had the standards removed.[3] This was reported because of the visible political effect of passive resistance, but most passive convictions received little coverage. The depth of passive convictions are more readily seen in teachings than in history, and these indicate the continuance of passive endurance. One author reported the non-resistant suffering of pious Jews who were killed in a cave rather than break the Sabbath. Theirs was a deliberate plan to motivate God to avenge their blood (*Hoc enim si faciemus et moriemur, sanguis noster vindicavitur coram Domino*) and reward Israel by restoring the kingdom (*regnum*).[4] The kingdom that later came was ruled by the Hasmoneans. Another teacher explained Israel's present hardship as an indication of the Lord's love for Israel. He did not want her account of merits to become so heavily overdrawn that he would have to foreclose, so he punished her little by little. He did not love the nations of the world, however, so he let them prosper so that he could justly destroy them when their sin had reached its height.[5] After the fall of Jerusalem, II Baruch was convinced that the nations had committed enough sins to be heavily overdrawn. He called them debtors (سبت) [6] and argued that the evil that came upon Israel

---

[1] I Mac. 2 : 32-38.

[2] I Mac. 2 : 39-41.

[3] *BJ* II (169-174).

[4] *Assump. Mos.* 9 : 1-10 : 10. See also J. Licht, "Taxo, or the Apocalyptic Doctrine of Vengeance," *JJS* XII (1961), 95-103. The idea of a vengeful god is not distinctive to Israel. W. G. Lambert, "ii) Counsels of Wisdom," *Babylonian Wisdom Literature* (Oxford, 1960), 101, quotes this Babylonian passage:

> "57. Do not insult the downtrodden and [. .]
> 58. Do not sneer at them aristocratically.
> 59. With this a man's god is angry,
> 60. It is not pleasing to Šamas, who will repay him with evil."

[5] II Mac. 6 : 12-15; see also 7 : 18-19, 32-33; 8 : 36-38; 10 : 4.

[6] II Bar. 13 : 11.

was allowed so that the nations might be perfectly chastised
(ܟܬܒܐ ܐܢܝܢ ܐܝܟܕ ܢܬܪܕܘܢ).[1] Jews, on the other hand, were
encouraged to comfort themselves concerning their hardships,
knowing that the Lord would avenge their enemies for this. Although
the nations seemed strong, prosperous, and receiving glory, they
would soon vanish like smoke.[2] A poet held that the man was
blessed (ܛܘܒܘܗܝ) whom God punished, because punishment would
purify him from sin (ܠܡܬܕܟܝܘ ܡܢ ܚܛܗܐ). The Lord was always good to those who received his punishment.[3] Also blessed
was the man whom the Lord remembered with poverty (συμμετρία
αὐταρκείας = ܒܡܣܬܝܢܘܬܐ) because the extent that a man exceeds
his portion is sin for him.[4] IV Ezra did not expect the new age
to begin until Zion's humiliation was complete.[5] That was the
punishment required before honor could be received. Jews objected
to the Pauline effort at converting Gentiles, because if they repented, their quota of sins would not be so rapidly filled up.[6] God
would not destroy them until their sins were filled up, and the
kingdom would not come until the nations were destroyed. Hence
a mission to the Gentiles seemed like a sabotage movement.

With this kind of theology, Israel should have been expected
to rejoice in her sufferings, because the more she suffered the more
sins would be cancelled and the sooner God would reward her.
This is similar to Emerson's theology: "Put God in your debt.
Every stroke shall be repaid. The longer the payment is withholden,
the better for you; for compound interest upon compound interest
is the rate and usage of this exchequer." [7] A similar teaching was
written in ancient Babylon: "The man who sacrifices to his god
is satisfied with the bargain. He is making loan upon loan." [8]
The treasury of merits investment theology prompted the passivity
of the Rule of the Community: "I will not give recompense to the
evil man; with good I will pursue man, because God judges every
living being and he will pay to each man his due; but I will not

---

[1] II Bar. 13 : 5; see also 24 : 1.
[2] II Bar. 82 : 1-9; see also 24 : 1; IV Ezra 6 : 5, 7, 40, 77; 7 : 17; 8 : 32-33;
Mt. 6 : 19-20.
[3] Ps. of Sol. 10 : 1-2; see also 9 : 9.
[4] Ps. of Sol. 5 : 18-19.
[5] IV Ezra 6 : 19.
[6] I Thes. 2 : 13-16.
[7] R. W. Emerson, "Compensation."
[8] Lambert, "The Dialogue of Pessimism," Op. cit., 147.

gain vengeance in an evil spirit and the wealth of a violent man my soul will not covet, and I will not become involved in a conflict with the man of the pit until the day of vengeance."[1] This did not mean the covenanter wished his enemy well, but that he believed God would hurt the enemy more than the covenanter could if he took the law in his own hands. He would increase his enemy's deficit of merits by doing good when the enemy deserved punishment. That made the enemy's sin the worse. The same document said, "And these are the rules for the teacher in these times with reference to his love and his hatred: let there be eternal hatred toward the men of the pit in a spirit of concealment, while giving up to them wealth and labor of hands like a servant to the one who rules him and submission to the one who dominates him. But let each man be zealous for the decree and the season, for the day of vengeance."[2] The same gratitude was expressed by another psalmist who had unfairly been made a debtor and had his spoil taken from him. He remained silent and bore their bitterness, so that he might redeem his people and inherit it (ܡܒܝܢ ܠܐܝ ܡܒܝܬܗ ܠܥܡ) and not make void the promises to the fathers.[3]

Rabbis believed that the merits of the patriarchs, primarily Abraham, would work on their behalf. The virtue as well as the sins of the fathers would be visited upon the sons of future generations.[4] Abraham's good deeds built up the treasury of merits for Israel.[5] Even though the law was not yet given to Israel, God personally taught Abraham the law in the most minute details.[6] Both he and Sarah kept the whole Torah from beginning to end, "not under compulsion but with delight."[7] More important was Abraham's faith, which weighed heavily in the accumulation of merit for Israel.[8] He ascended the mountain of the Lord with clean hands and a pure heart because of his belief.[9] He was rescued from the fiery furnace[10] and from battle because of his faith.[11]

---

[1] 1QS 10 : 17-19.
[2] 1QS 9 : 21-23.
[3] II Bar. 13 : 5.
[4] Dt. 5 : 6-10.
[5] Shab. 127a.
[6] Mid. Ps. 1 : 13.
[7] Mid. Ps. 1 : 13.
[8] Gen. 15 : 6; Mid. Ps. 119 : 78.
[9] Mid. Ps. 24 : 8.
[10] Mid. Ps. 118:11.
[11] Mid. Ps. 110 : 2-3.

Israel, in later history, drew upon the merits of the patriarchs in time of need. Because of the "guardian merit of the patriarchs," [1] the Lord brought Israel up from slavery and defeated Amalek.[2] Jews suffered in Babylon until the scale had tipped toward righteousness. Then the way across the desert was to be made completely open without obstacle.[3] This salvation would not come to those who fought but to those who waited in patience and trusted God to keep his word.[4]

The Sermon on the Mount encouraged Christians to lay up for themselves treasures in heaven; [5] and they were also to turn the second cheek, walk the second mile, and add the cloak to the coat required.[6] The motivation for this may have been to build up merits in the treasury so that God would reward them and punish their enemies. Paul's motivation was clear: "Beloved, never avenge yourselves, but leave it to the wrath of God; for it is written, 'Vengeance is mine. I will repay, says the Lord.' No, 'If your enemy is hungry, feed him. If he is thirsty, give him drink; for by so doing you will heap burning coals upon his head.' Do not be overcome by evil, but overcome evil with good." [7] Since vengeance belonged to God's department, the way to hurt your enemy most was to be good to him so that his sin would be greater and thereby require the worse divine punishment.[8] In this context, Paul urged the Christians to be subject to the governing authorities [9] and owe no one anything.[10] I Peter also called Christians' attention to the meritorious sufferings of Christ, from whose wounds later Christians have been healed.[11] The author also warned Christians to be sure

---

[1] Mid. Ps. 94 : 5; Mekilta, *Beshallah* 4 : 1-95.

[2] Mekilta, *Amelek* 1 : 94-98.

[3] Targ. Isa. 43 : 19b. By the same standard, the wicked would deserve their reward in this age and punishment in the future, whereas the righteous, who are punished in this age, will be rewarded in the future (*PRK* 9 : 1, 7-10).

[4] Targ. Isa. 40 : 30-31; 50 : 10.

[5] Mt. 6 : 20.

[6] Mt. 5 : 38-41. O. Betz, "Jesu Heiliger Krieg," *Nov.* 2 (1958), 116-137, observed that holy war theology in the scrolls was very much like that of the OT but insisted that Jesus had no part of this theology. Betz spiritualized holy war terms.

[7] Rom. 12 : 19-20; also T. Gad 6 : 7.

[8] See further K. Stendahl, "Hate, Non-Retaliation, and Love," *HTR* 55 (1962), 343-555, for a careful examination of non-resistant ethics.

[9] Rom. 13 : 1-2.

[10] Rom. 13 : 8.

[11] I Peter 2 : 21-25.

that their suffering was for righteousness; otherwise it had no merit. If they suffered in punishment for wrongdoing, they added to the debit column at the same time they may have added to the credit column of the ledger.[1] I Peter said those who suffered in the flesh had ceased from sin.[2] James said Christians who faced trials should rejoice because they could later receive a crown of life.[3] When Paul listed for the Christians his merits as a servant of Christ, he cataloged the number of tortures he had suffered for Christ.[4] Paul told the Philippian Christians that it was their privilege not only to believe in Christ but also to suffer for his sake.[5] He further spoke of his own impending death in terms of a sacrificial offering [6] and compared his sufferings with those of Christ.[7] Paul spoke negatively to the sinners who by their hard and impenitent hearts were storing up wrath for themselves on the day of wrath.[8] He said that the Jews tried to hinder him from speaking to the Gentiles because Jews wanted the Gentiles to fill up the measure of their sins.[9] For Paul there was laid up a crown of righteousness which the Lord would give him on that day.[10] To the Colossians, Paul said, "Now I rejoice in my sufferings for your sake, and in my flesh I complete what is lacking in Christ's afflictions for the sake of the body, that is, the church." [11] This meant that Paul believed that the sins of Israel had almost been balanced by the undeserved suffering and death of Jesus. When the scales were completely balanced, God would reward the new Israel, which was the church, by establishing the Kingdom of God. Paul followed the example of his Master by suffering for the church as Christ had done, in the belief that these hardships would cancel sins and gain merit for the body of Christ, the church.

Paul's conversion.—Farmer observed that there were in the OT only two examples of the qualities that the Lord reckoned as

---

[1] I Peter 3 : 13-17.
[2] I Peter 4 : 1; for further pacifistic exhortations, see *Clem. Hom.* XV.vi-vii.
[3] James 1 : 12.
[4] II Cor. 11 : 23-29.
[5] Philip. 1 : 29.
[6] Philip. 2 : 17.
[7] Philip. 3 : 10-11.
[8] Rom. 2 : 5.   [9] I Thes. 4 : 16.
[10] II Tim. 4 : 8. This quotation is not really Paul's, but it belongs to the "Pauline school."
[11] Col. 1 : 24.

righteousness.[1] One of these pictured Abraham, who believed against heavy odds, and his faith was reckoned to him as righteousness.[2] The other was Phineas who, in opposition to Hebrew mingling with Midianites, took the law in his own hands, and killed Zimri and the Midianite girl he had brought into his tent.[3] Because of this, the Lord stopped the plague that had been killing thousands of Hebrews, and he made with Phineas a covenant of peace,[4] a covenant of perpetual priesthood, because he had made atonement for Israel. The Psalmist said that that act of Phineas' was reckoned to him as righteousness from generation to generation forever.[5] Farmer correctly understood these two different types of ethics as bases for justification that Paul had considered, but the depth to which these two types of ethics were imbedded in conquest theology was greater than Farmer noticed. It was not just Phineas contrasted with Abraham but the exodus from Egypt contrasted with the exodus from Babylon. The struggles between these alternatives were not only necessary for Paul but for Jews generally from the Babylonian captivity to the defeat of Bar Cochba. Much blood was shed both in active aggression and passive suffering as the covenanters were given experiences by which to learn God's will.

Paul described his earlier life in Judaism as a period when he persecuted the church of God and tried to destroy it, so extremely zealous was he for the traditions of his fathers.[6] From the standpoint of law, Paul had been classed as a Pharisee; as to zeal, a persecutor of the church; as to righteousness under the law, he was blameless.[7] This activistic ethic was similar to the zeal of Phineas or that of the Maccabees who took up the sword against the Syrians in the name of their forefather Phineas. When Paul became a Christian, he changed from an activistic ethic to a pacifistic ethic, and his insistence on salvation by faith is best understood in opposition to his former belief in salvation by activistic zeal for the law. Both types of ethics had strong biblical support with illustrations of their success in Israel's history, and both were based on conquest theology.

---

[1] W. R. Farmer, "The Patriarch Phineas," *ATR* 34 (1952), 26-30.
[2] Gen. 15 : 1-7.
[3] Num. 25 : 1-8.
[4] Num. 25 : 10-13. [5] Ps. 106 : 3.
[6] Gal. 1 : 13-14. [7] Philip. 3 : 5-6.

Jesus' temptations.—The struggle, the religious zeal, the political turmoil, and the intense longing of Jews for freedom during the first century were so vital that no significant religious or political leader could have avoided the burning issues of his times. How should Jews react to Rome? Should they pay tribute to Caesar or not?[1] Should they fight Rome, collaborate with her, or suffer meritoriously under her heel? It is not easy to learn all Jesus' answers to these questions. The data is now included in literature that has been organized by some other principle than chronological order of events, and the material has been edited and supplemented by later Christians. Without engaging in the form-critical problem necessary to understand and distinguish the teachings of Jesus and his actions from those attributed to him,[2] some general observations will be considered here that relate to Jesus and the theology of holy war:

1) Jesus was a popular teacher and leader, so he must have been involved in problems that were vital to the Jews of his day.

2) His teachings centered around the Kingdom of God which meant his goals were the same as those of other conquest theologians.[3]

3) He was closely associated with John the Baptist who was beheaded by a political leader who was afraid John would initiate a rebellion.[4]

4) The initial impact of some teachings attributed to Jesus was militaristic: "I have not come to bring peace but a sword."[5] "Let him who has a purse take it, and also a bag; and let him who has no sword sell his coat and buy one."[6]

---

[1] Mt. 22 : 15-21; Lk. 20 : 21-25.

[2] This does not mean that nothing can be known of the historical Jesus. There are rather solid ways of testing which teachings were those of Jesus and which were added later. This requires a careful form-critical study that is far too extensive for this one chapter, but will receive separate attention in the future.

[3] Mt. 4 : 17, 23; 5 : 19; 6 : 33; 7 : 21; 9 : 35; 10 : 7; 12 : 28; 13 : 1-52; 16 : 17; 18 : 1-4, 23-35; 20 : 1, 21, 43; 23 : 13-14; 24 : 14; 25 : 1-13, 31-46; 26 : 29; Lk. 4 : 43; 8 : 1; 9 : 2, 10-11, 27; 12 : 32; 13 : 18-30; 16 : 16; 17 : 20-21; 18 : 16, 24-30; 19 : 11; 21 : 31; 22 : 16.

[4] *Ant.* XVIII.v, 2. Mt. 3 : 1-17; 4 : 12; 11 : 2-11; 14 : 1-13; 16 : 13-14; 21 : 23-27; Lk. 1 : 5-3 : 22; 7 : 18-34; 9 : 7-9, 18-20, 57-62; 10 : 9-11; 20 : 2-8.

[5] Mt. 10 : 34-38; Lk. 12 : 49-53.

[6] Lk. 22 : 36-38.

5) His disciples were not very passive: Simon Barjona (i.e. Simon the zealot); James and John, sons of thunder; Simon the zealot; Judas Iscariot (i.e. the dagger bearer). Two of them wanted to call down fire from Heaven against the Samaritans.[1] One had a sword at Gethsemane.[2] They seemed surprised by Jesus' behavior before the crucifixion. It was only at the last that Judas betrayed him and Peter denied him.[3] They seemed to have thought then that his willingness to suffer was sabotage.

6) He was crucified between two political insurrectionists by the Roman government as one who pretended to be king of the Jews, which meant they thought he was trying to lead a revolution against Rome.[4]

7) His willing acceptance of suffering and death did not surprise his followers so much that they failed to understand its meaning. By the time of Paul's conversion [5] the crucifixion was interpreted in relationship to the suffering servant and the faith of Abraham, and Christian ethics became identified with suffering servant ethics rather than activistic ethics.[6]

8) The gospels record two reports of struggles Jesus had with understanding the exact will of God for him in his own historical situation. These may not be historical accounts, but they were probably composed by some who thought they were representative of Jesus' experiences.[7]

The Gospels tend to depreciate John the Baptist, but still reflect Jesus' high regard for him. Jesus identified the power by which he worked with the authority of John's baptism.[8] Luke held that Jesus was a son of David and John a son of Aaron.[9] Some political

---

[1] Lk. 9 : 51-54.

[2] Mt. 26 : 51-54; Lk. 22 : 49-50.

[3] Mt. 26 : 20-25, 47-50; Lk. 22 : 3-6, 21-23, 47-48; Mt. 26 : 30-35, 69-75; Lk. 22 : 31-34, 54-62.

[4] Mt. 27 : 11-14, 29, 37, 42; Lk. 23 : 1-3, 32, 37, 39.

[5] No later than 37 A.D.—three years before he left Damascus which was during the reign of King Aretas (9 B.C.—40 A.D.). See Gal. 1 : 16-18; II Cor. 11 : 32-12 : 2.

[6] The only clear activistic ethics in the NT are found in the Book of Revelation, in parts which are probably not of Christian composition. The book has been questioned every time the books for the canon have been considered because it has not seemed Christian.

[7] Temptations: Mt. 4 : 1-11; Lk. 4 : 1-13; Gethsemane: Mt. 26 : 36-46; Lk. 22 : 39-46.

[8] Mt. 21 : 23-27.

[9] Lk. 1 : 5-80.

and religious expectations of Judaism anticipated two leaders:
one from Levi or Aaron [1] and one from Judah or Israel.[2] From
prison John asked Jesus if he were the one who should come or
should they look for another, reflecting his impatience. Jesus
responded by noting the fulfillment of Isaiah's prophecy:

> "In that day the deaf shall hear the words of a book,
> and out of their gloom and darkness, the eyes of the blind
>   shall see.
> The meek shall harvest joy in the Lord,
> and the impoverished man will rejoice in the holy One of
>   Israel." [3]

That which John may have been expected to understand, but the
Romans would not, was the continuing verse:

> "For the terrible one will come to nothing
>   and the scoffer, cease,
> and the evil doers will be cut off." [4]

God had been fulfilling prophecy. The rest would soon follow.
But it did not happen. John was beheaded and Herod continued.
This may have required Jesus to rethink his whole program and
reconsider the role of the Messiah. The temptation narratives
indicate that Jesus struggled to resist becoming a ruler of the
land, which would have required a war. This means that the two
kinds of conquest ethics were involved in this decision. At Gethsemane he still prayed that the "cup would pass." [5] The metaphor
of the cup was probably intended to recall the "cup" of God's
wrath that Jews "drank" who suffered after the fall of Jerusalem

---

[1] Zech. 6 : 9-13; T. Reuben 6 : 7-12; T. Sim. 5 : 4-6; 7 : 13; T. Levi
8 : 1-17; T. Judah 21 : 1-5; 25 : 1; T. Iss. 5 : 6-8; T. Naph. 5 : 3-6; 6 : 6;
T. Jos. 19 : 11-12; T. Ben. 11 : 2; 1QS 9 : 11; CDC 14 : 19. Num. R. 18 : 16
interpreted the sons of oil in Zech. 4 : 14 as Aaron and David. To one would
go the priesthood and to the other the kingdom.

[2] Zech. 6 : 9-13; T. Reuben 6 : 11-12; T. Sim. 5 : 4-6; 7 : 13; T. Judah
21 : 1-5; T. Naph. 5 : 3-6; T. Jos. 19 : 11-12; T. Ben. 11 : 2; 1QS 9 : 11;
CDC 14 : 19. H. Kosmala, *Hebräer-Essener-Christen* (Leiden, 1959), 93,
fn. 12-13; 94, fn. 18, has noted that these leaders are not always referred to
as messiahs.

[3] Isa. 29 : 18-19.

[4] Isa. 29 : 20.

[5] Mt. 26 : 39; Mk. 14 : 36; Lk. 22 : 42.

until they had paid double for all Israel's sin.[1] Jesus' followers, at least, understood afterward that he had struggled to learn God's will. If he had received a sign from Heaven that he should lead a war against Rome, he may have been willing to do so. But without divine command, he understood that his role was to suffer so as to cover the sins of Israel. By the time of Paul's conversion, Paul had Jesus' example and had understood Jesus' choice and the religious heritage that taught the effectiveness of suffering in preparation for the kingdom. The teaching of righteous suffering and the treasury of heavenly merits to be built up far outweigh the encouragement for active revenge in the NT. At a period when militant zeal for the law was encouraged as God's will, Jesus and his followers chose the alternative of meritorious suffering.

The interpretation here conjectured for the relationship of Jesus' militant zeal and meritorious suffering may be inaccurate, but the long heritage of conquest theology that directed both types of ethics is a necessary theological background for understanding Jesus' leadership in Palestine. This study has shown that conquest theology which was prevalent in the OT has a double aspect and that both types of ethics were continued into NT times. Those who suffered passively did so as slaves sold because they were unable to pay Israel's debt of sin. They anticipated release according to the rules of sabbatical eschatology.

Conquest theology was closely related to the nation the believers expected to establish after their enemies had been defeated. The kingdom begun by Saul and expanded by David and Solomon later came to be called the Kingdom of God or the Kingdom of Heaven. This conclusion has not been widely held by NT scholars of the last century, most of whom have understood the concept in non-political, non-nationalistic, and non-military terms. For this reason the next chapter will evaluate the views of other scholars and also the evidence available from early sources for understanding the nature of the Kingdom of God.

---

[1] Isa. 51 : 17, 22.

CHAPTER TWO

THE KINGDOM OF GOD

Introduction

Almost simultaneously, Gösta Lundström and Norman Perrin wrote books with the same title and the same basic undertaking—reviewing and analyzing the interpretations of NT scholars concerning the Kingdom of God in the teachings of Jesus.[1] Lundström began his survey with Ritschl, whereas Perrin began with Ritschl's earlier contemporary, Schleiermacher. Ritschl was strongly influenced by Schleiermacher and continued working at some of the same problems Schleiermacher undertook. The principal problem was presented still earlier by Reimarus, whose work received no attention from Lundström or Perrin. Both followed the example of previous scholars in keeping the skeleton hidden in the closet. Schweitzer, however, began his review of NT opinions about the historical Jesus with Reimarus, whose views he described as "makeshift" and "mistaken." But Schweitzer conceded that "Reimarus was the first, after eighteen centuries of misconception, to have an inkling of what eschatology really was." [2] What were the views of Reimarus that were ignored by Lundström and Perrin, on the one hand, but on the other hand, held to be original by Schweitzer? Reimarus began correctly by noting that Jesus nowhere explained what the Kingdom of Heaven was or in what it consisted. Reimarus therefore concluded that the expression must have been already known by Jews of that time, and the Jews must have understood the same meaning that Jesus expressed. If this were not the case, the idiom would not have been an effective term to use in communication.[3] The Jews, according to Reimarus, understood that the Kingdom of God would be revealed in the days of the Messiah on Mt. Zion when all the heathen would be gathered

---

[1] Gösta Lundström, *The Kingdom of God in the Teaching of Jesus*, tr. J. Bulman (Edinburgh, 1963); Norman Perrin, *The Kingdom of God in the Teaching of Jesus* (Philadelphia, c1963).

[2] A. Schweitzer, *The Quest of the Historical Jesus, a Critical Study of its Progress from Reimarus to Wrede*, tr. W. Montgomery (London, 1910), 23.

[3] H. S. Reimarus, „Von dem Zwecke Jesu und seiner Jünger," *Fragmente des Wolfenbüttelschen Ungenannten*, ed. G. E. Lessing (Berlin, 1895), 50.

together at Jerusalem before the God of Israel.[1] Reimarus further argued that the NT supported this position. Commenting on Mt. 24:3, Reimarus said the expression "end of the world" (συντέλεια τοῦ αἰῶνος) in Jewish concepts did not mean the end of the cosmos as the German translation indicated, but rather the end of the period before the Messiah would begin to rule. The disciples were really asking when the Jewish kingdom would be established.[2]

REACTIONS TO REIMARUS

After the first hundred years.—Schleiermacher's attempts to spiritualize the kingdom were resisted by Strauss[3] but generally followed by NT scholars who wrote more liberal lives of Jesus. In 1892, however, Weiss[4] wrote not only in opposition to Reimarus, but also to NT scholars who had composed the "liberal lives of Jesus." Reimarus had been previously opposed by Holtzmann,[5] Ritschl,[6] and other nineteenth century authors who denied any affiliation of the Kingdom of God with a political kingdom. They believed that Jesus spoke of an inner, ethical kingdom, and they explained the eschatological passages in the NT as views of the early church which had been written back into the life of Jesus. Weiss held that these sayings were genuine and that Jesus had anticipated a wholly future, other-worldly kingdom,[7] completely dissociated from a political messiahship, which he conceded continued in Judaism and was reflected in Rabbinic literature, II Baruch, and IV Ezra.[8] Weiss's theory was further supported by Schweitzer.[9] After depicting the futile attempts of the nineteenth

---

[1] Reimarus, *Op. cit.*, 50-51.

[2] *Ibid.*, 86.

[3] D. F. Strauss, *Der Christus des Glaubens und der Jesus der Geschichte* (Berlin, 1865). Schleiermacher was not the first to spiritualize the concept of the kingdom. That had been done long before Reimarus, but Schleiermacher's anti-rationalistic emphasis made it seem much less necessary to pay any attention to Reimarus than was previously the case.

[4] J. Weiss, *Die Predigt Jesu vom Reich Gottes* (Göttingen, 1892; 1900[2]), 58-59.

[5] H. J. Holtzmann, *Die synoptischen Evangelien, Ihr Ursprung und geschichtlicher Charakter* (Leipzig, 1863).

[6] A. Ritschl, *The Christian Doctrine of Justification and Reconciliation*, English tr. and ed. by H. R. Mackintosh and A. B. Macaulay (Edinburgh, 1902[2]).

[7] Weiss, *Op. cit.*, 58-59.

[8] Weiss, *Op. cit,*. 109.

[9] A. Schweitzer, *The Mystery of the Kingdom of God*, tr. W. Lowrie (New York, 1901, 1950[2]), 66-67, 86, 114-115.

century scholars to provide answers to the historical and sceptical
questions raised by Reimarus and Strauss,[1] Schweitzer concluded
that NT scholarship had two alternatives: either a thorough-going
scepticism or a thorough-going eschatology.[2] By thorough-going
eschatology, Schweitzer meant that the entire ministry of Jesus
was based on his conviction that he himself was destined to bring
history to a close in the immediate future with a final cosmic
catastrophe when he, the Son of Man, would appear on the clouds
of heaven. Charles correctly observed that Schweitzer made "no
fresh contribution to the subject" of eschatology, but Schweitzer's
eschatological explanation of the career of Jesus has deeply influenced NT scholarship. Charles, himself, did more than any
other person to interest scholarship in the study of eschatology by
making available apocryphal and pseudepigraphical writings, both
in the original languages and in English translation, together with
his own evaluations and extensive writings on subjects and literature related to eschatology.[3] He believed there were two types
of eschatology, prophetic and apocalyptic, one the child of the
other but in disagreement with its parent.[4] In disagreement with
Dalman, Charles held that the expression "Kingdom of God"
was used eschatologically and signified the divine community in
which the will of God would be perfectly realized.[5] Although
Charles thought later Judaism abandoned all hope of a restored
nation, he allowed a definition that would include it.[6] Under the
definition, eschatology, Charles included all "the teaching of the

[1] D. F. Strauss, *A New Life of Jesus*, 2 vols. (London, 1865).

[2] A. Schweitzer, *Op. cit.*, 328-395.

[3] R. H. Charles, *Eschatology: the Doctrine of a Future Life in Israel,
Judaism and Christianity* (New York, c1963[2]). A fuller appraisal of Charles'
work is given in the introduction to the reprinting of his book. Also included
is a selected list of Charles' major contributions to scholarship. This survey
is only a slightly revised version of the report of scholarship on the subject
of eschatology from 1900-1963 in that introduction.

[4] R. H. Charles, *The Religious Development Between the Old and New
Testaments*, 97.

[5] *Ibid.*, 48. Dalman, *Die Worte Jesu*, 75-119, has been a source of comfort
and assurance to many who have not wanted to consider the political ramifications of kingdom ethics. By holding that the Aramaic for kingdom
really meant "rule" rather than "kingdom," he has kept many scholars from
investigating the matter fully. Some who have followed him are: J. W. Doeve,
Jewish Hermeneutics in the Synoptic Gospels and Acts (Assen, 1954), 138,
144-145; K. G. Kuhn, "βασιλεύς, " *TWNT*, I, 570; J. Bonsirven, *Le Règne
de Dieu* (Aubier, c1957), 33.

[6] Charles, *Religious Development*, 57.

OT, of Judaism, and of the NT on the final condition of man and the world." [1] Eschatology included individual life after death, future national blessedness, the messianic kingdom, resurrection of the righteous dead, the role of Jesus, and the *parousia* or "second coming."

Gunkel compared Gen. 1, Rev. 12, and other biblical and apocalyptical passages with Babylonian etiological myths which reported the creation of the world and of man by the god Marduk. Gunkel concluded that these passages reflected a Babylonian origin. Israel had replaced Marduk with Jehovah [2] and had supposed that the end of time would be like the beginning.[3] At the end, the present world would be destroyed and there would be a new heaven and a new earth, a new paradise, and a new redeemer like Moses.[4] Bousset examined the apocalyptic literature of NT times and saw eschatological opinion within Israel changing from expectation of this-worldly, political kingdom[5] to expectation of a completely new aeon which was otherworldly and would come after this world should be destroyed.[6] Volz recognized a similar development, but said it could not be clearly traced in its temporal progress by one view completely replacing another. Instead, various views were held simultaneously and intermingled in many ways.[7] The Kingdom of God was identified with the Kingdom of Israel in nationalistic Jewish thought, but in broader Jewish eschatology it was the acceptance of God's rule.[8] Eschatology of the individual, Volz maintained, was a contradiction of terms. The destiny of the individual after death had nothing to do with eschatology unless the person who had died was a member of a community which was to be involved in some eschatological act such as a general resurrection.[9] Kohler said Jewish eschatology dealt

---

[1] Charles, *Eschatology*, 1.

[2] H. Gunkel, *Schöpfung und Chaos in Urzeit und Endzeit* (Göttingen, 1894, 1921²), 114.

[3] *Ibid.*, 87.   [4] *Ibid.*, 367-369.

[5] D. W. Bousset, *Die Jüdische Apokalyptik* (Berlin, 1903), 12.

[6] *Ibid.*, 31, 64-65.

[7] P. Volz, *Jüdische Eschatologie von Daniel bis Akiba* (Tübingen und Leipzig, 1903), 1-3, 60-61.

[8] *Ibid.*, 298-300.

[9] *Ibid.*, 1. Up to this point, dealing with eschatology at the turn of the century, Volz's first edition was used. Throughout the remainder of the discussion, his second edition, *Die Eschatologie der jüdischen Gemeinde im neutestamentlichen Zeitalter* (Tübingen, 1934), will be employed.

principally with the final destiny of the Jewish nation and the world generally, but he objected to the conclusions of Bousset and Schürer that this meant the triumph of the Jewish people and the annihilation of all other nations.[1] Kohler said Israel's messianic hope was to do God's will. Before this the kingdom of violence must be removed. Kohler failed to consider the way the kingdom of violence (i.e. Rome) would be removed peacefully. Many rabbis expected Rome to be destroyed when the kingdom of David was restored.[2] Jews did not always hope for the annihilation of all other nations, but for sufficient suppression of the competing or ruling nations to allow Israel freedom and prominence.

NT scholarship.—The "thoroughgoing" eschatology of Schweitzer and Weiss was reinterpreted by C. H. Dodd, who had been influenced by Otto,[3] Gloege,[4] Weiss,[5] and others. Dodd accepted the significance of eschatology in the NT but held that with the coming of Jesus, the prophecies were fulfilled, the Kingdom of God, the Messiah, and the Spirit promised "in the last days" had already come.[6] In the Fourth Gospel and Paul, eschatology was sublimated into mysticism.[7] At the same time, with Jesus there was an end to history but the beginning of the age to come, "which is not history but the pure realization of those values which our empirical life in part affirms and partly seems to deny." [8] Similar views were later expressed by von Rad,[9] Robinson,[10] Frost,[11] Ladd,[12] and others who thought of eschatology primarily as the manifestation of theological values in time. According to Dodd, the prophets and apocalyptists saw the mighty hand of the Lord in the remote past and again in the future, but not in the present.[13] For the early

---

[1] K. Kohler, "Eschatology," *JE*, V, 209-218.

[2] Mekilta, *Vayassa* 6 : 60-64; *Amalek* 2:155-158.

[3] R. Otto, *Reich Gottes und Menschensohn* (München, 1934).

[4] G. Gloege, *Reiche Gottes und Kirche in Neuen Testament* (Gütersloh, 1929), 108-111.

[5] Weiss, *Op. cit.*, 12.

[6] C. H. Dodd, *The Apostolic Preaching and its Developments* (New York, 1936), 32.

[7] *Ibid.*, 66.

[8] *Ibid.*, 84.

[9] G. Von Rad, *OT Theology*, II, tr. D. M. G. Stalker (Edinburgh, 1965), 99-125.

[10] J. A. T. Robinson, *Jesus and His Coming* (New York, c1957), 136.

[11] S. B. Frost, "Eschatology and Myth," *VT*, II (1952), 70-78.

[12] G. E. Ladd, "Why Not Prophetic-Apocalyptic," *JBL*, 76 (1957), 192-200.

[13] Dodd, *The Apostolic Preaching*, 80-81.

church, by contrast, the end had come. Futuristic elements within the NT, like II Thes. 2:7-20, Mk. 13, and the Book of Revelation were reversions to pre-Christian, Jewish eschatology,[1] and did not reflect normative apostolic eschatology.

Dodd's interpretation was promptly challenged by Craig [2] and later by Fuller,[3] both of whom admitted that the end began with the acts of Jesus in history, but neither of whom admitted that the end began with the declaration that the *eschaton* (i.e. the final stage of the apocalyptic process) had completely arrived. Both insisted that the future aspect of eschatology must be taken seriously. Dodd himself, in clarifying his position, explained it more moderately. He conceded that there were two kinds of eschatology in the NT, realized and unrealized, and that these two beliefs lead to some contradictions in most NT writings.[4] Kümmel,[5] after examining crucial passages and evaluating the variant views on the subject, concluded that Jesus did say, "The Kingdom of God has come upon you" (Mt. 12:28; Lk. 11:20),[6] but he also taught that the kingdom was still coming. Kümmel resolved this seeming conflict by saying that God, who would bring about his kingdom in the future, had already allowed his redemptive purpose to be achieved in Jesus. The intrinsic meaning of the eschatological event, then, is the realization of the kingdom of *that* God whom Jesus made known. Therefore Jesus was not primarily concerned with apocalyptic instructions about the date, premonitory signs, or the end of the world.[7] Kümmel also rejected any possibility that Jesus expected a national catastrophe which he deduced from the political situations.[8] These scholars have strained to propose theories that acknowledged, on the one hand, that Jesus expected

---

[1] *Ibid.*, 37-40; see also Robinson, *Op. cit.*, 98-99.

[2] C. T. Craig, "Realized Eschatology," *JBL*, 56 (1937), 17-26.

[3] R. H. Fuller, *The Mission and Achievement of Jesus* (Chicago, c1954), 20-29.

[4] Dodd, *The Interpretation of the Fourth Gospel* (Cambridge, 1954), 7.

[5] W. G. Kümmel, *Promise and Fulfillment*, tr. D. M. Barton (London, c1957); also "Futurische und präsentische Eschatologie im ältesten Urchristentum," *NTS* 5 (1958), 113-126.

[6] Kümmel, *Promise and Fulfillment*, 107.

[7] *Ibid.*, 149-153.

[8] *Ibid.*, 48. See also 100-102. Robinson's view is quite similar to Kümmel's. Robinson called the event that occurred when Jesus was raised and exalted to the right hand of God, "inaugurated eschatology" (pp. 81, 136, 185). This is the point at which the *eschaton* began; it has not yet been concluded.

the kingdom to come momentarily, and on the other hand, did not require them to admit that Jesus was mistaken at this point.

Under the influence of Barth, Bultmann gave a new turn to discussions of eschatology.[1] The end with which theology is concerned, according to Bultmann, is not the end of time, history, or the cosmos. Neither is the goal of prophecy fulfilled in Jesus. In the eyes of the church, the eschatological event began with the appearance of Jesus the Messiah, but the end continues to be realized in the life of the believer. In the preaching of the Christian church, the eschatological event becomes present in faith. Conversion is the time at which the old world reaches its end for the believer and he becomes a new creature in Christ. When a man makes a decision for Christ he is taken out of the world, yet he remains in the world —within its history. He is above history, yet he does not lose his historicity. This is the paradox of the Christian faith.[2]

Bultmann, Dodd, and others who emphasized the end in terms of meaning rather than time have moved away from the temporal, cosmic eschatology of Weiss and Schweitzer and still further from sabbatical eschatology of the Bible or any understanding of the Kingdom of God in terms of the nation of Israel as Reimarus proposed.

Cadoux [3] argued that Jesus, as a Jew, had normal nationalistic feelings, believing the Kingdom of God was for Israelites and that he and his disciples constituted the remnant. He thought Jesus had human difficulties in making decisions and could also make mistakes. Had he not followed Dalman in holding that the Kingdom of God was a human existence under "royal sovereignty" of God without any territorial involvements, he might have related his beliefs about Jesus to a different eschatology. He correctly noted Jesus' pacifistic acts and teachings, but he probably misunderstood his motivation. Cullmann observed a wide hiatus between eschatological theories and Jewish history. He said the NT must be understood against a Jewish rectilinear, rather than a Greek cyclical, concept of time. Eternity is, therefore, endless time seen

---

[1] One of the clearest and most succinct expressions of Bultmann's interpretation of eschatology is "History and Eschatology in the NT," *NTS* 1 (1954/55), 5-16. His best known treatment is *The Presence of Eternity* (New York, c1957).

[2] Bultmann, *The Presence of Eternity*, 151-155.

[3] C. J. Cadoux, *The Historic Mission of Jesus* (New York, n.d.).

in a straight line rather than a "platonic and modern philosophical sense" of timelessness.[1] The mid-point of history toward which Judaism aspired was the future coming of the Messiah. This, for the believing Christian, no longer lies in the future. The Messiah has come. This is a point in past history that occurred between the creation and the *parousia*.[2] The primary event for the Christian faith, then, is not the end which is still to come, but the resurrection which has already occurred and has determined the outcome of the future events.[3] Judaism was eschatologically oriented, but in primitive Christianity eschatology was dethroned and the resurrection was given central place. Nevertheless, primitive Christianity still expected an eschatological drama to take place on this earth within time.[4] Christians now live in the Kingdom of Christ, but the Kingdom of Christ has not yet become the Kingdom of God. This will come only at the end.[5] Feuillet noted that OT eschatological themes, such as those in Daniel, Isaiah, Jeremiah, Zechariah, Ezekiel, and Deuteronomy, were closely related to the theocratic nation of Israel, the dispersion, and final restoration of God's elect. He observed some of the same themes in the NT and concluded that Jesus' judgment on Jerusalem "certainly was not the end of the world . . . Jesus regarded it as the beginning of a new era." [6] If Jesus transcended OT thought, said Feuillet, he was nonetheless consistent with it.[7] Dahl saw that the eschatology of both the OT and the Dead Sea Scrolls anticipated an end in terms of the restoration of Israel as a nation in history. He also noted some similar trends in the NT and he thought eschatology should be reexamined in this light[8]. At the same time Kümmel insisted that the temporal aspect of Jesus' expectation must be taken seriously. Jesus' hope in the immediacy of the fulfillment cannot be dismissed, he said.[9] Hiers noted that Weiss thought

---

[1] O. Cullmann, *Christ and Time*, tr. F. V. Filson (Philadelphia, c1950), 45-46, 51, 69.

[2] *Ibid.*, 82-83.   [3] *Ibid.*, 84-85.

[4] *Ibid.*, 139-141.

[5] *Ibid.*, 208.

[6] A. Feuillet, "Le Discours de Jésus sur la Ruine du Temple," (Suite), *RB* 56(1949), 91.

[7] *Ibid.*, 66, 69, 77-78, 91-92.

[8] N.A. Dahl, "Eschatologie und Geschichte im Lichte der Qumran Texte," *Zeit und Geschichte*, ed. E. Dinkler (Tübingen, 1964), 3-19.

[9] W. G. Kümmel, "Die Naherwartung in der Verkündigung Jesu," *Zeit und Geschichte*, 31-46.

theology could no longer use the expression, Kingdom of God, as Jesus did.[1] Hiers said NT students have found the eschatological Jesus unknown to his own time but intended "for us today," and, as Schweitzer and Weiss did not, attributed modern theological needs to the historical Jesus, thus confusing the theological task with historical fact.[2]

There are a few scholars, like Cullmann, Feuillet, Dahl, Kümmel, and Hiers, who are beginning to reexamine the eschatology in the NT in terms of history or to note the discrepancies of those who do not, but there continue to be those who look only for "spiritual" meanings of the Kingdom of God. Bonsirven, for instance, insisted that the kingdom is spiritual and not national, but his effort to show that the twelve tribes of Israel really constitute the whole church, as used in the NT, is strained.[3] His confession that "glory" is non-nationalistic represents better piety than scholarship.[4] Doeve was sufficiently sensitive to time and space to notice that Jesus was very near the temple at Jerusalem where God's throne was when he referred to himself as the Son of Man.[5] This should have prompted a close inquiry into the political meaning of the Kingdom of God, but it did not. Doeve followed scholars like Weiss and Schweitzer in holding that Jesus anticipated the end of history rather than a political kingdom.[6] K. L. Schmidt, Kuhn, and von Rad distinguished the Kingdom of Israel from the Kingdom of Heaven. The latter, they declared, was a "purely religious concept of the ἔσχατον," which is expressed "in all its exaltation ("God all in all"), wherein there is no longer any place for the special national idea of the link with Israel."[7] Agreeing with Schleiermacher, they disagreed with Reimarus without mentioning his name. Perrin[8] followed Dalman[9] in avoiding the national implications of the Kingdom of God by emphasizing the "rule" rather

---

[1] R. H. Hiers, "Eschatology and Methodology," *JBL* 85 (1966), 174.
[2] *Ibid.*, 58.
[3] Bonsirven, *Op. cit.*, 33, 57, 194-195, 201-202.
[4] *Ibid.*, 54.
[5] Doeve, *Op. cit.*, 142-143.
[6] *Ibid.*, 144-145.
[7] K. L. Schmidt, H. Kleinknecht, K. G. Kuhn, and G. von Rad, *Basileia*, *TDNT*, I, 20-21.
[8] N. Perrin, *Rediscovering the Teaching of Jesus* (New York, c1967), 57. See also 54-57.
[9] G. Dalman, *The Words of Jesus*, tr. O. M. Kay (Edinburgh, 1902), 91-101.

than the sphere ruled. "The eschatological Kingdom of God," he said, was the ". . . final and decisive activity of God in visiting and redeeming his people; no particular form of this activity is necessarily implied and no particular accompanying phenomena must necessarily be present." The literature describing the manner in which the kingdom would come into being and the consequent effect on Israel and her enemies does not confirm this view.

OT scholarship.—Interest in eschatology was not confined to those who studied intertestamental literature or the NT. Gressmann [1] maintained that the pre-exilic prophets anticipated the same kind of cosmic end that was expected in NT times.[2] By this he did not mean sabbatical eschatology. He took the expression "end of days," for instance, as a technical term for thoroughgoing eschatology.[3] He then described passages, like Ps. 93:6 and Gen. 49:8-12 [4] (in which the expression does not occur!), as looking forward to the "end of days."[5] "The day of the Lord," "that day," together with the command to return, all belonged to eschatological rather than historical thought.[6] He agreed with Gunkel that the eschatological time would be a return to original chaos.[7]

Eichrodt agreed with Gressmann that OT prophecy must be seen as "bound up with the certainty that history will be finally broken off and abolished in a new age." [8] The imagery in later Jewish apocalyptic literature described the annihilation of the cosmos with floods of fire. Even the heavenly bodies would be

---

[1] H. Gressmann, *Der Ursprung der israelitisch-jüdischen Eschatologie* (Göttingen, 1905), revised and republished posthumously as *Der Messias* (Göttingen, 1929).

[2] Gressman, *Der Messias*, 74-75.

[3] *Ibid.*, 75-84.

[4] *Ibid.*, 217, 222.

[5] B. D. Eerdmans, *The Religion of Israel* (Leiden, 1947), 322-323, understood eschatology to mean the end of this world and therefore insisted that the references to "the end of days" did not hold this meaning in the OT. Th. C. Vriezen, on the other hand, thought "the end of days" was a technical term for eschatology, but on the basis of context gave eschatology a broader meaning which included a nationalistic hope. For a fuller treatment of this discussion, see "Eschatology and the 'End of Days,' " *JNES*, 20 (1961), 188-193.

[6] Gressmann, *Op. cit.*, 75-84, 147.

[7] *Ibid.*, 100, 110, 118.

[8] W. Eichrodt, *Theology of the OT*, I, tr. J. A. Baker (Philadelphia, c 1961), 385.

effected by this retribution. This was only an extension of the
prophetic picture of judgment which had the same meaning.[1] There
were, he admitted, also opposite trends in the OT. For instance,
the priestly writer of the Pentateuch subordinated eschatology to
history.[2] But whenever prophetic ideas were accepted the present
world order was thought only preparatory.[3]

Mowinckel, contradicting Gressmann,[4] maintained that there
was no thoroughgoing eschatology in Babylonia, Assyria, or Egypt
—nor in the prophets.[5] Even the prophets of doom expected the
restoration of Israel after the disaster, and this future hope left
no place for eschatology which anticipated the end of the world.[6]
As a result of Persian influences while in the diaspora, later Judaism
developed a new eschatology: "dualistic, cosmic, universalistic,
transcendental, and individualistic." [7] The new eschatology was
mingled unsystemmatically with the earlier political hopes for
the future. Sometimes attempts were made to reconcile the two
views by means of a millenium. During this time the Jewish
messianic kingdom would be established, after which there would
be a general judgment and the end of the world.[8] The beginning
of the new eschatology, Mowinckel thought, was evident in Daniel
and Deutero-Zechariah.[9] Coppens criticized Mowinckel for making
too sharp a limitation for messianism and eschatology. He thought
the concepts could have changed and developed with the passage
of time.[10] OT scholars were correct in noticing future hopes in the
NT to be similar to those in the OT. They erred in assuming that
the hopes in the NT or the OT were those described by contemporary
NT scholars. Not all OT scholars made that mistake.

---

[1] Eichrodt, *Op. cit.*, 470-471.

[2] *Ibid.*, 424-429.

[3] *Ibid.*, 268.

[4] S. Mowinckel, *He That Cometh*, tr. G. H. Anderson (New York, c1954),
127-133.

[5] V. G. Fohrer, "Die Struktur der alttestamentlichen Eschatologie,"
Theologische Literaturzeitung, 85 Jahrgang (1960), 402, 419, saw both national
and cosmic ends anticipated in the OT, although he would agree with
Mowinckel that the national hope appeared earlier chronologically. Fohrer,
however, called both expectations "eschatology."

[6] Mowinckel, *Op. cit.*, 131.

[7] *Ibid.*, 271.

[8] *Ibid.*, 277.

[9] *Ibid.*, 266, 271 ff.

[10] J. Coppens, "Les Origines du Messianisme," *L'Attente du Messie*, ed.
Cerfaux and others (Lovanii, 1954), 35.

One OT professor whose conclusions concurred with Reimarus was Kaufmann. The belief which Mowinckel called "future hope" he called "proto-eschatology," [1] if national, or "eschatology," if universal in its dimension. He held that both were based on the covenant; [2] and the belief that God would give Israel the Land of Palestine for an inheritance.[3] Universalistic eschatology thought that Israel's God would become the God of all the nations and that all nations would live in peace with Israel, whose holy city, Jerusalem, would become the religious center of the world.[4] These hopes could not be realized until opposing nations and unrepentant sinners within Palestine were suppressed and idolatry ceased.[5] The Messiah to come was to be a political ruler. The wars of Israel were fought against men and not gods.[6] There was no expectation of a redeemer other than God who would win Israel's battles for her. The God who ruled the Kingdom of Heaven also ruled the earth.[7] He sustained the idolatrous kings without their knowledge. In time he would be revealed so that the other nations would worship him.[8] OT eschatology, according to Kaufmann, does not anticipate the end of time, history, or the cosmos,[9] and in other ways differs from the mythological eschatology of other cultures.[10] Kaufmann's views have been upheld by the research done for this chapter, and he has support for his position from other Jewish scholars such as Klausner and Buber.

Klausner's belief about the messianic age was similar to Kaufmann's view of eschatology, but he did not call it eschatology. He believed the Kingdom of Heaven was Jewish, nationalistic,

---

[1] Y. Kaufmann, *Tôldôt Ha-ʾEmûnâh Ha-Yiśraʾelît* (Jerusalem, 1954), 4 vols. Originally in eight volumes. III, 651-653. Vols. 1-7 have been abridged into one volume and translated by M. Greenberg into English, *The Religion of Israel* (Chicago, 1960). The work is well done, but the major section on eschatology was omitted in the abridged edition.

[2] *Ibid.*, II, 288-293, 512-522; III, 641, 650, 655.

[3] *Ibid.*, II, 155-158, 512-522; III, 643, 648, 652-653, 655.

[4] *Ibid.*, III, 10, 39, 240-241, 249, 252-254, 262.

[5] *Ibid.*, III, 241, 249, 255, 468, 473; IV, 431, 436-438.

[6] *Ibid.*, III, 252, 640-641, 655.

[7] *Ibid.*, 641.

[8] *Ibid.*, III, 240-241, 262, 473; IV, 431, 434, 436, 438.

[9] *Ibid.*, III, 650, 652. Kaufmann made a distinction between cosmological and historical apocalypticism. Ezekiel, he held, did not explain cosmology and was not correctly called the father of apocalypses (III, 542, 626). Daniel is a historical apocalypse dealing with times (III, 16).

[10] *Ibid.*, III, 642-645.

and messianic,[1] but this was to be followed by the new world which would come *after* the messianic age. The expectation of a new world was similar to Schweitzer's eschatology, and Klausner also called it eschatology.[2]

Buber distinguished between the concrete, historical messianic faith, and the expectation of the "end," i.e. eschatology in the strict sense of the word.[3] Israel's expectations were closely tied to an everchanging history. The first literary prophets hoped "for the fulfillment of God's will regarding the right ordering of the people—and radiating from it to the right ordering of the world." This hope was closely linked to someone from the house of David.[4] The "end" expected was peace among the nations and the political and cultural centrality of Zion in the world affairs.[5] The Messiah would be God's viceregent, anointed to establish by human forces "the divine order of the human community." [6] He was to be a human being no "nearer to God than what is appointed to man as man." [7]

A different emphasis was given by the Christian scholar, Von Rad, who held that the coming event expected by the prophets provided a new foundation for faith which formerly had been based on past acts of God in history.[8] This new event would replace the old event in history: the new Jerusalem, new David, new exodus, and new covenant were so important to Israel that

---

[1] J. Klausner, *The Messianic Idea in Israel*, tr. W. F. Stinespring (New York, 1955), 235, 372.

[2] *Ibid.*, 272-273, 414.

[3] M. Buber, *The Prophetic Faith*, tr. C. Witton-Davies (New York, 1949), 142, 150. In this connection the views of the philosopher, H. Cohen, *Religion der Vernunft aus den Quellen des Judentums* (Frankfort, 1929²) deserves attention. Cohen held that the messianic idea of the future was the same as the concept of the suffering servant which was a corporate personality, composed of the remnant of Judaism and those pious Gentiles who shared in bearing the sufferings of mankind (304-305, 311-313). The end anticipated was the messianic era in which humanitarian ethics would be practiced (313). Because there is one God, the messianic age must be for all nations (284). Because the messianic era was bound to history it should thus be distinguished from eschatology (340).

[4] Buber, *Op. cit.*, 142.

[5] *Ibid.*, 150.

[6] *Ibid.*, 153.

[7] *Ibid.*, 153.

[8] G. von Rad, *Theologie des Alten Testamentes*, II (München, 1960). For similar views see P. S. Minear, *Eyes of Faith* (Philadelphia, 1946), 251-276; and R. Bultmann, *The Presence of Eternity*, 36-37.

the old were no longer to be considered.[1] In this, Von Rad was faithful to Jeremiah, and the term he gave to describe this conviction was "eschatology." [2]

Many others, such as these, both OT and NT scholars, have continued to express and reexpress the various possible non-nationalistic interpretations of the Kingdom of God. Some, following scholars like Schleiermacher and Otto, have given it a spiritual or ethical content, whereas others, following Weiss, have given the Kingdom of God a supraterrestrial meaning. The end was thought to be the end of the cosmos rather than the end of a political era. Still others, like Bultmann, have given it an individualistic, experiential meaning divorced from political and cosmic dimensions. Many attempts have been made to avoid the acceptance of a kingdom theology related to the political kingdom of Israel. Scholars have internalized, de-temporalized, de-historicized, cosmologized, spiritualized, allegorized, mysticized, psychologized, philosophized, and sociologized the concept of the Kingdom of God. This has all been done for the purpose of denationalizing it. But almost every scholar who has given some non-nationalistic interpretation of the kingdom has had to deny that there was any relationship between the Kingdom of God and the Land of Palestine or explain that it *once* held a political significance but that in pre-Christian times, it evolved into some other cosmic or spiritual concept. No one has proved these claims, and the political situations and expressions associated with the Kingdom of God are so obvious that the scholar who dislikes political and military associations most finds it necessary to deal with them in some way before appropriating or inventing a non-nationalistic interpretation.

Reimarus' thesis.—Reimarus did not even use the term "eschatology" which has since become popular. The term he used was the "Kingdom of God." He said that Jesus spoke of the same kingdom that his contemporary Jews expected. This was not a completely new idea. Much earlier Tertullian noted that Jesus spoke of preaching the Kingdom of God,[3] and concluded that Jesus was announcing the kingdom of that God whom he knew was the only God of those

---

[1] *Ibid.*, 121-122.
[2] *Ibid.*, 126-127.
[3] *Adv. Marc.*, VII.

listening to him. Although he was primarily arguing that the God
of Jesus was also the God of the Jews, Tertullian's argument also
implied that the kingdom preached by Jesus was the Kingdom
of God the Jews expected. Reimarus revived the idea, however,
but his study in Jewish literature was not very extensive. He
mentioned only targum passages on Micah 4:17, Zech. 16:9, and
Yalkut Shimoni, fol. 178, col. 1, [1] to clarify the type of kingdom
Jews were expecting. A reexamination of the problem here on a
much broader basis will support Reimarus' thesis. The first literature to be examined will be the OT, apocrypha and pseudepigrapha,
rabbinic literature, and Jewish liturgy to learn the way the expression "Kingdom of God" or "Kingdom of Heaven" was used. Once
this has been determined, the next step will be to show that the
idea of the Kingdom of God understood in the OT and later Jewish
literature was continued in the NT. This does not imply that there
was only one view but that the view Reimarus proposed had more
support than he mustered.

Theology and Politics

God's kingdom and God's Son.—The term "kingdom" occurs
many times in the OT, describing various nations with whom the
people of Israel came into contact. Except for a few instances, in
which the nation involved was the ruling nation of the Jews while
in captivity,[2] the expression was used with a definite article only
to describe the United Kingdom,[3] North Israel,[4] or Judah.[5] This
is not surprising. People normally use terms like, "the king" or
"the kingdom," to mean their own king or kingdom. Any other
kingdom needs a further definition. It is also normal for the
expression, "the kingdom" to occur most frequently in the books
of Samuel, Kings, and Chronicles, because those books describe
the political affairs in the Land of Palestine from the time of the
judges until the Babylonian captivity, when the last remnant of

---

[1] Reimarus, *Op. cit.*, 51. The reference in Yalkut Shimoni does not occur
in texts available. He presented much indirect evidence by showing similar
concepts between NT and OT literature.

[2] Ezek. 14:14; Dan. 2:41-42.

[3] I Sam. 15:28; II Sam. 3:10; 16:3; I Kgs. 1:46; 2:15, 22, 46; 11:11, 13,
31, 34, 35; 12:21, 26; 14:8; I Chron. 10:14; 29:11; II Chron. 11:1; 13:8;
Micah 4:8; Obad. 1:21; Hos. 1:4; Dan. 2:44.

[4] II Kgs. 15:19.

[5] II Chron. 14:5; 17:5; 21:3-4; 22:9; 23:20; 25:3; 29:21.

the United Kingdom was overpowered and taken into captivity. Judah was called "the kingdom" much more frequently than Israel because the literature was preserved by the Southern Kingdom. The kingdom in charge of Saul,[1] David,[2] and Solomon,[3] was the United Kingdom. The kingdom ruled by Asa,[4] Jehoshaphat,[5] Ahaziah,[6] Jehoiada,[7] Amaziah,[8] or Hezekiah,[9] was the Southern Kingdom of Judah and Benjamin. Jeroboam [10] and Menahem,[11] of course, were kings of the northern ten tribes. The books of the Chronicler related the rule of the kings over Israel to the rule of God over the same territory. When David was forbidden to build a temple for the Lord, Nathan interpreted the Lord as promising David that he (the Lord) would raise up one of David's sons and establish his kingdom (מלכותו).[12] David's son would build the temple and the Lord would confirm him in the Lord's house (ביתי) and in the Lord's Kingdom (מלכותי) for the age.[13] The son mentioned was Solomon. The kingdom belonged both to Solomon and to God. God was to be Solomon's Father, and Solomon was to be the Lord's son.[14] There was evidently a close relationship between sonship of God and kingship.[15] Of all David's sons, Solomon was selected to rule over Israel.[16] He was chosen to "sit on the throne of the Kingdom of the Lord" (מלכות יהוה) over Israel.[17]

---

[1] II Sam. 3:10.
[2] II Sam. 3:10; I Kgs. 12:26; 14:8.
[3] I Kgs. 2:46; 11:11, 13, 31, 34.
[4] II Chron. 14:5.
[5] II Chron. 17:5.
[6] II Chron. 22:9.
[7] II Chron. 23:20.
[8] II Kgs. 14:5.
[9] II Chron. 29:21.
[10] I Kgs. 12:26; 14:8.
[11] II Kgs. 15:19.
[12] I Chron. 17:11.
[13] I Chron. 17:12-14.
[14] I Chron. 17:13; 22:10.
[15] S. Mowinckel, *The Psalms in Israel's Worship*, tr. D. R. Ap-Thomas (New York, c1962), I, 54, compared the Psalms with the concept of sonship to a deity and kingship in Mesopotamia and Egypt. In both cultures, the deity adopted the king with the formula, "Thou art my son." In Egypt, the clause, "I have begotten thee," was added, as in Ps. 2:7. In Jn. 1:49 son of God was placed in parallel construction with king of Israel:
"Rabbi, you are the son of God;
you are the king of Israel."
[16] I Chron. 28:4.
[17] I Chron. 28:5.

David, certain that his kingdom was secure for his posterity, said,
"Thine is the kingdom, O Lord" (לך יהוה הממלכה).[1] After the
kingdoms had been divided, Abijah tried to regain control of the
northern ten tribes. When he was within shouting distance of the
enemy, the Chronicler presented him as saying, "Are you not
aware of the fact that the Lord God of Israel gave the kingdom
to David over Israel for the age ? to him and to his sons, [confirmed
by] a covenant of salt ? . . . And now you are saying that you will
establish yourselves in place of (לפני) the Kingdom of the Lord
(ממלכת יהוה) through the sons of David!" [2] For the Chronicler,
at least, the Lord's kingdom was the whole *Davidic* kingdom, with
the center of the government at *Jerusalem* and a Davidic king on
the throne. He was indignant to think that North Israel dared
to secede from the government that was not only David's but
Jehovah's. This was the Lord's kingdom because he established it.
The king was the son of God because the Lord chose him to be.
Since only in Chronicles does the expression "Kingdom of the Lord"
occur in the OT, it seems like a good starting point for research.
Unless other data contradicts it, the Chronicler should be expected
to have given the correct interpretation.

The Book of Obadiah is a vengeful prophecy against those who
had assisted the Babylonians in destroying Jerusalem and taking
its citizens captive. The poet, evidently from Judah before the
captivity, looked forward to the day of the Lord (יום יהוה) [3] when
all the nations that had injured Israel would be punished. In that
day Mt. Zion would be restored to a position of power.[4] Both the
northern and southern kingdoms would unite in burning Esau
like stubble.[5] At that time the kingdom would be the Lord's
(והיתה ליהוה המלוכה).[6] This seems to mean that when the people
of the Lord were ruling the kingdom, then the kingdom was the
Lord's. Otherwise it was not.[7] Later rabbis also understood this
to be the case.

---

[1] I Chron. 29:11.
[2] II Chron. 13:5, 8.
[3] Obad. 1:15.
[4] Obad. 1:21.
[5] Obad. 1:17-18.
[6] Obad. 1:21.
[7] There are some problems with the text in the last verse of Ps. 22, but
the quotation, ליהוה המלוכה (22:28), should probably be understood to
mean the Davidic kingdom, as in the similar expression in I Chron. 29:11.

God's rule and Israel's destiny.—The enthronement psalms [1] confessed that God had been made king or had begun to rule. This was true, even though he was from everlasting.[2] When he ruled, nations were subdued.[3] He reigned over the nations [4] who should take note [5] and tremble.[6] The Lord's victory made Zion glad,[7] because victory meant deliverance for the saints.[8] He remembered his steadfast love and faithfulness to Israel.[9] He became great over Zion,[10] and he executed justice in Jacob.[11] His rule was good news to Israel because he chose Israel's heritage,[12] so that his victory also meant Israel's victory. Mowinckel, who related the enthronement Psalms to Canaanite practices before the United Kingdom, believed they were used in annual festivals in which the Lord was declared king anew each year, as if he were only then being enthroned as king. He was probably correct in concluding that "the concept of Yahweh as a king would hardly be adopted by the Israelites until they themselves had got a king, and with him, an obvious occasion to bestow on Yahweh this highest title of honor." [13] The Lord set up his throne in the heavens so that his kingdom could rule over all.[14] His kingdom was glorious and everlasting,[15] but that did not prevent another king from ruling in Israel. In fact it was the Lord who established a Davidic king on Zion, his holy hill, and declared him to be the Lord's son.[16] It was the Lord who placed the king at Jerusalem at his own right hand and who shattered the king's enemies and overpowered all opposing nations.[17] Although the Lord had power over all nations, Israel alone was his chosen people. The Lord overcame other nations so that Israel could

---

[1] Ps. 47, 93, 96, 97, 99, 146
[2] Ps. 93:2.
[3] Ps. 47:3-4.
[4] Ps. 47:8; 98:2, 9.
[5] Ps. 96:10.
[6] Ps. 96:4-5; 99:1-2.
[7] Ps. 97:8.
[8] Ps. 97:10.
[9] Ps. 98:3.
[10] Ps. 99:2.
[11] Ps. 99:4.
[12] Ps. 47:4.
[13] Mowinckel, *Op. cit.*, 125.
[14] Ps. 103:19.
[15] Ps. 145:10-13.
[16] Ps. 2:6-7.
[17] Ps. 110:5-6; 2:8-9.

exist as an independent kingdom, destined to deal in international politics from a position of power which would make all other nations subject to Israel. Israel never did obtain this status, but the Psalms continued to be sung, copied, and perhaps composed. Either they were sung in anticipation of good days ahead, somewhat related to memory of the past, or they may have taken on another meaning which obscured or replaced their original meaning—a use which Mowinckel suggested. Whatever the correct explanation may be, Israel's dream of God's rule over Israel as a free nation in the promised land continued.

In the OT, kingdom theology was closely related to the memory of the Davidic kingdom which was called the Kingdom of the Lord in the books of Chronicles. The expression, Kingdom of God or Kingdom of Heaven, was never used in the OT, but since the Lord was God, the semantic difference is not important. This is the nearest expression in the OT to the NT expression, the Kingdom of God. Before examining the NT, however, other expressions in non-canonical Jewish literature will be considered.

GOD'S RULE AND THE NATION OF ISRAEL

God's kingship.—In the Eighteen Benedictions, God was frequently addressed as king.[1] One request is, "Rule over us, O Lord, Thou alone." This request belongs together with a supplication to restore Israel's judges as at first.[2] This seems to imply that when God was King there were charismatic leaders ruling as before the United Kingdom, and that when God ruled again, the situation would be the same. This is supported by other rabbinic resistance to the Davidic rule: "When he [Israel] heard from Mt. Sinai, 'For mine are the sons of Israel, servants, my servants are they,' she [Israel] broke from herself the yoke of Heaven (עול שמים) and made a king for herself, a yoke of flesh and blood."[3] But in the same Eighteen Benedictions is the request to restore Jerusalem, the Messiah of David, and worship in the temple at Zion.[4] There is also the petition to gather the exiles to Jerusalem,[5] and establish peace with Israel

---

[1] See also Ber. 28b.

[2] D. de Sola Pool (ed.), *The Traditional Prayer Book for Sabbath Festivals* (New York, c1960), 13. R. Johanan said a benediction in which the kingdom was not mentioned was not a benediction (Ber. 40b).

[3] T. BK 7:5 (358).

[4] Pool, *Op. cit.*, 15.

[5] *Ibid.*, 17.

for the age.[1] The views here are not completely unified, but God's activity was associated with more specific events than Perrin acknowledged. There were apparently some differences of opinion concerning which favorable time in the past should be restored, the time of the judges or the time of the great kings. Both systems of government had functioned for Israel in the promised land. Although these prayers did not mention the Kingdom of God, the requests for the return of the Land of Palestine, the restitution of the judges, and the Davidic rule were all closely related to God's ruling over Israel.

King without a throne.—In agreement with Obadiah, rabbis believed that God was not king when the land was not under control of Israel from the capital at Jerusalem, or at least when there was no chosen people to rule. Explaining the text, "He built him up" (יבוננהו,[2] they reasoned, "Until our father, Abraham, came into the world (לעולם), it was as if the Holy One blessed be He were King over the heaven only, as it is said, 'The Lord God of the heaven who took me';[3] but after our father Abraham came into the world, he [Abraham] made him [The Holy One blessed be He] King (המליכו) over the heaven and over the Land of Canaan, as it is said, 'And I will make you swear by the God of the heaven and the God of the land.'"[4] The covenant made with Abraham was the beginning of the Israelite people, the nation, and the promised land. Therefore when God ruled, his people were heirs of his promises, which meant that the land was in their possession, and the Kingdom of God was revealed. When the temple was destroyed and the land in possession of other nations, rabbis said that if Israel regularly met in assemblies to teach and learn the Torah so that they understood what was forbidden and what was permitted, the Holy One blessed be He would regard Israel *as if* it has made him King in his world.[5] This was the only alternative virtue possible for those who could not *really* make the Lord King by reestablishing the Davidic kingdom and worship at the temple. In a lamentation after the fall of Jerusalem, the covenanter said

---

[1] Pool, *Op. cit.*, 21.
[2] Dt. 32:10.
[3] Gen. 24:7.
[4] Gen. 24:3; Sifré *Debarim* 32:10.
[5] Yalkut I. 408 to *Vayakhêl*.

that even if Jews did not recognize their origin or acknowledge
the rule of Him who brought them up out of Egypt (ܪܚܐܘܝܙܝ
ܐܝܨܝ̈ ܠܝ ܠܝܨܚܐܪ ܗܘܢܘ) they would be grieved because of the
fall of Jerusalem.[1] According to IV Ezra, the Most High promised
that at the end those who were saved would see *his* salvation in
his land and within *his* borders which he had sanctified for himself.[2]

God's revelation.—Instead of reading, "Thus shall descend the
Lord of armies to join battle on Mt. Zion," [3] the targum has,
"Thus shall be revealed the Kingdom of the Lord of armies (מלכותא
דיהוה צבאות) to dwell on Mt. Zion." The announcement to the cities
of Zion of the good news that the captivity was over was, "The
Kingdom of your God' (מלכותא דאלהכון) is revealed," [4] instead of
"Behold your God!" The feet that were to bring the good news
were to tread on the mountains *of the land of Israel* and say to
the congregation of Zion, "The Kingdom of your God" (מלכותא
דאלהכון) is revealed." This is the interpretation of the Masoretic
text, "Your God has become King" (מלך אלהיך).[5] The Masoretic
text described the servant as one who "put his life [on the altar],
a guilt offering" and who would "see his seed." The Targum said
that the Lord wanted to test and purify the remnant of his people
to make them innocent of guilt. They would look upon the "kingdom
of their Messiah" and would multiply sons and daughters.[6] The
targumist understood the "Kingdom of the Lord of armies" to be
the same as the "Kingdom of your God." The kingdom of Israel's
God was to be revealed to the congregation of Zion and the good
news concerned the Land of Israel. The interpreter looked forward
to the kingdom of the Messiah where the posterity of the Babylonian
and other captives could dwell and multiply children after their
return from captivity. The Lord's becoming king was the same as
the kingdom of the Lord being revealed at Zion.[7] Instead of
"The kingdom will be the Lord's," the targum had "The Kingdom
of the Lord will be revealed over all those who dwell in the land." [8]

---

[1] II Bar. 75:8.
[2] IV Ezra 9:6-9.
[3] Targ. Isa. 31:4.
[4] Targ. Isa. 40:9.
[5] Isa. 52:7.
[6] Targ. Isa. 53:10.
[7] So also Targ. Micah 4:7.
[8] Targ. Obad. 21.

The prophecy in Zechariah was, "And the Lord will become King (והיה יהוה למלך) over all the land; in that day the Lord will be one and his name one."[1] The targum interpreted that to mean, "And the Kingdom of the Lord will be revealed (ותתגלי מלכותא דיי) over all those who dwell in the land; in that time they will serve the Lord [as] one shoulder. Behold his name will be established in the age (בעלמא) and there will be none beyond him." The targumists evidently believed that whenever the Lord became King, the Kingdom of the Lord would be revealed in Israel and vice versa.

Four things were called possessions in the OT: Israel, the Land of Palestine, the temple, and the Torah. They were summarized thus: "May Israel, which is called a possession, enter the land, which is called a possession, and erect the temple, which is called a possession, by virtue of the Torah, which is called a possession."[2]

THE KINGDOM AND ROME

Promises and obstacles.—The covenant with Aaron and the Torah were both given unconditionally, but the Land of Israel, the temple, and the kingdom of David were all given conditionally. If Israel kept covenant, these would be received; if not, they were withheld.[3] The Kingdom of God involved the establishment of all three. There were seven things that were hidden from men: "1) the day of death; 2) the day of comfort; 3) the depths of judgment; 4) no one knows in what he can profit; 5) no one knows what is in the mind of his fellow; 6) the kingdom of the house of David—how long until it is restored to its place; and 7) this guilty kingdom—how long until it is uprooted?"[4] The day of comfort was the time when the Kingdom of God was to be revealed, the land restored, and the captives set free. The depth of judgment referred to the amount of guilt weighed against Israel that had to be paid before she could be returned from captivity. The kingdom of David in its place was the political Kingdom of Israel. This could not be established until the wicked kingdom [Rome] was uprooted. Discussing the same enemy nation, R. Eleazar asked, "How long will it be until the name of these people is destroyed? At the time when idolatry will be uprooted and its idol worshippers;

---

[1] Zech. 14:9.
[2] Mekilta *Shirata* 9:124-126.
[3] Mekilta *Amalek* 4:132-143.
[4] Mekilta *Vayassaʿ* 6:61-64.

then the Lord will be the only [God] in the world; and his kingdom
(מלכותו) will be for the age and for ages of ages." [1] There could be
no halfway. It was either Rome or Israel. "R. Judah in the name of
R. Samuel, said, 'Whenever the Israelites are in exile, the Kingdom
of Heaven is not at peace, and the nations of the earth dwell in
serenity. But whenever the Israelites are redeemed, the Kingdom
of Heaven is at peace, and the nations of the earth tremble. Hence,
The Lord reigns! Let the peoples tremble'." [2]

When God's kingdom would appear, Jews visualized the Eternal
God arising from his royal throne to punish the Gentiles and destroy
their idols. Then Israel would be happy, because she would "mount
up on the necks and wings of the eagle [Rome] and they [the
Romans] shall be ended." [3] In her own judgment, Israel was destined
to judge the nations and rule the whole earth.[4] The poet who
confessed that the Lord was King and that the "Kingdom of our
God (ἡ βασιλεία τοῦ θεοῦ ἡμῶν) was forever over the nations in
judgment," [5] also reminded the Lord that he had chosen David
to be king over Israel [6] and urged the Lord to raise up for his
chosen people their king, the son of David.[7] The establishment of
a Davidic king over Israel would involve shattering unrighteous
rulers,[8] rescuing Jerusalem from the nations,[9] and gathering
together the saints at Jerusalem after it had been cleansed and
made holy.[10] The heathen nations would be subject to the Davidic
king,[11] who would be the anointed of the Lord[12] even though the
Lord himself would be King at the same time.[13] The Sibyl looked
forward to the time when God would raise up his kingdom over
men.[14] At that time the people to whom he had made promises
(i.e. Israel) would be blessed with prosperity and gladness,[15] and

---

[1] Mekilta *Amalek* 2:159-163.
[2] Mid. Ps. 99:1.
[3] Assump. Mos. 10:1-8. A reflection of Dt. 32:11 and Isa. 40:31.
[4] Jub. 32:19; Wis. 3:8.
[5] Ps. of Sol. 17:1, 4.
[6] Ps. of Sol. 17:5.
[7] Ps. of Sol. 17:23.
[8] Ps. of Sol. 17:24.
[9] Ps. of Sol. 17:25.
[10] Ps. of Sol. 17:28, 32, 34.
[11] Ps. of Sol. 17:32.
[12] Ps. of Sol. 17:36.
[13] Ps. of Sol. 17:38, 51.
[14] Sib. Or. 3:666-668.
[15] Sib. Or. 3:669-671.

gifts and frankencense would be brought to the temple of the great God which would then be the only temple in the world for future generations to know.[1] After Rome gained control over Egypt so that Gentile political force would be all concentrated in one country, "then the greatest kingdom of the immortal king will appear."[2] The Messiah would come and Rome be destroyed in the judgment of the eternal God, the mighty King.[3]

According to Amram's Kaddish, the Jews prayed that God's kingdom would reign (וימליך מלכותיה), his salvation spring forth, and his Messiah draw near.[4] Together with the request for God's kingdom they prayed that God would revive the dead, build up the city of Jerusalem, complete the temple, root out foreign worship from the land, bring holy worship in its place, and that the Holy One blessed be He would rule his kingdom.[5] This is combined with requests for peace from Heaven, life, abundance, salvation, comfort, liberation, healing, redemption, forgiveness, atonement, expansion, and victory for Israel.[6] This prayer does not identify God's kingdom with the Kingdom of Israel, but it discloses a relationship between God and Israel that understood that whenever God's kingdom was in power that the Land of Israel with its accompanying promises of prosperity would be restored to Israel. Hence to pray for God's kingdom was the same as praying for the restoration of the Davidic kingdom.

The yoke of the kingdom.—As part of their daily worship, Jews were required to recite the *shema'*. This recitation was called accepting the yoke of the Kingdom of Heaven (עול מלכות שמים).[7]

---

[1] Sib. Or. 3:672-676. [2] Sib. Or. 3:46-48.
[3] Sib. Or. 3:55-104. [4] Pool, *Op. cit.*, XII.
[5] *Ibid.*
[6] *Ibid.*, XIII. The prayer for the major feasts (תפלת מוסף לרגלים) acknowledges that it is because of Israel's sin that Jews cannot offer sacrifices in the temple at Jerusalem as the law prescribes. The Lord is requested to "rebuild it [the temple] quickly and magnify its glory" (ותבנהו מהרה ותגדל), (כבודו) reveal the glory of his kingdom(גלה כבוד מלכותך עלינו), exalt Israel before all people, gather in the dispersed Jews from among the nations, and bring them to Zion, the Lord's city (לציון עירך), to the Jerusalem temple (לירושלים בית מקדשך), where they might again fulfill the commandments of sacrifices prescribed in the Torah (S. Singer [tr.], *The Authorized Daily Prayer Book* (New York, 1915), 234—from Hebrew text there).
[7] Ber. 2:2, 5; 14b-15a; 16a; 21a. There are only fifteen passages in the total Mishnah containing the expression, "kingdom," and several of those use it in ways that do not apply to this study.

Rabbis said that the one who separated himself from sin, meaning that he observed such rules as dietary laws, took upon himself the Kingdom of Heaven (מלכות שמים). If he refused to separate himself, the person in question would belong to Nebuchadnezzar and his fellows rather than the Lord.[1] This means that a Jew in captivity could have allegiance to only one government. Either he mingled and became a real citizen of the country in which he lived, or he refused to mingle and remained a citizen of the Kingdom of Heaven. His recital of the *shemaʿ* was an oath of allegiance. The Kingdom of Heaven, of course, was closely related to Palestine— so much so that some Jews believed that "every Israelite who lived in the Land of Israel accepted the yoke of the Kingdom of Heaven" (עול מלכות שמים), and that every Israelite who left the land was as if he were worshipping idols. So it was with David when he left the land to settle near Philistia. He said, "Cursed be those before the Lord, for they have banished me today from becoming a citizen in the inheritance of the Lord, saying, 'Go worship other gods!' "[2] Rabbi Akiba said that the Israelite who accepted the prohibition against receiving interest from his brother accepted the yoke of Heaven (עול שמים), whereas if he charged interest to his brother, he classed himself with the Gentiles by casting off the yoke of Heaven (עול שמים).[3] Rabbis interpreted the scripture passage, *"The time of singing* (הזמיר) *has come near"* (הגיע),[4] as follows: "The time of the foreskin has come near that it may be cut-off (שתזמיר); the time of the Canaanites has come near that they may be cut-off (שיזמירו); the time of the Land of Israel has come near that it may be apportioned to Israel . . . *The time of singing has come near.* The time of the foreskin has come near that it may be cut-off; the time of the wicked has come near that they may be broken, as it is said, *The Lord has broken the staff of the wicked.*[5] The time has come near for the Babylonians to be destroyed; the time of the temple has come near that it may be rebuilt . . . The time of the Kingdom of the Cutheans has come near that it may be destroyed; the time of the Kingdom of Heaven has come near that it may be revealed (הגיע זמנה של מלכות שמים שתגלה), as it

---

[1] Sifra Lev. 20:26, 93b.
[2] Sifra Lev. 25:38; 109b.
[3] Sifra 190b.
[4] Song of Solomon 2:12.
[5] Isa. 14:5.

is said, *and the Lord will become king over all the land* [1] *and the voice of the turtle is heard in our land.*[2] What is this? This is the voice of the king messiah who proclaims (המכריז) and says, *How beautiful upon the mountains are the feet of the publisher of good news.*"[3] When the Kingdom of Heaven came, the faithful Jews who accepted the yoke of the kingdom with all of its risks and responsibilities would be rewarded with prosperity and the privilege of citizenship. Jews who accepted the yoke of the Kingdom of Heaven comprised a subversive force against any "wicked kingdom" which controlled Palestine.[4]

Scribes under surveillance.—The expression "Kingdom of Heaven" occurs only a few places in rabbinic literature and the term "Kingdom of God," not at all. There are several possible explanations for this phenomenon. One might be that, in opposition to Christianity, later Judaism discontinued many terms that were basic to Christianity. Another is that, following the Bar Cochba revolt, Romans observed Jewish activity so carefully in order to prevent further insurrectionist movements that Jews who wished to live no longer discussed openly or published widely their expectations that involved the restoration of the Davidic kingdom and accompanying destruction of Rome.[5] Hegesippus said that after the fall

---

[1] Zech. 14:9.   [2] Song of Solomon 2:12.

[3] Isa. 52:7; Cant. R. 2:13, 2-3; *PR* 15, 75a.

[4] This does not agree with Perrin's opinion that "no particular form of this activity [of God's rule] is necessarily implied" in Kingdom of God eschatology (p. 57). In straining to show that the Kingdom of God Jesus proclaimed was different from that described by the Jewish texts, Perrin, *Op. cit.*, 57-59, noted that in the NT the kingdom was to "come," which differed from Jewish hopes that it would be "manifested" or "established." This strains the accuracy of the Jewish reports and means only that many verbs were used synonymously. Rabbis expected the Kingdom of Jehovah (מלכותא דייי) to be revealed when the Messiah, who had been kept from before the bosoms of the congregation of Zion, would receive the kingdom which was destined to *come* to him (עתידא מלכותא למיתי) (Targ. Micah 4:7-8); and II Baruch expected the new age (ܐܠܡܐ ܐܬܐ) to come (ܐܬܐ) (44:12). R. Tanḥuma (3:28b), described the exodus from Egypt to which eschatological hopes were attached and on which they were based as "a time to be redeemed which had *come*" (שבאתה השעה להיגאל). "Coming near" (הגיע or ἤγγικεν) was used both by the NT and Jewish literature. Other terms like "coming," "being revealed," "happening," and "being established," were synonymous ways of describing the same event. If the kingdom were of a different character, as Perrin maintained, it would have to be shown in some other way.

[5] For stories of Roman censorship see BK 38a; JBK 4b, IV, § 5; Sifré *Debarim* 33:3, 143b, § 343.

of Jerusalem, Vespasian made a careful search to find any members
of the family of David so that this royal tribe might be completely
annihilated, leaving no possible pretenders to the throne.[1] In the
time of Domitian some sons of David were found and they were
questioned concerning their beliefs about the messiah and his
kingdom (περὶ τοῦ χριστοῦ καὶ τῆς βασιλείας αὐτοῦ). They explained that the messianic kingdom was not earthly but heavenly
and angelic. It would come at the "end of the age" (ἐπὶ συντελείᾳ τοῦ
αἰῶνος). Since this sounded innocent enough to Domitian, the
suspects were released.[2] Had Domitian known that a "heavenly"
kingdom could be very closely related to political aspirations and
that the "end of the age" could refer to the end of the Roman
rule, he probably would not have been so lenient. Since their
literary activity had to pass Roman censorship, political insurrectionist activity had to be disguised in seemingly meaningless terms
and visions which had meaning only to Israelites. One such seemingly innocuous narrative was Rabbi Yishmael's vision. He saw
the future tortures and rewards stored up for Israel to pay for
her sins and virtues. The climax of the vision came when King
David appeared with all his successors wearing crowns. The scene
was to take place in heaven, but the practical question was, when
would a descendant from David's line be restored as ruler in
Jerusalem?[3] Another eschatological story portrayed the Lord
building a temple of great splendor in heaven, but the political
message of the apocalypse was the question of the messiah, David,
to the Lord concerning the time when the Lord would lower the
temple to the earth.[4]

Reimarus' claim.—Reimarus said that the kingdom the Jews
were expecting was a political kingdom in the messianic age with
a son of David ruling from Zion. This investigation has confirmed
that part of his assertion. The kingdom in the OT usually referred

---

[1] *HE* III.xii.1.

[2] *Ibid.* III.xix.1-xx.6. Eusebius reported that these sons of David were
close relatives of Jesus. This is possible, but it does not ascertain that they
were Christians who anticipated the return of Jesus as Messiah. They may
have expected some other son of David to become the king over Israel in the
messianic kingdom.

[3] Y. Ibn-Shmu'el, *Midreshê Ge'ûlâh* (Jerusalem, 1953/54), "*Davîd, Melekh
Yiśra'êl,*" 8-10.

[4] *Ibid.,* "*Yerûshalayim shel Ma'alâh,*" 20-22.

to Judah, Israel, or the United Kingdom. The United Kingdom was called the Kingdom of the Lord and Solomon was called the Son of God. The understanding that the Kingdom of God was also the Kingdom of Israel continued into later Jewish documents. There seemed no conflict between the idea that God was King at the same time someone from David's line sat on the throne. There were very close relationships seen between the expectations to be fulfilled when the Kingdom of God or the Kingdom of Heaven was revealed and the expectations of the political kingdom of Israel. When Israel was not a free nation on the land, some believed that God was not King. He needed a nation and a people to rule in order to be the ruler. When the Kingdom of God came the good news would be proclaimed in the Land of Israel. The chief obstacle in NT times for the coming of the kingdom was the power of Rome. There was an either/or attitude toward the Kingdom of Heaven and the Roman Empire. Jews believed the latter would be destroyed, and to that end fought the war of 66-72 A.D. and later the war of 132-135 A.D. After the Bar Cochba failure, Jews were suppressed and their nationalistic hopes limited or disguised, but their political aspirations and religious convictions did not cease.

With such a long, continuous, and consistent relationship between militarism and religion, the nation of Israel and the Kingdom of God in earlier Israelite and later Jewish thought, it would be strange indeed if the Christianity, which arose from this environment, accepted the expressions of the major tenets of Israel's faith with a completely spiritual meaning. Reimarus was right. If this were done, Christians would have had to explain and define their terms to keep them from being confused. It is sound scholarship to expect that people who lived on the same land at the same time with the same religious background had the same meanings for the same terms unless distinctions were shown. Since the first half of Reimarus' claim was correct, the next investigation will be to examine the NT to learn the extent to which the second half of his claim was also right. Reimarus said Jesus also referred to the free Davidic kingdom on the promised land when he spoke of the Kingdom of God or the Kingdom of Heaven. He claimed the apostles revised some of the gospel accounts, particulary after Jesus' death, but he did not ask whether the rabbinic literature had preserved valid accounts of the sayings of the rabbis. Since Reimarus' time both Strauss and Wrede have further quertioned the reliability of the documents, and since rabbinic literature has no more basis for confidence than the NT, therefore this study will not attempt to deal directly with Reimarus' second claim. Instead of discerning the valid teachings and reports of Jesus, this work will show the relationship of the attitudes and expectations in the NT to those held by Jews prior to, during, and later than NT times.

THE NEW EXODUS

The good news.—The author of Hebrews, comparing the "rest" Christ gave with the "rest" offered the Israelites when they left Egypt, said, "We received the good news just as they did." [1] This is only one instance in the NT which compared the deliverance expected with Israel's deliverances in the past. Before Jesus' birth, the angel Gabriel was reported to have told Mary that Jesus would be given the throne of his father, David, and that he would rule the house of Jacob forever.[2] Apart from contradicting evidence, this appears to be a promise that Jesus would be the kind of king David was—a ruler over the promised land. Jesus, John the Baptist, and Jesus' apostles preached, "Repent, for the Kingdom of Heaven has come near" (ἤγγικεν).[3] The situation was very similar to the rabbinic report of the exodus from Egypt. The exegete pictured Moses recovering the bones of Joseph for the Israelites to take with them back to the promised land. Moses went to the Nile, engraved the Tetragrammaton on a golden tablet, threw it into the Nile and called: "Joseph, son of Jacob, the oath which the Holy One blessed be He swore to Abraham, our father, that he would redeem his sons, is ready to be fulfilled (הגיע).[4] This was

---

[1] Heb. 4:2.

[2] Lk. 1:32-33.

[3] Mt. 3:2; 4:17; 10:7; Mk. 1:15; see also Lk. 4:43; 8:1; 9:2, 11, 60; 10:9, 11.

[4] Mekilta, *Beshallaḥ* 1:93-96, 106-107. P. Seidensticker, "Die Gemeinschaftsform der religiösen Gruppen des Spätjudentums und der Urkirche," *LA*, 9 (1959), 94-198, has shown well the close relationships between Jewish sects and the OT upon which they were based. Then he strained to show that these features were not at work in the NT. One bold assertion is as follows: "Die neue Epoche, die mit *Jesus von Nazareth* angebrochen ist, wird also nicht mehr durch 'Gesetz und Propheten' bestimmt, sondern durch die Verkündigung des Evangeliums. Damit ist eine Ordnung des Heils grundgelegt, die nicht mehr von der im Exodus proklamierten Grundordnung Israels als des priesterlichen Volkes abhängt, sondern durch die Proklamation des Reiches Gottes geformt wird" (p. 179).

just as the Israelites were leaving Egypt. It meant that the chosen people had suffered enough to cover their sins and the Lord was ready to fulfill his oath by delivering his people from bondage to restore them to the promised land. R. Isaac used the same verb to say that the time of the Kingdom of Heaven had come near (הגיע זמנה של מלכות שמים). This was the same time that the wicked would be broken, the Canaanites cut-off, Cutheans destroyed, the Land of Israel apportioned to the Israelites, the King Messiah proclaim good news, and the Lord become King over the land.[1] In a similar Jewish background based on the same scripture and the same religious and political history, John, Jesus, and the disciples were also expecting a new deliverance and recovery of the kingdom. They, too, believed that the time was ripe for God to fulfill his oath.[2] This was the "good news of the kingdom" (τὸ εὐαγγέλιον τῆς βασιλείας) which Jesus announced was near.[3] The deliverance other Jews proclaimed was associated with the good news II Isaiah announced regarding the exodus from Babylon. The prophet told the cities of Zion that the Kingdom of God was being revealed.[4] The land was being restored. The temple would

---

[1] Cant. R. 2:13, 2-3; See also *PRK* V.ix; XII.xviii; XII. lv. J. Weiss, *Die Predigt Jesu vom Reiche Gottes* (Göttingen, 1892, 1900²), 70, preceded C. H. Dodd by many years in concluding that the Greek ἤγγικεν and ἔφθασεν were renderings of the Aramaic מטא, because מטא in Dan. 4:8 was rendered by Theodotian as ἔφθασε and by the LXX as ἤγγιζε. One instance is hardly enough to prove which term was translated *regularly* by Greek terms used. Contexts in which הגיע was used in rabbinic literature, for which there is no Greek translation, are much nearer the NT context than Dan. 4:8, and there are many more examples. See particularly *PR* 15:75a and Cant. R. 2:13; also *PRK* 5: 8, 11-13; 19:4, 9-13; Nid. 10:1, and Sifré *Bemidbar* 27:14 § 137, 51b. In Song of Songs R. 7:2 § 1 (35d) מטא was used with the same force usually given הגיע, showing the synonymous character of those terms. In the story, Gentile neighbors were planning to plunder and rob the houses of two wealthy Jews while they were in Jerusalem worshipping, but "when the time came" (מטא זמנא), God appointed two angels who looked like them to go in and out of their houses so the Gentiles thought the Jews were still there. This means מטא is one, but not the only, word used to describe the arrival of time. הגיע was used much more frequently. Dodd was admittedly dependant upon R. Otto, *Op. cit.* Seven years before Dodd's *The Apostolic Preaching and its Developments* (New York, 1936), 32, G. Gloege, *Op. cit.*, 108-111, had suggested that with the ministry of Jesus the beginning of the future had already started. The present and future do not stand in antithesis to each other, but are organically woven in and through each other.

[2] See further Sifré *Bemidbar* 27:14 § 137, 51b.

[3] Mt. 4: 23; 9: 25. See also p. 65, fn. 7.

[4] Targ. Isa. 40:9; 52:7.

be rebuilt, and the exiles would be returned. The author of Hebrews compared the good news proclaimed under the leadership of Moses, Aaron, and Joshua with the good news heralded by John and Jesus, and it seems quite likely that Jesus and John were preaching the same good news of the same kingdom.

The conflict before the conquest.—John from Patmos said that Jesus, the firstborn from the dead, was ruler of the kings of the earth and that he had also made a kingdom for Christians.[1] While John was in prison, it was evident that the kingdom had not yet been established on earth, but the conflict that was to bring this about was symbolically expressed. On the one side was the Lamb, the saints, angels, and the child; on the other side were such adversaries as Babylon, the harlot, the dragon, the beast, the devil and/or satan. The enemy was Rome, the harlot on seven hills,[2] who played the role previously played by Pharaoh, Nebuchadnezzar, or Antiochus Epiphanes. All the rest of the opponents were her collaborators. The child was the Messiah,[3] who was probably also the Lamb. The Lamb was also the Lion of Judah, son of David,[4] who shepherded those who had been cleansed.[5] There was war in heaven and on earth as in the conflict against Sisera.[6] When satan and his angels were thrown to earth, the voice from heaven declared: "Now is salvation and power and the Kingdom of God and the authority of the Messiah.[7]

The message was set in a typological format that would remind Jews who knew their scripture of earlier significant deliverances of the chosen people from foreign enemies and the restoration of their promised land. Like the trumpet blast announcing jubilee [8] when the land would be restored and the captives set free, so the trumpet blast of the seventh angel marked the end of the time specified for waiting,[9] after which the kingdom of the world would become the Kingdom of the Lord and his Messiah.[10] At that time

---

[1] Rev. 1:5-6, 9-10.
[2] Rev. 17:1-10.
[3] Rev. 12:1-17.
[4] Rev. 5:1-14.
[5] Rev. 7:15-17.
[6] Jdgs. 5:4-5, 20-21.
[7] Rev. 12:10.
[8] Rev. 25:8-17.
[9] Rev. 10:7.   [10] Rev. 11:15.

the "dead" would be judged and the servants of God rewarded.[1]
As in Daniel, the seventh angel swore by him who lived forever
and ever.[2] The two witnesses who were raised [3] were reminders of
the two olive trees and two lampstands which symbolized Joshua
and Zerubbabel, the two anointed ones who stood by the Lord
of the whole land.[4] They were the first priest and king of the land
after the captives returned from Babylon. The measuring stick,[5]
like the measuring line,[6] was to prepare for the New Jerusalem.
The plagues that worked against the enemy were like the plagues
of Egypt.[7] While the enemy, Rome, was burned with fire,[8] the
saints rejoiced [9] because this meant that the Lord God of armies
was reigning.[10] The enemy nations were described as "beasts" [11]
and "horns" [12] as in Daniel. The decisive battle was to be fought on
Mt. Megiddo, the strategic point of defense for the promised land.[13]
The song of the Lamb was sung together with the song of Moses,
a great victory cry describing the overthrow of the Pharaoh at
the Reed Sea in the first exodus.[14] The good news was that all
of this was expected to happen again.

Promises of the covenant.—The backbone of covenantal theology
was the belief that God had made certain promises to his chosen
people. These could not be rescinded. They would certainly be
fulfilled if only the covenanters met his requirements. The beatitudes
in the Gospel assured the covenanters that God would fulfill his
promises if his people behaved as did the suffering servant in the
Babylonian captivity. Just as the prophet promised that the Lord
would revive the spirit of the humble [15] and bring good tidings
to the afflicted and broken hearted who would be released to

---

[1] Rev. 11:18.
[2] Rev. 11:5-6.
[3] Rev. 11:1-13.
[4] Zech. 4:1-14.
[5] Rev. 11:1-2.
[6] Zech. 4:3, 11-14.
[7] Rev. 8:6-10; 16:1-21.
[8] Rev. 14:11.
[9] Rev. 18:20; 19:1-7.
[10] Rev. 18:6.
[11] Rev. 13:1-18.
[12] Rev. 17:7-18.
[13] Rev. 16:16.
[14] Ex. 15; Rev. 15:1-4.
[15] Isa. 57:15.

return to the Kingdom of Israel,[1] so the poor in spirit were those
who would become citizens of the Kingdom of Heaven.[2] The
prophet promised comfort for all those who mourned. These were
those who mourned for Zion during her humiliation.[3] The meek,
who, like the servant, had suffered without retaliation and had thus
borne the sins of Israel, would be doubly rewarded, according to
the prophet.[4] The beatitudes promised that the meek would
inherit the land, which has the same meaning.[5] The ones who were
hungry and thirsty for righteousness longed for a reestablishment of
the land where Levitical purity would be possible, sacrifices offered,
and dietary laws kept. When the kingdom would be established,
only orthodox Jews would be in the land; righteousness would be
possible; the saints would be satisfied.[6] Even the highway to Jerusalem would be exclusively for the redeemed of the Lord to avoid
any uncleanness.[7] God shows mercy to his people when he restores the
land and fulfills his promises. This would be done for the merciful.[8]
The pure in heart were those who had kept not only their bodies
ritually clean, but their motives upright. These would return to
worship in the temple where, like Isaiah,[9] they could "see God." [10]

---

[1] Isa. 61:1.

[2] Mt. 5:3; Lk. 6:20.

[3] Isa. 57:18; 61:2-3; Ezek. 9:3-4.

[4] Isa. 40:1; 53; 61:7.

[5] See also Ps. 22:26-28; 37:9-11. The Greek, ἡ γῆ, renders the Hebrew,
הארץ, which sometimes means "the world," but usually means "the land,"
namely the Land of Palestine. In the context of the reception of OT promises,
the meaning intended for the beatitude in Mt. 5:5 is the land rather than the
"earth" which most English translations give. Acts of Thomas 94 said that
the meek were counted worthy to inherit the heavenly kingdom, which
means Palestine, not the world. The Latin text of *Didache* 3:9, quoting
Mt. 5:5, rendered ἡ γῆ as *sancta terra*. It is not likely that *sancta* was
added by a late Christian editor; it is rather an accurate translation of a
different Greek text that read ἡ ἁγία γῆ or ἡ γῆ ἡ ἁγία.. See J. P. Audet,
"Affinités Littéraires et Doctrinales du 'Manuel de Discipline,' " *RB* 59
(1952), 217-238. 4Qp. Ps. 37:11, 21-22 interpreted the passage, "And the poor
will inherit the land (ארץ)" (the promise related to Mt. 5:5) referring to "The
Ebionites (האביונים)" who would "inherit the mount of the high place of
Israel, the mount of his holiness" (הר מרום ישראל והר[קדשו) (4Qp. Ps.
37:1, 8-11).

[6] Mt. 5:6.

[7] Isa. 35.

[8] Mt. 5:7.

[9] Isa. 6:1; also Ps. 24:34; 15:1-5.

[10] Mt. 5:8. The promise that anyone would ever see God seems strange
in the light of other biblical testimony. I Jn. 4:12 said that no man had
ever seen God. Israelites were warned to stay back from Mt. Sinai, with

The true Israelites were God's sons. [1] God would call those who

its smoke and fire, lest they look and perish (Ex. 19:16-21). Moses was told
that no one could see the Lord's face and live (Ex. 33:20), even though the
Lord's presence would go with his people (Ex. 33:14). Nevertheless, after
the commandments had been given, Moses, together with Aaron, Nadab,
Abihu, and the seventy elders of Israel went apart from the people and saw
the God of Israel (ויראו את אלהי ישראל). They saw God and ate and drank
(ויחזו את האלהים ויאכלו וישתו, Ex. 24:9-11). This took place at a festival
at the top of the mountain covered with a cloud (Ex. 24:15-16). Moses also
reminded the Lord that he was seen face to face (עין בעין נראה) and that
his cloud stood over his people and that the Lord went before them in a
pillar of cloud by day and a pillar of fire by night (Num. 14:14). Isaiah was
in the temple when the place was filled with smoke and he there saw the Lord
(ואראה את אדני, Isa. 6:1). Those who lived in the temple (i.e. the priests)
were required to walk blamelessly in certain specified ways (Ps. 15:1-5).
He who ascended the hill of the Lord was required to have clean hands and a
pure heart (Ps. 24:3-4). Rabbis understood the passage, "Because in a cloud
(כי בענן) I will be seen (אראה) on the ark cover" (Lev. 16:2), to refer to
the cloud of smoke made by incense offered by the priest on the Day of
Atonement when he entered the Holy of Holies. The incense was to be offered in such a way that the priest's vision there would always be blurred
by the smoke, lest he "see God" improperly (Sifra 81b; JYoma I, V, 39a-39b;
see also Ex. R. 34:1; RH 31a; Mekilta *Shirata* 10:24-43). Philo insisted that
even when he entered the holy of holies, the high priest could not see anything
(Spec. I.72; cf. Ebr. 136; Gig. 52; Leg. 306). J. Z. Lauterbach, *Rabbinic
Essays* (Cincinnati, 1951), 60-61, said, "It cannot be denied that the primitive
notion was that the tabernacle, and later on the temple in Jerusalem, were
the residences of God on earth and that the Holy of Holies within the temple
was especially the place where He dwelt, and the ark-cover with the two
Cherubim being, so to speak, His throne. The Rabbis often sought to suppress or modify these primitive beliefs, or at least, to remove from them the
crude anthropomorphic elements, but they were not always successful.
These primitive beliefs were retained by the people and echoes of them are
found in the Talmud and in the Midrashim." It seems, then, that the experience in which Isaiah saw the Lord in the temple with the smoke and the
fire was a situation much like that of the priests offering sacrifice and like that
in which Ezekiel saw the likeness of the glory of the Lord in the temple
(Ez. 10:1-2). Ezekiel said the throne held one whose appearance was like a
man (אדם, 1:26). Both experiences were related to smoky, fiery situations
in the temple, somewhat like that at Mt. Sinai when the leaders saw the God
of Israel while the mountain was covered with a cloud (Ex. 24:9-16), and
also the description of the Lord who was seen in the pillar of cloud [smoke]
and fire caused by the burning fire at the tent of meeting (Num. 14:14).

After the wilderness wandering, the place where God could be seen was
in the temple and there only by those who had clean hands and pure hearts.
In Mt. 5:8, then, those who had pure hearts were promised that they could
see God (τὸν θεὸν ὄψονται). In context of OT promises that were expected
to be fulfilled, the beatitude probably meant that those who had pure hearts
would live to worship in the temple, where they, like Isaiah and the priests,
could see God.

[1] Dt. 14:1.

made peace rather than reaping vengeance, who received persecutions rather than giving them, his sons.[1] All of these characteristics defined in the beatitudes represented the type of non-resistant behavior that was typical of the servant in II Isaiah, and all the promises made were standard expectations that would accompany the restoration of the land to the chosen people. The first generation in Babylon suffered for the sins of Israel. God, in turn, returned the captives to Palestine. Again in the first century, Jews expected that if they fulfilled the same requirements, God would in turn give them the Kingdom of Heaven.[2] This did not just mean that diaspora Jews would be returned, that the land—then under Roman rule—would be freed so that it could become God's kingdom and the local residents could become citizens. Matthaean promises were all centered around a new restoration like the one following the Babylonian captivity. Promises, such as mercy, comfort, inheriting, and being called God's sons, were all familiar OT promises. Also the land[3] and the Kingdom of Heaven[4] were the possessions Jews had traditionally wanted. This is another evidence that Christians in NT times were expecting the same deliverance and the same kingdom other Jews expected.

New heaven, earth, and Jerusalem.—According to Hebrews, the patriarchs sojourned by faith in the land of the promise, but they looked forward to a city that had foundations whose Builder and Maker was God.[5] The city mentioned was Jerusalem, "Mt. Zion, the city of the living God, the heavenly city,"[6] which was traditionally thought by the faithful to be eternal. The kingdom which could not be shaken[7] was probably the same as the kingdom of the Son of Man and the saints of the Most High.[8] That was to have been an everlasting kingdom in contrast to the four preceding kingdoms of the foreign nations which had all perished except the fourth, and it was destined to be destroyed within three and

---

[1] Mt. 5:9-10.
[2] Mt. 5:3, 10.
[3] Mt. 5:5.
[4] Mt. 5:3, 10.
[5] Heb. 11:8-10.
[6] Heb. 12:22.
[7] Heb. 12:28.
[8] Dan. 7:13-14, 27.

a half years. The everlasting kingdom reported in Daniel was the Maccabean state which followed after the downfall of the Seleucid Empire. Hebrews probably referred to the same city as Zion and the same kingdom as Palestine—the Davidic and Hasmonean kingdom.

The only real objection to this interpretation is the anticipation of a *heavenly* city.[1] Even though this was called "Zion" as well, it has led many scholars to interpret Hebrews in terms of Platonic philosophy.[2] Fritsch has shown that the Platonic interpretation of Hebrews is not only unnecessary, but unlikely.[3] He has done this by showing that Hebrews was not unique in comparing the earthly tabernacle with its heavenly pattern. Originally the tabernacle used in the wilderness was built according to the pattern or type which Moses was given on Mt. Sinai.[4] Hebrews referred to this fact to indicate the author's own familiarity with that OT belief.[5] Not only the tabernacle, but also the temple was built at Jerusalem according to the plan received from God's hand,[6] and God made his name to dwell there.[7] While in captivity, after the temple had been destroyed, Ezekiel was given a vision of the ideal temple which he described in detail so that the temple in Jerusalem might be built according to that plan when the land was restored.[8] Fritsch further gave examples of other ancient cities in the Near East which were claimed to have been antitypes of heavenly patterns. After the fall of Jerusalem, Jews believed that the temple God had recorded on the palms of his own hands (ܡ݂ܟ݂ܬ݂ܒ݁ܝ ܘ݂ܐ݂ܟ݂ ܡ݂ܟ݁ܐ ܓ݂ܠ݂ܝ) was taken from his people, just as Paradise was taken from Adam, because of sin. The temple was shown to Adam, Abraham, and Moses before it was built in the land. Then God preserved both the temple and Paradise with him (ܟ݂ܡ݂ܝ݂ܢܝ ܐ݂ܟ݁ܝ ܐ݂ܝ݂ܟ݁ ܐ݂ܬ݂ܝ݁ܟ݁ ܐ݂ܠ݂ܝ).[9] Afterwards Jews looked

---

[1] Heb. 12:22.

[2] W. Manson, *The Epistle to the Hebrews* (London, 1951), 124-126; J. Moffat, *Hebrews* (ICC), xxxi ff., 107 ff.

[3] C. T. Fritsch, "TO ANTITUPON," *Studia Biblica et Semitica* dedicated to Th. C. Vriezen (Leiden, 1966), 100-107.

[4] Ex. 25:9, 40; Num. 8:4; Acts 7:44; Fritsch, *Op. cit.*, 101-103.

[5] Heb. 8:5 referred to Ex. 25:40.

[6] I Chron. 28:11-19.

[7] I Kgs. 8:29; Ezek. 48:35.

[8] Ezek. 40-48.

[9] II Bar. 4:1-7.

forward to the time when the heavenly city and the heavenly temple would appear on earth still more luxurious than before in the position where the antitype formerly stood—at Zion.[1]

That the author of Hebrews related his theology to OT expectations and examples is evident from his comparison of Jesus with the old Joshua; the "rest" promised to the people of God with that into which Joshua was to lead the faithful;[2] the new high priest and sacrifices with the Levitical priesthood and their inferior sacrifices;[3] and the new covenant with the old.[4] In the same manner, the author contrasted the heavenly temple where Jesus ministered to the antitype previously located at Jerusalem. Some of the Dead Sea Scroll fragments seem to reflect an anticipation of the destruction of the temple and establishment of one built with God's hands.[5] Flusser has compared this to the report that Jesus planned to destroy the temple and build another not made with hands.[6] According to Pseudo-Philo, Joshua referred to the altar built across the Jordan by the two and a half tribes stationed there as an "altar made with hands" (*sacrarium manufactum*) associated with idols.[7] The expression "made with hands" (χειροποίητος) frequently referred to idolatry in the Septuagint, rendering אליל or אלילים. LXX Daniel rendered "gods" as "idols made with hands"; Stephen described both the temple and the golden

---

[1] IV Ezra 7:26; 8:52; *SO* 5:420-429; *Bereshith Rabbiti*—see Y. Ibn-Shmuʾel, *Op. cit.*, 20-22. Rabbis said that the earthly temple was like the heavenly temple (JBer. IV.5.8c) and that the Lord would not enter the heavenly Jerusalem until he had entered the earthly Jerusalem (Taʿanith 5a). There in the Holy of Holies the Lord consented to confine himself to one square cubit of space (Ex. R. 34:1; see also RH 31a; Mekilta *Shirata* 10:24-28). The Lord built the temple with his own hands (*Ibid.*, 10:29-42) and when he built it again with his two hands, he would again rule from there (*Ibid.* 10:42-43). Philo said that the temple not made with hands was in heaven. The temple made with hands (χειρόκμητον) Moses allowed, but he permitted only one temple for one God (Spec. I [66-67]).

[2] Ps. 95:7-11; Heb. 3:11-19; 4:1-11.

[3] Heb. 3:1; 4:1-5:10; 7:1-26; 9:11-14, 25-10:14.

[4] Heb. 8:6-13; 9:1, 15-22; 10:16-29; 12:24.

[5] 4Q Florilegium. See J. M. Allegro, "Fragments of a Qumran Scroll of Eschatological Midrâšîm," *JBL*, 77 (1958), 350-354.

[6] D. Flusser, "Two Notes on the Midrash on II Sam. 7," *IEJ*, 9 (1959), 99-104; and Mk. 14:58; Mt. 26:61; Jn. 2:9; Mk. 15:29; Mt. 27:40; and Acts 6:14; Also see Y. Yadin, "A Midrash on II Sam. 7 and Ps. 1-2 (4Q Florilegium)," *IEJ* 9 [1959], 93-98, and R. Hummel, *Die Auseinandersetzung zwischen Kirche und Judentum* (München, 1963), 106-107.

[7] Pseudo-Philo 22:5.

calf as objects "made with hands"; and Paul was quoted in relationship to the pagan temples in Athens as saying that the Lord did
not dwell in temples made with hands (χειροποιήτοις ναοῖς).[1]
Enoch told of the temple that had been folded up and carried
off. After that, however, the Lord of the sheep provided a new
temple (ቤተ፡ ሕዳስ) which was bigger, but placed where the old
one had formerly been.[2] IV Ezra thought that when the Messiah
was revealed then the city which had previously been hidden
would appear (وتظهر المدينة التي لم تكن تظهر).[3] When the Son is revealed
Zion will become visible to all men, prepared and built without
hands (*parata et aedificata . . . sine manibus*).[4] Like other Jews and
Christians after the fall of Jerusalem, the author of Hebrews probably expected the heavenly temple restored to Mt. Zion when
the people entered their promised "rest" in the Land of Canaan.[5]

The same kind of expectation was reported in the Book of
Revelation, with more extensive manifestations. Heaven and
earth were expected to pass away before the new creation. But in
the new creation was a new Jerusalem which would come down
from heaven[6] (insuring perfection in pattern) and also the twelve
tribes of Israel whose names would be written in the Lamb's book
of life.[7] The Petrine prophet after the fall of Jerusalem encouraged
Christians not to become discouraged because the kingdom had
been delayed in coming. He reminded them of the unlimited
power of God, who had once destroyed all the world and all the
living beings except the small remnant that escaped with Noah.
Christians might expect something like this to happen again.
Then after the disaster, God would create a new heaven and a new
earth.[8] The prophet did not promise a new Israel or a new Jerusalem. He and the author of Rev. 21 both mixed their kingdom
typology with the flood typology, but since both found biblical

---

[1] Isa. 2:18; 19:1; 31:7; LXX Dan. 5:4, 23; 6:27 (28); Acts 7:41, 48.
See further S. G. Sowers, *The Hermeneutics of Philo and Hebrews* (Zürich,
c1965), 110, fn. 57.

[2] Enoch 90:28-29.

[3] IV Ezra 7:26.

[4] IV Ezra 13:36.

[5] B. Gärtner, *The Temple and the Community in Qumran and the NT* (Cambridge, 1965), 11-122, believed the heavenly temple to be the Christian
community "not made with hands."

[6] Rev. 21:2, 10.

[7] Rev. 1:27.

[8] Gen. 9:8-17; II Peter 3:7-13.

bases for their prophecies, it is likely that they expected a continuation of the remnant of Israel after the destruction and the
fulfillment of God's promise. Hebrews and Revelation related their
heavenly expectation to the product on earth where God's promises
were to be fulfilled.

Kingdom and community.—Various sects in Judaism and Christianity believed themselves to be the only true remnant of Israel.
This meant that in their own judgment, they alone would be
admitted into the kingdom, whenever it was reestablished. The
Petrine community, for instance, believed that Peter was given
the keys to the Kingdom of Heaven.[1] Those whom he permitted
would be admitted by God and those whom he judged guilty would
be rejected.[2] Jesus told the man who wanted to inherit eternal
life that he must sell all his possessions and give the money to the
"poor" (probably the community which called itself the poor).
This was similar to the full membership requirements for the
Essenes.[3] After the man had declined the terms, Jesus said that
it was very difficult for a rich man to enter the Kingdom of Heaven.[4]
Having eternal life [5] was used here synonymously with entering
into life [6] and entering the Kingdom of Heaven.[7] This meant that
sectarian membership was necessary for entrance. When the scribe
supported Jesus' understanding of the first and second greatest
commandments, Jesus told him he was not far from the Kingdom
of God,[8] by which he probably meant that his doctrine was close
to that required for membership. There could be no vacillation
among the members. Those who put their hands to the plough and
looked back were not well set (εὔθετός) for the Kingdom of God.[9]
Those who were members were taught some secret knowledge, called
gnosis, torah shebe 'al peh, or mysteries of the Kingdom of God.[10]

---

[1] Binding and loosing, or forbidding and permitting, in Hebrew thought
frequently refers to court cases where the one bound becomes a prisoner
and the one loosed, set free.
[2] Mt. 16:18-19.
[3] *BJ* II (122).
[4] Mt. 19:16-25; Mk. 10:23-25; Lk. 18:18-25.
[5] Mt. 19:16.
[6] Mt. 19:17.
[7] Mt. 19:23, 24.
[8] Mk. 12:28-34.
[9] Lk. 9:62.
[10] See *Clem. Rec.* III.lxvii.

The Fourth Gospel records the term, "Kingdom of God" only twice, and the term "kingdom" was used only an additional three times in one verse. Since "eternal life" was frequently used by the authors of this book, scholars have concluded that "Kingdom of God" and "eternal life" were synonymous terms. Since eternal life was thought to be a known factor which meant immortality, therefore, the somewhat unknown factor, the Kingdom of God, which was frequently used in the synoptic gospels, should be understood, by transfer, in the same way.[1] Chapter IV concedes the possibility that membership in the Kingdom of God was believed to be eternal life, but it challenges the general assumption that eternal life regularly meant immortality in NT times. It will not be necessary to anticipate that discussion, however, because the usage of the expression "Kingdom of God" in the Gospel of John is not sufficiently frequent to provide a confident conclusion about its meaning. Nonetheless, the expressions that occur will here be examined to see the possible meanings suggested by the contexts.

Nicodemus was told that he must be born again or he could not see the Kingdom of God.[2] Being born again in Jewish concepts usually referred either to the forgiveness that takes place on the Day of Atonement or to proselyte baptism, and the latter is probably the meaning intended for Nicodemus. Nicodemus had to be born of the water and of the Spirit before he could enter the Kingdom of God.[3] Seeing the Kingdom of God [4] and entering it [5] evidently had the same meaning. Jesus seemed to be asking Nicodemus to give up his Judaism and become a Christian proselyte, which would be eternal life.

Before Pilate, Jesus said that his kingdom was not of this world,[6] which has led many scholars to believe that Jesus was talking about an other-worldly kingdom.[7] "The world" in the Gospel of John and the Johannine epistles, however, does not refer to the earth in contrast to heaven, but existence outside the sect as over against "life" inside the covenant community. The Jews, like

---

[1] See L. van Hartingsveld, *Die Eschatologie des Johannesevangeliums* (Assen, 1962), 39.
[2] Jn. 3:3, 5.
[3] Jn. 3:5.
[4] Jn. 3:3.
[5] Jn. 3:5.
[6] Jn. 18:36.
[7] Weiss, *Op. cit.*, 48-59.

Nicodemus, did not belong to the Johannine sect. Therefore they
did not have eternal life, and so belonged to the world. Pilate had
asked Jesus if he were the king of the Jews.[1] Jesus denied that he
was a king of a group whom he classed as belonging to "the world."
He acknowledged that he was a king and that he had come into
"the world," where he associated with non-sectarians like the
Judaeans,[2] but he did not want to be identified with that group.

Since the Gospel of John probably had its origin in a Samaritan
Christian community [3] and was distinctly anti-Judaic, it is under-
standable why that group would not endorse a kingdom whose
plan was the reestablishment of Jerusalem as the capital of all
twelve tribes of Israel, so its doctrines were modified. It may have
thought of the kingdom in relationship to Mt. Gerizim or the
Samaritan Christian community, but the usage of the expression
was not frequent enough to make that clear.

Before the jubilee.—Sabbatical eschatologists had no doubt that
the Lord would restore his kingdom to his chosen people. The only
question was, "When?" What would be the sign of his appearance
and the end of the age (συντελείας τοῦ αἰῶνος)? [4] The answers
given were different. Some held that it would come soon. The
ability of Jesus to work miracles, like Aaron in Egypt just before the
exodus, by the finger of God [5] should be sufficient testimony that
the Kingdom of God was just around the corner.[6] It was about
to appear suddenly.[7] There were certain signs that should be clear
to the disciples that the Kingdom of Heaven was near.[8] They
should be in constant expectation, like virgins waiting with lamps
trimmed and plenty of oil for the bridegroom to come to his
wedding.[9] The maximum time of waiting necessary would be the
time prophesied by Daniel: forty-two months,[10] one thousand two

---

[1] Jn. 18:33.
[2] Jn. 18:37.
[3] See further, "The Samaritan Origin of the Gospel of John," *Religions
in Antiquity. Essays in Memory of Erwin Ramsdall Goodenough* (Leiden,
1967), 162-188.
[4] Mt. 24:3.
[5] Lk. 11:20.
[6] Mt. 12:28.
[7] Lk. 19:11-12.
[8] Lk. 21:31.
[9] Mt. 25:1-10.
[10] Rev. 11:2; 13:5; Rev. 12:14.

hundred and sixty days,[1] or three and a half years.[2] The apostles
were sent to announce the immediate approach of the Kingdom
of Heaven [3] and were told that they would not finish their task in
Israel before the Son of Man would come.[4] Jesus told his disciples
that there were some standing there who would not "taste death"
until they saw "the Son of Man coming in his kingdom." [5] In Daniel,
when the Son of Man came he was given the dominion and glory
and the kingdom [6] at the same time the saints were also given the
kingdom and the dominion.[7] The kingdom given there was the
Maccabean state which followed many years under the subjection
of beasts. At the last supper with his disciples, Jesus vowed that
he would not eat the Passover again or drink any more wine until
he drank it anew in the Kingdom of God.[8] Vows of abstinence
such as this are usually taken in crisis situations shortly before
an important turning point is expected.[9]

There were others who urged Christians not to be anxious.[10]
There would be wars and rumors of wars, but the end was not yet.
Paul told Christians that they should not be so confident of the
kingdom's early coming that they did not take care of their own
necessary daily tasks.[11] In reply to the scoffers who had noticed
that the three and a half years predicted by Daniel had long since
passed, II Peter reminded them that one day is as a thousand
years with the Lord.[12] Christians should continue to wait for and
hasten the coming of the day of God.[13] Jesus compared the coming
of the kingdom to a mustard seed or leaven which grew quietly and
invisibly.[14] The strong man was probably the Roman government

---

[1] Rev. 11:3.
[2] Rev. 12:14.
[3] Mt. 10:23.
[4] Mt. 16:27-28.
[5] Lk. 9:27; Mk. 9:1 adds "in power."
[6] Dan. 9:13-14.
[7] Dan. 7:26-27.
[8] Mk. 14:25; Lk. 22:14-18.
[9] Such as Jdgs. 11:30-40; I Sam. 14:24; II Kgs. 3:27; Acts 23:12-13.
[10] Mt. 24:5-9.   [11] II Thes. 3:6-12.
[12] II Peter 3:3-8.   [13] II Peter 3:11-22.
[14] Mt. 13:31-33; Mk. 4:26-32; Lk. 13:18-21. For the use of "leaven" as
a negative infiltration movement as in Mt. 16:6, see Ber. 17a: "Master of
the ages, it is revealed and known to you that our will [should be] to do your
will. Now, what hinders? The leaven which is in the dough (שאור שבעיסה)
and servitude to the kingdom. May it be your will that we be delivered from
their hands."

which could not be taken without first developing an effective intelligence operation to weaken and sabotage the government from within.[1] When Jesus told the Pharisees that the kingdom would not come suddenly, he said it was already in their midst (ἐντὸς ὑμῶν).[2] This may have referred to an underground operation that was already at work, but not openly visible.

After the Israelites tested the Lord in the wilderness by spying out the land before entering, the Lord took an oath that none of the men of that wicked generation who were guilty of that sin would enter the promised land.[3] Only Joshua and Caleb would be allowed to inherit the Land of Israel, together with the toddlers (טפים) and teenagers (בנים) who were not legally accountable for the decision that evoked the Lord's anger.[4] Jesus told the disciples that they should not reject the children, for to such as these belonged the Kingdom of Heaven.[5] This may have meant that, just as for the Israelites who left Egypt (with two exceptions), only the children and youth lived to enter the kingdom, so the younger generation of Jesus' time would be the ones who really would live to be the leaders and citizens of the kingdom they were expecting. That would be true even if the kingdom were to come suddenly.

The problem with sabbatical eschatology was that it worked within a time table of sabbaths and jubilees. Prophets interpreted for the faithful when the periods of servitude began and when they were just about over. Since this was a subjective judgment, the

---

[1] Mt. 12: 29.

[2] Lk. 17:20-21. C. H. Dodd, *Historical Tradition in the Fourth Gospel* (Cambridge, 1963), 401, fn. 1, followed C. H. Roberts in translating ἐντὸς ὑμῶν "within your reach" or within your grasp, but did not explain how or in what way. Perrin, *Op. cit.*, 74, claims ἐντὸς ὑμῶν means "a matter of human experience." C. H. Roberts, "The Kingdom of Heaven (Lk. 17:21)," *HTR* 41 (1948), 1-8, quoted Cyril of Alexandria (Migne PG 72, *Comment. in Luc.* § 368 [col. 841]), σπουδάσατε δὲ μᾶλλον τυχεῖν αὐτῆς ἐντὸς γὰρ ὑμῖν ἐστι· τουτέστιν ἐν ταῖς ὑμετέραις προαιρέσεσι καὶ ἐν ἐξουσίᾳ κεῖται τὸ λαβεῖν αὐτήν, which could be translated as follows: "So, be very eager to attain it, for it is 'in your midst'; that is, it lies in your choice and authority to take it." Cyril may have understood this also to be a subversive movement which was prepared to take over governmental control. Even R. H. Charles, *Religious Development*, 68, however, thought the kingdom that was "within" was a personal, ethical preparation for the entrance into the coming Kingdom of God.

[3] Dt. 1:34-35.

[4] Dt. 1:36-39. See "OT Meaning of the Knowledge of Good and Evil," *JBL*, 75 (1956), 114-120.

[5] Mt. 19:13-14; Mk. 10:13-14; Lk. 18:15-16.

authorities differed on matters of schedule, both in Jewish and Christian circles, but the consistency was maintained that there would be an end.[1] The end expected by Jews was the reestablishment of the chosen people as free citizens of a kingdom on the promised land. The details of the Christian expectations were so similar that it is quite likely that, except for Samaritan Christians, they too were expecting the reestablishment of the Davidic kingdom.

The kingdom and the diaspora.—One of the important promises of sabbatical eschatology was that the Lord would gather to Palestine all of the Jewish slaves whom he had "pushed" into the diaspora

---

[1] The beginning and the *end* were eschatological terms sometimes expressed as the *alpha* and the *omega*, the first and last letters of the Greek alphabet (Rev. 1:18). This in Hebrew would be the *aleph* and the *tau*. The *tau* is made like the sign of the cross and may have been a sign used to express hopes for the end of the current evil era. The beginning had taken place, but the end would come only when the promises were fulfilled. Whether or not this conjecture is accurate, as early as the time of Ezekiel, those pious Jews in Jerusalem who lamented the wickedness of the city and longed for its *end* were said to be manted with the sign of the *tau* on their foreheads (Ezek. 9:4). Rabbis said that the angel Gabriel put a *tau* of ink on the foreheads of the righteous and a *tau* of blood on the foreheads of the wicked, so that the destroying angel might distinguish them and destroy the wicked. Rab said, "*Tau* [stands for] 'You shall live' (תחיה) and *tau* stands for 'You shall die' (תמות)" (See also Ps. of Sol. 15:8-10). Resh Lakish said *tau* was the end of the seal of the Holy One blessed be He (Shab. 55a). Other covenanters spoke of the Lord's "seal" (ܚܬܡܐ) worn by the elect archangels (Odes of Sol. 4:7-8) and the seal which the Lord put on the faces of those who were his (Odes of Sol. 8:14-15). The elect in the Book of Revelation (7:3; 9:4-5; 14:1) were the 144,000 from the twelve tribes of Israel who were sealed with a seal or the name of the Father and the Son on their foreheads so that they could be spared the plagues that would destroy the wicked. These are intentional allusions to the sign of the *tau* placed on the foreheads of the elect in Jerusalem. The followers of Jesus who took up the cross before the crucifixion may have been the faithful ones who wore the sign of the *tau* on their foreheads, admitting openly their Zionism—their longing for the end of the evil era and the restoration of Zion. Tertullian (Adv. Marc. 3:22) said the apostles suffered because they were the very ones of whom Ezekiel spoke who had been sealed on their foreheads with the letter *tau*, which, he explained, was like the Latin "T." Tertullian reminded Christians that they too wore the mark of the cross on their foreheads. The close relationship of the sign of the cross (*tau*) to covenantal faithfulness, longing for the end of the evil age and the restoration of Zion, and the early Christian symbols relating the *alpha* and the *omega* to the cross suggest that the sign of the cross was initially the sign of the *tau* which symbolized the hope for the end of the evil era.

until they had paid double for all their sins.[1] Therefore it was
proper for later Jews to expect the Messiah to gather in the Jews
from other nations. After Vespasian and Titus had successfully
captured Jerusalem and all of the fortresses on the promised land,
there continued to be uprisings in the diaspora as one messiah
after another arose, each to lead a group of insurrectionists who
hoped to regain the promised land.[2] Philo expected that in the
messianic age, the Messiah would rule from Jerusalem and would
have no international problems because he would rule the whole
Near East and Roman world.[3] Other Jews of the Greco-Roman
period expected that the righteous would judge nations and have
dominion over peoples.[4] They believed the Lord promised Israel
the entire world as a possession to be ruled by Israelite kings.[5]
When the disciples were reported to have asked Jesus about the
signs for the end of the age, his reply was that, among other things,
this good news of the kingdom must be preached in all the civilized
world (οἰκουμένη)[6] as a testimony to all the nations. Then the end would
come. This was something like gathering in the Jews of the diaspora.
Paul evidently understood that this would be necessary for the
coming of the kingdom, because he was eager to go beyond Asia
Minor to Rome and on to Spain, the end of the Roman Empire,
and probably from there around the southern shore of the Mediterranean Sea until he had fulfilled the requirement.[7]

The Acts of the Apostles described the disciples and early
leaders of the church preaching the gospel of the Kingdom of God
in the Roman world, from Jerusalem, to all Judaea, and Samaria,
to the ends of the world.[8] Those who believed were baptized and

---

[1] Jer. 31:1-9; 33:1-18; 50:4-7, 17-20; 51:5, 10; Ezek. 11:15-21; 20:40-
44; Isa. 49:5-6; so also *PRK* 16:8; Jer. 16:18; Isa. 40:2; 61:7.

[2] *BJ* VII (409-436).

[3] See H. A. Wolfson, *Philo* (Cambridge, 1948), I, 407-426, and E. R.
Goodenough, *The Politics of Philo Judaeus* (New Haven, 1938), 115-120.

[4] Wis. of Sol. 3:1-8.

[5] Jub. 32:18-19.

[6] οἰκουμένη usually refers to the whole Roman Empire; see Jos. *Ant.* VIII.
iii.4; Lk. 2:1.

[7] See J. Knox, "Romans 15:14-33 and Paul's Conception of his Apostolic
Mission," *JBL* 83 (1964), 1-11; and G. D. Kilpatrick, "The Gentile Mission
in Mark and Mark 13:9-11," *Studies in the Gospels* (Oxford, 1957).

[8] Acts 1:8. See also W. C. Van Unnik, "Der Ausdruck ʽΕΩΣ ʽΕΣΧΑΤΟΥ
ΤΗΣ ΓΗΣ (Apostelgeschichte 1:8) und sein Alttestamentlicher Hintergrund,"
Studia Biblica et Semitica, 335-349.

received the Holy Spirit.[1] The gospel of the Kingdom of God had a long pre-Christian history of relationship to political involvement. There is no certainty that the early church was free of this. One of the post-apostolic prayers thanked God for life (ζωῆς) he had made known through Jesus and prayed that he would gather together his church (ἐκκλησία) from the ends of the earth into his kingdom (βασιλεία).[2] If this prayer was consistent with the OT theology, that would have meant the elect of God were members of the church and the kingdom would have been a geographic location to which members could come.

Position in the kingdom.—The Pauline author of the Pastoral Epistles believed that Jesus would be the judge of the living and the dead, that he would appear, and that he would rule his kingdom.[3] To the disciples who were anxious about their future, he said that in the renewal (παλιγγενεσία), when the Son of Man ruled, then the twelve would also rule over the twelve tribes of Israel. Those who had given up a great deal to follow Jesus would receive in return many times more than they had given up and then they would inherit eternal life.[4] Without allegorizing, it would appear that the disciples and Jesus were both speaking in terms of national

---

[1] Acts 8:12.

[2] *Apos. Cons.*, Bk. VII, ch. xxv (see Schaff, 269-280).

[3] II Tim. 4:1.

[4] Mt. 19:27-29; Lk. 18:28-30 and 22:28-30. In similar contexts "renewal" or "establishing anew" was used in relationship to the establishment of the kingdom under Israelite leadership. After Saul defeated the Ammonites, Samuel agreed to go with Saul and the people to Gilgal to establish anew the kingdom (ונחדש שם המלוכה) with Saul as king (I Sam. 11:14-15). When II Isaiah promised the Jews that the Lord was about to do something new (עשה חדשה, Isa. 43:19), the plan was to restore the twelve tribes on the land under Davidic leadership. Jubilees said the Lord had four places on earth: the Garden of Eden, the Mountain of the East, Mt. Sinai, and Mt. Zion, thich would be sanctified in the new creation (ዕፅትል ፡ ሕዳስ) (Jub. 4:26). Mt. Zion was the center of the navel of the earth (Jub. 8:19). In relationship to the Lord's promises that he would send the messianic king, give his children the land, fulfill his oath, bring the end, redeem his people from captivity, and comfort his people, the rabbis taught that generations were afflicted according to their iniquities. "Said the Holy One Blessed be He, 'In that hour I will create it [the generation who has suffered for its quota of sins] anew (חדשה) and it will suffer hardships no more and I will give you your land' " (*PR* 84a; see also 31:146b). In a similar context of promises that the Lord would restore the kingdom was also the promise that the messianic king, the Son of Man, would come. "Said the Holy One Blessed be He, 'I am obligated to make him a new creation (בריאה חדשה). There-

politics. Paul said that at the right time the Messiah would put
down every rule, authority, and power, making all things subject
to him.[1] In his judgment, the kingdom would not come by means
of word, but by power.[2] The sons of Zebedee were not rebuked or
corrected for wanting chief seats in the kingdom.[3] Jesus told the
chief priests and elders [4] that the tax collectors and "harlots"
would have higher rank (προάγειν) than they in the Kingdom of
God (ἡ βασιλεία τοῦ θεοῦ). This was a threat to the positions of
importance that they then held, but it did not indicate that Jesus
was thinking of rank in any other kingdom than one which would
rule in Palestine where the chief priests and elders were then leading
citizens. Another report of the disciples asking Jesus who would be
the greatest in the Kingdom of Heaven evoked a rebuke. Jesus
said that if they did not repent and become as children they would
not enter the kingdom at all.[5] This did not answer the disciples'

---

fore it says, "Today I have begotten you" ' " (Ps. 2 : 7; Mid. Ps. 2; 14b).
The translation of Onkelos promised the Israelites, "Jehovah will bless
them alone in the age (בעלמא) which he will renew (לאתחדתא)" (Targ.
Dt. 32 : 23). He quoted the Lord, " 'I am the God of the covenant of the
age at the beginning,' says the Lord, 'I am the God appointed to renew
(לחדתא) the age (עלמא) for the righteous' " (Targ. Jer. 23 : 23). R.
Tanḥuma (Noah 12, 19a) anticipated the time when the Lord would
destroy the wicked from the age (עלמא) and make the righteous a
new creation (בריה חדשה) and give them breath. Baruch promised that
after the building of Zion had been destroyed, it would again be renewed
(ܠܡܬܒܢܝܘ) and completed for the age (ܠܥܠܡ ܕܐܠܗܐ ܡܕܝܢܬܐ, II Bar. 32:4).
That would happen when the Mighty One renewed his creation (ܒܪܝܬܗ ܡ
II Bar. 32:6). In the vision of the vine that destroyed the last cedar of the
forest, the interpretation explained that the last cedar was the fourth
kingdom. When its decreed time of existence was over, then the rule of the
Lord's Messiah would be revealed (ܕܡܫܝܚܗ ܡܠܟܘܬܗ ܬܬܓܠܐ, II Bar. 39:7).
The Sibyl who pictured a future international scene foresaw a celestial con-
flagration on earth, a new phenomenon (καινὴ φύσις, SO 5:211-212). This
did not do away with all nations, however, much less the cosmos.
India, Ethiopia, and Corinth would be destroyed, but Persia would have
peace and the Jews would continue to dwell in peace around the city of
God at the center of the earth (SO 5:206-254; see also 1QS 4:16-17, 25).
Ezra asked what would happen to the souls that died before the Lord renewed
his creation (IV Ezra 7:75). After a detailed answer, the Lord promised that
at the last times there would be for Israel Paradise, the tree of life, the
future age, the city rebuilt, and a rest appointed (IV Ezra 8:52). These were
all expectations that were to take place in Palestine on the earth.

[1] I Cor. 15:24-28.
[2] I Cor. 4:20.
[3] Mt. 20:20-22.
[4] Mt. 21:23.   [5] Mt. 18:1-3.

question, but it indicates that they were thinking of the kingdom in terms of political position. Jesus told them that innocence was required for admission. The child was probably used as an analogy because a child was not held accountable for any of his sins until his bar mitzwah.[1] Like covenanters forgiven on the Day of Atonement or newly baptized proselytes,[2] they were expected to be free from sin and also at the very lowest ecclesiastical rank. In the kingdom the ones who kept the law would have positions of importance, whereas the ones who were non-observant would have lowest rank.[3] Those whose righteousness was no more rigid than that of the scribes and Pharisees would not "enter" the Kingdom of Heaven.[4] The prayer that requested God's will to take place on the land as it did in heaven, also requested deliverance from the "evil one" and petitioned God's kingdom to come.[5]

In the NT, Jesus, John, and the disciples were shown preaching the good news of the Kingdom of God. The announcements resembled those of II Isaiah just before the captivity in Babylon was over and also rabbinic interpretations of the exodus from Egypt. The blessings promised were the same as the covenantal promises of the OT and were to be given on the condition that the covenanters behave like the servant in Babylon who suffered for the sins of Israel. In conformity to sabbatical eschatology, the belief that the end of the age was just about there motivated a missionary movement into the diaspora. Also consistent were the many varied attempts to approximate the length of time required before the end. Like the exodus from Egypt and the promise in II Isaiah, there were miracles that preceded the overthrow of the oppressive nation. As in other literature, there was a close relationship among the conditions of "life," covenantal observance within the community, and citizenship in the Kingdom of God. There was probably some variance among the sects at that point. The nature of the kingdom Christians expected involved a king, judges,

---

[1] After which he was no longer a child but a "son." See below, p. 181-184.

[2] *Gerim* 2:5; Yeb. 98a.

[3] Mt. 5:19; 7:21; Mt. 11:11 appears to be an anti-John-the-Baptist pol emic intruded into a passage that is otherwise in praise of John. The message of the intrusion, evidently added after John's death, held that the lowest rank of citizen in the Kingdom of Heaven would be greater than John, who would not be raised to enter. See also Lk. 7:28.

[4] Mt. 5:20.

[5] Mt. 6:9-13; see also Lk. 11:2.

rank, and international involvements. There are some usages of
the terms "Kingdom of God" or "Kingdom of Heaven" that
might be interpreted otherwise. Paul's claim that flesh and blood
could not inherit the kingdom apparently has some other meaning
intended, whatever it is. The Johannine assurance that Jesus'
kingdom was not of this world, and Luke's report that the kingdom
was ἐντὸς ὑμῶν could be given mystical or spiritual interpretations.
There may also be others that indicate a spiritualization, mysticiz-
ing, or psychologizing of the theological and political concept.
The extent to which this is so indicates the extent to which the
church moved away from its original heritage. But after all of
these variant possible interpretations have been conceded, there
remains a strong majority of the usages in the NT that are closely
related to similar expectations in earlier and later Israelite and
Jewish understanding of the Kingdom of God. There was much
more evidence than Reimarus mustered to indicate that Jews in
NT times spoke of the Kingdom of God or the Kingdom of Heaven
when they expected Rome to be overthrown and the political state
of Israel established. There was also a great deal of evidence to
suggest that Christians expected the same kind of kingdom. It
is quite likely that the good news Jesus proclaimed was related in
some way or another to the political position of Palestinian government in relationship to the children of Abraham and the foreign
powers.

Summary

Reimarus' claim that Jesus as well as his Jewish contemporaries
expected the near establishment of the political nation of Palestine
as the Kingdom of God has received more support in this chapter.
This does not mean that all NT teaching about the Kingdom of
God had only this meaning, but the percentage of references for
which the nationalistic meaning was clear was high enough to
justify further consideration of sabbatical eschatology in relationship to a certain geographic area in the Near East as the Kingdom
of God. Since this kingdom was territorial, the next chapter will
consider briefly the land itself—its topography, boundaries, and
position in the Near East. The testimony considered will be taken
from sources as old as the report of God's promise to Abraham
and as recent as Christian views in NT times.

CHAPTER THREE

THE LAND OF THE CONQUEST

INTRODUCTION [1]

In the covenant, the Lord promised Abraham:

"To your seed I have given this land,
from the River of Egypt to the Great River" (The river
Euphrates).[2]

The interpretive words, "The river Euphrates," break the poetry; but more than that, they leave the impression that the promise provided for Abraham's seed a land without good natural boundary lines to the north. It further indicates a promise that was not reasonably related to the size of the nation established. This suggests that the interpretative passage was a later erroneous gloss. To confirm this possibility, other passages will be considered that deal with boundaries of the same land. Texts on boundaries are ample but not uniform. They describe a land of three different sizes which will be discussed here, beginning with the most modest limits:

FROM DAN TO BEERSHEBA

When Moses was allowed to view the promised land, he was reported to have visualized the land as far south as the Negev and as far north as Dan.[3] These are not sharp boundary lines, but probably mark the northernmost and southernmost administration centers of a territory that included all the region between the Mediterranean Sea to the west and the water boundary from the headwaters of the Jordan to the southernmost tip of the Dead Sea to the east.[4] The extent of Joshua's conquest is more specific:

---

[1] Research for this chapter was done with the aid of a grant from the American Association of Theological Schools. Dr. N. Glueck, Dr. B. Mazar, and Dr. J. Aharoni have read this chapter and made helpful suggestions for its improvement.

[2] Gen. 15:18.

[3] Dt. 34:1-3. See also II Sam. 24:2; I Kgs. 5:5.

[4] Mazar has suggested that Dan and Beersheba were administrative centers. The location given by Israeli archaeologists as "Dan" is probably erroneously labeled. This site extends out from Mt. Hermon the way Megiddo

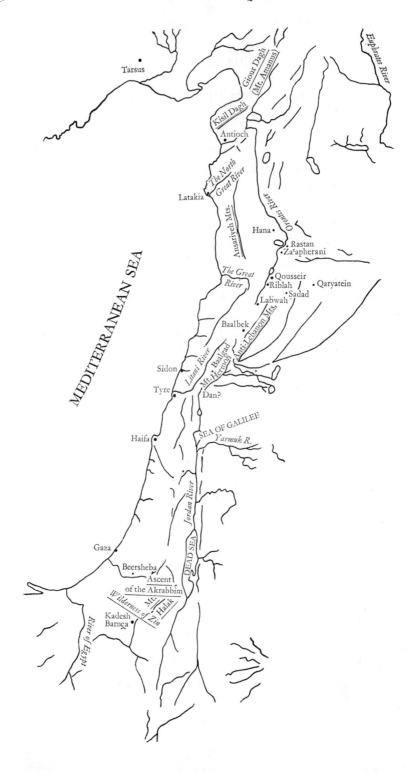

from Mt. Ḥalak in the south to Baalgad in the Valley of Lebanon below Mt. Hermon to the north.[1] The northern border had good natural protection. The Mountains of Galilee from the Mediterranean Sea to the Upper Jordan Valley had the Litani River north of the mountains to mark the boundary clearly.[2] The Sea of Galilee, Jordan River, and Dead Sea marked the limits to the east, and the Mediterranean Sea, the western boundary. Mt. Ḥalak was the most secure position of the southern border. It provided a natural barrier protecting the border northeast to the Dead Sea and west through the mountain range. The wide plain near the sea was always subject to capture. For this reason the west end of the southern border varied from time to time depending on the strength of the nation and its southern neighbors. During the reign of Solomon, Judah and Israel dwelt in safety, "from Dan to Beersheba." [3] In the same context, the limits were from Dan to the border of Egypt.[4] The border of Egypt was also variable, but was the same southern border as that administered by Beersheba, probably extending as far south as Mt. Ḥalak in agreement with the topography and the limits of Joshua's conquest. When David was provoked by the Lord to number Israel, he commissioned Joab for the task, "from Dan to Beersheba." [5]

The limits from Dan to Beersheba marked the northern and

---

extends out from Mt. Carmel and the way many other fortresses are built at the edge of the foothills to defend the mountains. The site Israeli scholars have partially excavated and called "Dan" has a strong wall to the *south* and *east* to protect it from possible attackers from those directions. This means it was the southwesternmost defense of Mt. Hermon and the territory to the northeast rather than a northeasternmost defense of the people to the southwest. It seems unreasonable for a country to build huge defense walls to protect itself from its own people. Dan, like Beersheba, was probably not a fortress on the boundary at all, but an administrative center somewhere in the Huleh Valley. The fortress Israelis now call "Dan" may be a better candidate for Baalgad.

[1] Josh. 11:17.

[2] That would be the most favorable border for Israel. The southern edge of the Mountains of Galilee, however, also provide an excellent natural boundary that favors the country to the north. This line begins with the sharp cliff at the edge of the Mediterranean Sea, the Ladder of Tyre (modern Rosh Ha-Nikra), and extends to the sharp banks west of the Upper Jordan and Lower Lebanon valleys. This is currently the border between Israel and Lebanon.

[3] I Kgs. 5:5.

[4] I Kgs. 5:1.

[5] II Sam. 24:1-2.

southern centers of the territory conquered by Joshua and ruled by David and Solomon, but other testimony claimed a larger country.

From River to River

The Great River.—The spies sent to examine the promised land, spied out the region from the Wilderness of Zin to the Plain of Labwah Ḥamath (רחב לבוא חמת).[1] The Wilderness of Zin is just south of Mt. Ḥalak. Mazar identified Labwah, which he called Labu, with ancient and modern Labwah, Lebanon. He also identified it with a city called Labwah in a forest, south of Kadesh on the Orontes. In the stele of Amenhotep II, Pharaoh was reported to have returned from North Syria, through Kadesh, and continued south to the forest around Labwah.[2] Labwah in the forest south of Kadesh was also mentioned as a place to hunt in the records of Ramses II.[3] Mazar now concurs that the village of Labwah only marks a city in a large forest which also bore the name Labwah.[4]

---

[1] Num. 13:21.

[2] 100, ([1946-1945] תש״ו) י׳׳ב , ידיעות ״מתקרים טופוגראפיים״ ,מזר ·ב See also his "Canaan and the Canaanites," *BASOR*, 102 (1946), 9; and, אנציקלופדיה מקראית, 610-609, 613. ״ארץ ישראל״ From the sources Mazar used alone Labu would seem the most reasonable pronunciation to conjecture, but the relationship of the name to the lioness goddess indicates the probability that the modern city, Labwah, Lebanon, has preserved a pronunciation that is approximately correct. See further note 4.

[3] *Ibid.*

[4] See also A. Alt, "Neue Berichte über Feldzüge von Pharaonen," *ZDPV*, 70(1954), 42, fn. 34. K. Galling, "Das Deutsche Ev. Institut für Altertumswissenschaft des Heiligen Landes," *ZDPV*, 70(1954), 99, said that Mazar's thesis is destroyed by the existence of a place called "Labu, Egypt" (II Chron. 26:8). Mazar has suggested that II Chron. 26:8 makes no sense as it is. "Why should a person's name reach to the 'entrance' of another country?" he asks. Since he found no answer, he assumes that words have fallen out of the text which originally read: עד [חמת] [מ]לבא [שמו וילך מצרים [נחל]. J. Simons, *The Geographical and Topographical Texts of the OT* (Leiden, 1959), § 283, says of Galling's argument: "This argument would be almost convincing but for the possibility that the expression in Ch. merely imitates the much older *'ad lebô ḥamath.'* "

J. T. Milik and F. M. Cross, Jr., "Inscribed Javelinheads from the Period of the Judges," *BASOR* 134 (1954), 5-15, reported javelin heads on which were inscribed ḥṣ ʿbdlbʾt. The second word would be ʿebed labiʾt/labît, "servant of labeʾt labaʾt," which Milik relates to the biblical place names, lebô(ʾ) Ḥamât, in the north and a Phoenician sanctuary of a lioness goddess at Bêt Lĕbāʾôt, in the south. Milik says both place names come from the word labi(ʾ) which means "lion." Another name for a Canaanite goddess is ʾAṭirat, also called Qudšu in several Egyptian stelae. Qudšu is near enough in pro-

The northern boundary of old Canaan, which was also the southern
boundary of Ḥamath and the Hittite territory, he now believes was
nearer the northern end of the valley than the village of Labwah.
He thinks that the biblical borders were simply the same boundaries
which had been accepted previously for Canaan when it was a
province of Egypt.[1] This dimension is in conformity with the
boundary limits of several biblical witnesses.[2] At Joshua's death,
he left unconquered of the areas outlined, the land between Mt.
Ḥalak and Shiḥor opposite Egypt on the south and from Baalgad
to Labwah Ḥamath to the north.[3] Although the text reporting
this is confused,[4] the coveted land apparently included all of the
Lebanon Mountains and possibly the Anti-Lebanon Mountains
as well. Included in this extension was the Land of the Gebelites
which extended to the northern border of the land occupied by
Amorites.[5] The uncertain territories included seem to fit well into

---

nunciation and spelling to the northern city of Kadesh, which is near Labwah
to suggest that both names were given in honor of the same lioness goddess
whom people in that area worshipped. This would preclude the possibility
that the name simply meant "entrance." It would also suggest that the modern Labwah, Lebanon, preserves the ancient correct pronunciation.

[1] Mazar, "מתקרים טופוגראפיים," 98.

[2] Josh. 13:3-5.

[3] *Ibid.*

[4] Simons, *Op. cit.*, § 295.

[5] The expression עד גבול האמרי does not mean "*up to* the (southern)
boundary of the Amorite territory," but "*including* the Amorite territory
up to the (northern) boundary" (Josh. 13:4). This is confirmed by the same
kind of an expression in the same context (Josh. 13:10): עד גבול בני עמון
"up to the border of the Ammonites," meaning the southern border, *including*
Ammon. More specifically, this border was marked by the Arnon River
between Moab and Ammon (Num. 21:13, 21-26). Furthermore, Amorite
territory, which in the north included Lebanon where the *Amurru* settled
close to Arvan, near the Great River and also Anti-Lebanon (Simons, *Op. cit.*,
§ § 108, 295), reached south as far as the Ascent of the Akrabbim on the
west side of the Jordan River (Jdgs. 1:36; see also Dt. 1:19-20). East of the
Jordan River, Amorites held the territory from the Jordan to the wilderness,
from the Arnon River to the river Jabbok (Jdgs. 11:22; see further Num.
32:39; Dt. 1:4; Josh. 2:10; 5:1; 9:10; 10:6, 12; 12:2; 13:10; 24:8, 12;
Jdgs. 10:8; 11:19-23; I Kgs. 4:8; Ps. 135:11-12; 136:19-20). Between the
Great River (Dt. 1:7) and the Ascent of the Akrabbim, Amorites were at
Gibeon (Josh. 10:6, 12; 24:11; II Sam. 21:2), Ai (Josh. 7:7; see also 24:11),
in the Jordan Valley near Dan (Jdgs. 1:34), Judah (Jdgs. 1:35), and Samaria
(Gen. 45:22; Josh. 24:12, 18). They held hill country (Num. 13:29; Dt. 1:7,
19-20; Josh. 11:3), plain (Jdgs. 1:34), and Negev (Dt. 1:19-20; Jdgs. 1:36).
They seem to have been pretty generally distributed throughout the land,
and attempts to distinguish Amorite territory from Canaanite territory have

the area from the Mountains of Galilee to the northern tip of Mt. Lebanon and the Forest of Labwah Ḥamath. The unconquered limits desired were the very same as those David held—from Shiḥor on the Nile River to Labwah Ḥamath.[1] The Land of Ḥamath held the cities of Riblah and Kadesh within its borders and lay north of the Anti-Lebanon Mountains and adjacent to the Land of Damascus.[2] The country of Ḥamath was probably the plain north of the mountains that fan out from Mt. Hermon. It may have extended north to Mt. Shomeriyah or farther.[3] It was probably bounded on the west by the Orontes River. Aharoni is probably correct in holding that the Land of Ḥamath sometimes extended as far south as the village of Labwah, but he agrees that the natural boundary is north of the mountain ranges.[4] The valley between the two mountain ranges would be difficult for a northern plain country to defend from adjacent mountaineers. The valley north of the Lebanon Mountains still provides the boundary between Lebanon and Syria. That valley is drained by *Nahr el-Kebir*

(نَهْر أَلْ كَبِير), "The Great River." If the interpretative gloss were

removed from Gen. 15:18, then its description of the size of the promised land would be the same as the kingdom Joshua was commanded to conquer, from the wilderness on the south to

---

been unsuccessful (such as K.M. Kenyon, *Amorites and Canaanites* [London, 1966]. Note her map on page 4).

The promised land was not only generally referred to as the Land of Canaan, but also as the Land of the Amorites (Num. 21:2, 34; Josh. 24:12, 18; Dt. 31:4; Jdgs. 6:10; Amos 2:9-10) which was to be given Abraham's seed after the iniquity of the Amorites was complete (Gen. 15:16). Ezekiel accused Jerusalem of originating from the Land of Canaan with a Hittite for a mother and an Amorite for a father (Ezek. 16:3, 45).

The picture is far from clear, but Canaanite and Amorite territory were used coterminously and synonymously at times as if the Canaanites were also called Amorites or as if the land once held by Canaanites had been earlier held by Amorites who were still in the land. In addition to the land included in the promise, Amorites also once held the land across the Jordan, later occupied by the two and a half tribes. Extra-biblical sources indicate that Amorites once populated most of the region west of the Euphrates (see Simons, *Op. cit.*, § 13; see also §§ 108; 295).

[1] I Chron. 13:5; J. Aharoni, *The Land of the Bible, a Historical Geography*, tr. A. Rainey (London, 1967), 58-59.

[2] II Kgs. 23:33.

[3] Jos. *Ant.* VIII. vi.1 said Solomon held the territory in Syria as far east as Palmyra.

[4] Aharoni, *Op. cit.*, 58-72, and in conversation.

the Great River on the north.[1] It is also the same as the land
Moses told the Israelites to go in and take forty years earlier, from
the Arabah and the Negev on the south to the Great River on the
north.[2] In all three cases, however, a later editor interpreted
"the Great River" to mean "the river Euphrates." In one instance,
the interpretation was "the river Euphrates, and all the land of
the Hittites to the Great Sea from the setting of the sun will be
your border." [3]

One of the reasons for thinking that the Great River was not
initially understood to be the Euphrates is that the Euphrates is
not in the same geographical area as Labwah Ḥamath, Kadesh, or
other points given as the northern boundary. At the dedication of
the temple all Israel came to the feast from Labwah Ḥamath to
the brook of Egypt.[4] Amos promised that a nation would oppress
Israel from the brook of the Arabah to Labwah Ḥamath.[5] The
brook of the Arabah runs into the southern tip of the Dead Sea
and marks about the same boundary as Mt. Ḥalak, the Wilderness
of Zin, the Arabah and the Negev, the Brook of Egypt, or Shiḥor.
The northern edge of the Forest of Labwah Ḥamath outlines the
same boundary as the Great River north of the Lebanon Mountains.
Ezekiel said the Lord would punish Israel from the wilderness
to Riblah, near Kadesh.[6] When Jeroboam restored Israel's border
to its proper place, the boundaries reached from the Sea of the
Arabah to Labwah Ḥamath.[7]

The Great River which has been interpreted as the river Euphrates is more closely related to other geographical locations near
Nahr el-Kebir than the Euphrates. The same is true of the expression
"the river" (הנהר) in these contexts: Solomon ruled all the kingdoms
from "the river" to the land of the Philistines, and on to the border
of Egypt.[8] The river was not named, but the RSV rendered הנהר
the southeast point of the Salt Sea, continued past the Ascent of

---

[1] Josh. 1:4.
[2] Dt. 1:7.
[3] Josh. 1:4.
[4] I Kgs. 8:65.
[5] Amos 6:14.
[6] Ezek. 6:14 as emended by Bewer in *Kittel-Kahle*.[3]
[7] II Kgs. 14:25.
[8] I Kgs. 5:1. The text now reads, "The river of the land of the Philistines
and to the boundary of Egypt." Something has probably dropped out of the
text.

"the Euphrates." The translators did not recognize the interpretations as later glosses. The possible identifications for "the
river" are: the Litani, the Great River, the Orontes, or the Euphrates. The most likely possibility is the Great River north of Mt.
Akkar.[1] The Lord promised to drive out Israel's enemies from the
Reed Sea on the south to "the river" on the north,[2] or from the
wilderness on the south to Lebanon and "the river" on the north.[3]
The Reed Sea, like Shiḥor is no farther south than the Wilderness
of Zin, but it reaches farther west than the Brook of Egypt. The
river associated with Lebanon was probably the Great River and
not the Euphrates, as the text now reads.[4]

Isaiah promised a great day when the whole land would be
threshed like grain, "from 'the river' to the Brook of Egypt. " [5]
Again, the RSV interpreted "the River" as "the river Euphrates,"
but their reasons for their interpretations were the same in all
instances and their likelihood of being right is the same. The
Isaiah expectation reflected the conditions after the Assyrian
captivity. Isaiah promised that the exiled faithful would be returned,
presumably to the same land with the same boundaries as it had
before the captivity. The Great River is the most likely northern
boundary for the land as its limitations were most popularly
understood. This will become still more evident after an examination
of the northern boundaries according to Numbers and Ezekiel.

Specific sites.—The Land of Canaan promised to Moses was
bounded on the south by a border that included the Wilderness of
Zin and provided also the northern border of Edom. It began at

---

[1] I Kgs. 5:1.

[2] Ex. 23:31.

[3] Dt. 11:24.

[4] Dt. 11:24. The fluctuation of the southern border may not have been
so great as it appears. The vacillation between *Wady el-Arish* (the Brook
of Egypt) and the Nile Delta might reflect a confusion of the River of
Egypt with *Wady el-Arish*. H. Bar-Deroma, "The River of Egypt (Naḥal
Mizraim)," *PEQ* 92 (1960), 37-56, although clearly apologetic, has made an
interesting case for identifying the River of Egypt with the Nile River. This
would also coincide with Shiḥor.

[5] Isa. 27:12. The author of Jubilees was fair to his text, so he also said
the promise extended to the Euphrates (Jub. 14:18), but in another context
he said the land Canaan usurped from the heritage of Shem, which Israel
later recovered, extended from Lebanon to the river of Egypt and from the
Jordan River to the Mediterranean Sea (Jub. 10-29).

the Akrabbim and on to Zin, Kadesh Barnea, Ḥazar Adar, Azmon, and along the River of Egypt to the Mediterranean Sea.[1] This was just a more explicit marking of the southern limit some- times summarized as "the River of Egypt," "the Wilderness of Zin," "Mt. Ḥalak," "the Brook of the Arabah," "The Sea of the Arabah," or "the Arabah and the Negev." The western boundary was the Mediterranean Sea.[2] The northern boundary, of greatest importance here, was to begin at the Mediterranean Sea, extend to "Mt. Hor," Labwah Ḥamath, Zedad, Ziphron, and Ḥazer Ainon. From Ḥazer Ainon, the border continued to Shapham, Riblah, the eastern shore of the Sea of Kinnereth, the Jordan River, and the Salt Sea.[3] There are no modern names to help in the identification of Mt. Hor, but its proximity to the Great River and the Mediterranean Sea make Mt. Akkar a good candidate. The towns, Riblah, Zedad, and Ziphron, were probably the pre- cursors of Arabic villages with very similar names today, but they may have changed their locations somewhat over the years. Rableh today is not east, but southwest of the only sizeable spring in that region.[4] The name Ḥazer Ainon, the Ḥazer Spring, should be a spring or a village adjacent to a spring. The village of Qussier

(قصر) has no spring, but it receives its spring water from Ain

Sukkin (عـيـن سـخـن) a few miles east at the foot of the moun- tains. The spring which was west of Riblah was evidently the Ḥazer Spring, also reported to have been west of Riblah.[5] The name, Qussier, resembles the name, Ḥazer, much more closely than Qaryatein does, but Qaryatein has been identified with Ḥazer Ainon because it has an abundance of water, is the last village east before the dessert, and seems to be in a better position to be on the northern border of the district of Damascus,[6] but it is

---

[1] Num. 34:1-5.   [2] Num. 34:6.

[3] Num. 34:7-12.

[4] Num. 34:11. J. P. Van Kasteren, "La Frontière Septentrionale," *RB*, 4 (1895), 27-29, said Mt. Hor was the Mt. Amanus at the southernmost end of the Lebanon range. K. Furrer, "Antike Städte im Libanongebiete," *ZDPV*, 8 (1885), 27, followed by Simons, *Op. cit.*, § 283, chose the northern- most of the mountains, i.e. Mt. Akkar. K. Elliger, "Die Nordgrenze des Reiches Davids," *Palästinajahrbuch*, 32 (1936), 70-71, concurred with Furrer but said the text had been confused by abbreviations.

[5] Num. 34:10-11.

[6] Ezek. 47:17. So Furrer, *Op. cit.*, 28, followed by F.-M. Abel, *Géographie de la Palestine* (Paris, 1933), I, 302, Elliger, *Op. cit.*, 66-67, and Simons,

still farther east of Rableh than Qussier is. Shapham has not been satisfactorily identified.[1] There is not much space between Qussier and Rableh| today| for another village. Zapharoni (زعــفــرونـي) today is a small village, five to ten miles south of a prominent city, Rastan.[2] It is located on a hill and has a good well, but it is too far from the Orontes River to receive water for water power or irrigation. These names seem to be the ones referred to in the scripture, and they probably all belonged to the district of Ḥamath, but their geographical relationship may have been changed.

Ezekiel noted that the border was from the Great Sea toward Labwah and farther on to Zedad by way of Hethlon.[3] Hethlon has been identified with Heitela,[4] near the mouth of the Great River. Ezekiel included some different names to his border list: Berothah, deep south into the valley, Sibraim, north of the Anti-Lebanon Mountains, near Mt. Shomeriyah. Sibraim was on the borderline between the districts, Ḥamath and Damascus.[5] Ḥazer Hattikon has not been adequately located.[6] Ḥazer Ainon was on

---

Op. cit., § 283. R. Dussaud, *Topographie Historique de la Syrie Antique et Mediévale* (Paris, 1927), 16, however, followed Van Kasteren, *Op. cit.*, 26, in identifying Ḥazer Ainon with Ḥadr at the southeastern foot of Mt. Hermon.

[1] Furrer, *Op. cit.*, 29, however, had Elliger's (*Op. cit.*, 72) support in identifying it with Atni, southwest of Qaryatein, and Van Kasteren, *Op. cit.*, suggested Ofni, south of Ḥadr.

[2] Furrer, *Op. cit.*, 28, and Abel, *Op. cit.*, 302, also made this identification. Van Kasteren, *Op. cit.*, 30-31, however, chose instead the location of Sanbariyah; Dussaud, *Op. cit.*, 15, fn. 5, held for Defne; and Elliger, *Op. cit.*, 68-70, identified both Ziphron and Sibraim with Hauwarin.

[3] Ezek. 47:15; 48:1.

[4] Furrer, *Op. cit.*, 27, followed by Abel, *Op. cit.*, 302. Van Kasteren, *Op. cit.*, 25-27, objected to Furrer's conclusions and claimed Adloun, between Tyre and Sidon for the location of ancient Hethlon. Dussaud, *Op. cit.*, 17, denied the correctness of Van Kasteren's analysis and held, instead, that the inland village of Aitroun met the requirements. All four scholars selected boundaries near the only two satisfactory places for a northern boundary. Furrer and Abel chose the plain and river north of the Lebanon range. Van Kasteren chose the plain and river north of the Mountains of Galilee. Abel, *Op. cit.*, 302, said of Dussaud's deduction, "Perspective grandiose qui s'adepte mal à la réalité."

[5] So 614, "ארץ ישראל," מייזלר. Elliger, *Op. cit.*, 60, identified present Ghuntur with ancient Berothah.

[6] Dussaud, *Op. cit.*, 16, Elliger, *Op. cit.*, 67-68, 70, and Simons, *Op. cit.*, § 283, all thought Ḥazer Ainon and Ḥazer Hattikon were the same place. Van Kasteren, *Op. cit.*, 31, thought Ḥazer Hattikon was modern Ḥazoreh, south of Ḥadr.

the boundary between the areas, Damascus and Ḥamath.[1] According to Ezekiel, the eastern boundary went from Ḥazer Ainon to Hauran, where it followed the boundary of Damascus adjacent to the boundary of Hauran to the river Jordan, down the Jordan southward along the eastern shore of the Eastern Sea to Tamar.[2]

Topography.—Because these names were given as biblical boundary sites and have claimed the attention of many scholars, they have also been considered here, but ancient boundaries can be more accurately deduced from topographical possibilities than by comparing present villages with ancient sites. If a country whose northern boundary had been the Litany River wished to extend its border northward, it probably would not have inched its way up the mountain range. A well-managed conquest would have taken the whole area between the Mountains of Galilee and the Great River or nothing at all, because no point in between would provide a natural geographical border.[3] The territory bounded by the Litani and Orontes valleys east and the Great River, north, had the whole Lebanon range to protect itself from invasion. The territory of Ḥamath, north and east, was comparatively level with an adequate water supply, but, except for Mt. Shomeriyah, it has hardly any natural protection from the north or east—only a barren desert. From the north and west it was always subject to capture by the countries that controlled the mountains. The country that controlled the Ansariyah Mountains could defend this plain better than any other country that would have had to cross the desert to attack or defend it. Its position in relationship to the Ansariyah Mountains on the west and the desert to the east, was very much like that of Bashan, Gilead, and Ammon in relationship to Canaan and the desert east. When the Israelites took Canaan they also added these eastern territories to Canaan's natural boundaries.

There is some confusion of locations in the Land of Ḥamath which make it difficult, if not impossible, to follow the northern

---

[1] Ezek. 47:15-17.

[2] Ezek. 47:17-18. It is difficult, if not impossible, to follow Ezekiel's text and understand where his boundary lines run within the limits of reliable knowledge of the locations mentioned. Damascus seems to have been the land east of Ḥamath and Hauran. See also Simons, *Op. cit.*, § 283.

[3] Ezek. 47:18.

boundary exactly, but the territory is closely related to the northern
end of the Lebanon mountain range and the Great River. The
Great River is not very big by some standards, and it would not
provide much resistance to an invading army, but that is not the
reason some rivers are chosen for boundary lines. Mountains,
like the Lebanon range, provide adequate defenses, but they are
so wide that they cannot be used to mark a boundary exactly,[1]
therefore the river at the foot of the mountain serves as a marker
to show that the whole mountain is included within the jurisdiction
of the country. For those who have seen the river Euphrates, the
Great River seems rather small, and so an interpreter might
innocently have added the words, "the river Euphrates," to the
text, because he thought the river Euphrates was the only river
in the Near East that deserved the description "big". Had he seen the
Mississippi or Amazon rivers, he might have thought the Euphrates
was also small. The people who named the river, however, evidently
thought it appropriate in comparison with other streams they knew.

The topography of the land east of the Mediterranean Sea was
such that there were only a few possibilities for boundaries on all
sides. The river that marked the northern boundary was closely
related to geographical sites either near the Litani river, or more
frequently, the Great River. This will become more evident when
the sites marking the north and south boundaries are placed in
parallel:

	South	North
1.	Mt. Ḥalak	Baalgad [2]
2.	Beersheba	Dan [3]
3.	Negev	Dan [4]
4.	Beersheba	Dan [5]

South	North	Interpretations
1. Wilderness of Zin	Plain of Labwah Ḥamath [6]	
2. River of Egypt	Labwah Ḥamath [7]	

---

[1] E.g., except for the Brook of Egypt, which is poorly defended, the
southern border has no sharp boundary lines, so the limits have been given
variously in terms of mountains and wildernesses, and they probably shifted
from time to time.

[2] Josh. 11:17; 12:7.

[3] I Kgs. 5:5.

[4] Dt. 34:1-3.

[5] I Sam. 24:2.

[6] Num. 13:21.

[7] I Kgs. 8:65.

South	*North*	*Interpretations*
3. Shihor opposite Egypt	Labwah Ḥamath [1]	
4. Shihor opposite Egypt	Labwah Ḥamath [2]	
5. River of Egypt	The Great River [3]	"the river Euphrates"
6. River of the Arabah	Labwah Ḥamath [4]	
7. River of Egypt	the river (הנהר) [5]	
8. Reed Sea	the river (הנהר) [6]	
9. Sea of the Arabah	Labwah Ḥamath [7]	
10. Wilderness	Riblah[8]	
11. Wilderness	Lebanon from the river (הנהר) [9]	
12. Wilderness	The Great River [10]	"The river Euphrates, and all the land of the Hittites to the Great Sea from the setting of the sun will be your border."
13. Boundary of Egypt	The river (הנהר) [11]	
14. Tamar, Meribath-Kadesh, the brook	Hethlon, Labwah Ḥamath, Zedad, Berothah . . . [12]	
15. Arabah and Negev	The Great River [13]	"the river Euphrates."
16. Salt Sea, Ascent of the Akrabbim, Zin, Kadesh-barnea, Ḥazar Adar, Azmon, River of Egypt	Mt. Hor, Labwah Ḥamath Zedad, Ziphron, Ḥazer Ainon [14]	
17. Tamar, water of Meribath-Kadesh, brook on the Great Sea	Way of Hethlon, Labwah Ḥamath, Ḥazer Ainon . . [15]	

The river that bordered the northern end of the extended kingdom is now called "the Great River" (نَهْر أل كَبِير) in modern Arabic.

---

[1] Josh. 13:3-5.
[2] I Chron. 13:5.
[3] Gen. 15:18.
[4] Amos 6:18.
[5] Isa. 27:12.
[6] Ex. 23:31.
[7] II Kgs. 14:25.
[8] Ezek. 6:24.
[9] Dt. 11:24.
[10] Josh. 1:4.
[11] I Kgs. 5:1.
[12] Ezek. 47:15-19.
[13] Dt. 1:7.
[14] Num. 34:3-9.
[15] Ezek. 48:1-2, 28.

The scripture that mentions the Great River (הנהר הגדל) was written centuries ago in Hebrew. Had the name "the Great River" not occurred as frequently and consistently as it did in relationship to the same geographical area as the river that is now called "the Great River" in Arabic, it would have been rash to assume that the Arabic of today had faithfully translated the earlier Hebrew. The fact, however, that the associations are so much closer in space to the Great River than the Euphrates River, and that the Great River marks a line that is much superior in position for a boundary than the Euphrates makes the conjecture seem reasonable and the supposition that the references to the river Euphrates are later glosses, sound. These boundaries also agree with other accounts of the land taken by Israel, including that formerly held by Philistines, Sidonians, Canaanites, the Hivites in Mt. Lebanon between Mt. Hermon and Labwah Ḥamath,[1] or, put differently, that had been Canaan, which seems to have been the same land ruled earlier by the Amorites,[2] reaching north to include the land of the Gebalites in the Lebanon Mountains, from Baalgad to Labwah Ḥamath.[3]

Dominion over the promised land.—This outline of the promised land clarifies a passage that has been previously given some strange interpretations. The context is as follows: Zechariah promised that the Lord would deal severely with enemy nations around the promised land. These nations included Damascus, Aram, and Ḥamath—the last being a country which Zechariah noted was on the border of Israel.[4] Since the southern border of Ḥamath was a long distance from the Euphrates River, its mention here as a boundary eliminates the Euphrates River from consideration as the boundary that the prophet had in mind. Places within the promised limits, like Tyre and Sidon, Ashkelon, Gaza, Ekron, and other Philistine cities would be destroyed because their land belonged to the jurisdiction promised Israel.[5] Israel would then have a king who had been victorious in battle.[6] For him the Lord

---

[1] Jdgs. 3:3.
[2] See p. 95, fn. 5.
[3] Josh. 13:1-5.
[4] Zech. 9:1-2.
[5] Zech. 9:2-6.
[6] Zech. 9:2.

would cut off the chariot and war horse from Ephraim and Jerusalem, and the king would maintain peace among the nations.[1]

> "His rule will be from sea to sea,
> from the river to the ends of the land." [2]

The seas under consideration here have been interpreted as the Indian Ocean and the Mediterranean Sea. The river has been assumed to have been the Euphrates, and "the ends of the land" (אפסי ארץ) understood to mean the ends of the earth.[3] This is so different from the dimensions in which Israel was interested that some other interpretation is both necessary and possible. Basing the interpretation on the understood land promised to Abraham and his seed, the territory bounded by two seas would be Palestine, between the body of water called the Great Sea,[4] the Western Sea,[5] or the Rear Sea,[6] on the west and the sea called the Salt Sea,[7] the Eastern Sea,[8] or the Sea of the Arabah [9] on the east. The couplet indicates that the territory between the two seas was the same as the land between the river and the ends or edges of the land. The river, then, would be the Jordan River, and the ends of the land would refer to the shore of the Mediterranean Sea.[10] This interpretation is consistent with Ben Sira who understood God's covenant to Abraham to be the territory upon which the twelve tribes settled, which extended

> "from sea to sea
> and from the river to the ends of the land." [11]

---

[1] Zech. 9:10.

[2] Zech. 9:10. The same couplet appears in Ps. 72:8, also in a nationalistic context. Therefore the same interpretation given Zech. 9:10 should be given Ps. 72:8.

[3] So C. A. and E. G. Briggs, *ICC Psalms*, (Edinburgh, c1907), II, 134-135; H. J. Kraus, *Psalmen* (Neukirchen, 1961), 498, and K. Elliger, *Das Buch der zwölf kleinen Propheten* (Göttingen, 1964), 150. For other interpretations, see H. G. Mitchell, J. M. Powis Smith, and J. A. Brewer, *ICC Haggai, Zechariah, Malachi, and Jonah*, 275.

[4] Num. 34:7; Josh. 1:4; Ezek. 47:15; 48:28.

[5] Dt. 34:2.   [6] Dt. 34:2.

[7] Num. 34:12.   [8] Ezek. 47:18.   [9] II Kgs. 14:25.

[10] The same limits were shown in Ps. 80:12. The vine that was brought out of Egypt and planted on ground that had been cleared so that its branches shaded the mountains (80:9-11) had branches that reached both to the sea and the river, namely the Mediterranean Sea and the river Jordan. The kingdom compared to a tree is similar to Ezek. 31:2-9; Dan. 4:4-27; and Mt 13:31-32.

[11] Sir. 44:19-23.

It also makes good sense geographically and poetically, and it fits properly into the context of a nationalistic psalm couched in war terminology. It also fits in with the theology of a people that believed a certain prescribed land was theirs by divine promise.

THE RIVER EUPHRATES

Eastern extensions.—Where there was only one line possible for a border, the boundaries were given very simply: The Great Sea to the west,[1] or from Riblah to the sea of Kinnereth, the Jordan River, and the Salt Sea to the east.[2] Where there were more ways than one, however, to get from one point to the other, several identifying places in between were added. This was true of the southern border,[3] and also the border north of Riblah.[4] Normal boundaries reached eastward only to the Jordan, Litani, or Orontes Valley. Ammon, Gilead, Bashan, and the Land of Ḥamath were extensions. Eastern borders of these territories did not need explicit landmarks, because no nation was there to challenge the ownership of the uninhabited desert. Therefore these territories extended as far east as there were villages and water. When wells went dry, whole villages might have moved westward and thus changed the border. This may explain why some of the locations mentioned by Numbers and Ezekiel have been relocated or can no longer be identified.

Although the promise did not include Ammon, Gilead, and Bashan, they were annexed because they could be taken. Desires for acquisition did not stop at that point. The Land of Ḥamath could not easily be taken or held by the country that controlled only the mountains to the south. The crucial region was Mt. Ansariyah. Since Israel wanted Ḥamath, she also had to plan to take the mountains west of Ḥamath as well. Once these were taken, it would not be hard to extend the borders east to the Euphrates River. So these dreams were added to the promise: "to the Great River (the river Euphrates—all the land of the Hittites to the Great Sea from the setting of the sun will be your border) . . ."[5] On the basis of that dream boundary, the Great River was interpreted to mean the river Euphrates.[6]

---

[1] Num. 34:6.   [2] Num. 34:11-12.
[3] Num. 34:3-5.   [4] Num. 34:8-11.
[5] Josh. 1:4.
[6] Gen. 15:18; Dt. 1:7; Josh. 1:4.

In NT times.—Since the sacred text included the land of the Hittites and the river Euphrates, Dan and Labwah Ḥamath were no longer considered limitations. The Genesis Apocryphon pictured Abraham viewing the promised land from the high point of Ḥazor. He saw the land as far south as the river of Egypt, northwest to the Lebanon Mountains and the land of the Gebalites, north as far as Kadesh, northeast to Mt. Senir, across Hauran and all the wilderness to the river Euphrates, and west to the Great Sea.[1] Since the Hittites were also to be conquered, the rabbis understood Mt. Hor to be Mt. Amanus,[2] modern Giour Dagh, north of Antioch. It may have been these boundaries that caused Paul's quarrel with Peter to occur at Antioch. It was agreed that Paul would go to the nations and Peter, James, and John would minister to the circumcised. Sometimes the term, "circumcised," referred to those within the land in contrast to those outside the land.[3] Antioch was just north of the tall Ansariyah mountains and across the Orontes River. Saman Dagh, in the Ansariyah range makes a formidable barrier right up to the mouth of the Orontes River, marking out a natural boundary, but the whole Orontes Valley to the north is south of Mt. Amanus. In this borderline territory, should Christians observe the rules of the land or those outside the land?[4] Peter apparently first agreed to follow Paul's rules here, but was persuaded to change his mind when some came from the party of James.[5] This issue might not have arisen if Peter and Paul had been together in Jerusalem or Asia Minor rather than Antioch.

The Amanus Mountains north of Antioch are certainly impressive. This range is long and tall, broken only by the Syrian Gates between Giour Dagh and Kissel Dagh. But it is not really a satisfactory northern border. Since this extension of the promise never materialized, it never had to be related to adequate military defenses. If the borders had ever come that far, better borders would

---

[1] Gen. Apoc. 21:10-12. The author of this text stayed within the limitations of Num. 34, Ezek. 47 and 48, accepting, of course, the interpolation, "the river Euphrates," of Gen. 15:18 and Dt. 1:7, but he did not extend the border to include the Ansariyah Mountains as did Josh. 1:4.

[2] Sheb. 6:1; JHallah 21a; 4d; Git. 8a; Ex. R. 23:5.

[3] Ned. 3:8.

[4] To note the effect of the territory in which a Jew resided to he rules he observed, see Sheb. 6:1 and JHallah 21a, 4d.

[5] Gal. 2:7-9.

have been required. To control the Orontes Valley and the Euphrates Valley, it would be necessary to capture also the Amanus Mountains and the whole range that cradles the Tigris-Euphrates Valley, because the Euphrates River, except for small cliffs, runs through a plain with no natural defense except the river itself. This would have encompassed all the territory assigned to Shem,[1] which was a larger area than Israel ever understood to have been part of the promise.

Conclusions

The evidence gathered suggests the following probable conclusions:

1. The reference to the Great River as a northern boundary of the promised land was to *Nahr el-Kebir*, north of the Lebanon Mountains.

2. The biblical references to "the river Euphrates" as the northern boundary are all erroneous later interpretations of the Great River.

3. The dominion referred to in Zech. 9:10 and Ps. 72:8 was the Land of Canaan, bounded on the east by the Eastern Sea and the Jordan River and on the west by the Western Sea.

4. Israel's "promise" was amended at least twice after its original borders were recorded. The three kingdoms are roughly outlined as follows:

a) From Dan to Beersheba—Joshua's conquest, but also reported as Solomon's kingdom.

b) From the River of Egypt to the Great River—somewhat similar to Solomon's kingdom. Solomon also ruled Ammon, Gilead, and Bashan, and there is some ancient authority for believing he ruled part, at least, of the Land of Ḥamath.[2]

c) From the River of Egypt or the border of Egypt in the south to include the Land of Ḥamath, or Ḥamath and the Land of the Hittites, north, to Mt. Amanus and the river Euphrates. This kingdom was never realized. Israel's two smaller dimensions had good natural boundaries, but the river Euphrates and Mt. Amanus are not good boundaries for territory south or southwest. The next size natural boundary would have been the Orontes River,

---

[1] Jub. 8:21. See also Jub. 9:4.
[2] See p. 96, fn. 3.

including Saman Dagh. After that had been made secure, Israel might have ventured to take the Orontes Valley east, as far as she could defend. She did this with Ammon, Gilead, and Bashan, to the south. She might even have reached out to the Euphrates River, but if she had done so she would have been left with a border that was difficult to defend against the mountaineers to the north. In Israel's early military campaigns, the natural boundaries were evidently considered very seriously.

The promised land commanded a lot of attention in the faith of the covenanters, both in the OT and in the NT. This small land bridge between Egypt and countries along the Euphrates was central to Jewish and Christian theology. It was the land God promised to the seed of Abraham for which they were obligated by the God of armies both to suffer passively and fight bravely in battle. So closely was this land related to Israelite theology that it was called the Kingdom of Heaven or the Kingdom of God. Another illustration of the significance of the land and the covenant to the faith of Israel was the custom of calling existence in the covenant on the promised land "life" and existence outside either the covenant or the land "death." The nature of "life" and "death" in relationship to the covenant community and the land will be considered in the next chapter.

CHAPTER FOUR

LIFE UNDER THE COVENANT

INTRODUCTION

The God who fought the battles of Israel and rewarded her
virtue by establishing the people upon the land he promised them
was called the God of life (אלהים חיים). He was the God who lives
forever. [1] He had life and he could give or create life. He made
heaven and earth,[2] beasts,[3] and man.[4] He also made of Abraham
a great nation,[5] Israel his people, the flock of his shepherding.[6]
He promised to make Israel a new heart and a new spirit.[7] He
would make Israel one nation in the land.[8] These life-giving
qualities of God were not all related to the origin of the species.[9]

---

[1] Also called אל חי and אלהים חי. See Josh. 3 : 10; I Sam. 17 : 26, 36; II
Kgs. 19:4, 16; Ps. 42:3 and possibly 42:9; 84:3; Isa. 37:4, 17; Jer. 10:10;
23:36; Hos. 2:1; Eccl. 7:12. In the NT, ὁ θεὸς ὁ ζῶν; θεὸς ζῶν (Mt. 16:16;
26:63; Acts 14:15; Rom. 9:26; II Cor. 3:3; 6:16; I Thes. 1:9; I Tim.
3:15; 4:10; Heb. 3:12; 9:14; 10:31; 12:22); and ὁ θεὸς ὁ ζῶν εἰς τοὺς
αἰῶνας τῶν αἰώνων (Rev. 15:7.) The word, life, appears often in oaths:
"by your life and the life of your soul (חיך וחי נפשך) (II Sam. 11:11) or
just by the other person's life (Gen. 42:15, 16; I Sam. 1:26; 17:55; II Sam.
11:11; 14:19). More often by the life of the Lord (חי יהוה) and frequently
the other person's life as well (Jdgs. 8:19; I Sam. 14:39, 45; 19:6; 20:3, 21;
25:26; 26:10, 16; 28:10; 29:6; II Sam. 4:9; 11:11; 12:9; 14:11; 15:21,
22; 22:47; I Kgs. 1:29; 2:2, 4, 6; 22:14; II Kgs. 4:30; 5:16, 20; II Chron.
18:13; Ps. 18:47; Ruth 3:13; Jer. 4:2; 5:2; 12:16; 16:14, 15; 23:7, 8;
38:16; Hos. 4:15), the life of God (חי האלהים) (II Sam. 2:27; Job 27:2;
Amos 8:14), the Lord God (חי יהוה אלהים), I Kgs. 17:12; 18:10), the Lord
God of Israel (חי יהוה אלהי ישראל), I Sam. 23:34; I Kgs. 17:1), the Lord of
armies (חי יהוה צבאות), (I Kgs. 18:15; II Kgs. 3:14), or the Lord Jehovah
(חי אדני יהוה) (Jer. 44:26). This use of "life" might be related to the study
here if enough were known about the vows to discern its meaning. See
"Some Oath and Vow Formulas in the NT," *HTR*, 58 (1965), 319-326, and
M. Greenberg, "The Hebrew Oath Partical *Ḥây/Ḥê*," *JBL*, 76 (1957), 34-39.

[2] Gen.2:4.

[3] Gen. 1:25.

[4] Gen. 1:26; Isa. 45:12; Jer. 27:5.

[5] Gen. 12:2; Ex. 32:10; Dt. 9:14.

[6] Ps. 110:3.

[7] Ezek. 18:31.   [8] Ezek. 37:22.

[9] God did create physical beings, however, and the use of the term "life"
to mean physical existence as a breathing creature is frequent in the OT.
The religious meaning takes its significance from the secular meaning to
which it is analogous. Here only the metaphorical usages will be considered.

At the time the Lord made a covenant with Israel, he gave her a new life, a new heart, and a new spirit. When God gave new life to the dead bones of Israel, the remnants would again become a community on the Land of Palestine as a united kingdom. [1]

Those who faced the decision of entering the covenant community or worshipping other gods were asked to choose between life and death.[2] Amos urged Israel to seek the Lord and live.[3] Those who loved the Christian brothers of the new covenant were changed from death into life.[4] Paul said that for him to live was Christ.[5] The author of the Fourth Gospel said that life eternal was knowing the only true God and Jesus Christ whom he sent.[6]

In some of these instances life meant something other than eating, breathing, and taking up space.[7] There seems to have been a close relationship between the God of life and the existence of his people with whom he was bound by covenant to be their God. The belief that Israel was a community bound under covenant to fulfill God's purpose and was promised sustenance and security was basic to OT theology and was continued in the NT. The close relationship between the existence in community under God's providential care and "life" will be examined in this chapter. This will be done by illustrating various metaphorical usages of the word "life" in Israelite, Jewish, Samaritan, and Christian literature. These will not only show that life and death were used metaphorically, but that the metaphor had a religious significance closely related to being included in the community or excluded from it. Those who belonged, had their names listed in the book of life; they had life or eternal life and the spirit. They were cleansed in the water of life, would eat from the tree of life, live on the land

---

[1] Ezek. 37:1-23.

[2] Dt. 30:15-20.

[3] Amos 5:4-6.

[4] I Jn. 3:13-14.

[5] Philip. 1:21.

[6] Jn. 10:28; 17:2.

[7] Contra G. Von Rad, "Life and Death in the OT," *TDNT* II, 843, who says of life (חיים) in the OT: "It indicates only physical, organic life, and this for the most part as the epitome of the interrelated forces and phenomena." G. Bertram, "ζωή and βίος in the Septuagint," *Ibid.*, 852, was also wrong in saying, "It is only in the hagiographa and apocrypha that the word really becomes a moral and religious term." H. Clavier, "Le Drame de la Mort et de la Vie," *Studia Evangelica* III, ed. F. L. Cross (Berlin, 1964), 166-177 has noticed a type of life which is not physical. He relates life and death to the two-ways doctrine.

of life, observe the commandments and walk in the way of life. Existence in covenant relationship with God and his chosen people was called "life" in the OT, and this religious meaning of life was continued in the NT. Different aspects of community existence will be examined, one after the other, as they are related to life in the biblical tradition.

LIFE AND DEATH

Decision for life.—Before his death Moses was pictured as addressing his most important ideas to the children of Israel who were to enter the promised land. They were urged to keep the commandments of the covenant so that they might live (תחיו) [1] and inherit the land promised their forefathers. They were reminded that the disobedient ones of their original group had been destroyed,[2] but those who held fast to the Lord were still alive (חיים) at that day.[3] Moses said that the covenant the Lord made at Horeb was not with their fathers, but with all of them who were alive (חיים) that day.[4] But if they entered the covenant and then served other gods, they would receive the curses of the covenant. All apostate generations would be cursed, but if wayward members remembered and returned to the Lord, he would gather them from the lands where they had been scattered and restore them to the promised land:[5] "And the Lord your God will circumcise your heart and the heart of all your children, so that you will love the Lord your God with all your heart and with all your soul, for the sake of your life" (למען חייך).[6] Toward the end of his speech, Moses reminded Israel that he had set before them life and good (את החיים ואת הטוב) and death and evil (את המות ואת הרע).[7] If they obeyed the commandments they would prosper and inherit the land. If not they would perish, without living long in the land.[8] In recapitulation, Moses said, "I call heaven and earth to witness against you this day, that I have set before you life and death, blessing and curse; therefore choose life (חיים), that you and your

---

[1] Dt. 4:1.
[2] Dt. 4:3.
[3] Dt. 4:4.
[4] Dt. 5:3.
[5] Dt. 29:16-30:5.
[6] Dt. 30:6.
[7] Dt. 30:15.
[8] Dt. 30:16-18.

posterity may live (תחיו), so as to love the Lord your God, obey his voice, and cleave to him; for he (it) is your life (חייך) and length of days, to dwell in the land which the Lord swore to your fathers, to Abraham, Isaac, and Jacob, to give them." [1]

It is not completely clear what antecedent was intended for the הוא in "He (it) is your life." [2] This could mean God; conduct described as loving the Lord, obeying his voice, and cleaving to him; [3] or length of days in the land. [4] Whatever the antecedent, in Deuteronomy the life of the Israelite was bound inseparably to existence under the covenant which involves the blessing of the land. Death is not only perishing, but also being scattered, having the community dissolved, and becoming outcasts among foreign nations. [5] Those who wanted to live had to keep the covenant. Ezekiel was faithful to Deuteronomy in relating death to wickedness and life to righteousness. He urged the wicked to turn away from his evil ways and live (וחיה). [6] Malachi reminded the priests who ignored the commandments that they would receive the promised curses and rejection, whereas God's covenant made long ago with Levi was a covenant of life (החיים) and peace (והשלום). [7] Another psalmist who walked before the Lord in right paths expected paths of glory, life, and peace (חיים ושלום) for the everlasting sabbath (להשבת לנצח). [8]

Continuous decisions.—The life and death decisions of ancient Israel were continued in later Judaism, Samaritanism, and Christianity. One poet said the Lord chose those who believed in him to be separated from the dead (ܡܦܪܫ ܐܝܢ ܡܢ ܡܝܬܐ). As in Ezekiel's vision, the Lord would cover the dead bones with bodies and give them energy for life (ܚܝܠܐ). [9] Philo said that it was life eternal (ζωὴ αἰώνιος) to take refuge in God, and death (θάνατος) to flee from him. The one capable of running should hurry to the divine word, the fountain of wisdom, so that he might

---

[1] Dt. 30:19-20.
[2] Dt. 30:20.
[3] Dt. 30:20.
[4] Dt. 30:20.
[5] Dt. 30:3-4.
[6] Ezek. 33:11.
[7] Mal. 2:1-5.
[8] 1QH 7:14-15.
[9] Odes of Sol. 22:7-10.

drink from the stream and be released from death to gain life
eternal.[1] Describing the Israelites as they entered the promised
land, Sifré said, "The living [i.e. the children ready to enter the
land] take possession of the dead [i.e. the patriarchs] and thus the
dead inherit life (חיים).[2] Baruch said of proselytes that some Gentiles at first did not know life (ܐܝܠܝܢ ܕܒܢ ܩܡܘ ܠܐ ܝܕܥܘ), but
afterwards learned (ܝܠܦܘ ܚܝܐ) and from that time on associated
only with the separated elect (ܒܓܒܝܐ ܦܪܝܫ).[3] An ancient Samaritan, commenting on the passage, "life and death," [4] said that
Adam ate for the death that was prepared, but Moses fasted for
the life that was prepared.[5] Moses taught Israel life and warned
her against death. He led her in the way of salvation and removed
her from the way of destruction.[6] In an *a fortiori* argument Paul
reasoned:

> 1) "For if, when we were enemies,
> 2) we were reconciled to God   3) through the death of his son;
>   1a) how much more, having been reconciled,
>   2a) shall we be saved   3a) in his life?" [7]

In this literary form, there is some parallel relationship between
1 and 1a, 2 and 2a, 3 and 3a. So those who are reconciled will be
saved, and that which happened through the death of his Son can
further happen in his life. What then is "life"? In accordance with
the meaning in Deuteronomy, Ezekiel, and Philo, it refers to the
existence within the covenant community. Here Christ's life is
membership in the body of Christ, the church.

In a similar form:

> 1) "For if, by means of the transgression of one [namely
>   Adam],
> 2) death ruled   3) through that one;
>   1a) how much more, those who receive the abundance of grace
>   and the free gift of righteousness,
>   2a) will he rule in life   3a) through the one,
>   Jesus Christ?" [8]

---

[1] *De Fuga*, 78, 97.
[2] Sifré, *Bemidbar* 48b § 132.
[3] II Bar. 42:5.
[4] Dt. 30:19.
[5] *Memar Marqah* IV § 5.
[6] *Memar Marqah* IV § 10.
[7] Rom. 5:10.
[8] Rom. 5:17.

In this case, the reign of death was contrasted to the reign of the recipients of grace and righteousness in life. The reign of death was through Adam, or the whole human race; the reign of the recipients of grace and righteousness took place in the covenant community, the Christian church, through Jesus who was the "initial leader" (ἀρχηγόν) of life, that is the founder of the new covenant.[1]

In still another similar analogy,

  1) "Then, as through the trespass of one [namely Adam],
  2) [the verdict went] to all men 3) for condemnation;
  1a) thus also through the righteous
       act of one [Jesus],
  2a) [the verdict went] to all men 3a) for justification of life."[2]

In this instance, the contrasts in the verdicts have universal application. The sin of Adam placed mankind in a relationship with God that decreed man to be guilty and therefore rejected. The righteous deed of Jesus brought about a verdict of "not guilty." This cleared the record for "life," or a new covenant relationship with God.

A further argument is:

  1) "Just as sin ruled,
  2) in death (ἐν τῷ θανάτῳ);   3) [incomplete]
  1a) thus also grace may rule
       through righteousness,
  2a) to life eternal   3a) through Jesus Christ
       (εἰς ζωὴν αἰώνιον),   our Lord."[3]

The rule of sin took place in the community of death, which is the whole estranged human race, originating with Adam. In contrast, the rule of grace reigns in life eternal (εἰς ζωὴν αἰώνιον) originating with Jesus Christ. So eternal life is the situation where grace reigns. That is the community of the new covenant. Throughout all of these arguments the reign of death through Adam was contrasted with the reign of life through Christ. One was marked by enmity, transgression, death, condemnation; whereas the other was asso-

---

[1] Acts 3 : 15; See also Heb. 2 : 10.
[2] Rom. 5:18. See also Didache 1 : 1ff.: Ep. of Barn. 18-19.
[3] Rom. 5:21

ciated with reconciliation, salvation, grace, righteousness, justification, and life eternal. "Life" and "life eternal" in these contexts
do not mean physical life but life in favorable relationship to God.
This is life within the new covenant.

Concerning the Jews, Paul said that if their rejection had such
a salutary effect that it meant reconciliation of the world; then
their acceptance of Christ would mean still more—life from the
dead.[1] Those who had broken the old covenant and were therefore
"dead" had another chance. Through Christ, they could become
members of the new covenant, which would mean "life" as the
term was used here.

The author of I John said that if any member of the community
noted his brother committing a sin, he could ask and God would
give the brother life, if the sin were not mortal.[2] This means either
that sin at once caused a member to be at least temporarily "dead,"
or that it would later cause him to become permanently so. But
as a result of prayer, he might be forgiven, restored to the community, and be "alive," or spared and so be alive in the future. The
implication is that for mortal sins this cannot be done, so the sinful
brother would be doomed to "death."

Christian life was more valuable than any material possession.
It was better to enter into life (ζωή) crippled than to be thrown
into eternal fire with a sound body.[3] The man who had many
possessions and was physically very much alive asked what he
must do to have eternal life (ζωὴ αἰώνιος).[4] In response, Jesus
said that if he wanted to enter into life (εἰς τὴν ζωὴν εἰσελθεῖν),
he should keep the commandments.[5] The life under consideration
was something a person could enter the way he might enter a country, a community, or a covenant. The prodigal son left his father's
house and went into a foreign country. After he became hungry,
he returned, defiled. He had sinned.[6] But his father rejoiced
because his son who had been dead was now alive; he was lost and
was now found.[7] Being "dead" in this context meant being away
from the father's house, being lost, out of reach; whereas being

---

[1] Rom. 11:15.
[2] I Jn. 5:16.
[3] Mt. 18:8-9; Mk. 9:43-45.
[4] Mt. 19:16.
[5] Mt. 19:17.
[6] Lk. 15:11-21.
[7] Lk. 15:24-32.

"alive" meant returning home, being restored to his own community, being found. Here life means acceptance within a law-abiding community, the community of the covenant.[1]

According to John, the time was foreseen when the "dead" would hear the voice of the Son of God and "live."[2] This would be possible because the son had life in himself (ζωὴν ἐν ἑαυτῷ) just as the Father did.[3] At that time those in the tombs would come forth. The ones who had done good would face the resurrection of life (ἀνάστασιν ζωῆς) and those who had done evil the resurrection of judgment.[4] Those who did not eat of the flesh of the Son of Man and drink of his blood had no life in themselves.[5] Jesus was the resurrection and the life; whoever believed in him even though he should die, yet he would live.[6] The signs that Jesus did were recorded so that people might believe and believing have life (ζωή) in his name.[7]

Eating the flesh and drinking the blood of the Son of Man probably referred to the fellowship meals of the community (body of Christ) that were restricted to the membership. The dead who heard the voice of the Son of God might have been those outside the community who would become proselytes and live. Judgment and resurrection were associated with life to show that community membership did not discontinue with physical death. When the dead would be raised, those who were really alive would be raised to live in the new community. The life-giving power of Christ had no limitations. Just as in Adam all died, so in Christ all should be made alive.[8] Those who had been baptized into Christ (i.e. the body of Christ, the Christian church) had been baptized into his death. They were buried in union with Christ when they were baptized, so that just as Christ was raised from the dead, Christians might also come up from the water to walk in newness of life, which means they practiced the way of conduct required of the new

---

[1] T. Barrosse, "The Death and Sin in Saint Paul's Epistle to the Romans," *CBQ* 15 (1953), 447, noted that in the very part of Romans (1:16f.) that Paul announced that he would devote to salvation, instead he discussed life.

[2] Jn. 5:25.

[3] Jn. 5:26.

[4] Jn. 5:29.

[5] Jn. 6:53.

[6] Jn. 11:25.

[7] Jn. 20:31.

[8] I Cor. 15:22.

covenant.[1] Every person confronted an either/or decision whereby
he chose either life or death and took the consequences of his
decisions. Those who bargained for sin would get death (θάνατος),
but the free gift of God was eternal life (ζωὴ αἰώνιος) in Christ
Jesus our Lord.[2]

When "life" and "death" are understood in terms of relationship
to the community, some confusing passages begin to make sense.
When one wanted to postpone following Jesus until he had buried
his father, Jesus said, "Let the 'dead' bury their own dead."[3] In
the physical sense corpses cannot be expected to bury other
corpses, but in the community responsible for the preservation
of this teaching, those outside the community were as defiling as
corpses even though they were physically alive and breathing.[4]
Those who joined such exclusive, legalistic communities had to
break all familiy ties. The only way that family members could
associate with such isolationists was to join the same group so
that they too could have life. The man who asked for permission
to bury his father was probably asking permission to fulfill the
commandment to honor his father and mother by providing for
them in their old age until they had died.[5] Decisions for "life" in
such exclusive communities meant considering family relationships
as "dead." In the tense, unstable political situation of first century
Palestine, the one who refused to give up his family ties, wealth,
security, and social position might expect to lose all of these
values, anyway, and finally be killed; but the one who gave up
his life (ψυχή) would preserve his life (ζῳογονήσει),[6] even though
he were martyred. The life (ζωή) in the new covenant was not
destroyed by the loss of physical life (ψυχή) or the broken pattern
of social behavior in the "world." The resurrection promised reunion
for members, and the new covenant provided a new "family"
and community.

---

[1] Rom. 6:3-4.
[2] Rom. 6:23.
[3] Mt. 8:22; Lk. 9:60.
[4] This is the interpretation given by Origen, *Fragment on Luke*, 156. The
scribes and Pharisees were so inwardly defiled that Jesus compared them
to dead bones and all kinds of uncleanness (Mt. 23:27). This sectarian
teaching is contrary to many of the anti-legalistic teachings attributed to
Jesus.
[5] Mekilta, *Baḥodesh* 8:1-4.
[6] Lk. 17:33.

The claim that Jesus was judge both of the living and the dead [1] might have had a double meaning: on the one hand, the physically living and dead and on the other hand those who were Christians and those who were not. An angel told Callimachus, "Die that you may live." Callimachus then told John he wanted to become one of those who hoped in Christ so that his faithless, disorderly self might be "dead" and that he might "live," being faithful, God-fearing, and knowing the truth.[2] When the angel released the apostles from prison, he commanded them to stand up in the temple to tell the people all the words of this life (τῆς ζωῆς ταύτης),[3] meaning the Christian religion. After Peter had told the circumcision party about his vision, the group glorified God and said, "Then God has given to the Gentiles repentance into 'life,'"[4] which meant Gentiles could be admitted into the covenant community where life was possible. From a non-Judaic point of view, the old covenant to which the Jews belonged was a handicap to them. They thought that in the scriptures they had eternal life (ζωὴ αἰώνιος), so they refused to come to him and have "life" (ζωή).[5] Here the antitheses were not physical life against life in the covenant, but the life under one covenant as over against another. The author of the pastoral epistles mixed his meanings when describing widows. The true widow was pious (and therefore "alive"). But the self-indulgent woman was "dead even while alive" (ζῶσα τέθνηκεν). The same author held that Paul was an apostle of Jesus Christ according to the promise of life (ζωή) which was in Christ Jesus.[6] Hermas said anyone who wanted to be "made alive" (ζῳοποιηθῶσιν) had to come up through the water. Otherwise it was not possible to enter the Kingdom of God. Whenever a person accepts the seal, which is the water, he puts away mortality (νέκρωσιν) and accepts life (ἀναλαμβάνει τὴν ζωήν). The dead (νεκροί) go down into the water and come up alive (ζῶντες). Enoch said the elect would inherit the land; they would be wise; and they would never again sin.[7] This was a dream of perfection, but after their religious war had failed and the temple was burned, the elect were confused. The

---

[1] Acts 10:43; II Tim. 4:1.
[2] Acts of John 76.
[3] Acts 5:20.
[4] Acts 11:18.
[5] Jn. 5:39-40.
[6] I Tim. 5:6; II Tim. 1:1.
[7] Shepherd of Hermas Sim. IX.xvi.2-4; Enoch 5:7a-b, 8.

life they expected they did not receive. Perhaps they had misunderstood, but where could they go for correction? "Where again
shall we seek the law, or who will distinguish for us between life
and death?" [1] The life they sought was more than physical survival.
It was real (ὄντως) life.[2]

The life described in the passages considered was not physical
life but some quality of existence for which people who were
physically alive could seek. Those who lived entered the promised
land, were obedient to God, kept the covenant, and made no covenant with other gods. Their hearts were circumcised; they loved
the Lord with all their being; they found refuge in God, were
reconciled, recipients of God's grace, justified, included, accepted
home, forgiven, saved, and found. Those who desired life had to
meet the terms so that they could enter or inherit life. Those
expressions were so closely related to the meaning of membership
in the covenant community that the two can be considered synonymous. The person who belonged to the covenant community
was alive; the one who did not, was dead. Since this is so, it would
not be surprising to find some relationship between covenant
membership and having one's name written in the "book of life."
This will be the next step of our investigation.

The Book of Life

Membership list.—When the captives from Babylon were
returned to Jerusalem, there were lists made of the entire community.[3] There were undoubtedly other times in the history of
the people when the nation was small enough to be recorded one
by one in a membership roll. Isaiah described the Jews left in
Jerusalem and Zion after the destruction as holy—everyone who
had been written down for life in Jerusalem (כל הכתוב לחיים
בירושלם)[4]. Those saints who were victorious would be saved. They
would wear the crown of the true covenant of the Lord (ܣܘܚܐ
ܚܠܠܐ ܟܣܝܡܗ ܫܝܪ ܘܢܪܝܐ) and be written in his book (ܟܗܒܐ).[5]
Those written down for life were the righteous remnant and members of the covenant. Their being written down may have meant

---

[1] II Bar. 46:3; See also *Congr.* xvii(93).
[2] I Tim. 6:19.
[3] Ezra 2:1-67; Neh. 11:1-12:43; see also Neh. 7:5.
[4] Isa 4:3-5.
[5] Odes of Sol. 9:6-13.

that they were destined to survive the destruction, or that the list of members recorded would all be righteous. The book of life probably referred as much to their holiness as to their being alive in the physical sense.

In the Psalmist's cry for vengeance, he complained because his enemies were Israelites—his mother's sons,[1] and therefore members of the covenant community. He asked that their names be blotted out of the book of life (ימחו מספר חיים), not written down among the righteous (עם צדיקים אל יכתבו).[2] Since the righteous were the approved members of the community and therefore "alive," it seems as if the book of life here was the membership list. He wanted his brothers excommunicated. The same connotation was given in the NT. Paul's fellow workers were among those whose names were written in the book of life (βίβλῳ ζωῆς).[3] The few in Sardis who had not "soiled their garments" were considered "worthy."[4] Their names would not be blotted out of the book of life.[5] All those whose names were not written down in the Lamb's book of life, worshipped the beast.[6]

Court record.—In all except the Isaiah prophecy, the people whose names were either included or excluded in the book of life were those who were physically alive at the time of the writing, so the basic meaning of the expression was not eschatological, but there was a judgmental quality about the use of the expression. The righteous, holy, worthy, and those whose garments were not soiled were included. If a person was excluded from the list he was not registered with the righteous. In an eschatological context, Enoch saw the righteous and wicked being judged before the Head of Days when the books of life were opened (ωσ²ሕፉት : ሕየዋን).[7] He also referred to a book where unrighteous deeds were recorded and held against a person on the day of judgment [8] and another which recorded the destruction of the evil shepherds.[9] Baruch

---

[1] Ps. 69:8.
[2] Ps. 69:28.
[3] Phil. 4:3.
[4] Rev. 3:4.
[5] Rev. 3:5.
[6] Rev. 13:8; 17:8.
[7] Enoch 47:3-4; see also 108:3.
[8] Enoch 81:4.
[9] Enoch 90:17.

foresaw the judgment day when the books would be opened which recorded sinners' sins and also the treasuries of righteousness in which the good deeds of the righteous were gathered.[1] Before the great white throne, the Johannine seer also saw the books opened. One of these was the book of life. Those whose names were not recorded there were thrown into the lake of fire.[2] Those saved had life and would live in the new Jerusalem where no unclean thing could enter. It would be completely free from defilement. In an eschatological sense, the book of life referred to the new community restored to the land after the period of servitude was over. Not all Jews would qualify, but those who did were the true members of the covenant. Therefore, the expression, "book of life," referred, on the one hand, to the regular membership of the righteous, and on the other, to the righteous of the future restored community. On the Day of Judgment, the Judge had some books which recorded the good and bad deeds of individuals and others listing those acquitted and those condemned. Those in the list of the innocent were enrolled in the book of life. Of course, the members who had life were expected to have long physical life and not receive the punishment of the wicked, but the book of life was probably not so important for listing those who were physically alive as those who were the righteous members of the covenant.

The rabbis contrasted darkness to light, slavery to freedom, and, in the same context, the yoke of iron to life. They believed that on the Day of Atonement and New Year's Day, the books of life and death were opened and Israelites were judged for "life" or "death,"[3] meaning exile or freedom to "live" on the land of the promise. Commenting on "from your midst,"[4] Sifré said, "But not from the membership" (ולא מן הספר).[5] The sons of Belial who left were not members of the covenant, the rabbis decided, so they were really among the dead. The expression "book of life" was not used many times, but the consistency with which it was used related it closely to the covenant members who had life. The next demonstration will show the relationship between the people who inherit life and those who inherit

---

[1] II Bar. 24:1; see Dan. 7:10; Enoch 90:20; IV Ezra 6:20.
[2] Rev. 20:11-15.
[3] *PRK*, Appendix 7:6-13.
[4] Dt. 13:14.
[5] Sifré 93a § 93.

the land. This will interpret the expression, the land of life, as Palestine.

THE LAND OF LIFE

OT testimony.—Since the members of the covenant, whose names were written in the book of life were those who inherited life and also inherited the land promised them in the covenant, it should not be surprising to find a close relationship between the promised land and the land of life. In Ezra's confession to God, he admitted that his people had been sinful from the days of their fathers until that day.[1] Because of this they had been given into the hands of the rulers of other lands as slaves.[2] But in Ezra's time the Lord had shown favor to his people. He restored a remnant to the holy place. In so doing, God had made the eyes of the Jews to shine (להאיר עינים) and given them life to a small degree (מחיה מעט).[3] That which Ezra called "granting life to a small degree" (מחיה מעט) meant permitting his people to rebuild the temple and walls and provide protection in Jerusalem and Judah.[4] Life was not complete because the entire land had not been restored. That was why Ezra called it "life to a small degree." Evidently Ezra had not considered the Jews in Babylon to have been "alive" so long as they lived in a foreign country without a temple and a land. Life began for them, with the first small installment, when they were returned to Jerusalem and could begin to reestablish the Davidic kingdom.

A psalmist was weary of God's anger and hoped it would soon cease. If God would just declare that the account of Israel's sins had been paid up,[5] then his salvation would draw near and glory would dwell in their land. This would be the way God would again give his people life (תחינו).[6] It was probably a Levite who had no portion in the promised land[7] who cried out to the Lord who

---

[1] Ezra 9:6.

[2] Ezra 9:7.

[3] Ezra 9:8. See also Odes of Sol. 6:16-17. In addition to life and strength, the Lord gave "light to their eyes" (ܘܢܘܗܪܐ ܠܥܝ̈ܢܝܗܘܢ) so they all knew the Lord (ܐܫܬܘܕܥ ܐܢܘܢ ܟܠܗܘܢ).

[4] Ezra 9:9; cf. also II Bar. 56:4.

[5] Ps. 85:9.

[6] Ps. 85:7, 10.

[7] Dt. 18:1-2.

was his "portion in the land of life" (חלקי בארץ החיים).[1] Another psalmist, who was probably a priest, wanted to spend all his life in the temple, protected and secure.[2] At the time of his prayer, his enemies were threatening his position.[3] They wanted him to be turned away, cast off,[4] but the psalmist had faith that he would see the Lord's goodness "in the land of life" (בארץ חיים).[5] Still another said that the evil man would be rooted up from the land of life (מארץ חיים), whereas the psalmist would continue like a green tree in the temple, which, of course, was in the promised land.[6] A psalmist who paid his vows to the Lord at Jerusalem[7] walked before the Lord in the land of life.[8] A non-canonical psalmist said death had been destroyed before his face. Deathless life had gone into the Lord's land (ܘܣܠܩ ܒ݁ܐܝܬ݂ܗܘܢ ܘܗܒ݁ܬ݂ ܚܝܐ ܠܐܪܥܗ) and was made known to all who believed in him.[9] Some of these psalms can be understood if the expression "land of life" were interpreted to mean the place where people are physically alive. In that case the person who was to be cast off would be killed rather than exiled. To see the goodness of the Lord in the land of life would mean while the psalmist lived rather than in Palestine. But the Levite whose portion was the Lord in the land of life was one whose portion in the Land of Palestine was also the Lord, and all of the other psalms also make good sense if the land of life is understood to mean Palestine.

When Hezekiah was ill he expected to see the Lord no more in the land of life. The Vatican text of this lament is:

"I will no longer see the victory of God in the
land of living (ἐπὶ τῆς γῆς ζώντων)
I will no longer see the triumph of Israel upon the
land (ἐπὶ τῆς γῆς).[10]

In this text, the land of living, which is a literal translation of the Hebrew "land of life" is the place where God's victory and

---

[1] Ps. 142:6.
[2] Ps. 27:2-5.
[3] Ps. 27:2-3, 12.
[4] Ps. 27:9-10.
[5] Ps. 27:13.
[6] Ps. 52:5-8.
[7] Ps. 116:18-19.
[8] Read with the Syriac ܒ݁ܐܪܥܗ ܕܚܝܐ; Hebrew בארצות החיים (Ps. 116:9).
[9] Odes of Sol. 15:10-11.
[10] Isa. 38:11.

Israel's triumph would both take place. The land of living here means "the land." When not accompanied by an adjective, הארץ or ἡ γῆ means either the earth or the Land of Palestine. Since the Land of Palestine was the land Hezekiah ruled and for which he desired salvation from foreign powers,[1] the land of living here probably also means the promised land. Jeremiah's enemies planned to cut him off from the land of life so that his name would not be remembered again.[2] This may have been a plan to kill Jeremiah,[3] banish him from the country, or both. The context is not clear. If the land of living were understood to mean Palestine, this would mean exile.[4]

After Jerusalem had fallen,[5] the temple burned, and the priests become defiled, the psalmist contrasted the people's high hopes with the actual tragedy.[6] The people had hoped to have life among the nations (נחיה בגוים) under the shadow of the Messiah—the Messiah of the Lord (משיח יהוה) who was the breath of the people's nostrils (רוח אפינו).[7] This entire lamentation was in relationship to the life of Israel as a free nation, prominent among the nations, with her own temple, government, and king—all of which were then gone. Without a king, the people were "dead."

Ezekiel prophesied that Nebuchadnezzar would utterly destroy Tyre, which was located within the boundaries of the promised

---

[1] See L. H. Brockington, "Septuagint and Targum," ZATW 66 (1954), 81.

[2] Jer. 11:19.

[3] Jer. 11:21.

[4] Jeremiah was exiled when he was taken against his will into Egypt (Jer. 43:4-7).

[5] Jerusalem fell in 586 B. C. and again in 70 A. D. There are some suggestive, though by no means conclusive, reasons for considering the latter date as the event about which this psalmist wrote. The events described *may* have occurred in 586 B. C., but Josephus (*BJ* VI) *reported* similar events to have happened in 70 A.D. There were such conditions that mothers killed and ate their own children (Lam. 2:20; 4:8-10)). People and priests killed the righteous (*BJ* IV [334-344]; Zechariah, see Mt. 23:35) in the temple area (Lam. 4:13); and priests were defiled by bloodshed (Lam. 4:14-16). If these events described in Lam. 4 referred to 586 B.C. the name "Edom" referred to Idumea. If it referred to the events of 70 A.D., then Rome was meant. Lam. 4:21 may be an allusion to Ps. 137:7. If any material was added to the canon after 70 A.D., Lam. 2 and 4; Ps. 74; and the following lamentations for Zion may have been some: Ps. 14:7; 51:20-21; and 53:7. These appear to have been added to completed psalms on other topics. Cf. the known post-70 A.D. lamentations in II Baruch and IV Ezra.

[6] Lam. 4:1-19.

[7] Lam. 4:20.

land [1] even though it was usually under the domination of foreign powers. In the future, however, the Lord would send Nebuchadnezzar to push Tyre off into the sea.[2] He would give pleasantness to the land of life (באָרץ חיים) but destruction to Tyre.[3] Ezekiel further prophesied that Assyria, Elam, Mesheck, Tubul, Edom, the princes of the North, the Sidonians, and Pharaoh—all of whom "spread terror in the land of life" (באָרץ חיים) [4]—would lie together, slain among the uncircumcised.[5] The countries listed were all enemies of Israel. Those who spread terror in the land of life were the ones who had terrified Judah and Israel. I Baruch criticized Israel for growing old in enemy territory (γῇ ἐχθρῶν), in a foreign land (ἐν γῇ ἀλλοτρίᾳ). Israel had become stained with the dead (συνεμιάνθης τοῖς νεκροῖς), reckoned with those in hades. The "dead" with whom they had been identified were the citizens of the foreign land (Babylon) in which they were captive. "Life" was not possible outside of Palestine, "the land of life." [6] III Baruch warned the transgressors not to boast that they had conquered Jerusalem. This had been possible only because of Israel's sins. But God would later have mercy on the Jews and return them to their city. The transgressors, however, would not then control Jerusalem and therefore should not have life (ὑμεῖς δὲ ζωὴν οὐχ ἕξετε).[7] In his prayer, Baruch said, "Take courage, virgin faith of mine, and believe that you will live (ζήσεις).[8] Rabbis said that all David and Solomon did was for the "life" of Israel.[9] David and Solomon established the kingdom for the people of Israel.

Since all of the OT and non-canonical passages considered make good sense when "land of life" is understood to mean "the promised land," and since some make much better sense with that interpretation than understood to mean "physically alive and breathing," it is more likely that the expression really was intended to mean Palestine. That is the way the rabbis understood it.

---

[1] For boundary limits that include the region of Tyre, see Gen. 15:18; Ex. 23:31; Num. 13:21; 34:3-9; Dt. 1:7; 11:24; Josh. 1:4; I Kgs. 5:1; 8:65; Isa. 27:12; Ezek. 6:14; 47:15, 19; 48:12, 28. See also Chapter IV.

[2] Ezek. 26:1-19.

[3] Ezek. 26:20.

[4] Ezek. 32:23, 24, 25, 27, 32.

[5] Ezek. 32:18-32.

[6] I Bar. 3:10-12.

[7] III Bar. 5:7-8.

[8] III Bar. 6:4.

[9] Dt. R. 2:20 (102c).

Later interpretation.—The likelihood that the expression, "land of life" referred to the promised land where life was possible becomes greater when it is confirmed by later Jewish authors. Rabbi Tanḥuma said, "The Land of Israel is called the land of life" (קורא ארץ ישראל ארץ חיים), and Jacob's hope to return to the land of Israel was his claim to his portion in the land of life.[1] Rav Kahana said:

> "Listen [to the people] in the land until you do not
>   hear [anyone] outside the land;
> pay attention to the living (חיים) until you do not
>   hear the dead (מתים)." [2]

In this couplet, those outside the land were called "dead" and those inside the land, "living." Rav Kahana also said that souls were judged on New Year's Day for "life" or "death." At that time the Lord would accept those who had repented.[3] Baruch called Israel to hear the commandment of life, reminding her that she was then in an enemy's land and thus defiled with the "dead," counted with those who go down to the grave.[4] R. Meir said that everyone who lived in the land of Israel, recited the *Shemaʻ* morning and evening, and spoke Hebrew was a member (בן) of the age to come.[5] R. Joḥanan said the ones who dwelled in the Land of Israel, reared their sons in the study of the Torah, or recited the *habdalah* over wine at the end of the Sabbath would inherit the age to come.[6] R. Nathan b. R. Joseph said the covenant was made for the land (לארץ), by which he meant the land of the promise.[7] According to Baruch, the Lord promised to protect those who were found in that land (ܒܐܪܥ ܐܝܢ) when the Messiah was

---

[1] *Tanḥuma, Vayêṣê* 8ob.
[2] *PRK* 14:4, 11-12.
[3] *PRK*, Appendix 7:11-13.
[4] Bar. 3:9-11.
[5] Sifré *Debarim* 32:43; 14ob § 333.
[6] Pes. 113a.
[7] Sifré *Debarim* 6:5; 73 § 32. *Ikkarim* IV.49, 10-16, also says, " 'Wait for the Lord and keep his way, and he will exalt you to inherit the land' (Ps. 131:34, 37). This means the reward of hope in particular and keeping the way of the Lord in general, is inheritance of the land of life" (ארץ חיים). According to the rabbis, inheriting the land refers to the land of life, as they say, "All Israel has a portion in the age to come (עולם הבא) as it is said, 'All your people will be righteous so as to inherit the land for the age' " (San. 9oa; Isa. 60:21).

revealed.[1] Abtalion admonished scholars to be careful in their words lest they incur a conviction of sin against Israel that required exile for punishment. Exile would be in a foreign land where there were "evil waters" (מים הרעים) from which future disciples would drink and "die" (וימותו).[2] The "waters" probably referred to something like foreign teachings that would draw disciples from the covenant. R. Simeon ben Lakish in the name of Bar Kapra, said that the land of life was the place where its dead would live at the beginning of the days of the Messiah. This raised a question about the disadvantage given the rabbis in the diaspora where the dead would not be raised. Since these neither lived nor were buried in the land of life, were they to be penalized for this misfortune? The rabbis reasoned some rather ingenious ways by which the Lord would have their bodies moved to the Land of Israel so that they could be raised on the land of life. Here the understanding that the land of life was the Land of Israel was taken for granted. The resurrection was associated with it to give further reason for calling it the land of life.

The suffering servant and the land.—When the land of life is understood as the promised land, some previously confusing passages begin to make sense. One of these is a difficult passage in II Isaiah. The "servant" was frequently identified with Israel,[3]

---

[1] II Bar. 29:2.

[2] Aboth 1:11.

[3] Isa. 41:8; 44:21; 45:4. S. H. Blank, "Studies in Deutero-Isaiah," *HUCA* 15 (1940), 1-46; L. J. Liebreich, "The Compilation of the Book of Isaiah," *JQR* 46 (1955-56), 259-277; 47 (1956-57), 114-138; H. G. May, "The Righteous Servant in Second Isaiah's Songs," *ZATW* 66 (1954), 236-244; W. M. Roth, "The Anonymity of the Suffering Servant," *JBL* 83 (1964), 171-179; and R. J. Tournay, "Les Chants du Serviteur dans la Seconde Partise d'Isaïe," *RB* 59 (1912), 355-512, all agreed that the suffering servant was a personification of all Israel. Blank, Roth, and C. R. North, *The Suffering Servant in Deutero-Isaiah* (Oxford, 1956), 39, said that the servant not only personified the people of Israel but also the prophetic movement. Blank noted a similarity between the servant and Jeremiah, but concluded as did North that the servant really symbolized no single prophet (p. 29). North thought the servant songs were deduced from the sufferings of the prophets. Blank emphasized the group character of the servant so much that he included all generations of Israelites in the personality: "To convey His message to humanity, nothing less than an entire people—an historic *continuity* [italics mine]—is adequate" (p. 32). R. A. Rosenberg, "Jesus, Isaac, and the Suffering Servant," *JBL* 84 (1965), 381, said, "It is unlikely that the nation or a portion of the nation is meant [as the

and yet he was assigned the task of bringing Jacob/Israel back to the Lord.[1] He was to raise up the tribes of Jacob, restore the preserved of Israel, and become a light to the nations [2] so that salvation might reach the ends of the earth.[3] How was it possible for the servant both to be a personification of Israel and yet have a ministry to Israel? [4] When ארץ חיים is understood as the Land of Palestine, this is at once clear. The first generation of Jews taken to Babylon represented the servant who suffered. The targum on Isaiah described the servant as the "remnant of his people," [5] and referred to these people in the plural. *They* were despised and rejected.[6] *They* hung up their harps on the willows and refused to sing the songs of Zion.[7] When Israel had such an accumulation of sins that its treasury of merits was bankrupt, it was necessary for the Lord to "foreclose," and take the Jews from the promised land. There the Jews had to stay until they had paid double for all their sins.[8] There the servant bore the griefs and sorrows for

---

servant], since the language of the prophet speaks clearly of an individual." Rosenberg thought the servant was a real individual who substituted for the figure of the king of the Jews in a ritual drama, known to have been practiced in Babylon much earlier than the exilic period (381-383). Liebreich, 271, however, thought David was the prototype for the servant. Roth said that like the beloved disciple in John, so the suffering servant in II Isaiah was intentionally anonymous because he represented the prophetic office itself (pp. 177-179). Tournay thought Moses was the prototype (p. 367) and said that the author intentionally neglected to distinguish the servant as a group from the servant as an individual.

[1] Isa. 49:5.

[2] Isa. 49:6.

[3] Isa. 49:6.

[4] J. Morgenstern, "The Suffering Servant—a New Solution," *VT* 11 (1961), 293-320, said, "From this passage it is plain that under no condition, even though the Servant's name be Israel, or at least even though he be called by that title, may the Servant be identified with the people, Israel" (p. 307). Instead the servant was a king of Israel and his name was Judah (p. 307). E. Sellin, "Die Lösung des deuterojesajanischen Gottesknechtsrätsel," *ZATW* 55 (1937), 177-217, claimed that the servant was II Isaiah himself (p. 215).

[5] Targ. Isa. 53:10.

[6] Targ. Isa. 53:3.

[7] Ps. 137:1-6.

[8] Isa. 40:1-2. The eldest son was the "chosen one" (הבכר, Dt. 21:17) just as Israel was the Lord's chosen (בכיר) people. Just as the eldest son inherited a double portion of his father's wealth, so Israel "inherited" a double portion of the Lord's wrath when being punished. The same significance was attached to Elisha's request for a double portion of Elijah's spirit. His receipt of this heritage meant that he was Elijah's chosen disciple

later generations of Jews who were liberated to return to Jerusalem.[1]
He, the first generation in Babylon, was wounded for the transgressions of all Israel. By the stripes of that generation all Israel
was healed.[2] The rest of Israel had strayed like lost sheep and the
Lord laid on the first generation the iniquity of all Israel.[3] "Now
as for his generation, he was cut off from the land of life" (ארץ חיים)
[Palestine].[4] "And they made his grave with the wicked [Gentiles
in Babylon], and with the rich in his death." [5] Like Moses, the first
generation of captives was buried outside the promised land.[6]
Like Moses, this punishment was taken as an atonement for the
sins of the rest of Israel.[7] Moses offered to be blotted out of the
"book" which the Lord had written, if only the Lord would forgive
the people's sins.[8] The book was evidently the "book of life" which
contained the names of all those admitted into the promised land
where "life" could take place. The Lord was not content to punish
only Moses. He destroyed all that generation except Joshua and
Caleb.[9] Like Moses,[10] the first generation in Babylon was called
the servant. But just as Moses was able to see the land from the
outside,[11] and know that the children of Israel would enter after
his death, so the servant in Babylon, after he had made himself an
offering for the sin of Israel, was able to see his offspring.[12] He would
be satisfied to know that his suffering bore fruit.[13] It was the chil-

---

(II Kgs. 2:9). More important was the relationship of servitude to sabbatical
year justice. The debtor worked off his debt at half wages (Dt. 15:18). R.
Kahana said, "They sin double; they are punished double; and they are
comforted double" (*PRK* 16:11, 7-10).

[1] Isa. 53:4.

[2] Isa. 53:5. There is no basis for Klausner's (*Op. cit.*, 161-163) view that
th e servant was Israel who suffered for the sins of other nations. The
chosen people were only thought to have been accountable for their own sins.
But here one generation of Jews suffered for other Jews. His idea of the servant as an example of "collective messianism" is also out of character.

[3] Isa. 53:6.

[4] Isa. 53:8. Instead of ארץ חיים Targ. Isa. 53:8 has ארעא דישראל.

[5] Isa. 53:9.

[6] Dt. 3:23-27; 34:5-6.

[7] Ex. 32:31.

[8] Ex. 32:31.

[9] Dt. 1:35-39; 2:15-16.

[10] Dt. 3:24; 34:5.

[11] Dt. 3:24; 34:5.

[12] Isa. 53:10. Instead of יראה זרע, Targ. Isa. 53:10 has יחזון במלכות משיחהון
יסגון בניו ובנן

[13] Isa. 53:11.

dren, the second generation, that could see release just over the horizon and understand that the previous generation had done all the suffering without receiving the reward of returning to the land of life. That generation wrote the servant hymns in praise and gratitude for their immediate ancestors who died in Babylon.

The community that made its decision for life when it entered into covenant relationship with the God of life and were promised the land of life as an inheritance also had responsibilities that covenant living required. Covenant ethics, then, will next be considered in its relationship to life.

THE ETHICS OF LIFE

The way of life.—The covenant involved God's promises, but it also required the covenanters to follow a prescribed pattern of life if they were to remain in God's favor. Ezekiel referred to the covenant as the statutes of life (חקות החיים). The one who walked in these would surely live (חיו יחיה).[1] The assigned pattern of behavior was called the "path of life" (ארח חיים) or the "way of life" (דרך חיים) which kept covenanters from wandering. It was the path of the wisemen who heeded instruction and observed the required discipline.[2] Because the covenant ethics were described in ways to walk, later Jews referred to rules of conduct as *halakah* or "walking."[3] The words of the Torah lead a man's knowledge from the ways of death (מיתה) to the ways of life (חיים). They bring life eternal (חיים לעולם).[4] Turning aside to serve other gods means turning from the way of life to the way of death.[5] The psalmist praised God for rescuing him from Sheol and showing him the path of life.[6] After the fall of Jerusalem Ezra asked God for the Holy Spirit so he could rewrite the law. This was necessary so that those who wanted to live might find the right path and at last live (*et qui voluerint vivere in novissimis vivant*).[7]

The way of life is the right path but it is hard and those who find it are few.[8] The new and living way Christ opened up for

---

[1] Ezek. 33:35.
[2] Prov. 2:19; 5:6; 6:3; 10:17; 15:24. Also Philo, *De Plantatione* viii (37); *De Fuge* xi (20); xv (78); xviii (97).
[3] See "Midrashim Pré-Tannaïtes," *RB* 72 (1965), 227-239.
[4] Sifré *Debarim* 11:13, 79b, 81b, § 41.
[5] IV Ezra 7:48.
[6] Ps. 16:10-11; Acts 2:28.
[7] IV Ezra 14:22.   [8] Mt. 7:11.

Christians allowed them access to the holy of holies.[1] The Christian church was called the "way," [2] meaning the right way to walk for those who wanted to enter life. It was the ethics of the new covenant. In both the old covenant and the new, the law and the teaching of the sages were important guides for finding the right way for covenanters to walk.

Wisdom and the word.—Bread was important for physical existence, but life did not consist of possessions,[3] so the covenanter lived by every word which proceeded from the mouth of God.[4] God's word was living (ζῶν),[5] so Paul urged his people to hold fast to the word of life (λόγος ζωῆς).[6] Stephen said that Moses had been given "living oracles" (λόγια ζῶντα).[7] Christians were those who had been born anew through the "living word" (λόγος ζῶν) of God. In the OT the word was received from God through the Torah and the prophets. The Torah was called the tree of life [8] and also the water of life.[9] Just as water gives life for the world, so the words of the Torah give life to the world. Just as water raises the unclean from his defilement by ablutions, so the words of the Torah raise a man from his evil way to the good way.[10] The Lord gave a perfect Torah to his servants for life (חיים) and length of days.[11] The saints of the Lord lived (ܚܝܘ) by the Lord's commandments.[12] Baruch was told to teach others the commandments and make them live (ܚܣܝ).[13] Those who learned from Baruch's teaching would live and not die at the last time.[14] Jeremiah said the Israelites had forsaken the Lord who was the fountain of the water of life.[15] Baruch said that because they had forsaken the

---

[1] Heb. 10:20.
[2] Acts 9:2; 19:9, 23; 22:4; 24:14, 22.
[3] Lk. 12:15.
[4] Dt. 8:3; Mt. 4:4; Lk. 4:4.
[5] Heb. 1:23.
[6] Philip. 2:16.
[7] Acts 7:38.
[8] Sifré *Debarim* 11:21, 83 § 37.
[9] Prov. 4:22; Sifré *Debarim* 11:22, 84a § 48.
[10] Sifré *Bemidbar* 40a § 119; *Debarim* 11:22, 84a § 48; see also Sifré *Debarim* 32:2, 131b §306; 33:2, 142b § 343.
[11] *Memar Marqah* II § 1.
[12] Ps. of Sol. 14:2.
[13] II Bar. 45:2.
[14] II Bar. 76:4.
[15] Jer. 2:13; 17:13.

fountain of wisdom (which Jeremiah called the Lord), Israelites
were defiled with the dead in an enemy's land.[1] Those who entered
the new covenant at Damascus but later turned away from the
"well of the water of life" (מבאר מים חיים) were no longer kept on
the membership rolls.[2] Those who held fast to the eternal commandments were appointed to life, but those who left it would die.[3]
The basic rule was "the more study of the law the more life." The
law gives life to those who practice it both in this age and in the
age to come.[4] The eternal covenant which God gave Israel for a
heritage was the law of life (νόμον ζωῆς).[5] Jesus said the one who
kept the commandments would live,[6] but Paul denied that a
law had been given that could make alive.[7] Although it was understood by many to give life, Paul found that instead it led to
death.[8]

Closely related to the Torah was the teaching of the wise. The
instructions of a wise man are "life" to him who finds them.[9]
Wisdom nourishes those who fear the Lord with the bread of
understanding and the water of wisdom.[10] At the feasts in the
temple of Jerusalem the Lord gave the children to drink from the
fountain of life.[11] The fountain of life was the mouth of a righteous
man,[12] the teaching of the wise,[13] the fear of the Lord,[14] or wisdom.[15]
Fear of the Lord and steadfast righteousness lead to life.[16] The
counsel of wisdom is a fountain of life.[17] Wisdom is the tree of life[18]
which is also the fruit of righteousness,[19] a good desire,[20] or a

---

[1] Bar. 3:10-12.
[2] CDC 19:34.
[3] Bar. 4:1-2.
[4] Aboth 2:7; 6:7.
[5] Sir. 17:11-13.
[6] Lk. 10:28.
[7] Gal. 3:21.
[8] Rom. 3:21.
[9] Prov. 3:22; 4:13; 4:22; 8:35.
[10] Sir. 15:3.
[11] Ps. 36:10.
[12] Prov. 10:11.
[13] Prov. 13:14.
[14] Prov. 14:27.
[15] Prov. 16:22.
[16] Prov. 11:19; 19:23.
[17] Sir. 21:13.
[18] Prov. 3:18.
[19] Prov. 11:30.
[20] Prov. 13:12.

healing tongue.[1] Those who love wisdom love life.[2] It is the one who accepts correction of life (תוכחת חיים) that will be associated with the wise.[3] The labor of the righteous man contributes to life.[4] The sage admonished:

"Hold fast to instruction; do not let her go;
guard her, for she is your life (חייך)." [5]

Through the knowledge of Christ, God granted Christians all things that pertain to "life." [6] Those who are thus equipped qualify for entrance into the kingdom.[7] Thomas said the person who instructed another and gave him the holy seal (i.e. baptism) caused the one baptized to live.[8] The study of the Torah, rigid obedience of the commandments, acceptance of required discipline, and avoidance of the teachings of other groups were the exclusive bases for ethics that separated the members of the covenant who were alive from the rest of the world that was dead.

The Christian spirit.—Life and spirit were closely related in the OT but only in a physical sense. Breath was given to bodies so that they could live. In the NT, however, spirit was related to life in a religious sense, and, to some extent, it replaced the law for members of the new covenant. It was the spirit that gave life, in contrast to the flesh which profited nothing. The words of Jesus were spirit and life (πνεῦμά ἐστιν καὶ ζωή ἐστιν).[9] The law of the spirit of life in Christ Jesus freed Paul from the law of sin and death.[10] Attention to the flesh leads to death, but attention to the spirit is life and peace (ζωὴ καὶ εἰρήνη).[11]

"But if Christ is in your midst,
your body is dead because of sin,
but your spirit is life (ζωή) because of
righteousness."[12]

---

[1] Prov. 15:4.
[2] Sir. 4:12; see also Syriac Sir. 23:12.
[3] Prov. 15:31.
[4] Prov. 10:16.
[5] Prov. 4:13.
[6] II Peter 1:3.
[7] II Peter 1:11.
[8] *Apos. Cons.* 1:12.
[9] Jn. 6:63.
[10] Rom. 8:2.
[11] Rom. 8:6.
[12] Rom. 8:10.

This final couplet seems to be a text Paul quoted and explained further in the next verse. By the spirit, Paul meant the spirit of him who raised Jesus from the dead. The same spirit would give life to the mortal bodies (τὰ θνητὰ σώματα) of Christians.[1] Paul changed from the singular to the plural from verses 10 to 11. Before Paul's interpretation, verse 10 seemed to contrast body, death, and sin with spirit, life, and righteousness. It may originally have meant either/or. Paul, however, offered good news when he claimed that the "dead" could "live." Life and death have more than a physical meaning here. Paul contrasted the first Adam who received the spirit and became a living being with the last Adam (Christ) who could provide the spirit and make other beings live (πνεῦμα ζῳοποιοῦν).[2] Paul contrasted the old covenant of Moses with the new covenant of which he was a minister. He said, "The written code kills, but the spirit gives life" (ζῳοποιεῖ).[3] This life is life within the new covenant. Members of the new covenant live by the spirit rather than the law; therefore they must conduct their lives according to the dictates of the spirit.[4] Another early Christian said that Christ who died for our sins, was on the one hand put to death in the flesh, but on the other hand, made alive in the spirit (ζῳοποιηθεὶς δὲ πνεύματι).[5]

The Christian life.—Christ was the motivation for the Christian life. He was the bread of life;[6] he was himself our life[7] who was sent into the world that Christians might live through him.[8] To live was Christ.[9] The death Christ died he died to sin; but the life he lived he lived to God.[10] He died so that those who lived might live for him,[11] or die to sin and live to righteousness.[12] Gentiles were foreigners to the life of God because of ignorance.[13] Christians

---

[1] Rom. 8:11.
[2] I Cor. 15:45.
[3] II Cor. 3:6.
[4] Rom. 8:4-8, 12-17.
[5] I Peter 3:18.
[6] Jn. 6:35, 48.
[7] Col. 3:4.
[8] I Jn. 4:9.
[9] Philip. 1:21.
[10] Rom. 6:10.
[11] II Cor. 5:15.
[12] Rom. 6:11; I Peter 2:24.
[13] Gal. 2:19.

like Paul died to the law that they might live to God.[1] They continually carried the death of Jesus in the body so that the life of Jesus might be manifested for the benefit of the churches.[2] Having been crucified with Christ it was Christ who lived in them and the lives they lived in the flesh they lived by faith in Christ.[3] It was not by the law but by faith that life was possible.[4]

In order to understand the religious meaning of the expressions "life" and "death" in the Judeo-Samaritan-Christian tradition, it has been necessary to consider: 1) the relationship of life and death to existence within the covenant community, 2) the relationship of the membership roll to judgment, 3) the relationship of life and death to the promised land, and 4) the ethics of the community that is alive. There remains but one more aspect to this investigation—the future life of the covenant community. This will be given next attention.

LIFE IN THE FUTURE

The world to come.—After Saul had defeated the Ammonites at Jabesh-gilead, Samuel consented to go with Saul and the troops to Gilgal and there newly establish (נחדש) the kingdom by anointing Saul as king.[5] When II Isaiah announced that the Lord was doing something new (חדשה),[6] he meant the Lord would make a way in the wilderness for the captives to return to the promised land to rebuild Jerusalem and reestablish the kingdom. A sabbatical eschatologist described the reestablishment of the Jews and reconstruction of the temple after the Babylonian captivity in terms of renewal (*renovantes*).[7] The covenanters whose manual was preserved at Qumran reasoned that the two spirits would rule over man until the determined end—the renewal (נחרצה ועשות חדשה).[8] The end anticipated was the day of vengeance at the last period (קץ אחרון) when oppressors would be punished.[9] Baruch said that with Abraham, Isaac, and Jacob was built up

---

[1] Eph. 4:18.
[2] II Cor. 4:10-12.
[3] Gal. 2:20.
[4] Rom. 1:17; Gal. 3:11.
[5] I Sam. 11:14-15.
[6] Isa. 43:19.
[7] Assump. Mos. 4:7; see also II Bar. 32:1-6 and IV Ezra 7:75.
[8] 1QS 4:25.
[9] 1QS 4:16-17.

the hope of the world that was to be renewed and the promise of a life that should come afterwards.[1] This apparently referred to the covenant and promise made with Abraham for his posterity —life in the Land of Canaan. This is also true of another apocalypse that expected portions of the tribes to return to their appointed place and fortify it, renewing (*renovantes*) it.[2] A first century Jewish prayer, Amram's Kaddish, asked for great peace (i.e. declaration that all sins had been paid for in suffering and good deeds), life (חיים) in abundance, salvation, comfort (i.e. restoration of the land), and relief for all Israel.[3] It also requested that God's name be exalted in the age (עלמא) which he was about to renew (לחדתא), when he made the dead live (לאחאה מיתים), built up the city of Jerusalem, completed the temple, uprooted foreign worship from his land, introduced the worship of the Holy One of Heaven in its place, so that the Holy One blessed be He could rule his kingdom.[4] The same nationalistic prayer asked that God's redemption spring forth and that his Messiah draw near and redeem his people.[5]

This was not an abstract prayer of generalities. Redemption meant that God would pay off the debt of Israel's sins so that the treasury of merits would at least equal the demerits. According to sabbatical eschatology, whenever that was done, Israel would be restored to the land of the promise. That was another way of saying Israel would receive comfort. The practical effects of comfort involved completing the temple, getting rid of foreign worship, and anointing a king to rule over Israel. Those who were dead would be raised to live on the promised land where life would be had in abundance when the kingdom was renewed,[6] as it had been earlier in the Persian period and afterwards in the time of

---

[1] II Bar. 57:2.

[2] Assump. Mos. 4:7.

[3] See D. de Sola Pool, *The Oldest Aramaic Prayer the Kaddish* (Leipzig, 1909), reprinted as *The Kaddish* (New York, 1964), XII. This prayer asks that the temple, which began construction about 20 B.C. and was not yet finished when it was destroyed in 70 A.D., be completed. Therefore the prayer was composed sometime between these two dates.

[4] *Ibid.*

[5] *Ibid.*

[6] The Essenes were among those who believed in the resurrection. Josephus said they laughed at their tormentors and resigned their souls, expecting to receive them again (*BJ* II.viii. 10; H. Kosmala, *Hebräer-Essener-Christen* [Leiden, 1959], 38).

the Maccabees. This was probably the same kind of renewal expected by II Isaiah, the author of the Assumption of Moses, the Rule of the Community, and Baruch. When the Jews outside Palestine were considered "dead" and those inside Palestine when there was no foreign rule there were "alive," the resurrection of the dead might mean nothing more metaphysical than the return to Jerusalem of the diaspora Jews after the kingdom has been restored. Those who had been dead would be alive again.

The future life expected when the kingdom was renewed was life on the promised land. This was also called life in the age to come. R. Eliezar of Modi'im said that God would give Israel six good portions if she kept the Sabbath: "The Land of Israel, the age to come (עולם הבא), the new age (עולם חדש), the kingdom of the house of David, the priesthood, and the Levites."[1] Samuel said, "There is no difference between this age (העוה״ז), and the days of the Messiah except for the servitude to the kingdom (עבוד מלכיות), which meant Rome.[2] One who confused clean with unclean would be a disgrace in the world to come (לעולם הבא) where purity rules would be kept. Silver and gold removed a man both from this world and the world to come, but Torah brought a man into life in the world to come (לחיי העולם הבא).[3] The age to come was expected in the future as the following couplet shows:

אני לשעבר   אני לעתיד לבא
אני בעולם הזה   אני לעולם הבא [4]

In the age of Rav Kahana, Jews took their grievances to a judge, but in the future (לעתיד לבא, "that which is destined to come"), they would take them to the anointed king at Jerusalem (מלך המשיח בירושלם) where life would be possible for covenanters.[5]

The renewal and the resurrection.—The age (עלמא) which God was about to renew, according to Amran's Kaddish, was not the age which then existed. He meant the age to come (לעלמא דאתי) although he did not use that expression. In other instances, עולם or חיי עולם was used with the same meaning expected of עולם הבא

---

[1] Mekilta *Vayassa'* 5:66-73.
[2] Ber. 34b; Shab. 63a, 151a; Pes. 68a; San. 91b, 99a.
[3] Sifré *Bemidbar* 18:20; 37b-40a § 119.
[4] Mekilta *Baḥodesh* 5:28-29.
[5] *PRK* 18:6, 1-3.

or חיי העולם הבא, as if עולם were understood in certain contexts to be an abbreviation for עולם הבא. Daniel "prophesied" a future time of trouble during which Daniel's people would escape— everyone whose name had been written in the "book." [1] The book was probably the book of life. Then many of those who had been sleeping in the dust of the earth would awake, some to life for the age [to come] and others to shame and contempt for the age [to come].[2] This is consistent with Amram's Kaddish where the dead would be raised to live on the Land of Palestine when the Messiah came and the kingdom was renewed. Those raised were not promised that they would never die but that they would have life in a kingdom of an age (מלכות עולם) that favored them [3] under the rule of the Son of Man and the saints of the Most High.[4] The resurrection both in Daniel and Amram's Kaddish were part of a theological under-standing of the age that would come when the kingdom was re-newed. It was a general resurrection of the saints of the nation when Israel would gain a political victory and the covenanters would live again.

One of the hero legends of the Maccabean Revolt described a mother's seven sons who were martyred for their convictions. They had no fear because they believed God would raise them again after death [5] to eternal life (αἰώνιος ζωή or ἀέναος ζωή). The seventh son said his brothers had fallen under the covenant of God for eternal life (ἀενάου ζωῆς ὑπὸ διαθήκην θεοῦ πεπτώκασι), so he gave up his own body and soul for the law of the fathers

---

[1] Dan. 12:1. E. Jenni, "Das Word 'Olam im Alten Testament," *ZATW* 65 (1953), III. Hauptteil, 19, cited Dan. 12:2 as a clear example of עולם used as an attribute of the "jenseitigen Welt." Jenni observed correctly, however, that חק[ת] עולם had no different meaning from חק[ת] and ברית עולם was no different from ברית (p. 21-22). S. Kraub, "Sanhedren-Makkot," *Die Mischna* ed. G. Beer and O. Holtzmann (Giessen, 1933), 264, defined עולם הזה as " 'diese (gegenwärtige) Welt,' irdische Welt," and עולם הבא as "himmlische Welt, Himmelreich."

[2] Dan. 12:2. In rabbinic literature אומת העולם הזה who rule העולם הזה are contrasted with the Israelites who are destined to rule העולם הבא. אומת העולם [הזה] may be the nations of [this] age in contrast to Israel who will rule the age to come rather than the "nations of the world," as the expression is usually rendered. S. G. Sowers, *The Hermeneutics of Philo and Hebrews* (Zürich, c1965), 92-93, followed H. L. MacNeill, *The Christology of the Epistle to the Hebrews* (Chicago, 1914), 17, in holding that αἰῶνες of Heb. 1:2 mean temporal ages rather than "worlds."

[3] Dan. 7:14.

[4] Dan. 7:27.

[5] II Mac. 7:9, 11, 14, 29.

and prayed that God might quickly be merciful to the nation.[1]
The sooner God showed mercy to the nation by restoring the land
to the Jews, the sooner the martyr would be raised to live on the
land. Living again in the land of life meant the fulfillment of the
promise of the covenant.

In a later political situation, after the victory of Constantine,
Eusebius described the effect of this military victory on the Christians. Before then the Christians were not just half dead (ἡμιθνῆτες),
but foul and stinking in tombs. God lifted up (ἀναλαβών) the
Christians and saved (σῴζει) them as in days of old.[2] When the
nation was under Christian rule, Christians had life whether tombs
were opened or not. Just as Jews were revived a little bit during
the time of Ezra, Christians then had been revived to a much
greater degree during the time of Constantine. After so many
years in subjection, Eusebius, like Ezra, rejoiced to be living.
Covenanters who lived in such favorable political situations were
actually living in the age to come (חיי בעולם הבא; ζωὴ ἐν τῷ αἰῶνι
τῷ ἐρχομένῳ) which sometimes seems to be abbreviated to be called
eternal life. After the Maccabean victory Simon was declared
"leader and high priest for the age" (εἰς τὸν αἰῶνα).[3] The fact

---

[1] II Mac. 7:36-37. The rabbis said the Lord showed Moses all the providers who were destined to serve Israel from the time they left the wilderness until the dead lived (יחיו המתים). That would be from the first conquest of Canaan until the one expected at the time of this writing after
70 A.D. (Sifré Bemidbar 27:17; 5a-5b § 139).

[2] Eusebius, HE X.iv.12; see also LXX IV Kgdms. 2:10-11; II Esdras
2:23-35.

[3] I Mac. 14:41. Whatever meaning be given this passage, it should be
related to the same term in Ps. 110:4, an acrostic Psalm for Simon. "The
age" may have meant the messianic age or the age of his dynasty.
It was probably the temporal factor in Jewish expectations that prompted
R. Reuben to note that לנצח (eternal) was a Greek expression (PRK
17:1, 4-6). Jenni, Op. cit. (1952), 221, said that the expression did not have
the meaning of a space of time (Aeon) in pre-Christian times. Nor did it have
the meaning of "world" or "people" until after the time of Christ. See also
Jenni, Op. cit. (1953), 24. Th. C. Vriezen, "Prophecy and Eschatology,"
Congress Volume, Supplement to VT (Leiden, 1953), 223, said the ʿolam
hazze was life on earth and ʿolam habba life in heaven. For the use of עולם to
mean both a limited and limitless time, see O. Cullmann, Christ and Time
(Philadelphia, 1950), 45-62. L. Van Hartingsveld, Op. cit., 58, said that life
in the OT meant long life and that in the course of time long life came
to mean eternal life as it was used in the NT. John was in agreement with
Ezekiel, said van Hartingsveld, 62-63, in promising death to those who did
not obey. Death, he said, meant premature death from unnatural causes.
To be sure, the promise for obedience to the law was long life but it was
also on the land. The length of duration was not the factor which distin-

that he was not expected to reign forever is clear by the following modification: "until a true prophet arises." In this case the age to come had come. Simon was leader and high priest for the age. The nation was free. Jews could live again. This was the age for which they had prayed, suffered, and fought. Resurrection would not have to mean more than the return of the diaspora Jews to the homeland free from foreign rule. For Eusebius the expression was possibly used with just about that sense, but in Daniel and II Maccabees, there seems also to have been a belief that those who had ceased breathing would have their corpses revived. But just a revival of corpses would not promise life in the religious sense. The important feature was not physical existence nor everlastingness, but existence of the covenant community in the land of life free from foreign rule. It meant being returned home on the sabbatical year or jubilee after the period of service required to pay indebtedness was over.

When the man came to Jesus and asked what he must do to inherit "eternal life" (ζωὴν αἰώνιον κληρονομεῖν),[1] Jesus told him to keep the commandments that Moses had left for those who wanted to "live" in the land. This was necessary if he, like the Israelites, would "enter life." [2] Aware that he lacked something, he asked for more requirements. Then Jesus said if he wanted to be "perfect" he must give his possessions to the poor (i.e. the community called the "poor") and follow Jesus.[3] When the man was unable to meet the demands, Jesus said it was hard for a rich man to enter the kingdom of heaven.[4] The change of terms used

---

guished life from death. R.B. Laurin, "The question of Immortality in the Qumran 'Hodayot,' " *JSS* 3 (1938), 344-355, argued convincingly that the forms like "eternal height" are metaphors that refer to conditions of the elect in an earthly kingdom. Although everlastingness was not the most important point of life after the resurrection, Enoch said:

"Then the righteous will be in the light of the sun, the chosen ones in the light of eternal life (ሕይወት ፡ H1ዓለም) ; there will be no number to the days of their life, and the days of the saints without number" (Enoch 58:3; Laurence ed. 56:3).

See also Mk. 10:30; Lk. 18:30 for the expression "age to come" in the NT.

[1] Mk. 10:17; Lk. 18:18; also Mt. 19:16.
[2] Mt. 19:17.
[3] Mt. 19:20-21.
[4] J. Weiss, *Die Predigt Jesu vom Reiche Gottes* (Göttingen, 1900), 118, conceded that having life was paralleled with entering the Kingdom of God, but insisted that eternal life was still more. It meant the absolute opposite of death, immortality. He did not deal with the parallelism of life and eternal life.

meant that the eternal life he asked for was citizenship in the kingdom of heaven. Mark and Luke both also employed the term
"inherit" in relationship to "eternal life," just as the Israelites
spoke of "inheriting" the land God promised to their forefathers.
In their amazement over the answer and concern of the disciples
that anyone might be saved, Peter volunteered: "'Lo, we have left
everything and followed you. What then shall we have?' Jesus
said to them, 'Truly, I say to you, in the rebirth (παλιγγενεσία =
לחדתא),[1] when the Son of Man shall sit on his glorious throne,
you who have followed me will also sit on the twelve thrones,
judging the twelve tribes of Israel. And everyone who left houses or
children or lands, for my name's sake, will receive a hundredfold,
and inherit eternal life'" (ζωὴν αἰώνιον κληρονομήσει).[2] The picture
portrayed was similar to that in Daniel, except that here the Son
of Man was unquestionably a king with a council of judges holding
office under his direction. The disciples were promised material
possessions and life in the kingdom. The gifts to be given were
both material and political. These were the spoils that belonged
to the victors, and they were to be received at the same time.

Mark and Luke both have a variant here. According to them [3]
the material goods were to be received in this time (ἐν τῷ καιρῷ τούτῳ),
and the age to come (ἐν τῷ αἰῶνι τῷ ἐρχομένῳ) was the time when
they would receive eternal life.[4] This looks like a later revision
after the fall of Jerusalem when the promises had not been fulfilled,
the kingdom was far from being in their possession, the age to
come was not very imminent, so eternal life had to be postponed.
Mark added to the things to be received in this time, "persecutions"
—again a prophecy after the fact.[5]

---

[1] Amram's Kaddish, XII. See also I Sam. 11:14; Isa. 43:19; 48:6-8 to
learn contexts in which this expression was used.

[2] Mt. 19:27-29; also Mk. 10:28-30; Lk. 18:28-30.

[3] Mk. 10:30; Lk. 18:30.

[4] V. Taylor, *The Gospel According to Mark* (London, 1955), 434-435,
has listed numerous scholars who have questioned the authenticity of all
or part of Mk. 10:30. His own judgment was: "On the whole, the best view
to take is that substantially the saying is authentic, but that in the phrase
'and in the world to come eternal life' it has been adapted to current views
by the Evangelist or a predecessor" (p. 435).

[5] Mk. 10:30. In a similar situation, Luke had a lawyer coming to Jesus
in the same manner, asking the same question and receiving the same answer,
except that he used it for an introduction to the Good Samaritan story.
This was probably not a second event, but a second way in which Luke used
the account (Lk. 10:25-37).

Another description of the Son of Man pictured him as a king after the battle with all the nations before him who had participated in the conflict deciding what treatment would be given to the various people. After the judgment, those on the left were destined to face eternal punishment, but the favored ones on his right hand would go into eternal life.[1] Apparently the same message was given here as in the previous anticipations. Those on the side of the king before the victory would share in the spoils afterward. Important among the rewards was eternal life. They could live in the king's favor in the land which they had all hoped to inherit.

Eternal life.—The associations found with eternal life relate the expression more closely to religious life than unending physical or metaphysical life. It has more kinship with covenant keeping than calendars; it is more closely allied with community and politics than pulse rate. For many Jews, eternal life could only take place on the promised land free from foreign rule. But the sects did not all agree at every point. Some, at least, considered that life within their communities was eternal life, even though the power of Rome had not been broken. This is most evident in the Johannine writings.

According to John the Jews erroneously believed that they had eternal life in the scriptures. The scriptures pointed to Christ and the new covenant.[3] The commandment of God was eternal life;[3] life eternal was knowing God and Jesus Christ whom he had sent;[4] God had given Jesus authority to give eternal life to his elect,[5] so that no one could come to the Father except by Jesus. Jesus was the way, the truth, and the life.[6] All three mean the same. The true religion was the way of life for the Christian. Jesus had the words of eternal life.[7] Therefore everyone who believed in him had eternal life.[8] It was not necessary to wait for the age to come when life on the land was possible. This was comparable to believing in the one who had sent Jesus. The one who did, would

---

[1] Mt. 25:31-46.
[2] Jn. 5:39.
[3] Jn. 12:50.
[4] Jn. 17:3.
[5] Jn. 10:28; 17:2.
[6] Jn. 14:6.
[7] Jn. 6:68.
[8] Jn. 3:15, 16, 36; 6:40.

not come to judgment because he had already passed from "death" to "life."[1] The community responsible for I John witnessed that eternal life already had been manifested in their midst.[2] The group knew him who was true and were themselves "in Christ." That was eternal life.[3] No one who hated his brother could be a member and have eternal life.[4] The one who "reaped" new members for the Christian community gathered fruit for eternal life.[5] Eternal life stood in direct contrast to wordly existence. The one who rejected his "position in the world" ($\tau\dot{\eta}\nu$ $\psi\upsilon\chi\dot{\eta}\nu$ $\alpha\dot{\upsilon}\tauο\tilde{\upsilon}$ $\dot{\varepsilon}\nu$ $\tau\tilde{\wp}$ $\kappa\dot{ο}\sigma\mu\wp$) would preserve his position ($\tau\dot{\eta}\nu$ $\psi\upsilon\chi\dot{\eta}\nu$ $\alpha\dot{\upsilon}\tauο\tilde{\upsilon}$) in life eternal.[6] It was only the qualified members of the community who could drink of the water or blood which Jesus gave,[7] and have eternal life. Only the food which the Son of Man provided endured to eternal life.[8] All other food was perishing.[9]

In agreement with sabbatical eschatological hopes, Jews and Christians looked forward to the time when the foreign powers were expelled from Palestine and the chosen people could return to the land of life. This would involve the renewal of the kingdom, rebuilding or completion of the temple, resurrection of the dead, purifying the worship in Jerusalem, the rule of the Messiah, and the punishment of enemies. Before these events had taken place, covenanters were living in this [evil] age, or this age of labor. But they looked forward to the age to come (*saeculum futurum*). That would be the age when they would be paid for their labor.[10] Then the enemies would be punished and the covenanters rewarded by receiving the gifts promised in the covenant. There seemed no difference between "life" on the land of life and "life in the age to come" or "eternal life" except that the last two expressions are

---

[1] Jn. 5:24.
[2] I Jn. 1:1-2; 2:25.
[3] I Jn. 5:11, 20.
[4] I Jn. 3:15.
[5] Jn. 4:36.
[6] Jn. 12:25.
[7] Jn. 4:14; 6:51, 54, 58.
[8] Jn. 6:27.
[9] Ancient Canaanites worshipped Baal who was the Lord of life and was in conflict with mot (Death). Baal worship made a strong impression on North Israelite religion after the kingdoms were divided. Perhaps that is the reason the terms, life and death, were such significant terms in Deuteronomy and the Gospel of John, since both documents probably came originally from North Israel or Samaria.
[10] *Clem. Recog.* II.xxi.

generally future expectations, whereas "life" on the land of life also happened in the past after the conquest of Canaan, the return from Babylon, and the Maccabean Revolt. Even this distinction is not always possible, because eternal life was sometimes used in the present tense when the nation was not free from Roman rule. The variant interpretation, however, probably still had a basically religious meaning that was closely related to existence within the true covenant community in a situation where it was possible to keep the covenant. For both the resurrection and eternal life the emphasis was not on physical resuscitation of bodies or endless physical existence, but rather the fulfillment of the promise of life in the covenant community on the land of life. Jews and Christians from the Jewish tradition anticipated a new Jerusalem as the capital city. Descriptions of this hope will receive separate attention.

Paradise regained.—Among the hopes for the future was a restoration to the sinlessness of the past. Before the watchers of heaven defiled themselves with women they had been holy, spiritual, and living life eternal.[1] Prior to Adam and Eve's sin, they were prohibited to eat the fruit of the knowledge of good and evil but allowed to eat of the tree of life (עץ חיים).[2] After they ate of the tree of the knowledge of good and evil, however, they were driven out of the garden lest they also eat of the tree of life.[3] In the future, Jews and Christians hoped to live eternal life and eat of the tree of life. They also hoped to have access to the water of life (מיים חיים). In secular usage, water of life was spring water, water from a stream, or from a well supplied by a vein.[4] It may have got its name, however, from the religious usage of this water that was necessary for ritual purity, which in turn was necessary for "life." It was used for cleansing people, clothes, and other objects that were defiled by leprosy, continuous discharges, and other sources of uncleanness.[5] Cyprian called the water for baptism water for life eternal.[6] An ancient Samaritan said Moses praised the letter *qoph* which stood for sanctification (cleansing from defilement),

---

[1] Enoch 15:4-7.
[2] Gen. 2:9.
[3] Gen. 3:23-24
[4] Gen. 26:19.
[5] Lev. 14:6, 51, 52; 15:13; Num. 19:17.
[6] Cyprian, Epistle LVIII To Fadus, 9.

because wherever there was sanctification there was life, but
without it, destruction.[1]

In the future, non-Samaritan covenanters anticipated the
restoration of Jerusalem which was pictured as Paradise before
the fall. One psalmist anticipated a broad stream of water that
would come to the temple and from there spread over the whole
land (ܐܪܥܐ). Those who drank from it were saved from death
(ܡܘܬܐ). The feeble were strengthened and their eyes were
lightened. Everyone of them would know the Lord and live by the
water of life for the age (ܒܡܝܐ ܚܝܐ ܠܥܠܡ).[2] This seems to
reflect Ezekiel's dream of water flowing out from the temple to
the Dead Sea south of Qumran. Wherever it went it would provide
fruitfulness and healing.[3] Another ode described the conversion
of the Gentiles (as booty taken in war) who had made confession,
walked in life, were saved, and became the Lord's people for
the age (ܟܠܗܘܢ ܠܥܠܡܝܢ).[4] Zechariah
said the water of life would flow from the temple.[5] One who drank
from the water of life (ܡܝܐ ܚܝܐ) changed his garments and
was taken to the Lord's Paradise (ܠܦܪܕܝܣܗ) which was the
Lord's land (ܒܐܪܥܗ).[6] In the Garden of Eden, which became
identified with the new Jerusalem, there was to be the light of
life eternal (חיי עלמא) for the righteous.[7] Repentance was to be
the gate of the garden whose trees were good. Those who ate from
them would receive the Lord's care and favor.[8] In the future sin
was expected to cease, and the gates of Paradise open. Then the
saints would eat of the tree of life (ξύλον τῆς ζωῆς) which was
in the promised land.[9] John of Patmos promised that those who
were faithful could eat of the tree of life in the Paradise of God.[10]
Enoch said the elect who dwelled in the garden of life (ገነተ : ሕይወት)
would bless the Lord of Spirits.[11] In the new Jerusalem there was

---

[1] *Memar Marqah* IV § 9.

[2] Odes of Sol. 6:7-17.

[3] Ezekiel 47:1-12; see also W.R. Farmer, "The Geography of Ezekiel's
River of Life,'" *BA* 19 (1956), 17-22.

[4] Odes of Sol. 10:1-8.   [5] Zech. 14:8.

[6] Odes of Sol. 11:7-18.

[7] Targ. Jerushalmi Isa. 45:7.

[8] *Memar Marqah* VI § 10.

[9] T. Levi 18:9-14; *Leg. All.* III.xxxv. (107).

[10] IV Bar. 9:14; Apocalypse of Elijah 39:7-12; and Rev. 2:7; cf also
SO 2:46-49.

[11] Enoch 61:12.

to be a tree of life (ξύλον τῆς ζωῆς) on either side of a river in which flowed the river of life.[1] This water would flow from the throne of God and the Lamb through the streets of Jerusalem.[2] The trees of life would produce fruit all the year around, and their leaves were to be for the healing of the nations.[3] The fruit was for the inhabitants of the city. Those were the ones who had washed their robes and made them white by the blood of the Lamb,[4] and were to serve God in the temple,[5] and the Lamb would guide them to the springs of the water of life (ἐπὶ ζωῆς πηγὰς ὑδάτων).[6] Those who were ceremonially clean would be admitted to the city through the gates,[7] and they could receive water of life without cost.[8] After those who were ready had been born again from the water and the Holy Spirit of life eternal, Christ was to lead Adam to the tree of mercy in Paradise.[9] Those outside, who could not eat of the tree of life or use the water of life were "dogs," sorcerers, fornicators, murderers, and idolators.[10] The curse at the end of the Book of Revelation promised that if anyone removed anything from the book of prophecy, God would take away his share in the tree of life and the holy city.[11]

These were not just heavenly dreams. They were some of the ramifications of sabbatical eschatology. They expected life in the land of life whose capital was the holy city, Jerusalem. There the covenant community would observe the covenant faithfully, being completely free from ritually defiling contacts. II Isaiah said even the way from Babylon would be holy, free from uncleanness. Only the redeemed would walk there.[12] The tree of life provided nourishment necessary for the covenanters, and the water of life provided the cleansing necessary for purity. Those who lived in the future would not sin as the watchers and Adam and Eve had done. They would live in Paradise in Jerusalem on the land of life. Such would be the life in the age to come.

---

[1] Rev. 21:10.
[2] Rev. 22:1-2.
[3] Rev. 22:1-2.
[4] Rev. 4:14.
[5] Rev. 7:15.
[6] Rev. 7:17.
[7] Rev. 22:14.
[8] Rev. 21:6; 22:17.
[9] Book of Adam and Eve 43:4-5.
[10] Rev. 22:15.
[11] Rev. 22:19.   [12] Isa. 35:8-10.

Summary

This investigation has shown a significant religious meaning for the word, "life," that began as early as Deuteronomy and continued in use through NT times. The same basic meaning was found in Jewish, Samaritan, and Christian sources. This did not mean that there was a different word for physical life, but that from the physical meaning was found the basis for the religious analogy. Life meant existence in a covenant community as a member when the community was receiving the promises of the covenant. The opposite of life was death which meant being outside the fold, away from the land, alienated from God, being lost. The book of life seemed initially to be the roll of the covenanters who assumed that God also kept a similar roll. Those whose names were inscribed in the book of life were judged members in good standing. Those expelled had their names blotted out of the book. The land of life was the promised land. Covenanters were required to walk in the path of life, heed instruction, which was life, obey God, the fountain of life, and study the Torah to have life. The basic requirements for religious observance were also the basic requirements for life. Eternal life usually referred to life in the messianic age, the age to come, or the age when the land was restored and covenanters returned to live there. This sometimes involved a resurrection which might mean the resuscitation of bodies, but whose main emphasis was not on physical existence but covenant community on the promised land, free from foreign rule. For the Gospel of John, probably of Samaritan origin, there was no plan for a new Jerusalem, but eternal life could be lived in the Christian community of the new covenant. For Jews and Jewish Christians, eternal life involved a new Jerusalem as sinless as the Garden of Eden or the watchers before the fall. In the restored community would be the tree of life and the water of life for a rigid, Levitically pure community. All of this was to take place on the land of life, Palestine.

In Chapter I there was shown a close relationship between the warfare and politics of Israel and her theology. Chapter II upheld Reimarus' thesis that Israel's religion was so nationalistic that the promised land was called the Kingdom of God or the Kingdom of Heaven. Chapter III indicated the close interest of Israel in a geographical territory by reviewing the record left of the boundary lines to which she laid political claim. Chapter IV pointed out the depth of emotional feeling invested in the land by showing that early Israelites and later Jews, Samaritans, and Christians called existence on the land free from foreign rule under covenant allegiance to God "life" and all other existence, "death." But most of Israelite and Jewish existence was spent outside the land while Palestine was ruled by some other power. Even though covenanters were upper class citizens of foreign lands with great political, social, and economic power, their existence was called "captivity" or "slavery"—terms based on sabbatical eschatology. The rest of the book will show the consequences of covenant observance on covenanters in the diaspora. The most obvious consequence is a deep consciousness of iniquity and the development of extreme ascetic habits. These will be dealt with in the next chapter.

CHAPTER FIVE

COVENANTAL ASCETICISM

INTRODUCTION

While Israel lived on the land and the temple was still in operation, Jews had some security of righteousness even though the
nation was under domination of another country.[1] Although laws
were being broken, the laws of Israel's own covenant were in effect.
The continual burnt offerings being given every day assured Jews
that the Lord was in their midst. The laws by which Israel was
governed were many of those now preserved in the books of Leviticus and Deuteronomy. Although some of the same laws are
contained in both books,[2] the laws in Deuteronomy are principally
those interpreted and enforced by kings, civil judges, or elders
at the gate, whereas the Levitical laws were interpreted and
administered by the priests. When the temple was destroyed and
many people taken into captivity, the picture changed and Jews
faced many necessary adjustments in thought and action. When
priests no longer functioned in the temple, it was necessary to
attempt to establish a priesthood of all believers. The purity of
the sanctuary was transferred to the home. The altar was replaced
by the hearth. Instead of large congregations gathering three
times a year for feasts and special sacrifices, small groups of ten
(a *minyan*) or more men who had observed purity gathered frequently to study the Torah and to offer prayers instead of sacrifices.

The destruction of the temple convinced the captives that
Jeremiah's prophecy was true. They were being punished by the
Lord for their sin. This meant that they would have to repent and
observe the law with special meticulousness to win God's favor
again. They were no longer in a position to enforce many of the
civil laws, because they were now in another land and forced to
abide by its laws. This meant that they needed to reconsider the
administration of law before the conquest of Canaan. In the wilderness the Lord was in their midst without a temple. Under certain
conditions he marched with their armies and won their battles for

---

[1] Jer. 6:13-14; 7:3-4; 8:8-11; 28:1-4, 10-11.
[2] E.g. Lev. 11 and Dt. 14.

them. The conditions were that they obey his laws. Some of these were the personal laws of purity administered by the priests, who frequently used the expression "clean" and "unclean" to mean good and bad, from a ritualistic point of view. While the temple functioned, many people may have been very lax about these rules, believing them to have been delegated to the priests. The Lord caused his name to dwell in the temple.[1] That was the area that must be kept pure the way the camp had formerly been. If the priests observed purity and the people were pure whenever they entered the temple area, that seemed adequate to maintain the Lord's favor.

After the temple had been burnt, however, this false security was shaken. It was then important for the whole community to observe priestly rules in an attempt to keep the community pure in a foreign land. When the priests could not function in the temple, it was important that all Israel become a kingdom of priests and a holy people.[2] These may have been some of the reasons for Ezekiel's strong emphasis on the importance of turning from sin and walking in the way of purity. His message described sin as an abomination to the Lord [3] and warned Jews against breaking the kind of personal laws that could be kept by Jews in Babylon, and which must be kept since the temple no longer provided a dwelling place for the Shekinah.[4] The frustration of covenanters in the diaspora without a temple is expressed in a prayer used on major feast days by Jews still in the twentieth century:

"But because of our sins we were exiled from our land and removed far from our soil. We are not able to go up and appear and prostrate ourselves before you and fulfill our obligations in the house of your choosing, the great and holy house over which your name has been called . . . Have mercy upon us and upon your temple in your great mercy, and rebuild it quickly and magnify its glory. Our Father, our King, reveal the glory of your kingdom upon us . . . and bring us to Zion, your city, with joy, to Jerusalem,

---

[1] I Kgs. 8:27-30.

[2] Ex. 19:6. One of the early attempts at establishing a priesthood of all believers.

[3] Ezek. 6:9-11; 8:5-6, 14-15, 17; 11:18, *et passim.*

[4] So also J. Klausner, *The Messianic Idea in Israel*, tr. W. F. Stinespring (New York, 1955), 173, fn. 43, who held that Sabbath observance and the role of circumcision were given more significance after the Babylonian exile.

the temple of your holiness as the exultation of the age. There we
will prepare for you our obligatory offerings continually as prescribed, and additional offerings as they are appropriate." [1]

It is not possible to know the degree or the number of Levitical
laws observed by the non-Levitical Israelites before the Babylonian
captivity, but it is certain that the rules were known by the time
of the captivity and emphasized from that time on. This emphasis
led to a kind of exclusive asceticism that later resulted in various
types of sectarian groups and celibate communities of covenant
observers.[2]

Since the consciousness of sin meant the emphasis on Levitical
rules, this chapter will give primary consideration to those rules
and their later interpretation. The first step in this study will be
to consider the various words for sin and the type of activity that
was considered sinful. Particular attention will be given to the
relationship between sin and impurity, since these terms were
not so carefully distinguished as scholars have usually thought.
This knowledge will have a bearing on the interpretation of concepts
held later in Judaism and Christianity.

SIN IN THE OLD TESTAMENT

Adultery.—Improper sexual relationships were considered sin
(חטא) [3] both against God [4] and against the woman's husband.[5]
David's affair with Bathsheba was sin (חטא).[6] The same act of
adultery, however, was also called defilement (טמאה) whether it
referred to a man who defiled himself by adultery,[7] a woman who
defiled herself by unfaithfulness,[8] a man who defiled a woman

---

[1] Translated from the Hebrew text of S. Singer, *The Authorized Daily
Prayer Book* (New York, 1915), 234.

[2] J. Thomas, *Le Mouvement Baptiste en Palestine et Syrie* (Gembloux,
1935), 22-26, 417, 434, thought the many ablutions taken by Essenes could
not be explained by Levitical code but were of Iranian-Babylonian origin.
He thought lustrations replaced sacrifices in normal evolution of religion
to a more spiritual faith. The captivity may have increased the use of
ablutions—not to replace sacrifice, but because sacrifice could no longer be
made. When the captives returned, sacrifices were resumed. Babylonian
religion may have influenced purity practices which were then incorporated
into the purity rules of the Pentateuch.

[3] Lev. 20:20; Neh. 13:26.

[4] Gen. 39:9.

[5] Gen. 20:6.

[6] II Sam. 12:13.   [7] Lev. 18:20; 21:4.

[8] Num. 5:13, 19, 20, 27-29.

by adultery,¹ or a woman who had been defiled by that act.²
Such pollution (טמאה) brought sin (תחטיא) upon the land.³ A
woman was unclean during her menstrual period⁴ and everything
she touched was unclean (טמא).⁵ Likewise a man or woman who
had a continual discharge was unclean with the same consequences.⁶
Menstrual flows and continuous discharges left the people involved
unclean for seven days after the flow stopped,⁷ and those afflicted
with continual discharges were required to make a sin offering
after the discharge stopped before pollution was removed.⁸ Less
serious, but still defiling, was a seminal discharge, whether it
happened in sexual intercourse or not. Men and women involved
were required to bathe, wash all objects they touched, and be
unclean until evening.⁹ The discharge of semen necessary for
sexual intercourse was always defiling, but when it was done in an
improper relationship it was also sin. Whenever an offering was
necessary for one who had been defiled (טמא) it was a sin offering
(חטאת).

Idolatry.—Any type of divination,¹⁰ worship of idols,¹¹ other
gods,¹² or Baals¹³ was considered sin (חטא), but idolatry was also
called defilement (טמאה). Idols made a city or a land defiled;¹⁴
Israelites could become defiled (טמא) by turning to wizards or
engaging in abominable religious practices,¹⁵ worshipping Baals,¹⁶
or being influenced by idols¹⁷ whose worship was called harlotry.¹⁸

---

¹ Gen. 34:5, 13, 27; Ezek. 18:6, 11, 15; 22:11; 33:26.
² Dt. 24:4; Ezek. 23:13, 17. A. Büchler, *Studies in Sin and Atonement*
(London, 1928), 212-374, has argued that the term טמאה was frequently
used analogously to describe moral or spiritual wrong rather than an actual
Levitical defilement. It sometimes describes activity in relationship to ghosts
and spirits (p. 224) as well as speech (p. 231-234; 271-284).
³ Dt. 24:4.
⁴ Lev. 15:25, 33; 18:19; Ps. 106:39; Ezek. 22:10; 36:27.
⁵ Lev. 15:20, 24, 26.
⁶ Lev. 15:2-30.
⁷ Lev. 15:13-30.
⁸ Lev. 15:13-15, 25-30.
⁹ Lev. 15:16-18.
¹⁰ I Sam. 15:23.
¹¹ Ex. 32:31; Dt. 1:16; I Kgs. 16:13; II Chron. 33:19; Ezek. 23:49; Isa.
31:7; Hos. 8:11.
¹² Ex. 23:33; Dt. 20:18; II Kgs. 17:7.
¹³ Jdgs. 10:10; I Sam. 12:10.
¹⁴ Ezek. 22:3; 36:18.
¹⁵ Lev. 18:24, 30, 31.   ¹⁶ Jer. 2:23.
¹⁷ Lev. 18:24; Ezek. 20:7, 18; 22:4; 23:7, 30-31.
¹⁸ Ezek. 23:7, 30.

The Lord approved of the defilement of idols, other gods, or the banishment of unclean spirits,[1] and the Lord promised to cleanse (טהר) Israel from all her idols.[2] Notorious for idolatry was Jeroboam, in Judah's opinion, who sinned and made Israel to sin (חטא ואשר החטיא את ישראל) by erecting a separate temple in Israel.[3] Other kings continued in the sins of Jeroboam, Baasha, or Elah,[4] thus provoking the Lord's anger;[5] or else they failed to turn aside from those sins.[6] Judah also had kings which had made the people of Judah to sin.[7]

Sin and atonement.—When Israelites committed sins (חטאות),[8] some of which were noted to be unintentional,[9] a sin offering (חטאה) was required.[10] The sin offering usually was a male goat[11] or a bull[12]—very rarely a lamb.[13] For the poor, the sin offering was a pigeon, turtle dove, or a tenth of an ephah of fine flour.[14] These sin offerings were part of the requirement for atonement.[15]

Sinners and the angry God.—Provisions had been made for people's sins because no one was without sin (לא יחטא),[16] but sin provoked the Lord's anger.[17] Sin was not limited to individuals. A city or a land could sin.[18] Sin against a king also provoked the king to anger.[19] Sometimes provoking the king's anger "sins a

---

[1] II Kgs. 23:10, 13, 16; Isa. 30:22; Jer. 19:13; Zech. 13:2.

[2] Ezek. 36:25.

[3] I Kgs. 13:16, 34; 15:26, 30, 34; 16:2, 26; II Kgs. 17:21.

[4] I Kgs. 16:13, 19; 21:22, 53; II Kgs. 3:3; 13:2; 15:30; 16:13, 31; 23:15.

[5] I Kgs. 16:13; 21:22, 54; 15:30; 16:13.

[6] II Kgs. 10:29, 31; 13:6, 11; 14:24; 15:9, 18, 24, 28.

[7] II Kgs. 21:11, 16; 24:3; Jer. 32:35.

[8] Lev. 4:14, 23, 28, 35; 5:10, 11, 13.

[9] Num. 15:24, 25, 27, 28.

[10] Lev. 4:25, 33, 34; 5:8, 9, 12; 6:18; 9:10, 22; 10:19; 16:25; Num. 6:16; Ps. 40:7; Ezek. 45:19, 25, 27.

[11] Lev. 4:24; 9:3, 15; 10:16; 16:5, 9, 15; 23:19; Num. 7:16, 22, 34, 40, 46, 52, 58, 64, 70, 76, 82, 87; 28:15, 22; 29:5, 16, 22, 25, 28, 31, 34, 38; II Chron. 29:21, 23; Ezek. 43:25.

[12] Ex. 29:14; Lev. 4:8, 14, 21; 8:2, 14; 9:2; 16:3; Num. 8:8; Ezek. 43:19, 21-22.

[13] Lev. 4:32; Num. 6:14.

[14] Lev. 5:11; 14:22.

[15] Ex. 29:36; 30:10; 32:30; Lev. 4:20, 26; 5:6; 6:23; 9:7; 12:8; 14:31; 15:16; 16:6, 11, 27; Num. 6:11; 8:12; 15:28; 29:11; II Chron. 29:24; Ezek. 45:17; Neh. 10:34.

[16] I Kgs. 8:46; II Chron. 6:36; Eccl. 7:20.

[17] Num. 32:14; Dt. 9:18; I Kgs. 16:2; Isa. 13:9; 64:4.

[18] Lam. 1:8; Ezek. 14:12.

[19] Prov. 20:2; Eccl. 10:4.

man's soul" (חוטא נפשו), which probably meant it would prompt a death sentence.[1] A man might sin against another person forever even though this was but one act.[2] This probably meant he would never receive forgiveness or that he would become the other person's slave forever. There was a definite relationship between God's anger and the covenanter's sin.[3] The covenanter, however, was not supposed to sin even though he became angry.[4] When a king sinned, the people suffered.[5] Sinners had good reasons to be afraid.[6] If a man sinned against another man, God might mediate for him; if he sinned against the Lord, that was a much more serious matter.[7] Sinners sometimes rebelled,[8] disobeyed,[9] or worshipped idols;[10] at other times they sinned with their speech. This was usually false witnessing,[11] vowing,[12] or cursing God.[13] Sinners not only deserved punishment; they were fools.[14] Israelites should warn one another not to sin,[15] because those who had transgressed the covenant had broken the commandment,[16] and if they were not forgiven they were removed from the membership list of the elect.[17] Those who turned from their sin received instruction in the way and kept the commandments.[18] The one who was unlearned in the law was sure to sin.[19]

Any person who sinned was guilty even though he was not aware of the sin.[20] A ruler who sinned was guilty (אשם).[21] So was

[1] Prov. 20:2.
[2] Gen. 43:9; 44:32. See Staples, "Some Aspects of Sin and Atonement," *JNES* 6 (1947), 69. Also *Tanḥuma, Vayiggash* 103a.
[3] Ps. 38:4.
[4] Ps. 4:5.
[5] II Sam. 24:17; I Chron. 21:17, 18.
[6] Isa. 33:14.
[7] I Sam. 2:25.
[8] Num. 21:7; Ps. 78:17.
[9] Dt. 1:41; Neh. 9:29; Isa. 42:24; Jer. 3:25; 40:3; 44:23.
[10] Hos. 13:2.
[11] Isa. 29:21.
[12] Dt. 23:22, 23; Eccl. 5:5.
[13] Lev. 24:15; Job 1:5; 31:30; see also Job. 2:10; Ps. 39:2; and Ps. 59:13.
[14] Num. 12:11; I Sam. 26:21; II Sam. 24:10; Prov. 24:9.
[15] Ezek. 3:21.
[16] Josh. 7:11; I Sam. 15:24; Dan. 9:5, 11.
[17] Ex. 32:31-33.
[18] I Sam. 12:23; Ps. 25:8; Ezek. 18:21; 33:14.
[19] Ps. 119:11; Prov. 19:2; Eccl. 9:18.
[20] Lev. 5:5, 17; 4:27; Num. 5:6, 7; II Chron. 28:13.
[21] Lev. 4:22.

the anointed priest. But an anointed priest brought guilt upon the whole people when he sinned.[1] When a man's guilt was expiated, his sin was removed.[2] A person who was guilty sometimes brought a sin offering (חטאת) to atone for his guilt,[3] but at other times a guilt offering was given.[4] Sometimes a guilt offering was brought for a sin offering.[5] Both effected atonement.[6] The rules for the sin offering also applied to the guilt offering.[7] A ram was specified on some occasions for a guilt offering, although this was never prescribed for a sin offering.[8] The offerings were somewhat alike but somewhat different, and the difference is not clear.

Sin (חטא) and iniquity (עון) were frequently used in parallel construction.[9] This means that when a person confessed his iniquity, he was sorry for his sins;[10] when his iniquity was forgiven, his sin was pardoned.[11] In a record book of bad deeds to which sins contributed, the iniquity seems to have been the "debt" or claim of an offense or bad deed which made a person's or people's account overdrawn. So sins and iniquities were listed together (לעוננו ולחטאתנו),[12] and prophets spoke of iniquities (עונות) which people sinned (חטאו)[13] as if every sin had a recorded iniquity. Iniquity was remembered or reckoned against a person.[14] It was like a burden to be carried,[15] which left the sinner guilty and obligated to be punished.[16] Iniquity could be forgiven or forgiveness

---

[1] Lev. 4:3.   [2] Isa. 27:9.

[3] Lev. 4:3; 5:6, 7.

[4] Lev. 5:15, 16, 22-23; 19:22.

[5] Lev. 5:6-7.

[6] Lev. 5:16; 19:22.

[7] Lev. 6:10; 7:7, 37; 14:13; 18:9; II Kgs. 12:17; 40:39; 42:13; 46:20.

[8] Lev. 5:15.

[9] Lev. 5:1; I Sam. 20:1; Job 10:6; Ps. 38:19; 51:7, 11; 103:10; 109:14; Prov. 5:22; Isa. 1:4; 5:18; 6:7; 40:2; 43:24; 59:2; Jer. 5:25; 14:10; 16:10; 18:23; 30:14, 15; 31:34; 50:20; Lam. 4:6, 13, 22; Hos. 8:13; 9:9; Mic. 7:19.

[10] Ps. 38:19.

[11] Ps. 85:3.

[12] Ex. 34:9; Neh. 9:2; Jer. 16:18; 36:3.

[13] Jer. 14:7, 20; 33:8; Hos. 12:9.

[14] Gen. 15:18(16); Ps. 32:2; Isa. 64:9; Ezek. 29:16; Dan. 9:24.

[15] Ex. 28:38; Lev. 10:17; 22:16; Num. 18:1; Isa. 1:4; 53:6; Ezek. 4:4-6; 44:12.

[16] Gen. 44:16; Ex. 28:43; Lev. 26:41, 43; Num. 5:31; Josh. 22:17; I Sam. 20:8; 25:24; 28:10; II Sam. 14:9, 32; 19:20 (19); II Kgs. 7:9; Job 31:11, 28; 33:9; Ps. 32:5; 39:12(11); 59:5(4); 69:28(27); Isa. 26:21; 27:9; Jer. 30:14-15; Lam. 4:6; Ezek. 3:18-19; 7:13, 16; 9:9; 16:49; 18:18; 21:30(25), 34(29); 33:6-9; 35:5; Hos. 12:9(8); Zech. 3:9.

could be refused and the offender left to face punishment.[1] This debt of guilt could be handed down from father to son [2] so that if the fathers sinned (חטאו) the children had to bear their iniquities (עונותיהם), meaning they had to pay their fathers' "debts." They could then speak of their fathers' iniquities as well as their own sins [3] and also the iniquity of a man's sin (עון חטאת).[4] Thus the confession that said, "We have sinned; we have added iniquity to the offense ledger; we have done wickedly" (חטאנו העוינו ורשענו) was redundant but showed the various aspects of offenses. The same was true when the priest confessed all the people's iniquities, transgressions, and sins (עונות, פשעים, וחטאות).[5] The transgressions and wicked deeds were also sins which added iniquities to the debit column of the ledger.

The calf which the Israelites made in the wilderness was called their sin (חטאת).[6] If an Israelite's eye was evil (רעה) toward his brother, this became sin when the mistreated brother cried to the Lord.[7] Sin was called making the straight (ישר) crooked (עוה) [8] or being filled with violence (חמס).[9] It was doing evil (לעשות הרע) [10] or walking in evil ways (דרכים רעים).[11] A person who had been tried in court and found guilty was called "wicked" (רשע). The one tried and found innocent was called "righteous" (צדיק). "Sinners" and "wicked people" were frequently described rather synonymously in parallel constructions.[12] The same was true of wickedness and sin.[13] The wicked was classed with the sinful in contrast to the righteous (צדיק).[14] In confessions, wickedness, crookedness, transgression, cheating (לעשות עול), and sin (חטא)

---

[1] Num. 14:19; I Sam. 3:14; II Sam. 24:10; I Chron. 21:8; Ps. 78:38; 85:3(2); Prov. 16:6; Isa. 22:14; 33:24; Jer. 50:20; Hos. 14:2; Micah 7:18.

[2] Ex. 20:5; 34:7; Lev. 26:40; Num. 14:18; Dt. 5:9; Jer. 14:20; 31:29-30; 32:18.

[3] Dan. 9:16.

[4] Ps. 32:5.

[5] II Chron. 6:37; Ps. 106:6; Lev. 16:21.

[6] Dt. 9:21.

[7] Dt. 15:9; 24:15.

[8] Job 33:27.

[9] Ezek. 28:16.

[10] I Sam. 12:19; I Kgs. 16:19; II Kgs. 21:16; Ps. 51:6; Isa. 3:9.

[11] II Chron. 7:14.

[12] Ps. 1:1, 5; 104:14.

[13] Ps. 109:7.

[14] Prov. 10:16; 11:31; 13:6, 21.

were classed together as belonging to the same order.[1] Cheating
(לעשות עול) was also called sin (חטאת).[2]

The word which is usually rendered "transgress" means "to be
profane," "to rebel," or "to transgress," which in legalistic ethics
means to break a negative commandment.[3] It is not surprising to
find transgression (פשע) frequently written in parallel construction
with sin (חטא) which also involved being ungodly and breaking
commandments.[4] The one whose transgression (פשע) was forgiven
had his sin (חטאה) covered;[5] the servant who bore the sin (חטא)
of the many accepted the burden for the transgressors (פשעים),
since the Lord laid upon him the iniquity (עון) of all covenanters.[6]
Micah[7] was commissioned to tell Jacob his transgression (פשעו),
Israel, his sin (חטאתו). In Job[8] transgression was in parallel construction with iniquity, and in Isaiah[9] transgression paralleled both
sin and inquity. Transgression was listed together with sin several
times[10] and in larger lists that also included iniquity and doing
evil.[11] The brothers who had done evil needed their transgressions
and sins forgiven,[12] which probably referred to one set of events
only. The seventy years decreed for Israel and the holy city was
the time required to finish the transgression (לכלא הפשע), seal the
sins (לחתם חטאות), and atone the iniquity (לכפר עון).[13] This
probably was not understood as three sets of offenses, but rather

---

[1] Dt. 9:27; I Kgs. 8:47; Ezek. 33:12; Dan. 9:15.

[2] Ezek. 3:20; 18:24.

[3] פשע is most regularly rendered by some form of ἀσεβεῖν, which means
to profane or be ungodly. S. J. De Vries, "Sin, Sinners," *IDB*, 4, 361-362,
and A. Shusterman, "Sin," *UJE* IX, 552, hold that *pesha* means revolt or
rebel against God. DeVries says *'avon* means "perversity, iniquity, guilt"
(p. 362), and Shusterman gives a similar definition. DeVries says *pesha*
always consists of willful disobedience, but he gave no evidence for his
claim. Shusterman mentioned only II Kgs. 1:1 where *pesha* describes a
rebellious sin, but that is not enough to prove that the term always meant
rebellion.

[4] Gen. 31:36; Lev. 4:2; Josh. 24:19; Job 35:6; Ps. 25:7; 32:1; 51:15;
Isa. 43:25, 27; 44:22; 53:12; 58:1; Ezek. 33:10; Amos 5:12; Micah 1:5;
3:8.

[5] Ps. 32:1.

[6] Isa. 53:6, 12.

[7] Micah 3:8.

[8] Job 13:23.

[9] Isa. 59:12.

[10] I Kgs. 8:50; Job 8:4; 34:37; Isa. 1:28; Micah 1:13.

[11] Gen. 50:17; Ex. 34:7; Ps. 59:4; Ezek. 21:29; Dan. 9:24.

[12] Gen. 50:17.

[13] Dan. 9:24.

as repetition for emphasis. At the end of the seventy years the transgression would be completed which means the sin was sealed and the iniquity atoned.

An additional factor classified together with sin and transgression was defilement (טמאה). On the Day of Atonement, the priest made atonement for uncleanness (מטמאת), transgressions (מפשעים), all their sins (לכל חטאתם).[1] This could have meant three different types of offenses, one offense with three labels, or two offenses (transgressions and defilement) which constituted all of Israel's sins. When the Lord turned away the people's uncleanness and transgression [2] he may have dealt with one offense or two. The Koheleth contrasted clean with unclean, the good man and the sinner,[3] by which he may have referred to the same persons or just different types of desirable and undesirable people. But when II Isaiah said all Israel was like something unclean (כטמא) and described the type of uncleanness further as being like testimony garments (כבגד עדים) used to witness tokens of virginity, he did so to explain the meaning of his earlier confession, "We have sinned" (נחטא), and Psalms of Solomon spoke of being "cleansed" (καθαρισθῆναι) from sin (ἁμαρτία).[4] Ezekiel further forbade his people to defile themselves (לא יטמא) indicating that transgressions defiled and that a person who had sinned, transgressed.[5] This suggests that sin, transgression, and impurity were not thought of as completely distinguishable or that in some instances one could effectively describe the others. This is further made clear by references to cleansing (טהר) from sin (חטא),[6] rather than defilement (טמאה) and also the use of the same root word that means sin (חטא) to mean "purify" or "undefile" as well.[7] The cleansing that was described by the verb טהר was the very same as that described by חטא.[8] It meant that a person should be cleansed with a special kind of sprinkling water (במי נדה יתחטא) [9] which

---

[1] Lev. 16:16, 30.

[2] Ezek. 39:24.

[3] Eccl. 9:2.

[4] Isa. 63:4-5; Ps. of Sol. 9:12; 10:1-2.

[5] Ezek. 14:11; 37:23.

[6] Lev. 16:30; Num. 8:7; 9:13; Zech. 13:1; Prov. 20:9.

[7] Lev. 8:15; 14:49, 52; Num. 8:21; 19:12, 13, 19, 20; 31:19, 20, 23; 51:9; Ezek. 43:20, 22-23; 45:18.

[8] Lev. 16:19; Ezek. 24:13.

[9] Num. 31:23. D. Hoffmann, *Das Buch Leviticus Übersetzt und Erklärt* (Berlin, 1905), I, 358, says נדה comes from דוה, "to be sick." The woman who

the Mishnah described using the same word that means "sin" (מי חטאת).[1] A person who had "unsinned" himself (יתחטא) was clean (טהר).[2] If he was defiled (טמא) and did not cleanse himself (יתחטא) he would have remained defiled (טמא).[3] Indeed, water of impurity was itself called "cleansing," using the word which also meant "sin" (למי נדה חטאת הוא).[4] It is evident, therefore, that Israelites not only used words like sin, transgression, cheating, and iniquity synonymously. They also used defilement synonymously with these terms. The priest who atoned for sin, transgression, and wickedness also atoned for defilement. Since this was true it will be important to consider more carefully the various ways by which people could sin or transgress by becoming defiled.

DIETARY LAWS

The rules.—Among the rules that could be kept even in a foreign land were dietary laws. Food prohibited by these was unclean (טמא).[5] Food that had touched unclean food or objects was defiled.[6] Any Jew who ate forbidden food or even touched meat from animals improperly slaughtered was defiled.[7] He, by that act of becoming defiled, also sinned (חטא). Proper care and consumption of food was very important to the early Jews, Samaritans, and Christians. By NT times, at least, there was no knowledge of the origin of reason for these laws,[8] and there may not have been during the Babylonian captivity either. They were commanded; therefore they had to be obeyed. Animals that chewed the cud and

---

is defiled by נדה, like the one unclean from giving birth, is separated or removed from the community because of her sickness or defilement. Rabbinic נדוי means "bann." Sprinkling water (מי נדה) is used on those separated from the community so that they might return.

[1] Parah 9:4-8; Mik. 10:6.

[2] Num. 19:12, 19; Ps. 51:9.

[3] Num. 19:13, 20.

[4] Num. 19:9.

[5] Lev. 7:21; 11:4-47; 20:25; 27:11, 27; Num. 18:15; Dt. 14:7-19; Jdgs. 13:4, 7, 14; Ezek. 4:13; Hos. 9:3.

[6] Lev. 7:19; 11:35. .

[7] Lev. 11:24, 29, 36; 17:15; 22:8; Ezek. 4:14; Hos. 9:4.

[8] Rabbi Johanan ben Zakkai said that corpses did not defile and water did not purify, but these rituals must be observed because they have been commanded (Num. R. 19:8). It was considered better to eat a stinking fish (because it was "clean") than from dishes that were unapproved, even though sanitary (Ker. 6a).

had hoofs cloven in two could be eaten. This excluded camels, hares, rock badgers, and swine.[1] All fish that had scales and fins were permitted (כשר);[2] and all birds except eagles, vultures, ospreys, buzzards, kites, ostriches, night hawks, sea gulls, hawks, owls, water hens, pelicans, carrion vultures, cormorants, storks, herons, hopoes, bats, and winged insects were permitted.[3] The objection to most of these flying creatures was that they were scavangers that ate of carcasses or animals that died of themselves— a practice also forbidden to covenanters.[4] Exceptions to the winged insects were those that went on all four legs and hopped, such as locusts,[5] which were permitted.

The fence.—Covenanters were forbidden to boil a kid in its mother's milk.[6] Observing the rule that you should build a fence around the Torah, many precautionary measures were taken to be sure that covenanters did not boil a kid in its mother's milk. Perhaps the first step was to avoid boiling kids in any goat milk; the next step, to refrain from boiling any goat meat in goat milk; then to avoid boiling goat meat in any milk at all; further precaution was taken by refraining from boiling any meat in any milk. To avoid even this offense, covenanters did not serve meat and milk at the same table and had two sets of vessels; one for cooking meat and one for cooking milk dishes.[7] This also involved the refusal to consume any dairy products within a specified time after eating meat and vice versa. Perhaps the final step was to have two kitchens, one for cooking meat dishes and the other for dairy products. This kind of carefulness was designed to be sure that Jews never ate any meat that touched any object that had ever touched any milk products or vice versa, much less eat goat meat that had been boiled in its mother's milk. Most people who still observe these rules no longer include either goat milk or goat meat in their diet, and so they are in no danger at all of ever eating meat from a kid that had been boiled in its mother's milk, but they have been so carefully trained in the precautionary measures that they keep them even if they are unrelated to the original commandment.

---

[1] Dt. 14:3-8. [2] Dt. 14:9.
[3] Dt. 14:11-20. [4] Dt. 14:21.
[5] Lev. 11:20-23.
[6] Dt. 14:21; also Ex. 23:19; 34:26.
[7] See Sifré *Debarim* 12:24; 90b § 76.

The danger of mixing milk with meat really only applied to mammals. Therefore some rabbis permitted cheese and fowl to be served at the same table,[1] since most birds do not have mothers who give milk.[2] Probably for the same reason, eggs, fish, and locusts were not classed as meat, so they could be served together with dairy products.[3] Also a man who vowed that he would eat no meat could eat fish or locusts.[4] John the Baptist, who came in the way of righteousness,[5] neither eating nor drinking,[6] ate locusts and wild honey.[7] This diet would have protected him against eating anything that was not approved by all the dietary laws. Locusts could be eaten on the same table together with either meat or milk without offending this law. The same was true of wild honey.[8] According to law, he might also have eaten eggs and fish without fear, but these products probably were not available in the wilderness of Judah.

The claim that John did not eat or drink did not mean he starved. It meant that he did not eat or drink any food or liquid forbidden by dietary laws. Jesus, on the other hand, came eating and drinking, and people said:

"Behold an eater and a drinker of wine,
a friend of tax collectors and sinners." [9]

In the contexts of dietary laws, Jesus would not have been called a "glutton and a drunkard" as most English translations interpret

---

[1] Hullin 8:3-4; Shab. 13a; 130a.

[2] The duckbilled platypus is a mammal, but it was not known in Palestine when these laws were formed, and it is not a bird.

[3] R. Kahana said there were seven hundred varieties of clean fish, eight hundred kinds of clean locusts, and countless kinds of fowl that were edible (*PRK* 13:10). See also Sifra 39a; Sifré *Debarim* 95a § 103; Kerithoth 5:1; 21b; Acts 21:25.

[4] Hullin 8:1; 65a; JNed. 40b.

[5] Mt. 21:32.

[6] Mt. 11:18.

[7] Mt. 2:4.

[8] Judas Maccabeus reportedly kept a *minyon* of his comrades alive in the wilderness on food that was not defiled (II Mac. 5:27). Makshirin 6:1 noted that honey was one of the liquids that could make goods susceptible to defilement, but that hornets' honey (דבש ארעים) was not. If there were only evidence to show that "wild honey" was hornets' honey, then this would indicate a still further precaution against breaking any law, but evidence to establish that possibility is lacking at present. The Ethiopic translation for "wild honey" is "honey of the wilderness" (መዓረ፡ገዳም).

[9] Mt. 11:19.

this text.[1] The offense had nothing to do with the quantity of food
he ate or the amount of wine he drank. It either referred to the
type of food he ate, the people with whom he ate, or both.

The division between John and Jesus over the care with which
dietary laws should be kept continued in the later Christian church.
Paul argued with other apostles over eating food "offered to idols,"
which probably referred to food sold on the secular meat market,
or eating with Gentiles.[2] The emphasis given to dietary laws in
the Babylonian captivity continued in Judaism and Christianity
through NT times, but it was only one of the rules dealing with
purity. Another was the rules pertaining to leprosy.

LEPROSY

General mingling was forbidden by the rules of Leviticus. It was
against the law to breed different kinds of cattle, sow two kinds
of seed in the same field, or wear a garment made of two kinds of
material.[3] By extension, then, it was unlawful for people of different
races or religions to marry.[4] Likewise, it was unlawful for a person
to have any kind of discoloration of skin. This was a mingling of
skin colors and was called leprosy. If a person had some kind of
skin disease that colored his skin, he was pronounced by the priest
to be unclean.[5] If, however, the disease covered his whole body,
so that his skin was of one color, even though unnatural, he was
pronounced clean.[6] If he began to recover from the disease, so
that parts of his skin were not diseased, then he would be declared
a leper again.[7] A leper was required to let his hair hang loose, cover
his upper lip, and cry, "unclean, unclean!" wherever he went to
prevent people from touching him and thus becoming defiled.[8]
He was also required to dwell outside the camp where he would
not be available for others to touch accidently.[9] Although the
exact medical description for the affliction is not known with cer-

---

[1] RSV: "Behold, a glutton and a drunkard"; King James': "Behold a
man glutonous and a winebibber"; Doway: "Behold a man that is a glutton
and a winedrinker."

[2] I Cor. 8:1-13; Gal. 2:11-16.

[3] Lev. 19:19.

[4] See II Cor. 6:14-7:1.

[5] Lev. 31:1-8.

[6] Lev. 13:9-13.

[7] Lev. 13:14-17.

[8] Lev. 13:45-46.

[9] Lev. 13:46.

tainty, leprosy was held to be such a defilement that David included it along with having discharges, holding spindles, lacking bread, and being slain by the sword as those curses which he called down upon the descendants of Joab.[1] It was therefore quite daring for Jesus to have touched a leper in order to heal him,[2] and it was part of the good news of the kingdom that the lepers should be cleansed.[3]

Uncleanness Among Men

A man who had a seminal discharge, either in sexual intercourse with a woman or beast [4] or as a nocturnal emission was considered unclean. Objects or persons he touched became unclean. If he had a continual discharge, he defiled also the objects he touched. Anyone who later touched any of these would be unclean until evening. Should he have spat on someone, that person would have been unclean until evening. The woman with whom he had had sexual intercourse was unclean until evening. If a man had intercourse with a woman during her menstrual period, he was unclean for seven days.[5] Intercourse with a beast demanded the community to "cut him off" from the group.[6] It was more important for a priest to be clean than an Israelite, because he was not permitted to offer sacrifice while he was unclean.[7] For that reason the high priest was taken away from his wife seven days before the Day of Atonement and kept in the Counsellor's Chamber.[8] There he was kept free from touching anything unclean. On the eve of the Day of Atonement the high priest was given only a small amount of food and kept awake all night, lest he have a nocturnal emission in his sleep and so be unqualified to conduct the service the next day.[9] The same type of rules applied to women.

Uncleanness Among Women

A woman who had intercourse with a man was unclean until evening.[10] If she had intercourse with a beast she should be "cut off"

---

[1] II Sam. 3:29.　　　[2] Mt. 8:2-3.

[3] Mt. 10:8; 11:5; Lk. 7:22.

[4] Lev. 15:16; 18:23. The two offenses are not of equal degree.

[5] Lev. 15:1-18, 24.　　[6] Lev. 18:19.

[7] Lev. 22:1-9.　　　[8] Yoma 1:1.

[9] Yoma 1:4-7. This may also have been to avoid any elimination needs that would defile the "camp."

[10] Lev. 15:18.

from the community.[1] She was considered unclean for seven days
after her menstrual period stopped.[2] In order to build a fence
around the Torah, rabbis decreed that in some instances, not only
was everything she touched unclean during those seven days, but
in some instances everything she touched for twenty-four hours
prior to her menstrual flow.[3] During the period of seven days the
woman was considered unclean (טמא). Thus Bathsheba, bathing
on the roof when King David saw her, was reported to have been
sanctifying herself from her impurity (מתקדשת מטמאתה) after her
menstrual period was over.[4] Women were instructed to examine
themselves frequently to learn when the menstrual period began
so that they could remain in isolation, being careful not to sit or
lie on anything someone else might use and avoiding sexual intercourse that would defile their husbands.[5] If a woman gave birth
to a boy, she would be unclean for seven days, just as for a menstrual period. If she bore a girl, she would be unclean for fourteen
days.[6] One explanation for girls requiring a longer period was that
Eve was not shown to Adam until the second week of creation.[7]
If a woman suffered an abortion and the sex of the child was not
determined, the woman was treated as unclean for both the period
required for a boy and that required for a girl.[8] If anyone touched
an object that an unclean woman touched or an object that was
under an unclean woman, such as her chair or bed or an object
under either of them, he would be unclean until evening.[9] Should
a woman hemorrhage longer than seven days, during an ordinary
menstrual period, she would be unclean as long as her period lasted[10]
plus an additional seven days.[11]

In the Gospel of Luke, some later editor who did not know
Levitical rules probably added to the report that Mary gave birth
to Jesus in a stable the explanation, "because there was no room

---

[1] Lev. 18:23; 18:19.
[2] Lev. 12:2.
[3] Nid. 1:1-7.
[4] II Sam. 11:4.
[5] Nid. 2:1.
[6] Lev. 12:2-5.
[7] Jub. 3:8-12. M. Noth, *Leviticus* tr. J. E. Anderson (London, c1965), 97,
said the double uncleanness period required for the birth of a girl expressed
"the cultic inferiority of the female sex."
[8] Nid. 3:5.
[9] Lev. 15:19-23, 26-28.
[10] Lev. 15:25.   [11] Lev. 15:28.

at the inn." [1] A woman acquainted with Levitical rules was not
likely to have asked to be in an inn when her baby was to be born
and thus defile others in the building. Mandeans avoided unnecessary defilement by regularly arranging for births to take place in
stables while they kept their houses clean.[2] It was because of her
uncleanness that the woman whose period continued for twelve
years was afraid when she ventured to touch Jesus.[3] For twelve
years she had been prohibited from touching other people. All these
matters relating to sex were governed by purity rules, but they
were not the only defiling contacts.

OTHER RITUAL DEFILEMENT

Midras uncleanness.—The person who had a seminal discharge
or a menstrual flow by which he or she was unclean, also made
unclean all the objects he touched or over which he sat or lay.[4]
So long as these objects were unclean, anyone who sat on the
same objects or touched them obtained midras uncleanness (מדרס
טמאה) and his garments conveyed uncleanness until they were
cleansed.[5] Because it was not always possible for a person to
know whether or not every object his garments touched was free
from ever having had contact with someone unclean and because
some people were more careful than others. Pharisees always
considered the clothes of an 'am-haaretz to be suffering midras
uncleanness; whereas, the priests considered the clothes of the
Pharisee to be unclean on this score.[6] Essenes bathed and changed
garments before each meal just to be sure.[7]

Corpse uncleanness.—If a person touched a corpse or a bone of
a skeleton or entered a tent in which a person had died, he would
be unclean for at least seven days.[8] Priests were forbidden to

---

[1] Lk. 2:1-7, 12, 16.

[2] See further E.S. Drower, *The Mandaeans of Iraq and Iran* (Leiden,
1962), 41.

[3] Mk. 5:25-34.

[4] Lev. 15:4, 9-12, 20-24, 27. Purity rules were not unique to Israel.
Similar customs were practiced by Babylonians and Egyptians, and have
been reported by Herodotus, *Hist.* II. 37; Porphyre, *De Abstin.* IV. 7; and
Strabo. See Thomas, *Op. cit.*, 299.

[5] Lev. 15:7-8, 10-12, 16-17, 21-24, 27.

[6] Hag. 2:7.   Jos., *BJ* II (129-130).

[8] Num. 19:11-22; Lev. 11:32; 19:11; Num. 5:2; 6:7, 9; 9:6, 10, 16;
21:1, 3, 11; Ezek. 44:25; Hag. 2:13.

become defiled by corpse uncleanness for any except their nearest relatives: mothers, fathers, sons, daughters, and virgin sisters.[1] The anointed high priest was not allowed to touch a dead body at all—not even for his father or mother.[2] This partially explains why the priest and Levite would not stop to help a man who was "half dead." Had he died while they were helping him, they would have become defiled by someone not of their nearest kinship. The parable is an anti-priestly teaching. It shows that however high the social status of these officials, they were unable to help people in real need.[3]

Cleanliness in camp.—Military camps had to be free from uncleanness because the Lord walked in their camps, and they could not allow him to see anything indecent in the camp or he would not have won Israel's battles for her. Therefore a man who had a nocturnal emission had to leave camp, and all excrement had to be discharged from the body outside camp.[4] Women, who stimulated seminal discharges and had menstrual periods, and children too young to be responsible for their toilet habits were excluded from camp.[5] Also lepers, cripples, men with blemishes, or any type of physical uncleanness were excluded.[6] The priest, Ahimelech, allowed David and his soldiers to eat holy bread reserved for priests, only after David promised that his troops had kept themselves from women and therefore had vessels that were holy. Priests were not allowed in battle where they could become defiled with the slain,[7] and in the temple they were forbidden to wear garments that would make them perspire.[8]

Since it was excrement, discharges, hemorrhages, perspiration, and other types of emissions from the body that were so closely related to defilement, Jesus was reported to have said that it was not that which went into a man that defiled him but that which came out of a man.[9] Before the Lord would appear to the Israelites

---

[1] Lev. 21:1-3; Num. 6:11.
[2] Lev. 21:10-11.
[3] Lk. 10:30-37.
[4] According to 1QM 7:7, two thousand cubits from camp. Dt. 23:9-14.
[5] 1QM 7:3.
[6] 1QM 7:4-5.
[7] 1QM 9:7-9. For the contrast between holiness and defilement see O. Procksch, "ἅγιος . . .," *TDNT* I, 93, 113.
[8] Ezek. 44:18.
[9] Mk. 7:15; so also Sifra 84b.

to give them the ten commandments, Moses had to sanctify them, and forbid them from going near women until after the third day when the Lord appeared.[1] Later rabbis declared that Moses always kept away from his wife after the commandments were given because he did not know when God would speak to him.[2] This was the normal conclusion to be reached by those ascetics who, because of the covenant, took seriously all of the purity rules they were expected to observe. Add to these requirements the obligations for fasting, some of which were also motivated by purity rules, and a biblical basis for the most extreme type of asceticism is established.

In this study so far it has been shown that transgression (פשע), doing evil (לעשות רע), cheating (לעשות עול), and wickedness (רשע) were all considered sin (חטא) and that for each sin there seemed to be a corresponding iniquity (עון). But more important for this study, defilement (טמאה) was also sin (חטא) and people who sinned were defiled. Committing adultery, worshipping idols, or eating prohibited food was both sinful and defiling. On the Day of Atonement the priest atoned both for sins and impurities. A person who was unclean (טמא) had to be cleansed (הטהר) before he could be clean (טהור), but sins (חטאות) were also cleansed (טהר) leaving the cleansed sinner pure (טהור). Water used for sprinkling was called both by terms related to defilement (מי נדה) and also those related to sin (מי חטאת). In some instances people who were defiled (טמא) brought a sin offering (חטאת) so that they could be cleansed. This does not necessarily mean that these terms had no distinction of meaning, but that in many cases the definitions overlapped. If a person broke a commandment, for instance, that was sin. But if he were commanded to keep himself undefiled, defilement would also be sin. Priests who offered sacrifices while unclean were not only defiled but sinful. A person who had taken vows of celibacy and then had sexual intercourse, was not only defiled but sinful. Defilement had such a distasteful connotation that acts that were technically sinful might be described more repulsively if called acts of impurity or abominations.[3]

---

[1] Ex. 19:9-15.

[2] *ARN* 2.

[3] Shimoni said that every one who was proud (גבה לב) defiled the land (גורם לטמא את הארץ) and drove out the Shekina (Yalkut 178a [89c]). Thomas, *Op. cit.*, 285-436, having shown the numerous religions in the

In Babylon, where there was no Jewish temple, Jews were under greater obligation to keep their communities free from ritual defilement than they had been in the land. They faced obligations similar to those of an army camp of duty. If they failed then the Lord would not be in their midst. Under these circumstances defilement became much more seriously offensive than some sins. If they had not previously considered the difficulty, or impossibility, involved in trying to maintain even a small pure community, they undoubtedly realized it in Babylon. It was under such concepts and pressures that the doctrine of original sin probably came into being. The importance of the word study will be understood when original defilement at birth will be considered as the real meaning of original sin. The interchange of sin and defilement in the OT makes the transfer of original defilement to original sin a small hurdle. The next step will be to check the likelihood that the original defilement of conception and birth of every child was the condition that early Jews and Christians called original sin.

ORIGINAL SIN

Present doctrine.—The doctrine of original sin has been accepted by both Jews [1] and Christians,[2] but has become a more prominent belief among Christians than Jews.[3] Closely related to the doctrine

Orient and Greek world that bathed for healing, cleansing, forgiveness, and initiation, said these religions did not originally distinguish between bodily defilement and moral sin. Only later was the spiritual factor added and then purity terms were still used—cleansing the heart, inner purity, and other moral factors.

Speaking of Oriental religions, Thomas, *Op. cit.*, 311, said, "De là, un même rite baptismal écarte les causes de maladie, efface la souillure causée par le contact d'un cadavre ou par la menstruation et purifie l'homme coupable de quelque crime. Sainté, pureté, innocence; aspects divers, semble-t-il, d'une seule et meme realité physique, d'une qualité qui s'attache au corps et qui, perdue, peut se récupérer par un bain."

[1] The Jewish scholar, S. A. Cohon, "Original Sin," *HUCA* 21 (1948), 275-330, commenting on Ps. 51:7, said the sinfulness mentioned was not the act of generation, "but the general instability of the race of humans who are prone to sinfulness from the very womb" (p. 283).

[2] B. L. Conway, *The Question Box* (New York, c1929), 14, 243-244. Conway said the dogma of original sin cast a white light on the problem of evil, and he quoted the Council of Trent, sen. V, can. 2, for saying that because of Adam's sin all mankind is defiled and required to suffer and die (p. 14).

[3] L. H. Silberman, Jr., "Original Sin," *UJE*, denied that Judaism accepted a doctrine of eternal transmission of spiritual blemish. Instead he said Judaism "believes in the unsullied purity of each newborn soul" (p. 324). That has not always been true.

of original sin is the belief that baptism is necessary to save people from damnation. Therefore the conviction is strong that baptism should be administered to infants. Original sin is usually related to the "fall" of Adam and Eve in the Garden of Eden. For most Christians there is no good explanation for the effect of Adam's activity on the twentieth century baby that is born in sin before he has made any willful decision. Sometimes it is psychologized and explained in terms of feelings of guilt and the sense of sinfulness experienced by adults, but that has not adequately explained the doctrine from the point of view of scripture and Near Eastern tradition.[1] This study will attempt to provide a more likely explanation.

Universal sin.—One biblical narrative that has been interpreted as the cause for universal sin is the story of the sons of God (בני אלהים) who were lured by the daughters of Adam (בנות האדם). They came to earth and had intercourse with those women who became pregnant and gave birth to giants.[2] After that there was so much wickedness in the world that the Lord finally decided to destroy everything but Noah, his family, and necessary animals for reproduction.[3]

This story received a lot of attention in later Judaism. The "sons of God"[4] were called angels or watchers in inter-testamental literature.[5] The sin of the watchers was not only before the flood in sequence of the text, but later Jews understood that their sin was responsible for all the destruction that followed.[6] Their whoring after the daughters of men made the beginning of uncleanness.[7] Before they defiled themselves, the watchers hoped to live eternal life (ἐλπίζουσι ζῆσαι ζωὴν αἰώνιον);[8] in fact, they were spiritual, holy, living life eternal at that very time,[9] but they

---

[1] S. J. DeVries, "The Fall," *ID* II, 226, admired the story of the fall "for its psychological perceptiveness." Describing every human being who has sinned, DeVries said, "He knows that he too would hide in the trees of the Garden, would tell Yahweh half-truths to disguise his guilt, and would blame others for his sin." Perhaps that is true, but what has that to do with the newborn baby?

[2] Gen. 6:1-8.
[3] Gen. 6:5-7:24.
[4] Gen. 6.
[5] Jub. 4:15, 22; Enoch 91:15.
[6] Jub. 5:1-32; T. Naph. 3:5.
[7] Jub. 7:21.
[8] Enoch 10:10.   [9] Enoch 15:4-7.

mingled with women and defiled themselves (συμμίγεντες ταῖς
θυγατράσι τῶν ἀνθρώπων τοῦ μιανθῆναι ἐν αὐταῖς ἐν τῇ ἀκαθαρσίᾳ),[1]
and became unclean. They took wives which the Lord had not
appointed for them; they lusted; they begat children; which they
should not have done because they were spiritual.[2] It was after
the angels slept (συνεκοιμήθησαν) with women, having become
defiled with them (ἐν ταῖς θηλείαις ἐμιάνθησαν) that they demonstrated all the sins in those women (πᾶσας τὰς ἁμαρτίας)[3] and the
whole land was filled with unrighteousness (ἀδικίας).[4] Although
their act involved defilement, it was also called the origin of sin.
Prior to their fall, the watchers, like other angels, were celibate.[5]
After they had become defiled with women, there was so much
evil on earth that the flood was necessary to purify the land of
its defilement.[6]

The story of the fall of man and the story of the fall of the angels
belong to the same collection of etiological stories in Genesis, and
they were related by Jews in NT times. One of the angels that fell
was reported to have seduced Eve and caused her to sin.[7] The
same author understood that men were created exactly like angels
for purity and righteousness, which if they kept would have
preserved them from death. The knowledge of good and evil,
however, was the cause of their perishing.[8] This means that some
Jews, at least, thought Eve was defiled and came to know good
and evil by having sexual intercourse. One of these seems to have
been Philo, who compared the serpent to pleasure, the most violent
of all pleasures being sexual intercourse (αἱ περὶ τὰς γυναῖκας
ὁμιλίαι).[9] The serpent, he said, stirred up intemperance and
sexual lusts.[10] He said further that bodily pleasures (τὴν τῶν
σωμάτων ἡδονήν) is the beginning (ἀρχή) of unrighteousness and
lawlessness, and it causes mortality.[11] All of this was involved in

---

[1] Enoch 10:10; also 15:4-7.
[2] Enoch 15:1-7.
[3] Enoch 9:7-9.
[4] Enoch 9:9.
[5] II Bar. 56:14.
[6] Jub. 7:20-21; T. Naph. 3:5.
[7] Enoch 69:6.
[8] Enoch 69:11. In the garden Adam and Eve ate the food of angels (Adam
and Eve 4:2).
[9] Leg. All. II.viii (74).
[10] Op. 157-158.
[11] Op. 152.

Philo's interpretation of the Garden of Eden story rather than the fall of the watchers. Another exegete said the devil was the serpent who came disguised as an angel. Eve took an oath to him, after which he poured lust upon the fruit she ate. This lust was the beginning of all sin.[1] When they repented of their "sin," Adam and Eve stood in water up to their necks, as if being cleansed from defilement.[2] Adam and Eve's sin caused the death of all later human beings.[3] In addition to the passion of parents, the begetting of children began with the sin of Adam and Eve.[4] Ben Sirah said a woman (i.e. Eve) originated sin (ἁμαρτία) and caused death for all.[5] Jews who lamented the condition of the world grieved because Adam and Eve thus sinned. It was not Adam alone, but also his descendants who sinned. The Lord promised them the eternal age, but their own works brought about death. Moses encouraged Israelites to choose life, and the faces of all those who have practiced abstinence are destined to shine like the stars, but the faces of all others will be blacker than darkness.[6] Only the ascetics, only the celibate ones avoid the perpetuation of Adam's sin and lead pure lives.[7]

Clement of Alexandria opposed this type of asceticism which was practiced by a sect who lived according to the Gospel of the Egyptians. This sect taught that the Savior said, "I came to destroy both the works of sexual lusts (τὰ ἔργα τῆς θηλείας μὲν τῆς ἐπιθυμίας) and the works of creation and destruction." A certain Salome asked how long men would continue to die. The Lord answered, "As long as women bear children." She responded, "Then I did well not to bear children." Whereupon, the Lord replied, "Eat every plant, but do not eat the bitter plant" (τὴν δὲ πικρίαν ἔχουσαν μὴ φάγῃς).[8] Clement understood this to be a strong teaching by a group who called marriage "the bitter plant." They apparently took the expression from the tree of the knowledge of

---

[1] Apoc. Mos. 17:1; 19:3.
[2] Adam and Eve 5:1-11:3.
[3] IV Ezra 7:116-126; II Bar. 54:15-19; Adam and Eve 8:2; Apoc. Mos. 14:3; II Bar. 17:2; 23:4; 48:42; 54:15; 56:5-6; Tanḥuma, Ḥayyê Sârâh, 60a; ʾAdham Ḥôtêʾ (Tôldhôt, 69b): "וכי אדם הראשון כשחטא."
[4] II Bar. 56:5-6.
[5] Sirah 25:24.
[6] IV Ezra 7:116-131.
[7] IV Ezra 7:116-126; II Bar. 54:15-19.
[8] Stromata III.ix(63:1-67:2).

good and evil which they contrasted to the other trees of the garden
that were "pleasant to see and good to eat." [1] This was the tree
from which Adam and Eve ate when they were expelled from the
garden. Harris noted the same expression in a similar context in
the Odes of Solomon 11.[2] The author of that ode had drunk of
the water of life, given up folly (ܟ݂ܐܠܐ ܚ݂ܠ݂ܐܬ ܚ݂ܠ݂ܐ݁ܬܐ), was clothed
in a new garment, had his eyes lightened, and was taken to the
Lord's Paradise. He was one of the Lord's servants who turned
away from the bitterness of the trees (ܠ ܐܘܡ̈ܝ ܟ݂ܐܠ̈ܝ ܟܐ݁ܝܬ ܐ݁ܕܐܡ݁ܐ).[3]

Another psalmist thanked God for not reckoning him with the
sinners and asked the Lord to save him from the wicked sinful
woman (ܟ݂ܐܝܬ ܟ݂ܐܠ̈ܝ), not to let the beauty of a wicked
woman lead him astray (ܟ݂ܐܠ̈ܐ ܟ݂ܐ݁ܕܘܝܪ̈ ܡܝܬܐ ܟܝ݁ܝܬ ܟܠܐ),
and to remove from him all anger and unreasonable passion
(ܟ݂ܐܠ݂ ܟ݂ܝ݁ ܟ݂ܕܘ݁ܐ).[4]

In opposition to celibate heresies that were evidently prominent
in Clement's time, Clement said Moses' commandment not to touch
anything unclean did not refer to those who were married (οὐ τῶν
γεγαμηκότων) but those nations who were still living in fornication.[5]
Clement's objections reflect the views of those he opposed. St.
Isidore de Puluse (fifth century, A.D.) said baptism removed the
defilement caused by Adam's transgression.[6]

Adam's fall.—It is quite clear that later Jews and Christians
understood the sin of Adam, like the sin of the angels who fell, to
have been sexual intercourse. On what grounds did they arrive at
that interpretation? The narrative itself never mentioned either
sin or defilement. It did speak of the Lord's commandments,
however, and the disobedience of Adam and Eve.[7] Disobedience
would have been sin, and the act symbolized by the forbidden
fruit is suggested by the story itself to have been sexual intercourse.
Prior to the act, Adam and Eve did not know "good and evil." [8]
The expression "knowing good and evil" in the OT and later
Judaism referred to maturity. At about twenty years of age, every

---

[1] Gen. 2:9.
[2] J. R. Harris, *The Odes and Psalms of Solomon* (Cambridge, 1909), 70-71.
[3] Odes of Sol. 11:9-18.
[4] Ps. of Sol. 16:7-10.
[5] *Stromata* III.x(73:3-4).
[6] S. Lyonnet, "Le Péché Originel en Rom. 5:12," *Biblica* 4(1960), 349-354.
[7] Gen. 2:16-17; 3:11.   [8] Gen. 2:17; 3:3-5.

Jewish boy who had grown at least two hairs became an adult. He was then considered old enough to know good and evil, to marry, pay taxes, bear arms, and accept other adult responsibilities.[1] Prior to eating the forbidden fruit, Adam and Eve were comparatively well cared for without having to work excessively. Afterward they were aware of their nakedness; Eve became pregnant and had to face the pain of childbirth.[2] Adam had to work for a living in the world where thistles grew.[3] Eve had enticed Adam into the act just as the daughters of Adam enticed the watchers of heaven to defile themselves.[4] The Lord had warned Adam and Eve that they would "die" whenever they ate the fruit of the tree of the knowledge of good and evil.[5] After they committed the act, however, the Lord did not punish them with immediate *physical* death; he expelled them from the garden.[6] They continued to exist, but not in the garden where the tree of life grew. Instead they faced existence in "the world." This may mean that the "life" discussed was religious life in a covenant relationship with God and "death," excommunication from such a life. The details of the story provide enough information that later Jews did not

---

[1] Nid. 5:9. This thesis was first proposed in "The OT Meaning of the Knowledge of Good and Evil," *JBL* 75(1956), 114-120. It was attacked by R. Gordis, "The Knowledge of Good and Evil in the OT and the Qumran Scrolls," *JBL* 76 (1957), 123-138; but defended by M. Burrows, *More Light on the Dead Sea Scrolls* (New York, 1958), 167-168; H. S. Stern, "The Knowledge of Good and Evil," *VT* 8 (1958), 405-408, and P. Borgen, " 'At the Age of Twenty' in 1QSa," *RQ* 3 (1961), 267-77. Stern's attack on Gordis, insisting that the knowledge of good and evil was unrelated to sexual knowledge was overstated. The acceptable age for acquiring this knowledge was twenty years and the expression came to refer to that age, but it was not free from sexual concepts. See also JBik. 64c-64d.

S. B. Hoenig, "The Age of Mature Responsibility in 1QSa," *JQR* 48 (1958), 371-375, and "The Age of Twenty in Rabbinic Tradition and 1QSa," *JQR* 49 (1958-59), 209-214, sustained the same thesis against Baumgarten, "1QSa 1:11—Age of Testimony or Responsibility ?" *JQR* 49 (1958), 157-160, without either scholar acknowledging any acquaintance with the discussion of the subject that preceded their writing. These views are all quite different from some of the older opinions. See Windsch, "Zum Problem der Kindertaufe in Urchristentum," *ZNTW* 28 (1929), 132-133, for instance. He held that seven was the age for such knowledge as good and evil and guilt.

[2] Gen. 3:7, 16; 4:1.

[3] Gen. 3:17-19.

[4] Gen. 3:6; 6:2; T. Reuben 5:3-7.

[5] Gen. 2:17.

[6] Gen. 3:23-24.

have to read much between the lines to deduce that the event which brought "death" was the same as that which made Eve pregnant. The original intention of the story may have been to teach celibacy.[1]

The new paradise.—In NT times the stories of the fallen watchers and the sin of Adam and Eve were given a great deal of attention, and they were used to teach the virtues of celibacy and the wickedness of lust. In the new Jerusalem, the one hundred and forty-four thousand who were redeemed were the ones whose names had been written in the Lamb's book of life.[2] They had not defiled themselves (οὐκ ἐμολύνθησαν) with women, because they were celibate (παρθένοι).[3] In the city where they dwelt, there would be nothing

---

[1] Jacob referred to his eldest son, Reuben, as "My strength and the first fruit of my sin (ראשית אוני)" (Gen. 49:3). Tanḥuma (*Vayeḥî*, 109b) elaborated further that Reuben was the first drop of semen (טפה ראשונה) that went out from Jacob (see also *Vayêṣê* 77a). The relationship of conception and birth to sin was further expressed by Micah 6:7:

"Shall I give the first fruit of my transgression (בכורי פשעי) ?
the fruit of my belly (פרי בטני), for the sin of my pleasure (חטאת נפשי) ?"

Here the sin against the psalmist's life was his eldest son, the fruit of his belly. The question the psalmist asked, which others in his culture took for granted, was, "Should the eldest son be offered as sacrifice to atone for this sin of original defilement necessary for the father's sensual pleasure and the son's conception and birth ?" חטאת נפשי may be the "sin offering for my pleasure," meaning that the child might be given as the sin offering required by Lev. 12:6-7. That offering was required by the woman who bore the child, and therefore would consider the child to be the fruit of her womb. The words used in both instances were for sin or transgression rather than defilement, although intercourse was the act to which reference was made.

If the fruit of the tree of the knowledge of good and evil did not suggest sexual intercourse so readily it would not be necessary for scholars to deny that this was the meaning intended. J. H. Hertz (ed.), *The Pentateuch and Haftorahs* (London, 1947), 459, said if Eve's sin were related to the mother's defilement after birth, then "motherhood would thus in itself be a sinful thing, and its occurrence require purification and atonement . . . If impurity were associated with childbirth as a fact in nature, the child who is the cause of the mother's defilement, would itself have been unclean." Even though Hertz refused to accept this possibility, his logic was correct and not so absurd as he intended to show.

[2] Rev. 13:8.

[3] R. H. Charles, *ICC Revelation* (New York, 1920), II, 8-9, acknowledged the necessity of understanding this passage to refer to celibate males. Since he could not accept that conclusion, however, he was "forced to adopt the latter" conclusion that the text was interpolated. But even if that were so, it still has the same meaning. See Rev. 14:4.

unclean (κοινός), but there the Garden of Eden would be restored to its original purity.[1] Those who entered the Lord's Paradise gave up folly and rejected the "bitter plant" accepted by those who married.[2] Streams of the water of life would flow through the city in whose midst was the tree of life (τὸ ξύλον τῆς ζωῆς) which had been available to Adam and Eve before their knowledge of good and evil.[3] Paul contrasted the sin of Adam to the gift of grace in Christ.[4] In another context, Paul also strongly recommended celibacy for those unmarried and abstinence from sexual intercourse for those married, even though he did not require it.[5] Jesus said that in the resurrection there would be no marriage, but all would be like angels.[6] He may have meant that they would be celibate like the watchers before the fall.[7]

Conceived in sin.—According to Levitical purity laws, every man and woman who engaged in sexual intercourse became defiled by that act.[8] Furthermore, every woman who gave birth to a boy was unclean for seven days and for a girl, fourteen. During that time everything she touched was also unclean. Care was taken to see that no more people became defiled by this birth than was necessary. She could be kept in comparative isolation and thus avoid contact with people generally, but she could not avoid touching her own child while giving birth and afterwards while caring for it. Therefore every child born was defiled at birth, and his parents had become defiled at his conception. This may have prompted Job to ask rhetorically, "Who can produce something clean (טהר) from something unclean (מטמא)? Not one."[9] The

---

[1] Rev. 21:27.
[2] Odes of Sol. 11:9-18; see also Clem. Alex., *Stromata* III.ix (66:2-3).
[3] Rev. 21:22-22:4.
[4] Rom. 5.
[5] I Cor. 7.
[6] Mt. 22:30.
[7] II Bar. 56:14.
[8] Lev. 15:18.
[9] Job 14:4. Büchler, *Op. cit.*, arguing strongly and mostly correctly that טמא has a moral quality, was probably wrong when he said of Job 14:4, ". . . it is not doubted that not levitical purity and impurity were intended" (p. 242). Instead of simply having a moral quality, it is more accurate to say that moral offenses were often described in Levitical terms and vice versa. M. H. Pope, *Job* (Garden City, c1965), 101, says of Job 14:4: "It is *a propos* of vs. 1 that from an unclean thing (woman) no clean thing can be expected."

reason for this was that man was born from a woman,[1] who became unclean when giving birth. Job asked further:

"What is man, that he can be clean (יזכה)?
or that born of woman (ילוד אשה) that he can be righteous (יצדק)?"[2]

The psalmist who wrote the Hodayoth (1QH) lamented man's sinful character. He continued through life as a lawbreaker, but he began at conception and birth being related to defilement:

"But I am formed of clay, and a mixture of water,
a basis of sexual impurity and a fountain of menstrual defilement; (סוד הערוה ומקור הנדה)
an origin of iniquity and a construction of sin, (כור העוון ומבנה החטאה)
a spirit fallen and wayward without understanding."[3]
"And who is flesh such as this?
or what is that formed of clay to magnify marvelous deeds?
He is in iniquity from the womb to old age in
guilt of sacrilege (והוא בעוון מרחם ועד שבה באשמת מעל)."[4]
"But from the dust I have been [taken and from clay sn]atched,
belonging to a fountain of menstrual defilement and shameful sexual impurity—
a collection of dust and a mixture of water."[5]

This is in contrast with God who is "a source of glory and a fountain of knowledge."[6] In comparison, man seems weak:

"And what born of woman [will understand] all the terrible mysteries of your wonder?
He is a formation of dust and a mixture of water,

Of Job 14:1, Pope says, "Christian exegetes have seen in this passage an allusion to original sin, but the concern is perhaps more with physical and ritual uncleanness" (p. 101). Pope did not ask what the early nature of original "sin" was.

[1] Job 15:14.
[2] Job 15:14.
[3] 1QH 1:21-23. Text as amended by J. Licht, מגילת ההודיות (ירושלים, תש״ג).
[4] 1QH 4:29-30.
[5] 1QH 12:24-25.
[6] 1QH 12:29. For מקוי read מקור.

of wh[om iniquity and si]n are origin,
shameful sexual impurity [and a fountain of]
  menstrual defilement (ערות קלון [ומקור ה] נדה),
and a spirit of waywardness is securely established in him." [1]

Apparently absorbed with the uncleanness surrounding conception
and birth, the psalmist confesses:

"For I have been rolled in menstrual defilement (בנדה),
and from an origin of [sexual defilement I was f]ormed." [2]
Another lament of the same nature may be expressed in a biblical
Psalm:

"Thus I was brought forth in iniquity (עוון);
and in sin (חטא) my mother conceived me." [3]

It would have been more certain that the biblical psalmist
referred to the defilement of childbirth if he had used words that
meant defilement and uncleanness rather than iniquity and sin
to describe his original condition, but the Dead Sea psalmist also
used the same terms to describe his origin which was further
classified in categories of impurity. Poets sometimes vary their
vocabulary and utilize more synonyms than prose writers to express
a desired feeling in meter. This is usually considered poetic license,
but even in prose, rabbis said "everyone who commits a transgression (עבירה) is as if he were defiled with corpse uncleanness"
(מיטמא בנפש מת) and that after childbirth a woman was a sinner
(חוטאת היא).[4] The examination of words for sin and defilement
used in the OT indicates that neither psalmist was unique in
speaking of defilement as sin or iniquity or of sin and iniquity as
defilement. The seven day period when the mother was defiled
was a period when her son would have been defiled by her touch.[5]
That was probably the original stage of sinfulness about which
the Dead Sea psalmist and Job spoke. It may also have been the
condition about which Ps. 51 complained.

---

[1] 1QH 13:14-16.
[2] 1QH 17:19.
[3] Ps. 51:7.
[4] Mid. Ps. 51 § 2, 141a; Sheb. 8a.
[5] Not only in the Near East and East, but also in Hellenistic religions,
women were required to be purified from menstrual defilement and children
from the defilement of birth. See Thomas, *Op. cit.*, 315-316.

Christian interpretation.—De Ruspe said Jesus Christ was one who, "without sin was conceived (*sine peccato conceptus*), without sin was born (*sine peccato natus*), without sin died (*sine peccato mortuus*)," but who had nonetheless been made sin for us.[1] The implication of this claim is that it was not ordinary to be conceived, born, or to die without sin. This probably refers to the defilement attached to all three. Origen, however, did not claim Jesus to have been born without defilement. He admitted Luke's report that Jesus, as well as Mary, had to be purified.[2] But he was quick to mention that Job "did not say, 'No one is free from sin (*peccato*),' but rather, 'No one is free from defilement (*sorde*).'"[3] Origen said that the scripture ruling was that a mother was unclean for seven days after the birth of a son and then she had to bring a burnt offering and a sin offering forty days after his birth. Origen said the sin offering implied that the woman had sinned. In some way that Origen could not fathom there must have been a hidden and secret cause that made the woman unclean and also her child, who bore some mysterious stain. Every child, said Origen, was defiled by the stain of unrighteousness and sin (*iniquitatis et peccati sorde polluitur*).[4] As many exegetes since, Origen could understand that a baby was born defiled; he could not understand how he could be sinful; but since the word used in Ps. 51:7 was "sin," then a child must be born with original sin. He did not make the normal transfer of relating Lev. 12:2-8 to Job 14:4, Ps. 51:7, and Lk. 2:22, however, to explain the basis for his conviction of original sin. Nor did he observe the number of times in the OT that defilement was called sin, and sin, defilement. A Jewish scholar noted the three transgressions that caused women to die at child-birth: carelessness about purity in relationship to menstrual periods; failure to give the first fruits of dough; and the failure to light Sabbath candles. The commandment regarding menstrual care, he said, was given so that she could atone for her sin in causing Adam's death; the commandment regarding first fruits was given because Adam was the first fruit of the world, but then Eve came

---

[1] This quotation has been erroneously attributed to Augustine rather than Fulgence de Ruspe (d. 533 A.D.), so L. Sabourin, *Rédemption Sacrificielle* (Desclée de Brouwer, 1961), 65. The quotation is from *De Fide, seu de Regula verae Fidei, ad Petrum*, XXVI, reg. 23; PL 65, 701.

[2] Lk. 2:22.

[3] *Homily on Luke* XIV. 18833.B.

[4] *Homily on Leviticus* (Lev. 12: 2-8).

and defiled him (וטימאתהו). By offering first fruits she might be atoned for having defiled Adam.[1]

Since St. Augustine,[2] at least, theologians have called the offense of Adam "original sin" (*originale peccatum*), not original defilement. For St. Augustine, sin and lust were so closely identified that the defilement of concupiscence was also sin, but the traditional basis for a new born baby's impure state was more likely related to Levitical defilement than to any inborn rebellion or natural wickedness on the part of the child. There are rules that define the conditions at conception and birth as defilement. Later concerns about the condition of man at birth are related both to birth and conception. Original sin was attributed to the fall of the watchers and the fall of Adam, both of which were understood to have been sexual intercourse. In the new Jerusalem there would be no defilement; the Garden of Eden would be restored with the tree of life; and the place would be reserved for celibates who had not been defiled. Adam's sin had been repeated by all of his descendants except those who had abstained from sexual intercourse. Job said that an unclean mother (ῥύπος = טמא) could not produce a Levitically clean baby (καθαρός = טהר); therefore no one born of woman could be innocent (ἄμεμπτος = זכה) or righteous (δίκαιο = צדק).[3] It may have been in relationship to the same rules that the Psalmist said he was brought forth in iniquity (ἀνομία = עוון) and conceived in sin (ἀμαρτία = חטא).[4] The frequent interchange of sin and defilement in the OT support the Jewish interpretation of Adam's act that was responsible for original sin to have meant original defilement. For the interpretation of the NT, it makes little difference how much earlier than Jesus' time this belief was held. It was clearly known in Jesus' time, but it also seems not to have emerged suddenly *ex nihilo*. It appeared in intertestamental literature, the works of Philo, and the Dead Sea Scrolls. It seems also to have been as old as Job, and it *may* have been the traditional background that the authors of Ps. 51 and the Genesis story of

---

[1] Tanḥuma, *Noaḥ* 1-13, 14b.

[2] *De diversis quaestionibus ad Simplicianum* i.1,4.

[3] Job 15:14.

[4] When the child was born defiled, he was already in "debt." He had an iniquity (עוון) against his record already which required a sin offering (חטאת) to cancel. Hence the poet was not out of order when he used עוון and חטא to describe a condition of defilement usually described by טמא.

Adam and Eve assumed as familiar concepts by which their writings would be understood.

Levitical rules were very important in NT times. Some passages written by and for people who understood them do not make sense to twentieth century students of the bible who do not know them. One such passage is Romans 7, which will be interpreted here with the thesis that "life" and "death" in that chapter refer to existence within and without the covenant community.

PAUL'S BAR MITZWAH

Bar Mitzwah tradition.—In modern Judaism, a boy at the age of thirteen is considered to have reached the age of religious duty and responsibility. He is then religiously mature and held accountable for his own sins. Leopold Löw held that this rite did not become a fixed custom until the fourteenth century in Germany.[1] Kohler, however, correctly contended that its origin was much earlier,[2] but there is more support for the belief that the bar mitzwah was the earliest stage for accepting legal responsibilities than Kohler noted. As early as Deuteronomy, males were classified as toddlers (טפים), sons (בנים), and men (אנשים) who knew good and evil.[3] The men who knew good and evil were twenty years of age.[4] Those old enough to hold important positions of community leadership were at least thirty.[5] Boys became "sons" and were held responsible for the commandments (מצות). When a boy ceased being a "toddler" he could be condemned as a "stubborn and rebellious son." [6] Rabbis said a boy reached this age whenever he could produce two hairs. That would have been at the early

---

[1] L. Löw, *Das Lebensalter in der Jüdischen Literatur* (Szegedin, 1875), 210-217: "Diesselbe ist ihrem Wesen nach und ihrer Praxis nach eine antitalmudische Reform. Deutschland ist ihr Heimat" (p. 210).

[2] K. Kohler, "Bar Mizwah," *JE* II, 509-510.

[3] Dt. 1:34-35, 39.

[4] "The OT Meaning of the Knowledge of Good and Evil," *Op. cit.*

[5] "Dates, Discrepancies, and Dead Sea Scrolls," *The New Christian Advocate* (July, 1958), 50-54.

Just before this manuscript was sent to the press, J. K. Zink, "Uncleanness and Sin, A Study of Job 14:4 and Psalm 51:7," *VT* 17 (1967), 354-361, appeared surveying the scholarly views on these passages and holding that both should be understood in relationship to defilement. He supported Kaufmann and Yerkes in his belief that the חטאת offering was an exorcising sacrifice for the purpose of removing cultic disqualification.

[6] Dt. 21:18-21.

stage of his teens.[1] A boy who was twelve years of age could make vows, but they had to be examined throughout his thirteenth year.[2] If he became twenty years of age and had not grown two hairs, he had to bring proof that he was twenty. If that was established he was declared a eunuch, and he was not permitted to submit to *halitzah* or contract levarite marriage.[3] A male's good inclination was not believed to begin until he was thirteen years old. His evil impulse was thirteen years older, having gone uncurbed since birth; but at thirteen, the commandment prohibited the function of the evil impulse.[4] A boy could be trained in school from six years of age on, but he could not be threatened until after the first twelve years of his life were over.[5] R. Eleazar b. R. Simeon said that a man was responsible for his son until the age of thirteen. After that he said, "Blessed be he who has now freed me from the responsibility of this boy." [6] Maimonides said a boy at thirteen was responsible for matters dealing with sexual immorality (עריות).[7] At the age of twelve Luke reported Jesus astonishing the scholars with his wisdom.[8] This may have been intended to show that Jesus was unusually precocious, but it may also reflect Luke's acquaintance with a custom that demonstrated a boy's knowledge of the law at about that age.

The age of thirteen, when a boy became a "son" and was responsible for the commandments, would have been an age when he was accepted as a more mature member of the community where there was "life." He was not yet required to pay taxes but was accountable for all of his personal ethics. The regularity with which Paul used the terms "life" and "death" in relationship to the covenant community helps to clarify Paul's personal testimony in relationship to Levitical rules.

Paul's "life" and "death."—For the Jewish boy, "life" began at eight days, when he was purified from his original defilement

---

[1] San. 8:1; see also Nid. 6:11; 52a.
[2] Nid. 5:6.
[3] Nid. 5:9.
[4] Eccl. R. 4:13 § 1; *ARN* 16; *PRK*, Appendix 3.
[5] Ket. 50a.
[6] Gen. R. 63:10.
[7] Maimonides, *Mishnah Commentary* to San. 7:4.
[8] Lk 2:42-47.

and circumcised.[1] This, of course, refers to his religious life. His physical life began earlier. From eight days of age until his bar mitzwah age, however, he was not responsible for his behavior regarding the law. Paul's situation was not unique in this regard. During the time he was being instructed—until about thirteen years of age—his father was legally responsible for Paul's actions. During that time Paul was "alive apart from the law." [2] He had been circumcised so that he was as much a member of the covenant community as he could be without accepting his own responsibility toward the law.[3] Then when the commandment came, Paul was a "son of the commandment." Then he became responsible and sin revived (ἀνέζησεν), so Paul "died." [4] The very commandment which promised "life" to Paul, instead brought "death."[5] At Paul's bar mitzwah, when theoretically he should have been more fully accepted into the "life" of Judaism, he was also made responsible for the law which he could not keep. Therefore, he broke covenant and "died." The law was good, but sin brought death.[6] Apart from the law (from age eight days until thirteen years) sin was dead,[7] but once the commandment was accepted, then sin had an opportunity to work "death." [8] Paul then found a conflict between his reason (νοῦς) and his members (ἐν τοῖς μέλεσιν),[9] as most conscientious boys would that had been trained in all of the ascetic Levitical prohibitions. At the very time when his sex urges were most active, he was responsible to keep from having any defiling seminal emissions.[10] Paul wanted to do what the law commanded, but he could not control his members, so he was left captive to the law of sin, in need of deliverance from this body of death.[11] The deliverance he needed he found in the Christian

---

[1] According to the Gospel of Thomas 81:4-8, Jesus said that in the kingdom the old man would not hesitate to ask the child of seven days about the place of life (ⲡⲧⲟⲡⲟⲥ ⲙ̄ⲡⲱⲛϩ) and he would live (ϥⲛⲁⲱⲛϩ). The difference between conditions at the time of the author and those expected in the future kingdom was that the child of seven days, before circumcision or baptism, would have life, whereas in the author's day, life just began at eight days of age with circumcision and baptism.

[2] Rom. 7:7-8.

[3] When a boy was circumcised his father prayed that as he had been admitted into the covenant, so might he also enter the Torah (bar mitzwah), marriage canopy, and good deeds (Shab. 137b).

[4] Rom. 7:9-10.   [5] Rom. 7:10.
[6] Rom. 7:13.   [7] Rom. 7:8.
[8] Rom. 7:8.   [9] Rom. 7:22-23.
[10] Lev. 15.   [11] Rom. 7:15-24.

church.[1] This did not mean he was delivered from human passions, but that there was no condemnation for them in the Christian community.[2] Covenantal exclusivism which was fostered by Levitical laws and which nurtured asceticism also developed some derisive expressions that were used against outsiders. Two of these terms were "harlots" and "dogs."

HARLOTS AND DOGS

Descendants of Rahab.—Prostitution and adultery were both well established practices in the ancient Near East. Therefore prophetic invectives against it should not be surprising. But not all of the activity labeled adultery or harlotry makes sense in the usual understanding of these terms. Offering child sacrifice to Molech, for instance, was called harlotry (לזנות) with Molech.[3] Jeremiah, describing the faithlessness of Israel, said that she bowed down as a harlot (צעה זנה); but bowing is more the posture of a worshipper than a harlot. Jeremiah further said Judah and Israel were "harlots" who committed adultery with stone and tree.[4] Harlotry here, of course, was used metaphorically to describe idol worship. It was "whoring after strange gods" (זנה אחרי אלהי נכר) rather than women.[5] Hosea accused North Israel of playing the harlot, but the activity to which he objected was worshipping Baals,[6] idols,[7] or at the temple in Samaria.[8] Ephraim's "mingling" which was called "harlotry" involved international agreements with her "lovers," Assyria and Egypt.[9] Israel had made herself kings that were not of the seed of David who ruled from a capital in Samaria rather than Jerusalem.[10] Ezekiel's exposition on Hosea[11] interpreted Judah's faithlessness as harlotry, and like Hosea, he meant Judah's international agreements with Egypt and Assyria.[12] Judah's "lovers" were foreigners[13] who could later be expected to

---

[1] Rom. 7:23.

[2] Rom. 8:1.

[3] Lev. 20:1-5.

[4] Jer. 3:6-9.

[5] Dt. 31:16; Assump. Mos. 5:3. Shepherd of Hermas Mand. IV. i.9 said adultery referred not only to defilement of flesh but also behavior like that of the Gentiles.

[6] Hos. 2:7-8, 13; 7:16; 11:2.

[7] Hos. 4:12-13, 17.

[8] Hos. 8:5-6.

[9] Hos. 5:11-13; 7:8-11; 8:9-10; 10:13; 12:1.

[10] Hos. 8:4.   [11] Ezek. 16.

[12] Ezek. 16:26-29.   [13] Ezek. 16:32-34.

come against Judah with armies.[1] All of this amounted to breaking covenant with the Lord,[2] which meant that Judah had sinned.[3]

The use of the term "adultery" to describe worship of foreign gods,[4] or "harlotry" to describe unfaithfulness probably had its origin in sacred prostitution which was a standard practice in some neighboring religions and may even have been practiced in Israel in devotion to the Lord. Later religious leaders objected to it wherever it was practiced as the following prohibition indicates:

> "There shall not be a feminine prostitute (קדשה)
>   from the daughters of Israel;
> there shall not be a masculine prostitute (קדש)
>   from the sons of Israel.
> You shall not bring the wages of a harlot (זונה)
>   or the salary of a dog (כלב)
> into the temple of the Lord your God." [5]

The law ruled against the cult of the feminine prostitute (קדשה) who was also called a harlot (זונה), but the term was not restricted in its metaphorical use to sacred prostitution in worship. It described the faithlessness of Israelites who mingled with foreign nations and ways of worship. The law also prohibited practicing the cult of the male prostitute (קדש) who was also called a dog (כלב). Another example of that is:

> "You shall not eat any *nevelah* (that which dies of itself).
> To the stranger (גר) within your gates it shall be given—
> or, sell it to the foreigner (נכרי),
> because you are holy to the Lord your God." [6]

---

[1] Ezek. 16:39-40.

[2] Ezek. 16:59-60.

[3] The medieval Karaite, Al-Qumisi, said the "adulterers" (Mal. 3:5) were the rabbis who permitted niece marriage, a Gentile practice. See N. Wieder, *The Judaean Scrolls and Karaism* (London, c1962), 131.

[4] Philo said people who made idols were children of a harlot (ἐκ πόρνης) since they did not know their one true Father (*Decal.* II [8]), as was true of polytheists (*Spec.* I [331-332]; *Conf.* XXVIII [144-145]; *Mig.* [69]). The sons of a harlot were contrasted to the sons of God (*Conf.* XXVIII[145]), and quoted Dt. 33:2, prohibiting children of harlots to enter the congregation of the Lord.

[5] Dt. 23:17-18.

[6] Dt. 14:21.

A different version of the same basic law is:

> "You shall be holy men to me.
> Flesh in the field, *terefah* (torn by beasts),
>   you shall not eat.
> to the dogs (כלבים) you shall throw it." [1]

Flesh found dead in the field which dies of itself or is killed by beasts has not been properly slaughtered, so the saints are forbidden to eat it. Ezekiel says priests are not permitted to eat *nevelah* or *terefah*.[2] Both were classed in the same category. Deuteronomy says it should be given to the stranger or sold to the foreigner. Exodus says it should be thrown to the "dogs" which might be just an insulting way of saying it should be given or sold either to strangers or foreigners, because they, like dogs, eat anything. It is also possible that real dogs were intended by Deuteronomy, but "dogs" sometimes had a metaphorical connotation, and that usage deserves more attention.

A dog's life.—The dog as an animal was not despised in the Near East. Dogs were known for being friendly, faithful, and dependable guards.[3] The term was applied to masculine prostitutes as a tribute rather than an insult. The masculine prostitute was honored within the cult for his faithful service to the god.[4] When Israel tried to root out the practice of sacred prostitution from her community, the terms "harlot" and "dog" were both used metaphorically in contempt. The latter term may have been used as a synonym for foreigner quite early and continued through NT times. R. Judah interpreted the scriptural passage, "For you," [5] to mean

> "'For you' and not for the non-Jews (לנכרים);
> 'for you' and not for the dogs (לכלבים)." [6]

---

[1] Ex. 22:30.

[2] Ezek. 44:31.

[3] See W. G. Lambert, *Babylonian Wisdom Literature* (Oxford, 1960), 193-205; *PR* 52a; *Nat. Hist.* VIII.6 (140); Tobit 6:1; 11:4; *Praem.*, XV (89).

[4] The inscription from the temple of Astarte at Larnaka referred to "dogs" and "young ladies" as those employed by the temple (ולעלמת לעלמת בזבח [ ] לכלבים ולגרים קר 22 (3 (See H. Donner and W. Röllig, *Kanaanäische und Aramäische Inschriften* [Wiesbaden, 1964], III vols., 37: CIS I 86 AB; pl. XII; KI Nr. 29; NSI nr. 20). The "dogs" were male prostitutes.

[5] Ex. 12:16.

[6] Meg. 6b. H. Koester, "The Purpose of the Polemic of a 'Pauline Fragment,'" *NTS* 8 (1961/62), 319-320, not knowing the use of the term "dog"

In this couplet, R. Judah intended non-Jews to be labeled "dogs" in a way similar to Ex. 22: 30 or as a reasonable extension of the term once used by cults Israel disliked and wished to keep outside the community. Enoch insulted foreigners whom he called "dogs (አኅጓብ), eagles, and kites" who devoured the Israelite sheep.[1]

In an undated letter from one Jew to another, the writer said he had sent the letter with "dogs" (כלבים) who would tell the recipient about it. He assured the recipient that under the present conditions their going to someone about something would not be as though they had gone to a church (كنيسة) of idol worship, because there was no Jew there.[2] The "dogs" who would tell the recipient about something were obviously people. The church of idol worship was evidently a Christian church. The Jews in correspondence had to deal with Gentiles or Christians because there were no Jews nearby, but they did not like it and, like R. Judah, described them disrespectfully as "dogs."

It was a Gentile woman who came to Jesus asking that her daughter be healed, which prompted the reply, "It is not good to take the children's bread and throw it to the dogs (κυναρίοις)." [3] Pseudo-Clement, in reference to that passage, said it was not lawful to heal the Gentiles who were like dogs (τὰ ἔθνη, ἐοικότα κυσίν) because they ate various kinds of food [not approved by dietary laws]. This anti-Gentilic author justified Jesus' decision to heal the Syro-Phoenician's daughter, however, by claiming that when she replied that she wanted the crumbs that fell from the table, she had assured Jesus that she was living like the sons of the kingdom (τῆς βασιλείας υἱοῖς) and therefore received healing. Had she

---

in Jewish circles, mistakenly said, "The insulting address, 'dogs,' should not be used as an indication of the identity of the opponents. However, it must be kept in mind that this word was one of the strongest invective terms possible. This means that the deliberate aim of the polemics here is not to describe the opponents, but to insult them." Koester should have explained how the term "dog" got to be such an insulting word if it had no identifying significance. See also D. W. Thomas, "*Kalebh* 'dog': its Origin and Some Usages of it in the OT," *VT* 10 (1960), 410-427, and Astour, *Op. cit.*, 185-196.

[1] Enoch 90:4 (Laurence, 89:6); cf. also 89:42-49 (Laurence, 88:68-79) where the dogs were Philistines.

[2] W. H. Worrell (ed.), *Fragments from the Cairo Genizah in the Freer Collection* (New York, 1927), III, 4, 13-15 (p. 19, 21).

[3] Mt. 15:26. W. S. McCullough, "Dog" *ID* (New York, c1962), I, 862, thinks "dogs" in Mt. 15:26 = Mk. 7:27 means non-Jews.

continued to live like a Gentile (dog), Pseudo-Clement maintained that Jesus would never have healed her.[1]

One warning in the Sermon on the Mount was, "Do not give that which is holy to the dogs (κυσίν)."[2] Pseudo-Clement again interpreted this as a prohibition against missionary activity among the Gentiles: "He has received the commandment not to cast the pearls of his words before swine and dogs (*ante porcos et canes*), who, striving against them with their arguments and sophism, roll them in the mud of carnal understanding, and, by their barkings and base answers, break and exhaust those who proclaim God's word."[3] Cyril of Jerusalem said prospective Christians must be carefully examined and trained to be sure they are worthy (ἄξιος) of admission so that holy things would not be given to the "dogs" (κυσίν).[4] The Didache said those who had not been baptized were "dogs" who should not be allowed to partake of the eucharist.[5]

The continuation of derision.—It is clear that the term "dog" was used in NT times and later to refer to non-Jews, non-Christians, or Gentiles. This was true of R. Judah, the Didache, and Pseudo-Clement. Pseudo-Clement understood the NT to have given the same meaning to the term. This is not so certain, but it is possible.[6] To the extent that the term "dog" was used metaphorically and in contempt it was probably a continuation of the OT derision for foreign worship that once involved sacred prostitution. In the examples studied, the "dog" was used in contrast to the covenanter, and in some cases warnings were given not to mingle with them. The metaphorical use of the term "harlot" in the OT did not refer to Gentiles, but to Israelites that had mingled with Gentiles, either in worship or in international politics. The same might be true of the "harlots" in the NT who were classified together with the tax collectors who were Jews that mingled with the Romans. This is not so easy to ascertain as the metaphorical use of "dogs," because harlots are people whether the term is used metaphorically or not. Since there continued to be harlots in the usual sense of the term,

---

[1] *Clem. Hom.* II.xix.
[2] Mt. 7:6.
[3] *Clem. Rec.* III.i.
[4] *Cat.* 1:3.
[5] Didache 9:5.
[6] See also Mt. 21:31; Lk. 15:11-32; Phil. 3:2; II Peter 2:22; Shab. 33b.

distinctions are difficult to make, but the possibility is open for consideration. In the New Jerusalem, those who would not be admitted were dogs (κύνες), sorcerers, "masculine harlots" (πόρνοι), murderers, idolators, and liars.[1] Since all other items in the list are people, it is quite likely that the "dogs" mentioned also meant people, namely Gentiles. Since the term used for harlots has a masculine ending rather than the usual feminine term used for harlots, the "harlots" in the list may have meant the Jewish minglers who associated with Gentiles. Terms of derision, such as these, reflect the conviction that was deeply rooted in covenantal theology: the chosen people must keep themselves segregated from the peoples of the world, even when forced to live in foreign lands. This could be done more effectively if the peoples of the world were considered despicable and labeled accordingly. To some degree the observance of the Sabbath day has also helped to separate Jews from Gentiles.

Sabbath Observance

Foreign influence.—The observance of the Sabbath day did not originate in Israel. It was practiced by other nations before Israel's existence, and it was enforced with a superstitious taboo.[2] While Israel was in the wilderness it is not likely that she observed the Sabbath. Sheep had to graze seven days a week and those who earned their living as shepherds also had to work seven days a week. As late as the eighth century, B.C., the foreign practice of observing feasts, new moons, and Sabbath was resisted by Hosea[3] who considered it a Baalistic practice.[4] Perhaps an early approval of Sabbath observance is reflected in the commandment to rest on the Sabbath day "in plowing time and in harvest time."[5] Those were the seasons of the heaviest work of the year, and Israel may have conceded the Sabbath as a labor law in interest of the un-

---

[1] Rev. 22:15. Lightfoot, II, 230 says, the following quote is from Mdr. Tillin fol. 6:3. He must have used a text no longer available: אומות עולם נמשלו ככלבים. For πόρνη see T. Levi 14:5-6; Mt. 21:31-32; Lk. 15:30; Rev. 17:1, 5, 15-16; 19:2; see also Rev. 2:14, 20; 17:2; 18-3, 9.

[2] H. and J. Lewy, "The Origin of the Week and the Oldest West Asiatic Calendar," *HUCA*, 17 (1942/43), 1-152c. See especially 105. Also Lambert, *Op. cit.*, 39.

[3] Hos. 2:11.

[4] Hos. 2:13.

[5] Ex. 34:21.

employed. In the same chapter which commended Sabbath observance are also rules for dealing fairly with others. The covenanter
was warned not to reap all of his field or pick all of his grapes. These
must be left for the poor and the sojourner.[1] In a land where there
were always poor people and unemployed men, this was the way
the community provided some opportunity for them. Sabbath
observance would also have had the same effect whether intended
or not—especially during the heavy working seasons. Sowing and
reaping had to be done within certain limits of time. The farmer
who could not do this work alone within the necessary limits had
to hire more help. The requirement that the farmer also observe
the Sabbath during those seasons made it necessary for him to
hire still more unemployed men. Further evidence for relating the
Sabbath institution in Israel with labor regulation is the list of
people commanded not to work: sons, daughters, servants, and
beasts of burden. The farmer was also forbidden to work, but
his wife was not.[2] Her work may not have been closely enough
related to production of crops to have seriously effected the labor
situation.

   This is all conjectural, based only on a few facts such as these:
1) the institution was old and probably practiced in Canaan before
Israel's conquest; 2) it was resisted by Hosea who associated it
with Canaanite Baal worship; 3) probably the earliest commandment accepted by Israel was to be enforced only during heavy
working seasons; 4) wives were not forbidden to work on the Sabbath; and 5) Israel had other laws designed to help the poor, the
stranger, and the unemployed.

   The foot in the door.—Between the Assyrian captivity and the
Babylonian captivity, prophets seem to have reversed their position
on the Sabbath. Not only was it permitted, but it was commanded
for every week of the year. Death penalties were inflicted for its
infraction.[3] Jeremiah interpreted his whole eschatology of Israel
in relationship to the Babylonian captivity and return as a Sabbath
rest, which meant peaceful existence as free citizens on the land.
In Leviticus the warning given, probably after the captivity,

---

[1] Lev. 19:9-10.
[2] Dt. 5:13-14.
[3] Ex. 31:14; 35:2; Num. 15:32-36. It is not certain that these decrees
were formulated between the Assyrian and Babylonian captivities.

promised captivity for the number of years the land had not been given its scheduled sabbath rests.[1] The captivity following Jeremiah's prophecy probably increased the importance of the Sabbath to Israel, if it had not been so established beforehand.[2] In Babylon it also probably developed into a day of congregation and study as well as rest. By that time, it had also some of the same religious taboos attached to it as other nations knew.

Man for the Sabbath.—During the Babylonian captivity, the Sabbath was probably a very meaningful day for the Jew; later it sometimes became a burden. In the second century B.C., Jews allowed themselves to be killed on the Sabbath rather than fight or flee on that day.[3] Some Jews in NT times were allowed to pull a sheep out of a pit on the Sabbath,[4] but others were not.[5] Two thousand cubits from camp was the farthest distance a Jew could walk on the Sabbath,[6] whereas some were restricted to one thousand.[7] Because of these restrictions, the evangelist hoped that the destruction of Jerusalem would not be on the Sabbath when Jews could flee no farther than the Mt. of Olives.[8] Some Jews did not even get out of bed on the Sabbath.[9] Jesus broke the Sabbath when he healed on that day,[10] and his disciples offended others when they plucked grain on the Sabbath.[11] Care had to be taken not to begin any labor that would have to be continued on the Sabbath.[12] Taboos associated with beginning labor on Friday have continued as superstitions among Christians who no longer observe the Sabbath on Saturday. Some are: "If you begin a task on Friday, you will never finish it." In opposition to moving on Friday is the warning "Friday flit, short sit." [13]

---

[1] Lev. 26:34-35.
[2] So also Klausner, *Op. cit.*, 173.
[3] I Mac. 2:29-38.
[4] Mt. 12:11-12.
[5] CDC 11:36.
[6] 1QM 7:7.
[7] CDC 11:28.
[8] Mt. 24:20.
[9] Hippolytus, *Philosophumena* IX. lx. 25.
[10] Mt. 12:10-14.
[11] Mk. 2:23-27.
[12] San. 35a.
[13] This proverb makes best sense in Semitic thought forms in which "sit" and "dwell" are expressed by the same word.

To be and not to be.—So extensive were the minute developments related to Sabbath observance that there are two tractates, Shabbath and Erubin, in the Mishnah, Tosefta, and Talmud, which explain ways to continue planned activity on the Sabbath without breaking the letter of the law. A man might plan the day before and walk nearly two thousand cubits from his house and there make an *erub*, which technically made that spot his property. He was then allowed to walk that far, come to his *erub*, and since he was still on his property, he might walk another two thousand cubits. Neighbors could declare their property common, so that for the Sabbath day, a long line of properties was considered as one. Therefore any person from any of these houses was permitted to walk to the end of their joint property and then walk two thousand cubits farther on the Sabbath. Since in the ancient Near East there was no distinction between religious and community laws, laws that had some beneficial purposes sometimes became laden with details of interpretation which later had no purpose. If they were community laws only, they could have been dropped, but since they are enforced with divine commandments and taboos, they sometimes become burdensome. Then many kinds of manipulative legislation were required to counteract the law without interfering with the taboo.

SUMMARY

The previous chapters were closely related to the land of the promise. This chapter, however, has dealt mostly with rules that could be observed in the diaspora. These were the personal laws governing purity which was compared with other types of sin. Rules dealing with sex, discharges, and consumption of food were seen to have far reaching implications. When it was wrong to touch objects as well as to perform intentionally violent acts, life became circumscribed to known objects and persons who also observed the same rules. Not only did these rules provide the basis for asceticism and probably the doctrine of original sin, but they nurtured the type of self-consciousness and feelings of guilt that Paul expressed. Wherever these rules originated, they were understood as requirements of the covenant and probably were intensified in Babylon and other diaspora experiences during which Israel concentrated on ridding herself of every sin so that the land might be restored. It was impossible to keep from breaking many of the numerous rules under which covenanters were bound, so it was necessary to have ways of receiving atonement and cleansing from offenses and impurities that had stained the community. These will be considered in the next chapter.

CHAPTER SIX

COVENANTAL PROVISIONS
FOR FORGIVENESS AND RECONCILIATION

INTRODUCTION

Whenever an Israelite committed some Levitical or Deuteronomic offense, an obstacle was placed between himself and the Lord, on the one hand, and himself and the community, on the other. Whether he stole property belonging to a fellow Israelite, broke the Sabbath regulations, or unknowingly walked over a grave, he was in disfavor with the Almighty and needed some means by which he could find remission and reconciliation. There were specified ways for dealing with each situation. Objects that had been defiled could be broken, burned, or washed, depending on the object. Persons who had sinned or defiled themselves could either be atoned by the priest, cleansed by bathing, or both, depending on the act. This chapter will consider first repeated cleansings from various types of ritual impurity, second, special baptisms related to initiation and cleansings from defilement at birth, and third, the conditions whereby sin could be forgiven on the Day of Atonement.

RITUAL CLEANSINGS

Objects and persons.—Meat from peace offerings and thanksgiving offerings had to be eaten on the days immediately after they were offered. After the first day, thanksgiving offerings had to be burned with fire. After two days the peace offering was considered impure (פגול), and was also required to be burned.[1] Any meat that touched anything unclean (טמא) was burned,[2] and any person who ate of peace offerings while he was defiled was "cut off" from his people.[3] Also the Israelites who ate meat from animals not properly slaughtered were "cut off" from the community.[4] This is somewhat like lepers who were made to leave camp[5] until they were

---

[1] Lev. 7:15-18; 19:6-8.
[2] Lev. 7:19.
[3] Lev. 7:19-21.
[4] Lev. 7:22-27.
[5] Lev. 13:46.

pronounced clean by the priest, except for these offenses no provision was made to restore those who were "cut off" to the community. Garments could be cleansed from defilement by washing,[1]
as was true of objects of wood or skin, any sack or vessel. They
were washed or put in water as soon as they became defiled and
they remained unclean until evening. An earthen vessel that became
defiled was broken.[2] After battle, all objects of metal or other
material that could stand fire were passed through fire. Goods
that would burn were purified with sprinkling water.[3] Garments
that were leprous were washed under certain conditions, but under
more extreme cases they were burned.[4] When a house was leprous,[5]
the priest commanded that the stones be removed and put in an
unclean place, the plaster scraped off, new stones replaced, and
the house replastered. If the "disease" continued, the house was
broken down, and its parts carried to an unclean place.[6] The priest
determined whether or not any person or object was leprous. He
also supervised the cleansing which involved the proper sacrifices
as well as the methods listed above. The land was cleansed by the

---

[1] Ex. 19:10, 14; Lev. 11:32; 15:16, 21-22, 27.

[2] Lev. 11:33-35; 15:12.

[3] Num. 31:21-23.

[4] Lev. 13:47-59. It is interesting to note that John baptized with water
and promised that Jesus would baptize with the Holy Spirit and fire (Mt.
3:11). In the prayer for mourners for Zion, the worshipper affirmed, "For
you, O Lord, destroyed it [the temple] with fire. With fire you will rebuild it."
(Singer, 59-60). According to Büchler, "The Levitical Impurity of the Gentile," *JQR*, n.s. 17 (1926-27), 48, fn. 139, Samaritans purified the ground on
which Christians and Jews walked—with fire. Bagatti, *L'Eglise de la Circoncision*, tr. A. Storme (Jerusalem, 1965), 197, thinks baptism with fire
referred to branding a cross permanently on the foreheads of Christians with
a hot iron. The context of baptism with water as over against baptism with
fire seems to be analogous to the Levitical cleansing of objects taken as booty
in war. Those that could stand fire were made to pass through fire; those
that could not were baptized in water. Amos (1:7, 10, 11, 14; 2:2, 5) used the
figure "fire" to mean war.
The idea that John's (and therefore Christian) baptism differed from sectarian baptism because it was a "once for all" baptism in contrast to sectarian repeated washings continues to be affirmed with no new evidence
for its support. One recent advocate is J. Pryke, "Baptism and Communion
in the Light of Qumran," *RQ* 5 (1966), 546. Some Christians, at least, were
expected to continue practicing ablutions after the "once for all" Christian
initiation, wheras various Jewish sects that continued to use ablutions also
probably used only one "once for all" baptism for initiation of new members.

[5] Which probably meant "mouldy."

[6] Lev. 14:33-35.

Lord driving the people who were unclean off the land or the community "cutting off" the unclean members from the community.[1] The fruit of a tree was considered "uncircumcised" for the first three years. This may have meant that it was left unpruned for that length of time, but the reason "uncircumcised" was used to describe this condition is uncertain. During the first three years, the fruit was not allowed to be eaten.[2] Fruit from the fourth year was given as first fruits. This was probably in the background of the parable of the farmer who was impatient to find that his fig tree had not produced after three years.[3] The first three years would have netted him no profits, anyway, but after the fourth year, the produce was his.[4] By that time, his own interests were at stake.

The cleanness or defilement of objects, houses, corpses, or garments were important to Israelites only because they might defile persons or places, where persons lived. It was generally believed that the Lord would not be present with his people when they or their surroundings were defiled.[5] The person who was meticulous to see that every object in his house was properly cleansed whenever it became defiled was much less likely to become defiled himself from touching unclean objects. Even if he were free from touching unclean things, he could still become defiled from his own bodily discharges or from contact with some defiled person. Therefore it was more important that there be rules for cleansing persons than objects.

Cleansing from contacts.—A person who touched any object, beast, bird, fish, insect that was unclean for touching, or any person who had become defiled to the extent that he could defile others was considered unclean from the moment of contact until evening. If he had bathed his body in water before evening, then he would be considered clean at evening.[6] Ashes from a red heifer were necessary for some cleansing ceremonies, but the priest who

---

[1] Lev. 18:24-30.

[2] Lev. 19:23.

[3] Lk. 13:6-9. But unless he transplanted a fig tree he should not have expected fruit within three years, anyway.

[4] Lev. 19:25.

[5] Later rabbis declared, however, that the Shekinah would dwell with Israel even when Israelites were unclean (טומאתם) (Yoma 56b).

[6] Lev. 15:4-12; 22:5-6.

officiated, the man who actually burned the heifer outside the
city, and the man who gathered the ashes of the heifer, were all
required to wash their clothes and bathe their bodies. The men
who burned the heifer and gathered the ashes were unclean until
evening, but the priest was cleansed at once and therefore admitted
into camp immediately after bathing and washing his garments.[1]
The person who touched a corpse or entered a dwelling where a
man had died before the tent had been purified was required to
bathe on the third day and the seventh day and remain defiled for
seven days. He was also required to be sprinkled with water from
a spring or flowing stream mixed with ashes from the red heifer,
both on the third and seventh days, by someone who was not
defiled, and on the seventh day, he had to wash his garments as
well [2] and be unclean until evening. If a man had a running discharge he was unclean for seven days after the discharge stopped.[3]
On the seventh day he washed his clothes, bathed his body in water
from a stream or spring, and was unclean until that evening. On
the eighth day he was required to present two turtle doves or two
young pigeons to the priest, one for a sin offering and one for a
burnt offering, after which he was atoned for his discharge.[4] Any
man who had intercourse with a woman during her menstrual
period was unclean for seven days also.[5] The man who had a
seminal discharge was required to bathe his whole body and be
unclean until evening. If the discharge came while he was having
intercourse, the woman involved was also required to bathe and
be unclean until evening. If any of their garments or skins came in
contact with semen, they had to be washed and were unclean until
evening.[6] A woman during her menstrual period was treated in
exactly the same way as the man with the seminal discharge except
that she was considered unclean for seven days.[7] If her discharge
continued many days, she was treated like the man with the
running discharge. She was unclean during the period of her
discharge and for seven days after that. Then she took two turtle

---

[1] Num. 19:1:10.

[2] Num. 19:11-19; 31:19-20, 24.

[3] Toh. 8:2-5.

[4] Lev. 15:1-3, 13-15. The importance of being clean at evening was for
evening prayer and also for sexual intercourse.

[5] Lev. 15:24.

[6] Lev. 15:16-18; also Ber. 3:5-6.

[7] Lev. 15:19.

doves or two young pigeons to the priest for her atonement on
the eighth day, after which she was atoned.[1] After the birth of a
son, the mother was unclean for seven days and for a daughter,
for fourteen days.[2] After that time, she brought her gift to the
priest, a lamb for a burnt offering and a turtle dove or a young
pigeon for a sin offering.[3] If she could not afford a lamb, she
offered instead another pigeon or turtle dove.[4] This whole psychol-
ogy and cleansing was closely related to the baptismal cleansing
of adults before being admitted into a sect in Judaism or Christianity.

ADULT BAPTISM

Ritual baptism for priests and laymen.—Oddly enough, no
mention was made in Lev. 12 or 15 of the necessity for a woman
to bathe her body and wash her garments after a period of
uncleanness, but this certainly was required. Water was regularly
used for cleansing purposes for a person who had been defiled in
some way. When David noticed Bathsheba from his palace roof,
she was bathing (רחצת)[5] or sanctifying herself from her menstrual
impurity (מתקדשת מטמאתה).[6] Rabbis assumed that immersion
was required,[7] and that it should take place after sunset, i.e. at
the beginning of the eighth day.[8] On special occasions when cere-
monial purity was necessary, people washed their garments and
bathed their bodies for the occasion, just in case they may have
been defiled. Thus when Moses sanctified the people (ויקדש את העם),[9]
they washed (ויכבסו) their garments and were told not to touch
women.[10] On the Day of Atonement the high priest was required
to immerse himself five times and also to "sanctify his hands and
his feet" (קדש ידיו ורגליו).[11] Priests were always required to bathe

---

[1] Lev. 15:25-30.
[2] Lev. 12:1-5.
[3] Lev. 12:6-7.
[4] Lev. 12:8.
[5] II Sam. 11:2.
[6] II Sam. 11:4; see also Toh. 8:5.
[7] Ned. 4:3; Ber. 3:6.
[8] Sifra 78a-78b; see also Yoma 88a.
[9] Ex. 19:14; cf. 19:10.
[10] Ex. 19:14-15; Philo, *De Decalogo* X (45), says they also bathed. He
probably deduced this in the same way the rabbis did.
[11] Yoma 3:6; 4:5; 7:3,4; Parah 3:8; cf. Yoma 3:2; and 1QS 3:4-9.

and change their garments before entering the holy of holies.[1]
Especially when the temple was not standing or believed by some
Jews to be defiled, laymen observed the same strictness in their
homes as priests in relationship to the sanctuary. Without the
normal function of the priests in the temple it was necessary for
all believers to act as priests in matters of purity. Josephus'
instructor, Banus, for instance, washed frequently, by day or night,
for purity's sake, whether or not he was defiled.[2] Essenes bathed
(ἀπολούονται) so as to be ritually clean (καθαροί) before each meal.[3]
Some rabbis commanded that a person must wash his hands,
feet, and face daily.[4] The Sibyl called mortals to wash their whole
bodies in everflowing streams, praying for forgiveness of their
former deeds. If this were done, God's anger might be turned
away.[5] Marqah said it was immersion that cleansed from all
uncleanness and blotted out all sin (מצבוע מדכי מכל טמא ומחי לכל
חוב).[6] Rabbis promised that the Lord would cleanse Israel, just
as the immersion pool (מקוה) cleansed the unclean.[7] R. Tanḥuma
said the immersion pool (מקוה) was for the water of repentance
(למי שיבא).[8]

Baptism and hospitality customs.—In purifying from ritual
defilement the three most frequently allied demands were: 1)
bathing, 2) washing garments, and 3) waiting a prescribed length
of time. These were so frequently required together that the rabbis
concluded that even though Moses did not say that the children of
Israel should bathe before washing their garments [9] it was certainly
done. Their reasoning was that there was no case in the Torah
where washing of garments was prescribed without the accom-

---

[1] Ox. Pap. 840:18-29; T. Levi 9:11; Middoth 1:9; Ex. 29:4-9; Lev.
8:1-13. Philo (*Spec.* 1[230]) said the true high priest was free from sins (ἀμέτοχος
ἁμαρτημάτων) by which he apparently meant that he was not defiled
(κοινός = טמא). Care was taken to see that he was free from *defilement*,
but had he been free from *sin* he would not have had to offer a bull as an
offering for his sins (Lev. 16:3, 6; Yoma 3:8; Heb. 5:1-3).

[2] *Vita* ii (10-12).

[3] *BJ* II (129).

[4] Shab. 50b.

[5] *SO* 4:165-169

[6] *Memar Marqah* VI § 6.

[7] Yoma 8:9.

[8] Tanḥuma *Ḥayyê Śarâh* 61b.

[9] Ex. 19:14-15.

panying requirements of immersion (טעון טבילה). Since even in cases where washing of garments was not legislated, bathing was required, in those places where washing of garments was specified, immersion was understood.[1]

A covenanter who was very careful about his own purity (i.e. a חבר or other person who was נאמן) could not admit into his own house a person who may have been defiled or whose garments contained some defilement. If he had, then the objects of his house that the guest touched would become defiled and his own purity would be difficult, if not impossible, to maintain. Neither could he enter a house whose purity was uncertain, lest he sit on objects that were defiled, eat food that was defiled, or become tainted in some way.[2] If a man was careful about ritual purity but his wife was not, then a person who wanted to maintain ritual cleanliness could buy produce from the husband but not accept hospitality the wife provided. If, on the other hand, the wife was a careful observant, another observant could accept the hospitality of the family that the wife provided but was not permitted to buy the goods her husband sold.[3] An observant Jew (חבר) was forbidden to admit a less observant Jew ('am haaretz) into his home *in the less observant Jew's own clothing.*[4] This precaution was taken so that the guest's clothing did not touch anything in the house. The qualification, "in his own clothing," indicates that there were cases when an 'am haaretz was admitted into the house of a haver (חבר). Since the caution was against midras uncleanness, he could be admitted if he were bathed and wore clean garments. The text does not specify bathing, but the logic would follow that the guest would have to bathe or he would defile his host's garments, having touched his own garments and possibly having defiled them in the first place. The Essenes bathed and changed their own garments every time they entered the dining hall, just to be sure that the area surrounding the food was not defiled and perhaps to gain merit for excessive righteousness.[5] The relationship, then, between bathing, changing garments, and being admitted into a house was a custom that developed in the interests of ritual purity and

---

[1] Mekilta *Baḥodesh* 3:28-32; Yeb. 46b.
[2] Demai 2:3.
[3] T. Demai 4:9 (49-50).
[4] Demai 2:3.
[5] See also Ezek. 42:14; 44:15-19.

was easily transferred from the etiquette of the private home to
the community center.[1] This probably accounts for the ceremony
of adult baptism in the first place. The fact that early Christianity
required baptism but not circumcision may show a closer relationship to sectarian practice than to Gentile proselytization. The less
observant, circumcised Jew, wanting to become a proselyte to the
sect, was required to bathe and change his garments upon admission
into the community. The Gentile would first have been circumcised
before his bath to be admitted. Since existence within the covenant
community meant "life," being baptized upon admission was
passing from death into life or being born anew.

Proselyte baptism.—The rabbis said that the Gentile proselyte
who separated himself from his foreskin was as one who separated
himself from the grave.[2] This may have had a double meaning:
Since the word "foreskin" also meant uncircumcised, it may refer
to separation from his former contacts with Gentiles who were
considered "dead." Another possible or additional significance
might be that his foreskin was treated like a corpse from which
he was defiled and would require the normal prescription for
corpse uncleanness before being admitted into the community.[3]
Every proselyte began life in the new community as a child born
that day (כבן יומו).[4] When he became a proselyte, he was born
again.[5] These terms were even understood to apply to the first
covenanters at Mt. Sinai: "R. Berachiah says, 'Why do they call
Sinai, "My mother's house"?—because from there Israel was
made (נעשו) like a child born that day (כתינוק בן יומו) . . . Just as
the danger passed your mother bore you; just as pain passed over
you, you were made a new creature (ברייה חדשה).'" [6] Proselytes
entered the covenant by circumcision, a bath of purification
(בטבילה), and a gift.[7] The gift was to take the place of such sacri-

---

[1] See Ox. Pap. 840:18-29.
[2] Eduyoth 5:2; Pes. 8:8; Pes. 92a.
[3] Num. 19:14-19. Sprinkling of infants on the third day may reflect the
practice of sprinkling on the third and seventh days as Numbers prescribed
for corpse uncleanness (Shab. 9:3). If this were so, however, it is strange
that no mention is made also of the seventh day. See further Büchler, *Op. cit.*,
17, 80-81.
[4] Gerim 2:5; Yeb. 48b.
[5] Jn. 3:1-10.   [6] Cant. R. 8:2, 5.
[7] According to Ex. R. 23:12, circumcision is a witness that Israelites
are clean in the same way that a woman is clean after her immersion from
menstrual uncleanness.

fices as the two turtle doves or the two young pigeons required
of a Levitically unclean person,[1] which further relates proselyte
baptism to Levitical purification. Some rabbis did not require the
offering.[2] One who became a proselyte the day before Passover
by being circumcised could immerse himself and eat the Passover.[3]
If shreds of his circumcision remained, he had to be circumcised
again. Except for Passover, it was customary for the wound of
circumcision to heal before baptism.[4] The circumcision had to be
performed so as to cause the blood of the covenant to be shed.
If blood did not flow, the circumcision was considered ineffective.[5]
Therefore, according to these rabbis, baptism and circumcision
were the essential requirements for admission into the covenant
community.[6] The gift might be passed over as of secondary
importance and some rabbis said circumcision might not even be
required, but baptism was always essential.[7] After baptism, the
proselyte, like the woman cleansed from her menstrual period,[8]
was in a state of sanctification.[9] In some contemporary Christian
groups, the practice was first to anoint the proselyte with the holy
oil (ἐλαίῳ ἁγίῳ) and second to baptize him with water (βαπτίσεις
ὕδατι). The final step of initiation was to seal him with myrrh
(τελευταῖον σφαγίσεις μύρῳ). Anointing was to admit the initiate
to the Holy Spirit; water was a symbol of death, and myrrh was
the seal of the covenants (σφραγὶς τῶν συνθηκῶν). But if there was
no oil or myrrh, water was sufficient to serve the purpose of all
three.[10]

Defilement and Gentiles.—Rowley said that for Jews baptism
was more than Levitical ablution, but had no *ex opere operato*

---

[1] Lev. 12:6-8; 14:1-7, 19-32; 15:13-15, 29-30.
[2] Gerim 2:4-5; see also Yeb. 46b; Ker. 9a; Philo, *De Decalogo* ii (11).
[3] Eduyoth 5:2; Pes. 8:8; 92a; Kid. 70a: Mekilta, *Pisḥa* 15:121-125.
[4] Yeb. 47b.
[5] Shab. 137b; Yeb. 71 a.
[6] Yeb. 46a; see also D. Daube, *The NT and Rabbinic Judaism*, 108-109.
[7] Yeb. 46b; 47; Ker. 9a; AZ 57a; Shab. 135a; see also T.F. Torrence,
"Proselyte Baptism," *NTS* 1 (1954-55), 150-154; H. H. Rowley, "Jewish
Proselyte Baptism and the Baptism of John," *HUCA* 15 (1940), 313-334.
[8] II Sam. 11:4.
[9] Keth. 4:3; Yeb. 11:2; T. Bek. 6:3 (540); T. Yeb. 12:2 (254); San. 57b,
58a; Yeb. 42a, 98a; Cyprian, *Epist.* 64:2
[10] *Apos. Cons.* VII (Schaff, p. 275-276); see also Cyril of Jerusalem, *Baptism*
I, 1-III. 5.

efficacy.[1] He did not show good reasons for thinking that it was non-Levitical or that it had no *ex opere operato* efficacy. Levitical rules, if followed explicitly, were expected to cleanse from defilement.[2] This was *ex opere operato*, so that there was no real contrast between Levitical ablutions, on the one hand, and *ex opere operato* ablutions on the other, as Rowley implied. Neither is there a clear reason for discarding the close relationship between proselyte baptism and Levitical cleansing. Daube said that proselyte baptism "was essentially quite outside the Levitical sphere: pagans were not susceptible of Levitical uncleanness, so in principle there was simply no room for purification." [3] In support of that position were assertions that blood stains from Gentiles are clean;[4] Gentiles, their clothes, nor their houses are susceptible to uncleanness from leprosy signs,[5] and they are not defiled by the house of a leper. This tempts the conclusion that Gentiles were judged undefiled, but the data are not uniform. On the other side of the scale is the fact that Gentiles, because of their uncleanness, were not admitted into the temple: Antiochus III decreed that no foreigner (ἀλλόφυλος) or Jew who was not properly sanctified (ἀγνισθεῖσαν) was permitted to enter the temple.[6] Herod's temple had four courts. Foreigners (*alienigenae*; ἀλλόφυλοι; ἀλλοεθνῆ) and women not defiled by menstrual uncleanness were admitted to the outer court only. The next court admitted all Jews who were not defiled (*cum essent ab omni pollutione munaei*). The third admitted only Jewishmales who had been properly purified (*mundi existentes atque purificati*), and the sanctuary was limited to priests who were undefiled.[7] Titus accused the defenders of the temple of having defiled it by foreign blood

---

[1] Rowley, *Op. cit.*, 313-334.

[2] See *Ant.* XVIII.v.2 and Pseudo-Phocylides 228-229 for attempts at spiritualization.

[3] Daube, *Op. cit.*, 107. Also R.J.Z. Werblowsky, "On the Baptismal Rite According to St. Hippolytus," *Studia Patristica* II.ii. ed. K. Aland and F.L. Cross (Berlin, 1957), 95. Werblowsky, however, has since changed his mind on this point.

[4] Ned. 4:3; 7:3.

[5] Neg. 3:1; 11:1; 12:1; T. Neg. 7:10.

[6] Ant. XX (145).

[7] *Contra Apion* II (103-104); *BJ* V (193-221, 227). The admission of foreigners but not menstruating women meant foreigners were not susceptible to *this* type of uncleanness. If they were susceptible to no uncleanness, they should not have been forbidden entrance to the temple for purity reasons, as seems to have been the case according to this report of defilement and exclusions from the areas of the temple.

(αἵματι ξένῳ).[1] The high priest's vestments that were stored by the Romans were purified before they were worn, evidently because they had been touched by Gentiles, but maybe just as a special precautionary measure.[2] A person who worked in a mill in close contact with a Gentile or a woman defiled by menstrual impurity must consider his garments defiled by midras uncleanness.[3] When, on the Day of Atonement, the spittle of an Arabic king fell on the clothes of the high priest, the high priest's brother ministered in his place because the high priest's garments were treated as if defiled.[4] R. Naḥman said the schools of Hillel and Shammai decreed that daughters of Gentiles should be considered defiled from menstrual impurity from their cradle, that a Gentile boy was classed as one who caused defilement by seminal discharge from the day of his birth,[5] and that a Gentile child was considered defiled by gonorrhea.[6] Implements received from a Gentile must be cleansed either by heat or immersion. After mingling with Gentiles it is necessary to be immersed when leaving the defilement of the Gentiles to enter the sanctification of Israel (שיצאו מטומאת הגוי ונכנסו לקדושת ישראל).[7]

The rabbis could not decide whether a Gentile woman who had been immersed after defilement was clean or not.[8] The practical problem was that the Torah had no legislation saying that Gentiles were unclean at all, yet Israel was expected to keep separate from Gentiles just as from defiled Israelites. Therefore it was natural to treat Gentiles *as if* they were defiled. The high priest acted *as if* the Arabic king's spittle had been defiling; one who touched a Gentile at work was just as defiled *as if* he had touched a menstruant woman; Gentile girls were treated *as if* they were menstruants from the cradle although they were not; Gentile boys were treated *as if* they caused defilement by seminal discharges from birth, although they did not; all Gentile children were treated *as if* they were infected with gonorrhea, even though

---

[1] *BJ* VI (126).
[2] *Ant.* XVIII (93-94).
[3] T. Toh. 6:11.
[4] T. Yoma 4(3):20; Yoma 47a.
[5] AZ 36b.
[6] Shab. 17b.
[7] JAZ 45b. See also G. Alon, *Studies in Jewish History* (Hebrew) (Israel, 1957), II, 121-147.
[8] Nid. 43a-43b.

they were not. Those associating with Gentiles became defiled by
"Gentile uncleanness" (מטומאת הגוי) even though the Torah defined
no such defilement.

There seems to have been a ready transfer from the priestly
practice of bathing and changing clothes before entering the temple,[1]
the practice of an observant Jew requiring the less observant
Jewish guest to change garments, probably after bathing, the
Essene practice of full members bathing and changing garments
before eating, and the practice of baptism and a change of garments
for initiates into sects before admitting them to the table fellowship.
Since the first practices were motivated by Levitical purity, probably
the same observant communities required baptism for admission
for purity reasons also. The exact relationship of these customs
and their development is not completely clear since source material
has come from different sects of Judaism and Christianity whose
practices probably developed in different ways. Furthermore the
literature was written by and for people who understood the
practices, so they did not have to spell out all of the details or
reasons. Customs also continued after reasons were forgotten.
In Christianity, however, there are still more reasons for relating
adult baptism to Levitical cleansing practices.

Baptism and a change of garments.—Vermès noted the following
parallels between Paul's doctrine of baptism and the Jewish
belief about circumcision: 1) Just as the newborn child enters the
covenant by circumcision, so the newborn child enters the Christian
community of the new covenant by baptism; 2) just as circumcision
is the external sign of membership of the covenant, so baptism is
the 'seal' of faith for Christians; 3) just as circumcision of the flesh
is a symbol of the circumcised heart, so baptism is a circumcision
not made with hands.[2] Grail observed that the Greek world of
Paul's day seldom used the expression, "putting on," or "being

---

[1] *Ox. Pap.* 840:18-29; T. Levi 9:11; Mid. 1:9; Ex. 29:4-9; Lev. 8:1-13.
[2] Rom. 2:28-29; Philo, *Spec.* 1:6; col. 2:11; Vermès, "Baptism and
Jewish Exegesis; New Light from Ancient Sources," *NTS* 4 (1957/58), 308.
J. Gnilka, "Die Essenischen Tauchbäder und die Johannestaufe," *RQ*
3 (1961), 185-207, said John the Baptist's baptism was once for all baptism,
but not proselyte baptism. It was for Jews to become the holy remnant.
J.A.T. Robinson, "The Baptism of John and the Qumran Community,"
HTR 50 (1957), 175-191, said John's baptism may have been repeated
abluti ons a ld that later Jewish sects baptized many times. See also p. 195, fn. 4.

clothed with." Yet he noted correctly that Paul used the idiom as if it were familiar to his readers. Grail concluded that it was a term familiar to the LXX with which Paul was familiar.[1] Grail did not call attention to a single Levitical reference dealing with the changing of garments after defilement, but this is a necessary part of the picture. Just as the unobservant Jew had to put on the garments of his host if he were to be admitted into the home of an observant Jew,[2] so Paul told the Galatians, who were then sons of God,[3] that those who had been baptized into Christ had put on Christ (Χριστὸν ἐνεδύσασθε).[4] Hebrews who had been baptized "into Moses" became members of the body governed by the laws of Moses.[5] Those baptized "into Christ" became members of the body of Christ, the new covenant. They became Christians.

In Judaism, baptism was required for a woman; baptism and circumcision for a man; and a gift from both. There were circumstances whereby a slave might obtain his freedom by being baptized. If he had been baptized before his master, who was becoming a proselyte, was baptized, then he was set free. If, while in the water, he should declare that he had been baptized so as to become a free man, he was free if he did not have any bonds on him at the time. Masters who wanted their proselyte slaves to continue as slaves held them firmly during the ceremony. They loosened the chains around their necks so that no part of the skin was protected from being washed, but they immediately tightened them again before they could declare their intention to become free men. As soon as they raised their heads up above the water, a bucket full of clay was placed on each slave's head to maintain his status as a slave. He was then ordered to take the clay to his master's house.[6] The ceremony for admitting slaves, freemen, and women into Judaism was quite different. Christians under Paul's jurisdiction, however, had no formula or assurance that membership in the Christian community put an end to their slavery.[7] Therefore the same ceremony was used for all: males who had already been circumcised,

---

[1] A. Grail, "Le Baptême dans l'Épître aux Galates," *RB* 58 (1951), 503-520.
[2] Demai 2:3. Or, hypothetically, he could enter naked.
[3] Cf. Dt. 14:1.
[4] Gal. 3:26-27.
[5] I Cor. 10:1-2.
[6] Yeb. 46a; see also Mekilta, *Pisḥa* 15:121-125 and Yeb. 47b.
[7] I Cor. 7:21-24; Col. 4:7-17; Philemon.

males who had not been circumcised,[1] slaves, and females—all were
admitted with the same ritual of baptism. Therefore Paul could
say that there was neither Jew nor Greek, neither slave nor free,
neither male nor female, for they were all one in Christ Jesus,[2]
and heirs according to the promise of Abraham. This did not mean
that males stopped being males or slaves stopped being slaves,
but that all were admitted by the same ceremony. Those who were
in Christ had been washed and sanctified;[3] therefore they were
warned to avoid fellowship with unbelievers and idolators, being
careful to cleanse themselves from every defilement of body and
spirit so that they might be perfect in holiness in the fear of God.[4]
Colossians were initiated into Christianity by a circumcision not
made with hands, through which they put off the body of flesh
just as effectively as Jews removed the foreskin.[5] This was done by
putting to death immorality, passion, evil desire, and covetousness.
They put away anger, malice, and foul talk.[6] This was done just
the way a person discarded an old garment. So they put off the
old man (ἀπεκδυσάμενοι τὸν παλαιὸν ἄνθρωπον)[7] when they were
buried with Christ in baptism and raised with him through faith.[8] In
that ceremony, those who had been "dead" in their trespasses and
uncircumcision of their flesh as Gentiles, God made alive together
with Christ by acceptance into the Christian community. At that
time their sins were forgiven,[9] and they put on the new (ἐνδυσάμενοι
τὸν νέον) man, being renewed in the image of their creator.[10] The
baptized Christians who were then alive, raised, forgiven, and
dressed in a new nature, were urged to put on (ἐνδύσασθε) compas-
sion, kindness, lowliness, meekness, and long suffering[11] to show

---

[1] I Cor. 7:17-19.
[2] Gal. 2:28-29; Col. 3:11; see also Eph. 2.
[3] I Cor. 6:11.
[4] II Cor. 7:1; also Eph. 5:1-20.
[5] II Cor. 2:11.
[6] Col. 3:5-8.
[7] Col. 3:9. The sin of Adam was closely allied to the "old man" or old
garment removed and replaced at baptism. Symbolism is taken too literally by
D. Noltat, "Symbolismes Batismaux chez Saint Paul," *Lumière et Vie* 26
(1956), 72; "En 'revêtant le Christ,' le néophyte devient réellement 'un'
avec lui; non par fiction juridique, mais par communication de vie."
[8] Col. 2:12; see also Eph. 2:5-6.
[9] Col. 2:13-14.
[10] Col. 3:10.
[11] Col. 3:12-17.

that they were the elect and beloved ones of God, the saints
(ἅγιοι).[1] This passage [2] contrasted the existence of the Colossians
as dead, sinful, uncircumcised, and immoral before their baptism.
Then they put off these "old garments," were baptized, forgiven,
cleansed, and dressed in new garments, that were the characteristic
uniforms of the new community, which was considered holy, elect,
and beloved of God. The members were raised and alive in the new
covenant. Using the same metaphor, Paul described the resurrection as a time when the perishable nature would put on the imperish-
able and the mortal would put on immortality.[3] Optatus of Mileue
(Numida) described Christ as a garment which Christians put on
at baptism which fit infants, women, and men.[4] The Coptic
version of the Gospel of Mary referred to "putting on the perfect
man" (ⲛ̄ⲧⲛ̄ϯ ϩⲓⲱⲱⲛ ⲙ̄ⲡⲣⲱⲙⲉ ⲛ̄ⲧⲉⲗⲓⲟⲥ).[5] An early description of
a Christian baptism employed terminology also used in sectarian
hospitality customs: A certain procurator had asked St. John
what he and his people must do. John answered,

"'Remove your garments.'"

After he had undressed, St. John made a cross on his forehead
and anointed his whole body with oil. Then he took him to the
baptismal pool and said,

"'Go down, my brother, who is the new first fruit and who
goes up at the head of the flock in the Master's sheep fold. Go
down, my brother, whom the lambs watch, and hurry to go
down, become white, and acquire new wool in exchange for that
torn by wolves.'

The procurator asked,

'What must I say as I go down?'

John replied,

'Whatever you have seen, found true, and believe.'"

---

[1] Col. 3:12.
[2] Expanded in Eph. 2:1-22; 5:1-20; 6:11-17; see also Rom. 13:11-14.
[3] I Cor. 15:51-54.
[4] *Contra Parmenianum* V. 10.
[5] 18:16f.; so R.McL. Wilson, "The NT in the Gnostic Gospel of Mary,"
NTS 3 (1956/57), 242, fn. 2.

After a silence, the procurator spread out his hands to heaven and cried,

"'I believe in the Father, the Son, and the Holy Spirit.'

Then, leaping, he went down to the baptismal pool. The saint drew near and placed his hand on the procurator's head and immersed him (ܘܐܥܡܕܗ) once, crying out,

'In the name of the Father.'

Again,

'In the name of the Son.'

And a third time,

'In the name of the Holy Spirit.'

When he came out of the water, [St. John] clothed him (ܐܠܒܫܗ) in a white robe, gave him [a kiss of] peace, and said,

'Peace be to you, new bridegroom who had grown old and worn out in sin (ܒܚܛܝܬܐ) but who today has become young (ܛܠܝܐ) and your name is written in heaven.'" [1]

Cyril of Jerusalem, describing the Christian initiation rite, said that after vows were taken in the proper manner, the initiate was led into the holy of holies where he immediately removed his robe (ἀπεδύεσθε τὸν χιτῶνα) which was the image of the old man and his deeds. There he stood naked (γυμνός) before all but unashamed, like Adam before his sin. Then he was anointed with oil, confessed his belief, was immersed three times, and anointed with myrrh. At that point he was called worthy (ἄξιος) and a Christian (Χριστιανός). In place of the old garment he removed, the new Christian was clothed (ἐνδυσάμενον; περιβεβλῆσθαι) with a white garment (λευκὰ ἱμάτια). [2]

An earlier covenanter, telling of his admission to a celibate sect, said he gave up folly (ܠܫܛܝܘܬܐ), stripped it off (ܘܐܫܠܚܗ), and threw it away. Then the Lord renewed him with his own garment (ܚܕܬܢܝ ܒܠܒܘܫܗ) and gave him rest in incorruption. [3] When the Lord raised an initiate by his grace to salvation, the believer stripped off darkness (ܘܐܫܠܚܬ ܚܫܘܟܐ) and clothed himself (ܘܠܒܫܬ)

---

[1] W. Wright, *Apocryphal Acts of the Apostles*, I (London, 1871), 43-44. See also *CH* c. 112-135, and the *ECO* c. 46.

[2] Cyril of Jerusalem I, 1-II, 5; IV, 8.

[3] Odes of Sol. 11:9-10.

with light.[1] Only the saints can put on (ܕܠܒܫܝܢ) joy and love.[2]
A sinner who was freed from his bonds and saved by grace had
his old raiment taken from him and was instead clothed with the
covering of the spirit (ܘܐܬܒܣܡ ܒܒܣܡܐ ܕܪܘܚܗ).[3] It is not
certain whether these last confessions were Christian or Jewish,
but they clearly relate initiation to changing garments.

The new creation.—In Judaism a new convert was one who became
a new creature. When the Lord called Moses to deliver his people
he promised to make Moses a new creature (בריה חדשה), "just as
a woman when she conceives and gives birth." [4] When he called
Abraham to leave his home, the Lord promised to make him a
"new creature (בריה חדשה) fruitful and great." [5] When Israel
entered the covenant at Mt. Sinai, she became a new creature
(בריה חדשה).[6] The rabbis said, "Whoever brings one creature
(בריה) into [the community so that over him are] the wings of the
Shekinah [the one who brought him] is given credit of having
created him (בראו), formed him (ויצרו), and shaped him (וריקמו)." [7]
The same was true of Christianity, where in addition to the change
of garments with the cleansing in baptism, the convert was reborn.[8]
Paul said that if anyone was in Christ he was a new creature
(καινὴ κτίσις).[9] The old had passed away (at baptism); the new
had come.[10] Jesus told Nicodemus that he had to be born again
(γεννηθῆναι ἄνωθεν), by which he probably meant that he would
have to be reinstructed and rebaptized into the new community.[11]
This was being born of the water and of the spirit.[12] Justin Martyr
said Christians, after instruction and vows, were led to the water
where they were reborn (ἀνεγεννήθημεν) and their sins were forgiven.

---

[1] Odes of Sol. 21:2.
[2] Odes of Sol. 23:1-3.
[3] Odes of Sol. 25:1-8.
[4] Tanḥuma, *Shemot* § 18, 5b; see also Ex. R. 3:15.
[5] Gen. R. 39 (Gen. 12:2), 806; see also Num. R. 11:2. (end)
[6] Cant. R. 8:2.
[7] Cant. R. 8:3, 3. For a careful study of the meaning of Rebirth, see E.
Sjöberg, "Wiedergeburt und Neuschöpfung im Palästinensischen Judentum,"
ST 4 (1951), 44-85; and "Neuschöpfung in den Tote-Meer Rollen," *ST* 9
(1956), 131-136.
[8] Gerim 2:5; Yeb. 48b; Jn. 3:1-10.
[9] Gal. 6:15.
[10] II Cor. 5:17.
[11] Jn. 3:3-8.
[12] Jn. 3:5.

This fulfilled the demand Christ made of Nicodemus if he would enter the Kingdom of Heaven.[1] Irenaeus said that Jesus came to save all who through him (*per ipsum*) were born again (*renascuntur*).[2] According to *Canones Hippolyti*, at baptism the initiates were addressed as ones who were "worthy" (*dignos*), who had been born again (*qui iterum nascerentur*).[3] Pseudo-Clement described baptism as the means by which a man could be "born again to God" (ἀναγεννηθῆναι θεῷ; *regenerato ... deo renato*) through the saving water (διὰ τοῦ σῴζοντος ὕδατος; *ex aquis*).[4] Those who were baptized were perfected (τέλειος; *perfectam vitam sequentes*),[5] according to Pseudo-Clement, just as the rabbis claimed that circumcision made Abraham perfect (תמים).[6] Just as Moses required the Israelites to wash their garments and stay away from women until the Lord appeared on the third day,[7] so Peter prescribed a purification period[8] of three days before beginning to baptize.[9] By baptism a person was made pure (καθαρός), at which time he cast off presumption which was an unclean spirit and a foul garment (ἀκάθαρτον πνεῦμα καὶ μιαρὸν περίβλημα) and received the garment (ἔνδυμα) of the Divine Spirit.[10] Baptism itself was referred to as a clean garment (καθαρὸν ἔνδυμα) for the remission of sins.[11] Those baptized into the Christian church were cleansed from iniquity, sins, and defilement (ἁμαρτιῶν καὶ ῥύπου;[12] *iniquitatis et peccati, sorde*).[13] The Egyptian Church Order dismissed before baptism those who had received the prescribed training but had not kept themselves ritually clean (καθαρός).[14] Those who had been baptized into the Clementine sect were obligated to keep other

---

[1] *Baptism* 61.

[2] *Adv. Haer.* II. 33, 2; *MPG* 22.4, 7, 784.

[3] H. Achelis, *Die Canones Hippolyti*, TUGAL 6, 276, c. 136.

[4] *Hom.* VII. viii; XI.xxvi; *Rec.* VI.ix.

[5] *Hom.* XI.xxxvi; *Rec.* I.xxxix. For other instances when baptism was the factor that changed death into life, see Hermas, Sim. 8:11, 3; 9:1, 1-3, 17, 4; Justin, *Apologia* 1:61; *Adv. Haer.* 2:22, 4; Basilius, *De Spiritu Sancto* 12:28; 15:35-36; 16:38; 27:66.

[6] Ned. 32a; Tanḥuma, *Lek Leka* 39b. The perfection was in physical form for Abraham.

[7] Ex. 19:14-15.

[8] *Hom.* XIII.ix.

[9] *Hom.* III.lxxiii.

[10] *Hom.* VIII.xxiii.

[11] *Hom.* VIII.xxii.

[12] *Epist. Barn.* 11:11.

[13] Origen, *In Lev. Hom.* 8:3.

[14] *ECO* c. 45.

purity rules, being careful to eat only with those who had been baptized into the community, eating only food approved by dietary laws, washing after intercourse, refraining from intercourse during a woman's menstrual period, and, if women, being careful to keep the law of purification.[1] Although chastity was considered a great blessing, Gentiles who were not baptized, even though they were celibate, could not enter the kingdom.[2]

Baptism and community privileges.—Pseudo-Clement warned those baptized not to eat from the table of devils where the food would not be approved by dietary laws.[3] A person who had not been baptized was not admitted to eat with Clementine Christians,[4]

---

[1] *Hom.* VIII.viii; XI.xxviii, xxx, xxxiii; *Recog.* I.xix, liv; II. lxxii; VI.xi; VII.xxix.

[2] *Hom.* XII.xxi.

[3] *Hom.* VII.viii, xxix; VIII.xxiii.

[4] *Hom.* XIII. lx; *Recog.* I.xix; II. lxxii; VI.xxix. The acquaintance with purity laws required of members raises a question about the assumption that Christians at first dispensed with catechesis. See Werblowsky, *Op. cit.*, 94. Werblowsky, *Op. cit.*, 59, also believed demon exorcism prior to baptism an important innovation. Neither assumption seems accurate. By the time of the composition of the *Apos. Cons.* three years (τρία ἔτη) of training were required in preparation for membership (*Apos. Cons.* VIII. c31). The Zadokite Document, which was written earlier than the rabbinic literature considered, said that when a person takes an oath to return to the Torah of Moses (by joining the sect, which involves baptism), then the angel Mastemah leaves him (יסור מלאך המשטמה) if he keeps his words. The same was true of Abraham who was circumcised on the day his knowledge (of the necessary catechism) was adequate (על כן נימול אברהם ביום דעתו). The sect then compared the initiation of its members, when Mastemah was exorcised, to the circumcision of Abraham, implying that he, too, was properly instructed before circumcision at which time the evil angel was exorcised (CDC 14:13-16:10, especially 16:4-6). It is clear, then, that exorcism was no new development in Christianity, unknown to Judaism. It is true that a Christian who was possessed of demons was instructed, but not admitted to the fellowship until he had been cleansed (καθωρισθῇ) from the demon even if his instruction was complete (*Apos. Cons.* VIII. c31). The bishop's prayer at baptism included a request that the evil spirit (*malignum spiritum*) leave the members of the initiates (*CH* 108; see H. Achelis, *Die Ältesten Quellen des Orientalischen Kirchenrechts, Erste Buch, Die Canones Hippolyti,* TUGAL 6, 276 (Leipzig, 1891), 78-93). The demons in the NT were "unclean demons" possessed by menstruants and lepers, i.e. people known by Levitical rules to be unclean. Also in *CH* and *Apos. Cons.*, about which Werblowsky wrote, the person freed from a demon (δαίμονα) was "cleansed," meaning that the demons, like those in the accounts of Mark and Luke, were "unclean" (πνεύματα ἀκάθαρτα). Even though rabbis failed to mention it, demon exorcism was practiced in early Judaism, and in relationship to baptism.

but once he had been baptized he was prepared to receive the Eucharist.[1] The Didache warned Christians not to let unbaptized people share in the Eucharist. This was giving that which was holy to the dogs (τοῖς κυσίν).[2] A certain Theon asked Peter to baptize him if he considered him "worthy" (*dignus*). After baptizing him, Peter took bread and gave thanks to the Lord who had accounted Theon "worthy" (*dignatus*) of his holy ministry.[3] The practice of initiating a proselyte by baptism before allowing him to eat the common meal with the covenant community was not only true of Christianity, but also of Judaism. Proselytes were not admitted to eat the Passover meal if they had not been previously baptized.[4] Essenes were admitted to share the "purer water of sanctification" (καθαρωτέρων τῶν πρὸς ἀγνείαν ὑδάτων) after a year of probation. After two more years of training, if found "worthy" (ἄξιοι), they were fully admitted into the group and allowed to touch the common food.[5] The purer water of sanctification was not water for drinking, but for purification.[6] The sect whose rules were recorded in the Rule of the Community admitted a member to touch pure objects after one year,[7] but he was trained for two more years before he was counted among "the many." [8]

Conclusions.—From many different angles, the practices of baptizing adults have reflected the priestly practice of observing purity rules in the temple area and the sectarian practice in relationship to sectarians' homes. Just as neither laymen nor priests could be admitted to the temple area without washing and changing garments and as a guest who was not observant could not be admitted into the home of an observant Jew whose food he could then receive, unless he bathed and changed garments, so outsiders were not admitted into Jewish or Christian sects to receive the common food of the observant members, unless they bathed and changed garments. Other details of form emphasized both in Christian baptism and Levitical ablutions strengthen the possibility

---

[1] *Hom.* XI.xxxvi. Also *ECO* c. 46 and *CH*. c. 141-156. Didache 9:5.
[2] Didache 9:5.
[3] Acts of Peter V.
[4] Eduyoth 5:2; Pes. 8:8.
[5] *BJ* II (138-139).
[6] Cf. *BJ* II (129).
[7] 1QS 6:19.
[8] 1QS 6:19-21.

that they belong to the same origin. For instance, rabbis said it was better to be immersed with flowing water running over the defiled person than to be immersed in stagnant water even if there were forty seahs of water in the pool. Many early Christian pictures and statues show converts being baptized in shallow water while water flowed over them. At the same time, by each convert there was shown another Christian with his hand on the head of the initiate.[1] Expressions such as changing garments, bathing, being cleansed, transferring from death to life, and being born again were related both to Jewish circumcision and Christian baptism. Many of the contexts in which baptismal rites were practiced were those in which other Levitical ablutions, dietary laws, and purity rules were encouraged or required. Therefore it seems more than likely that the Jewish and Christian practice of adult baptism had its origin in Jewish sects that were careful in their observance of purity laws.

There were some superficial differences in the practices as reflected in the limited literature: the relationship of changing garments to baptism was not clearly evident in Jewish sources,[2] but was frequent in Christian sources and in relation to Jewish practices like the baptism that occurred before Essene common meals. Jewish sources indicated no baptism of the Spirit, or baptism in the name of the Father, Son, and Holy Spirit, the sign of the cross, or the kiss of peace.[3] Some of these may have been practiced in Judaism of NT times but not reflected in rabbinic literature which is primarily *haggadic* and *halakhik* in nature rather than liturgical.[4] It is difficult to be sure of the meaning of silence when so many of the bits of evidence necessary for deducing these practices are only accidentally disclosed in literature whose main message was something else. There probably were real differences in practice, because the sects were different. The majority of rabbinic writings were composed in the diaspora after the fall of

---

[1] See Mik. 1:6-8. Also W. A. DeVier, "Water Baptism in the Ancient Church," *BS* 116 (1959), 136-144; 230-240; 317-321.

[2] Odes of Solomon may be Jewish. If so, that is an exception.

[3] Of course, most of these are distinctively Christian practices, not expected in Judaism.

[4] Had there been a Deuteronomic or Levitical law that would have justified baptizing Gentile adults, the rabbis probably would have used it to defend a practice that then existed. Since there was none, they justified their treatment of Gentiles by decrees or rationalization.

Jerusalem and therefore do not always indicate accurately Palestinian sectarian practices on the land before the fall of Jerusalem.
This may account for the reason rabbis only spoke of baptism as
it applied to Gentile proselytes, whereas Christian writings reflect
proselyting from non-sectarian Jews and therefore are more
sectarian in their emphasis. There are undoubtedly other differences
and other reasons for the differences in the broad spectrum of
Jewish and Christian sectarian practice, but the close relationship
between form and reason for baptism and form and reason for
Levitical purifications provides the most adequate answer for the
origin of adult baptism.

This discussion has been completely centered around adult
baptism, but in modern Christianity many churches baptize
infants more frequently than adults, so it will be necessary to show
the close relationship between Levitical ablutions and the current
practice of infant baptism.

INFANT BAPTISM

Current scholarship.—Two of the most important books recently
published which claim infant baptism as a practice of the early
church are Jeremias, *Infant Baptism in the First Four Centuries* [1]
and Cullmann, *Baptism in the NT*.[2] Neither book has succeeded
in demonstrating its author's belief that Christians baptized
infants in NT times, but both have presented convincing evidence
to strengthen the probability that their deductions were accurate.
Jeremias collected material related to infant baptism from rabbinic
literature, the NT, inscriptions, and the church fathers to show
that the practice was firmly established and probably practiced
quite early. Cullmann opposed Barth's claim that consciousness
of the event was necessary for baptism to be effective. Like Jeremias
he related infant baptism to circumcision. He said there were no
traces in the NT of the baptism of adults born to Christian parents
and reared by them.[3] Nonetheless, he agreed with Jeremias that
"the hypothesis ... that the step to child baptism was already
taken in NT times, attains a high degree of probability." [4] Like

---

[1] J. Jeremias, *Infant Baptism in the First Four Centuries*, tr. D. Cairns
(Philadelphia, 1962).
[2] O. Cullmann, *Baptism in the NT* (Chicago, 1950).
[3] Cullmann, *Op. cit.*, 26.
[4] *Ibid.*, 44.

Jeremias, he related Christian baptism to Jewish proselyte baptism, holding that Christian baptism "takes over at the same time the function of proselyte baptism *and* circumcision." [1] One of Cullmann's most important contributions, approved also by Jeremias,[2] was his appendix, suggesting that κωλύειν was used in a baptismal formula and that Mk. 10:13-16 was therefore a reflection of a baptismal service[3].

Neither book dealt directly with the relationship between infant baptism and Levitical purity.[4] In his defense against Aland,[5] Jeremias,[6] largely influenced by Williams,[7] quoted church fathers who seemed to relate baptism to Levitical purity, but Jeremias' only interest in this material was to show that infant baptism was practiced by the early church. The relationship suggested by Origen and Cyprian will be examined here by considering Levitical rules involved and their interpretation in rabbinic literature.

Defilement at birth and baptism.—According to the Levitical commandment, a woman who bore a son was unclean (טמא) for seven days afterward, just as for a menstrual period (כימי נדת דותה).[8] Menstrual uncleanness required a bath before a woman was made ritually clean so that she could be in contact with other people without defiling them. The whole process of purification was called "sanctifying." [9] Until a woman had immersed herself after childbirth, her blood was unclean.[10] After her immersion, on the eighth day, her hemorrhaging might continue, but it was not considered

---

[1] *Ibid.*, 44. See also Tertullian, *De Baptismo* I.1 and Epist. Barn. 11:11.

[2] Jeremias, *Op. cit.*, 44-55.

[3] Cullmann, *Op. cit.*, 71-79.

[4] Cullmann said, "In fact it is characteristic of Christian baptism that in it purity, i.e. the forgiveness of sins through Christ, is realized *in and through* reception into the community of Christ by the Holy Spirit" (p. 64). Jeremias, commenting on Pes. 8:8, "He who separates himself from his foreskin, separates as it were from the grave," said that the phrase, "as a description of the removal of Levitical impurity is quite without analogy" (p. 33).

[5] K. Aland, *Did the Early Church Baptize Infants?*, tr. G. R. Beasely-Murray (Philadelphia, c1963).

[6] Jeremias, *The Origins of Infant Baptism*, tr. D. M. Barton (Naperville, c1963), 66, 70-74.

[7] N.P. Williams, *The Ideas of the Fall and of Original Sin* (New York, 1927), 167-314.

[8] Lev. 12:2.

[9] II Sam. 11:4; cf. also Lev. 15:13-15.

[10] Nid. 4:3.

unclean. From the time of her immersion the woman "sat in the blood of her purity" for thirty-three days for a boy.[1] During this time she was forbidden to touch anything holy or to enter the temple.[2] She was not permitted to pour out the water for washing the Passover-offering,[3] but she was allowed to eat of the second tithe and set-apart dough offering. If any of the blood of her purifying fell on a loaf of heave offering, the loaf remained clean. The school of Hillel said she did not need another immersion at the end of the thirty-three day period.[4] Before her immersion she was unclean, and made unclean all that she touched. After her immersion she was clean, even though she saw her blood.[5] Both Luke and Origen were fair in their interpretation of Leviticus to mean that the son born was defiled for the same length of time as the mother.[6] Job also asked rhetorically, "Who can produce something clean (טהר) from something unclean (מטמא)? Not one."[7] The reason for this was that man was born of a woman,[8] who became unclean when she gave birth.[9]

Infant defilement and baptism.—In the very next verse after a woman was declared unclean for seven days after giving birth to a son, Lev. 12:3 said that on the eighth day the son should be circumcised.[10] Rabbis said that the boy was washed either before

---

[1] Lev. 12:4.

[2] Lev. 12:4. [3] Nid. 10:6.

[4] Nid. 10:7. Both child and mother were defiled twice as long for a girl. Aland, *Op. cit.*, 82, fn. 1, said that for girls born in the earliest church, nothing at all was prescribed. On the fifteenth day, however, when the mother was cleansed (Lev. 12:5), the daughter was probably cleansed also. Since it was unaccompanied by circumcision, this may not have been a ceremony that merited extensive discussion. Rabbis recorded some instances when a daughter was immersed before her mother (והטבילוה קודם לאמה) (Nid. 32a). These would probably have been instances in which those who baptized the daughter kept her from her mother until she was also baptized.

[5] Lev. 15:19-28; Sifra 58d; § 2, 4, Lev. 12:5.

[6] Luke said that the time had come for their (αὐτῶν) (i.e. Mary's and Jesus') purification (Lk. 2:22). See Origen, *Homily on Luke* XIV (87.18-88.18) and Jeremias, *The Origins of Infant Baptism*, 70.

[7] Job. 14:4. See also Ps. 51:7.

[8] Job 14:1.

[9] Cyprian said a newborn child had not sinned. Baptism was not for the child's sin but for the sin of another (*aliena peccata*) (Ep. 64:5, CSEL 3.2, pp. 720 f., Kraft, no. 19a). Origen concurred that every soul born of flesh was defiled by iniquity and sin (*sorde pulluitur iniquitatis et peccati*) (*Homily on Lev.* VII. 3 [on 12:2]).

[10] The boy might be bathed again on the third day after circumcision even if that day fell on the Sabbath. The rabbis said that was to cleanse the

circumcision or after circumcision.[1] If circumcision occurred on
the Sabbath, they had to sprinkle water on him by hand (ומזלפין
עליו ביד,) but they could not use a vessel, presumably either to
immerse him in it or to pour water from it over the boy, as they
might on another day of the week.[2] The same held true for the
proselyte who was born after his mother's baptism (טבלה). But if
he were born before his mother was baptized into Judaism then he
would have been circumcised on the same day that she was baptized.[3] The son's baptism evidently took place so as to cleanse
him from the ritual impurity with which he was born—his original "sin." [4] "Just as Israelites (כשם שישראל) entered the covenant by three commandments, so proselytes enter by circumcision,
baptism (טבילה), and a gift (קרבן)." [5] This means that Israelites
as well as proselytes were baptized. This baptism evidently took
place on the eighth day. The rabbis were not in complete agreement about the gift. R. Eliezer said a gift was required and
R. Simon said it was not. But the requirement of baptism and
circumcision for both proselytes and Israelites was generally
accepted. Infant baptism, then, was a standard practice of Jews
who followed rabbinic rules, and it took place on the eighth day,
either before or after circumcision.

---

wound. If that were really so, the wound would have needed cleansing on
the second and fourth days as well, or could have been cleansed in advance
of the Sabbath. The requirement seems more of a ritualistic than a medicinal or
comfort measure. The Sabbath was only broken to fulfill commandments
that could not be postponed. This was true of circumcision and also for
corpse uncleanness, for which a person was sprinkled on the third and seventh
days, even if these fell on the Sabbath (Shab. 9:3; 19:3; Pes. 8:8; 92a;
Num. 19:14-19). The question left unanswered is, if this were the case, why
was not the provision also made for the seventh day after circumcision?
If water of purification were originally used for sprinkling on the third and
seventh days, that would have been treating the foreskin as if it were a corpse
(see Pes. 8:8).

[1] Shab. 19:3. The rationalization that the water was for the wound seems
like a later addition. If it had been for the wound, it would not have been
used before the wound had been made.

[2] See Shab. 9b. This probably is the origin of baptizing infants by sprinkling, since these services usually have been performed before the congregation
on the Christian Sabbath.

[3] Gerim 2:1.

[4] The water of sprinkling (מי נדה) was also called מי חטאת in Mik. 10:6
and Parah 9:4-8.

[5] Ger. 2:4.

Christian baptism of infants.—After Paul had convinced some churches of Asia Minor, at least, that circumcision was unnecessary, then the sole initiatory rite was baptism. Since children were no longer circumcised, there was for infants still the purification rite to be performed for the son on the eighth day and the daughter on the fifteenth—the same day the child's mother was sanctified from her defilement. As Levitical ablutions became less important to some branches of the Christian church, there also developed a greater division between Christianity and Judaism. Christians were urged not to fast on the same days the Jewish hypocrites did.[1] It was probably partially in opposition to Judaism that Christians changed the day of immersion from the eighth day to the second or third. Jews, probably also in opposition to Christians who had given up circumcision and held to baptism, continued to circumcise on the eighth day but discontinued the ablution rite that had formerly accompanied circumcision. This change did not take place all at once. Cyprian, in behalf of the council, wrote a letter in response to a certain Fidus who had requested that a general policy be made to baptize infants on the eighth day, holding that a newly born infant was not pure.[2] The council overruled the suggestion quoting a Pauline epistle, "To the pure all things are pure," [3] and arguing that the Jewish rite of circumcision on the eighth day had been made unnecessary by Christ. Spiritual circumcision, then, should be administered as soon as possible, baptizing the infant to admit him to the grace of Christ. In response to Fidus' claim that the child could not be ritually clean before the eighth day, the council quoted Acts, "'The Lord has said to me that I should call no man common or unclean.'" [4] Cyprian, justifying the council's anti-Jewish position, quoted II Isaiah, urging Fidus to forget the former things such as circumcision and the idea that women were unclean at childbirth. God was at that time fulfilling his promise of doing a new thing.[5] Among the Gentiles who had previously been "dry," rivers were now flowing to regenerate those whom God had admitted by receiving the grace of Christian baptism.[6] Had Cyprian been consistent, he could have

---

[1] Didache 8:1.
[2] Epistle 58:1-4.
[3] Titus 1:15.
[4] Acts 10:28; Epistle 58:5.
[5] Isa. 63:18-21.
[6] Epistle 58:5.

said that since there was nothing common or unclean, neither circumcision nor baptism was necessary. But religious bodies do not always change logically or very much all at once. The bases for the theology of infant baptism have been reinterpreted from time to time and from one religious group to another, but the practice of baptizing infants has continued.

Jewish Christian conflicts.—The fact that Fidus was understood to have been upholding Jewish practice when he recommended baptizing a boy on the eighth day after the boy's mother had been purified implies that Jews at that time also baptized male infants on the eighth day together with circumcision. This is further supported by Luke's simple statement that Origen later admitted; namely, that Mary and Jesus went to Jerusalem when the time came for *their* purification.[1] If Jews had not generally accepted the premise that all babies were defiled at birth, there is almost no probability that either Luke or Origen would have attributed to Jesus any extraordinary defilement. In fact, Luke said Jesus was born of a virgin and Origen, commenting on Lev. 12:2, noted that it was the male sperm that defiled a woman at conception and said Mary became pregnant without being so defiled (μὴ οὖσα ἀκάθαρτος ἡ μαρία).[2] The fifth century St. Isidore said baptism removed the *defilement* communicated by Adam's transgression. There has continued to be some opposition to the idea of origina sin. Up to the fourteenth century, Greeks refused to admit that children were born sinful, and more recent scholars admit that they prefer a doctrine of original defilement to original sin.[3]

Other evidence for believing that Jews formerly baptized infants to cleanse them from the defilement of birth is that Jews still accept infant proselytes by baptism, and in the case of a boy, circumcision. This happens when a father becomes a proselyte and wishes his children to become proselytes as well. With the approval of the Beth Din, his children, even those under three years of age,

---

[1] Origen, *Homily on Luke* XIV (87.18.8818= *Werke*, IX, p. 85 [947-948].
[2] *Homily on Lev.* VII. 3.
[3] S. Lyonnet, "Le Péché Originel en Rom. 5:12," *Biblica* 41 (1960), 354. For a step by step report of the reactions of Christians to the doctrine of original sin in history, see M. Jugie, "Péché Originel," *Dictionnaire de Théologie Catholique*, 12 (Paris, 1933). See p. 199, fn. 1.

may be immersed and received into the Jewish community. If they wish, when they are old enough to make mature decisions, they may reject the faith of their father or be confirmed in it.[1] Since adult proselytes are baptized to cleanse them from defilement, it would follow that infant proselytes would also be baptized for the same reason. There was a close relationship between the mother's defilement and purification and her son's. Rabbis, commenting on Lev. 12:2-3, denied this relationship, saying that in spite of the connection in the text of Leviticus there was no connection between the mother's seven day period of defilement [2] and the following statement about the son's circumcision on the eighth day.[3] They argued that the son who defiled his mother at birth was not himself defiled (היא טמאה ואין הוולד טמא · · · הוול שגרם לטומאה אינו דין שיהא טמא).[4] The conclusion that the son was not defiled is quite surprising. It was dogmatically made in contradiction to the normal understanding of the text interpreted. It is also contrary to the rules related to a mother's defilement during those seven days. Were she to touch her husband or anyone else, that person would be defiled. It seems reasonable, then, to assume that the son would be defiled at birth the way Luke, Fidus, Origen, and later St. Isidore said would be the case, and the way the proselyte infant is still treated upon admission to the Jewish community.[5] The polemic the rabbis upheld in this interpretation was in opposition to some people who believed otherwise, just as Cyprian's arguments were against some who believed otherwise. The difference is that Cyprian identified his opposition as the Jews and those Christians under their influence. The rabbis argued against some who would have believed baptism was necessary on the eighth day, as some Christians did.

It is reasonable to suspect that the rabbis, in their discussion upholding circumcision of infants but disclaiming any need for baptism, represent the Jewish reaction to Christians who baptized, but did not think circumcision was necessary, but this is not certain. From the limited materials it is not possible to reconstruct with complete confidence the adjustments that Christianity and Judaism

---

[1] Ket. 11a.
[2] Lev. 12: 2.
[3] Lev. 12:3.
[4] Sifra Lev. 12:2-3; 58a.
[5] Ket. 11a.

made in response to each other. Changes probably did not all take place at once. Fidus may have represented the view of many Christians of his day who preferred baptism on the eighth day, and there may have been many Jews who took objection to the rabbis' decree and continued to baptize on the eighth day because they believed the children to have been defiled at birth and later contact with a defiled mother. St. Isidore, as late as the fifth century, believed in infant baptism for removal of original defilement. There may have been divisions on the subject before the Christian era. These the Christians only increased by taking one side. This would have prompted Jews to gather around the opposition. This is all imaginary reconstruction with inadequate evidence for tracing every point, but the scripture, the Levitical rules, the Christian admission that Jesus was defiled at birth, and later belief in original defilement rather than original sin provide an adequate basis for understanding the opposition to the rabbis' dogmatic statement that babies were not defiled at birth. This means that before the division was formed, some Jews probably baptized infants on the eighth day, either before or after circumcision. After his mother had been ritually cleansed from her defilement, her son also needed to be cleansed from the defilement with which he was born. This defilement came to be called original sin which many Christians still believe is removed by infant baptism.

Adult and infant baptism are both continuations in modern Christianity of ancient purity practices related to midras uncleanness and the defilement that always accompanied childbirth within the covenant. These ablutions were practiced any day of the year— sometimes even on the Sabbath. But sins and defilements that occurred after baptism were dealt with on one special occasion each year, the Day of Atonement.

THE DAY OF ATONEMENT

Divine justice and human need.—The Day of Atonement filled a very practical need in the religious life of Israelites with their understanding of justice and mercy. They believed strict justice was exacted, an eye for an eye and a tooth for a tooth.[1] No matter

---

[1] Dt. 19:21.

how angry the offended person may have been, he was not allowed
to take revenge on his offender by putting out two eyes for one. But
justice was closely related to Hebrews' understanding of God's
activity. Therefore a person who had committed an offense should
have wanted his sin punished at once, lest God punish him more
severely. Sins were understood to accumulate in a ledger both for individuals and for nations, just the way a banker recorded the money
others borrowed from him. So the Amorites were disinherited after
their sins became complete,[1] and Jews who killed Jesus and the
prophets were filling up the measure of their sins.[2] Once the allotted
credit was completely withdrawn, foreclosure proceedings followed. An individual Hebrew who failed to pay his debts was
taken into slavery, but not for life. He could be released whenever
someone paid his debt for him, i.e., redeemed him. If not, he worked
for his creditor until the debt was paid at half wages. If he owed
more money than he could pay back at those terms, he worked
until the Sabbath year, when he was released. If he had sold
his property that was not in a walled city to pay his debt, the
property was kept from him until the jubilee year, when it
was again restored to his family. Sin[3] was considered a debt
(חוב) against a fellow Hebrew, against God, or both. A person
who had committed many sins had just as much reason to be
anxious as a person who had borrowed a great deal of money.
The latter could know the length of time he was expected to serve,
but a sinner could never be sure how much was recorded against
him. He might have walked over unmarked graves unknowingly,
touched defiled persons without realizing that they were defiled,
or unwittingly have broken more serious commandments. He
believed that God was just, but the ledger sheet was not available
and the offender could not know the extent of his debt. The
same logic was transferred to the nation. When Israel was
taken captive, it was assumed that God would punish according
to rules for the Sabbath year, either seven, seventy, or seventy
times seven, at which time the slavery should be over and the
captives set free. If it was the jubilee year, then the land should
also be restored to its original owners. God also recorded virtues,

---

[1] Gen. 15:16.
[2] I Thes. 2:16.
[3] Or, rather, "iniquity."

however, so it was important for Hebrews to do as many good works as possible to cancel their indebtedness.

In NT times the deepest longing in the heart of pious Jews was for the Kingdom of God. God had promised to give the Land of Palestine to the seed of Abraham, but at that time, Jews were under subjection of the Roman government. This did not mean that God's promise had failed, but that Israel had sinned. She had overdrawn her treasury of merits. She was in debt to God. How could the debt be overcome? Could it be paid? Could it be forgiven? It seemed impossible that all Israel would ever become free from iniquity, but some Jews attempted to be perfect, to keep the whole law. They took vows of poverty, chastity, and obedience. They strained every nerve to build up the account of merits credited to Israel.

Just as Hebrew law provided sabbatical years when slaves were freed and debts cancelled and jubilee years when land was restored to its original owners, so the Day of Atonement was established so that Israelites' sins could be forgiven. On that day every year Israelites had the opportunity to be born again, like the proselyte who was baptized as a child born that day with no more sins against his record than a newly born baby, cleansed of his mother's impurity. Abraham was made a new creature (בריה חדשה) when he was circumcised and given a "new" name, and a Jew who "brought" an idol worshipper "near" as a proselyte was credited with having made him.[1] In Judaism a boy was judged innocent until his *bar mitzwah* at about thirteen years of age. In the same way Israelites could become new creatures on the Day of Atonement. The rabbis, commenting on Ps. 102:18, *a people created will praise the Lord*, said, "These generations which were like corpses (כמיתים) in their deeds, come and pray before you on Rosh Ha-Shenah and you create them a new creation" (בריה חדשה).[2] The Lord promised Israel that if she would do penance even for the ten day period between New Year's Day and the Day of Atonement, then on the Day of Atonement he would judge Israel to be innocent (מזכה) and create her a new creature (ברית חדשה).[3] Furthermore, if Israelites would accept the yoke of the Torah, then the Lord would say to them, "Just as you enter into judgment before me on New

---

[1] Gen. R. 39 § 11, 14.

[2] Makiri Ps. 102:18. See also Mid. Ps. and Yalkut, *loc. cit.*

[3] *PR* 40, 169a.

Year's Day and leave in peace (בשלום, i.e. with all sins forgiven),
I will redeem you as if you had been made a new creature . . . as
if you had never sinned" (לא חטאתם מימיכם).[1] Any Israelite for
whom a miracle had been performed should know that his iniquities
had been forgiven and he had been made like a new creature
(בריה חדשה).[2] It was against this background that Jesus told his
disciples that if they did not repent and become as children (i.e.
either before the *bar mitzwah* when they were legally innocent or
after the Day of Atonement when they became new creatures), they
would not enter the Kingdom of Heaven.[3] The Kingdom of Heaven
was to be composed of citizens as innocent as children.[4] Nicodemus
was told that he must be reborn, even though he was old.[5] Paul
said that those who were in Christ were new creatures.[6] Those
baptized into the Christian community were all reborn.[7] If the
nation was to be reestablished, the people would have to repent
and become as innocent as children so that Israel would not have
an obligation of sin which had not been cancelled. Rabbis said
God would restore the promised land if all Israel repented for just
one day.[8] That day would be the Day of Atonement, when each
year Israel had a chance to have its debt to God forgiven. But
there were limitations under which these institutions functioned.

The terms of atonement.—"If a man brings his guilt offering and
does not bring the goods he has stolen, no sacrifice will be offered
until he brings the goods he has stolen, but [his offering will remain
there and] deteriorate until it is removed to a place of burning."[9]

"The sin offering and the unquestionable guilt offering atone.
Death and the Day of Atonement atone *together with repentance*
[italics mine]. Repentance atones for light offenses, both positive
and negative, and for serious offenses it suspends [them] until
the Day of Atonement comes and atones.

"If a man said, 'I will sin (אחטא) and repent, and sin again and

---

[1] JRHS IV.i, 59c, 60.
[2] Mid. Ps. 18, 69a.
[3] Mt. 18:1-3.
[4] Mt. 10:14.
[5] Jn. 3:3-8.
[6] II Cor. 5:17.
[7] See above p. 87, fn. 4.
[8] Cant. R. 5§2, 2.
[9] TBB 10:18(368).

repent,' he will be given no chance to repent. [If he said], 'I will sin
and the Day of Atonement will effect atonement,' then the Day
of Atonement effects no atonement. For transgressions between
man and God, the Day of Atonement effects atonement, but for
the transgressions that are between man and his fellow (לחבירו),
the Day of Atonement effects atonement only if he has appeased
his fellow (עד שירצה את חברו)." [1]

Forgiveness in the NT.—The covenanter who desired forgiveness
for his sins had to know that he had not sinned with any conscious
intent of seeking release on the Day of Atonement. Further, he
had first to be reconciled with his brother for his sin; he had to
repent; and he had to bring his sin and guilt offerings to the temple
of the Lord. It is against this background that Jesus was reported
to have said: "So if you are offering your gift at the altar, and
there remember that your brother has something against you,
leave your gift there before the altar and go; first be reconciled to
your brother, and then come and offer your gift." [2] God's forgiveness was dependent upon man's reconciliation to his fellow. Because
this was true, a person who had sinned against his fellow could
not be forgiven by God if his fellow refused to forgive him for the
sin he had committed against him. This was well illustrated by
a story from the Talmud: [3]

"Once R. Eleazar, son of R. Simeon, was coming from Migdal
Gedor, from the house of his teacher, and he was riding leisurely
on his ass by the riverside and was feeling happy and elated because
he had studied much Torah. [20b]. There chanced to meet him
an exceedingly ugly man who greeted him: 'Peace be upon you,
Sir.' He, however, did not return his salutation but instead said
to him, 'Raca, how ugly you are! Are all your fellow citizens as
ugly as you are?' The man replied: 'I do not know, but go and
tell the craftsman who made me, "How ugly is the vessel which
you have made." ' When R. Eleazar realized that he had done
wrong he dismounted from the ass and prostrated himself before
the man and said to him, 'I submit myself to you. Forgive me.'
The man replied: 'I will not forgive you until you go to the craftsman who made me and say to him, "How ugly is the vessel which

---

[1] Yoma 8:8-9.
[2] Mt. 5:23-24.
[3] Taʿanith 20a-20b.

you have made." ' He [R. Eleazar] walked behind him until he reached his native city. When his fellow citizens came out to meet him greeting him with the words, 'Peace be upon you, O Teacher, O Master.' The man asked them, 'Whom are you addressing thus?' They replied: 'The man who is walking behind you.' Thereupon he exclaimed: 'If this man is a teacher, may there not be any more like him in Israel!' The people then asked him: 'Why?' He replied: 'Such and such a thing has he done to me.' They said to him, 'Nevertheless, forgive him, for he is a man greatly learned in the Torah.' The man replied: 'For your sakes I will forgive him, but only on the condition that he does not act in the same manner in the future.' "

It was very important to R. Eleazar to obtain forgiveness from the man whom he insulted. Even though he was highly respected and well versed in the Torah, if the man whom he insulted had refused to forgive him, he could not have been forgiven his sins against God on the Day of Atonement. Therefore the man whom he insulted "had" something against him. Reconciliation was necessary between these two men, before the rabbi could be reconciled to God. Because the reconciliation between the believer and his brother was closely related to the reconciliation between the believer and God, the Lord's prayer said, "Forgive us our debts as we also forgive our debtors." [1] This comment follows: "For if you forgive men their trespasses, your heavenly Father will also forgive you; but if you do not forgive men their trespasses, neither will your Father forgive you your trespasses." [2] This teaching placed the responsibility on the person who had been offended rather then the offender, but both teachings reached the same end and were taught for the same purpose: to get all of the brothers reconciled to one another so that all Israel might be forgiven on the Day of Atonement. The unforgiving servant parable was told to emphasize a previous teaching that a man should forgive his brother "seventy times seven." [3] Just as the servant was delivered to the jailer until he should pay all his debt, "so also my heavenly Father will do to every one of you, if you do not forgive your brother from your

---

[1] Mt. 6:12.
[2] Mt. 6:14-15.
[3] Mt. 18:22.

heart." [1] If your brother sins you are to rebuke him, "and if he repents, forgive him; and if he sins against you seven times in a day, and turns to you seven times, and says, 'I repent,' you must forgive him."[2] Because the community to which a believer belonged had the right to forgive or withhold forgiveness, Peter, who represented the Petrine sect of Christianity, was understood by his community to have been given authority either to bind or forgive sins on earth; they believed that the Lord would follow suit.[3] Other groups of Christians and Jews, each of which considered itself to be the only true Israel, held similar beliefs. Individual Christians were to tell their brothers their faults so that they could repent and continue as brothers. This was not considered "fault-finding." It was done to keep the community completely free from sin so that its merits would atone for all Israel. If the brother who had been told of his sin, which he might have committed without realizing it, did not repent, his fellow Christian was next obligated to take two or three witnesses. If this failed, the matter was taken to the church. If there he acknowledged before all the act that he had done, but refused to repent, the church excommunicated him and classed him as a tax collector and a Gentile.[4] This admonition was followed with the statement, "Truly I say to you, whatever you bind on earth will be bound in heaven, and whatever you loose on earth will be loosed in heaven." [5] In these exclusive communities, members had either to repent of their sins or get out, so that the remaining community might be sinless. It was the narrow way that led to "life." [6] Sins were classified as debts, and Israel was in debt more than she could ever hope to pay. Her only hope for salvation lay in the possibility that her members might be reconciled to one another so that the Lord would forgive them on the Day of Atonement. This could only happen if, in addition to forgiveness and reconciliation with one another, they also brought the proper gifts in sufficient quantity to pay for the misdeeds. If the proper terms were met, then God would restore them the land he promised to Abraham. It was understood that God wanted to give Israel

---

[1] Mt. 18:35.
[2] Lk. 17:3-4; see also T. Gad 6:3-7.
[3] Mt. 16:19.
[4] Mt. 18:15-17.
[5] Mt. 18:18.
[6] Mt. 7:13-14.

the kingdom,[1] but Israel had filled up the measure of her sins, so God would not let the kingdom come until the account had been corrected. Therefore the same prayer that asked, "Thy kingdom come," also requested, "Forgive us our debts as we forgive our debtors."[2] Ritschl was correct when he said forgiveness was a fundamental attribute of the community Christ founded.[3] The pious Jew yearned for the Kingdom of God, so every effort had to be made to expose and forgive the sins of fellow Israelites. For the sake of the Kingdom of God, men were asked to neglect their parents in their old age so as to devote all of their money and energy to one movement.[4] Followers of Jesus were separated from their nearest relatives.[5] The Kingdom of Heaven was like a treasure hidden in a field or a precious jewel for which men would sell all they had to acquire.[6] Wealthy men were asked to give all they had to the movement, so that they might inherit life in the King-dom.[7] Jesus' followers had been required to leave families, houses, and land, in order to prepare for the Kingdom of God.[8] But all of this sacrifice would have been futile if Israel's sins could not be forgiven. When the kingdom was not in Israel's possession, Israel-ites pondered at length to determine which factor of the require-ment had been overlooked or improperly fulfilled.

The Christian sin offering.—It was against this concept of for-giveness that Paul understood Christ to be the sin offering made for Israel's sins on the Day of Atonement. Like Micah, Paul knew that the Lord could not be appeased with "thousands of rams, with ten thousands of rivers of oil."[9] Israel's sin was so great that there were not enough sacrificial beasts available to make the gift required on the Day of Atonement. Therefore God took the ini-tiative. It was God "who through Christ reconciled us to himself and gave us the ministry (διακονία) of reconciliation; that is, God was in Christ (i.e. the body of Christ, the church) reconciling the

---

[1] Lk. 11:32.

[2] Mt. 6:10, 12.

[3] A. Ritschl, *The Christian Doctrine of Justification and Reconciliation*, tr. "several hands" (Edinburgh, 1902), 543.

[4] Mt. 20:22.

[5] Mt. 10:34-39.

[6] Mt. 13:44-46.

[7] Mt. 19:16-24.

[8] Mt. 19:25-30.

[9] Micah 6:7.

world to himself, not counting their trespasses against them, and entrusting to us the reckoning (λόγος) of reconciliation." [1] The sacrifice of Christ, according to Paul, was a sin offering that God made on our behalf. For atonement to take place, three things were necessary: 1) the believer had to repent; 2) he was required to be reconciled to his brother; and 3) sin and guilt offerings were required to pay for the debt. God through Christ had made the offering which Israel could not make. That which was left for Christians was the business of reconciliation. They had to forgive one another and repent of their sins so that atonement could be completed.[2] This was good news and the exhortation given the Colossians. In their behalf, the author prayed, "May you be strengthened with all power, according to his glorious might, for all endurance and patience with joy, giving thanks to the Father, who has qualified us to share in the inheritance of the saints of light. He has delivered us from the dominion of darkness and transferred us to the kingdom of his beloved Son, in whom we have redemption, the forgiveness of sins." [3] The forgiveness of sins provided redemption and qualified the Colossians to share in the inheritance of the saints. As part of the New Israel, they could draw on the treasury of merits accumulated to cancel their sins. Although the Colossians had once been estranged and hostile in mind, God had reconciled them through the sacrifice of Christ so as to present the Colossians blameless and irreproachable before him.[4] The condition was that the Colossians continue in the faith steadfastly.[5] God took these Colossians who had been "dead" both from the standpoint of transgression and their lack of circumcision, and he gave them "life" by bringing them into the covenant with Christ, declaring the debit account of sin that had been recorded against them to be null and void. It could no longer hold any legal force to be used against them.[6] Their new status required new ethical obligation of the Colossians. Now that they were "alive," i.e. raised with Christ, they must conduct themselves in a manner becoming to those who belong to the new covenant.[7]

---

[1] II Cor. 5:18-19.
[2] Cf. also Rom. 5:6-11.
[3] Col 1:12-14.
[4] Col. 1:21-22.
[5] Col. 1:23.
[6] Col. 2:13-14.
[7] Col. 3:1.

Colossians had been made alive by God's grace when he forgave them their accumulated debt of sin. In response to this, Colossians must also forgive one another and be patient with each other.[1]

The change from disfavor to favor with God was sometimes called "reconciliation." The word usually translated "reconcile" is καταλλάσσειν which basically means "change." It seldom occurs in the LXX. In a secular sense it referred to changing a garment,[2] or it was used in counsel concerning celibacy and marriage. In that context, Paul said those who could stay married should, but if they separated, the married woman was permitted to be "reconciled" (καταλλαγήτω) to her husband, meaning she could give up her celibate state and resume marital life.[3] Other usages, however, involved a "change" that affected the fortune of a people because of God's change in attitude toward it. Thus Moab's change (κατήλλαξεν) in fortune was for the worse. She was turned back in shame. [4] The author of II Maccabees prayed for the Jews in Egypt, that God might be reconciled (καταλλαγείη) to them. If that happened he would pay attention to their requests and not forsake them when times were bad.[5] He said Jerusalem had suffered calamities when the Almighty became angry and forsook the place, but afterwards he became reconciled (καταλλαγῇ), i.e. he changed his attitude, with the result that the city was again restored to full glory.[6] There was a direct relationship between Israel's measure of sin and her chastisement which justice required, on the one hand, and her change of fortune after she had been adequately punished and God became reconciled (καταλλαγήσεται) to his servants, on the other.[7] Baruch urged Israel to pray constantly and sincerely that the Mighty One might be reconciled (ܢܬܪܥܐ) to them so that he would not count (ܢܚܫܘܒ) their numerous sins (ܣܘܓܐܐ) against them, but instead give them credit for the merits of the patriarchs. If this would be done, then the promise given to Abraham could be fulfilled and Israel could be restored to the promised land.[8] When Judah the Maccabee and his followers

---

[1] Col. 3:13.
[2] LXX Isa. 9:4; μετὰ καταλλαγῆς for Hebrew בדמים.
[3] I Cor. 7:11.
[4] LXX Jer. 31:39.
[5] II Mac. 1:5.
[6] II Mac. 5:20.
[7] II Mac. 7:30-35.
[8] II Bar. 84:10.

had won an astonishing victory against Nicanor, then the troops
rested on the Sabbath and prayed that the Lord would be completely reconciled to his servants.[1] This was a prayer for complete
victory over the Seleucids and the reestablishment of the land
promised to the seed of Abraham, to the Lord's chosen people.
The change that took place in this reconciliation was twofold:
The first change was in the Lord's feelings about his people. He
repented, and changed from anger to beneficence. The second
change was the result of the first and assured the covenanters
that the first had really taken place. This was the change in Israel's
fortune. While unreconciled, Israel suffered hardship, abuse,
embarrassment, and poverty. When reconciled, Israel won battles,
gained prestige, regained possession of the land, and became
prosperous. Whenever Israel lived in undesirable conditions it
was a sign to the people that God was angry and had to be appeased
before Israel's lot would improve. This meant that Israel was not
reconciled with God.

In the letters of Paul, reconciliation was used synonymously
with justification, both in contexts speaking of salvation from
God's wrath or into the "life" of Christ. In one *a fortiori* argument,[2]
the clause, "When we were still sinners, Christ died for us," was
paralleled by the following clause in another *a fortiori* argument,[3]
"When we were enemies, we were reconciled to God through the
death of his son." The second halves of the same arguments also
shed light on the meaning of reconciliation: "How much more,
having been justified (δικαιωθέντες) now by his blood, shall we be
saved (σωθησόμεθα) through him from the wrath of God," [4] was
written in parallel construction with, "How much more, having
been reconciled (καταλλαγέντες) shall we be saved (σωθησόμεθα)
in his life. " [5] In both arguments, the death of Christ or Christ's
having died, changed the whole legal relationship of the believer
to God. Before Christ's death, covenanters were under God's
wrath; afterwards, Christians were saved from God's wrath or
saved into "life" in the body of Christ, the church. Through Christ,
God reconciled covenanters to himself, not counting their trespasses

---

[1] II Mac. 8:12-29.
[2] Rom. 5:8-9.
[3] Rom. 5:10.
[4] Rom. 5:9.
[5] Rom. 5:10.

against them.[1] This means that they were "justified" or declared
innocent which had the same meaning as having been reconciled.
In the ledger of offenses, the believer was given a clean slate—
justified, reconciled, sins not counted. The time II Isaiah foretold
had come: the old passed away. The "new thing" that God was
going to do had been done.[2] The main work had been done by
God in Christ, but believers had to be reconciled to one another
and forgiven by each other before God would complete the process
by forgiving their sins and reestablishing the kingdom. In two
other parallel *a fortiori* arguments, Paul argued that God had
used Israel's transgression or rejection to bring riches to the
Gentiles or reconciliation of the world. Since this was so, Israel's
full inclusion would be "life" from the "dead."[3] Here reconciliation
of the world means riches for the nations. This further indicates
the close relationship between blessings and reconciliation.

The temple and forgiveness.—In the Gospel of Matthew, the
teachings of forgiveness presupposed the existence of the temple
where sinners could come before the altar bringing their sin and
guilt offerings. Therefore, these teachings were evidently composed
before the fall of Jerusalem in 70 A.D. Paul also understood forgiveness in terms of sacrifice and the Day of Atonement, so he
interpreted the death of Jesus as the sacrifice necessary for forgiveness. But he did not exclude the continuing advantage of adding
to the treasury of merits. Indeed, Paul himself rejoiced in his
sufferings on behalf of the Colossians and he filled up that which
was lacking of the tribulations of Christ. This Paul did in behalf
of the church, and he considered himself appointed in God's
economy to fill up (πληρῶσαι) the reckoning (λόγος) of God.[4] The
"reckoning" or "lack" in God's economy was the debt of sins not
yet atoned. Christ's sufferings were sufficient to remove the
punishment for most of them, but Paul also believed that his own
sufferings were necessary to balance the account. Hebrews,[5]
however, argued that Jesus' offering of himself once for all (ἐφάπαξ)[6]
was adequate. Hence no further sacrifices were needed, by contrast
to the temporary attonement effected by the Levitical priesthood.

---

[1] II Cor. 5:18-19.
[2] Isa. 43:18-19; II Cor. 5:17.
[3] Rom. 11:12, 15
[4] Col. 1:24-25.
[5] Heb. 7:22-28.
[6] Heb. 7:27.

This may reflect a Christian adjustment to life without the temple, necessary after Jerusalem had been destroyed, but in any case, it recognized the requirements for sacrifice and the Day of Atonement for the forgiveness of sins. The author of Hebrews was consistent, however, in also saying that, once forgiven, there was no opportunity for further backsliding and forgiveness. Since the sacrifice of Christ was enough to cover all the sins committed before belief, there was no further sacrifice available for additional sinfulness.[1]

The heavenly court.—Without surrendering the bookkeeping analogy of sin and forgiveness in terms of debt and cancellation of obligation, Hebrews also thought of the covenanter in relationship to God as of an accused criminal being tried in court on a day of judgment. From the standpoint of the individual believer, R. Eliezer b. Jacob said,

> "Whoever performs one good deed (מצוה)
>   acquires for himself one defense attorney (פרקליט);
> whoever commits one transgression (עבירה)
>   acquires for himself one accusing attorney (קטיגור)."[2]

R. Simon said that a sin offering (חטאת) was like a defense attorney (פרקליט) because just as a defense attorney enters [the court] to win favor of the judge, so the gift (דורון) enters [to win favor].[3] Rabbis taught that each illness was a sentence for a transgression. Anyone who was so ill that he was bedfast should imagine that he had ascended the scaffold to be punished. He could be saved only if he had great defense attorneys (פרקליטין גדולים). The effective defense attorneys were repentance and good deeds.[4]

After a battle with Gorgias, Judas Maccabeus and his soldiers recovered the bodies of those soldiers who had fallen in battle to give them proper burial. When they discovered idols under the shirts of all the slain, they knew at once why their brothers had fallen. The soldiers all prayed that the sin of those men would be blotted out. Judas took up a collection from every soldier in camp and sent the money to Jerusalem for a sin offering (περὶ ἁμαρτίας

---

[1] Heb. 6:1-12.
[2] Aboth 4:11.
[3] Sifra 72b.
[4] Shab. 32a.

θυσίαν). Judas did this because he believed in the resurrection and thus made atonement for those who had been killed that they might be free from sin and that their offense might not be listed against Israel.[1]

It was in the context of a case in court that the author of I John told early Christians that Jesus Christ was a sin offering (ἱλασμός) [2] for their sins. As a sin offering he acted as a defense attorney (παράκλητος) before the Father to win the Father's favor for the Christians when they were judged. It was because he could win the Father's favor that the Christian's sins would be forgiven.[3]

The priestly benediction was a prayer for God to show favoritism toward his chosen people when he judged them. It requested that they be given peace, which meant that he would consider whatever merits they had to be sufficient to offset all of their sins. Since, by actual reckoning, this would not be the case, the priests requested a special dispensation that would judge them innocent even though they really were not. The following translation calls attention to the judgmental nature of the prayer:

> "The Lord bless you and guard you;
> the Lord look upon you with favor and be kind to you;
> the Lord show you favoritism when he judges;
> and declare your account, 'paid in full.'" [4]

When an accused person was brought before a judge to be tried for an offense, the judge was supposed to judge fairly, without being in any way partial toward or prejudiced against the person accused, no matter whether he was prominent, wealthy, a personal friend, poor, or old.[5] For this reason he was not to "lift up his face" toward the person to see who he was. A good judge who judged impartially was "no respector of persons." Malachi warned the people that their offerings were such that if the Lord saw them, he would not on that account "lift up his face" toward the Israelites to grant them special favor.[6] It was because of Nehemiah's special

---

[1] II Mac. 12:40-45.
[2] See also II Mac. 12:45.
[3] I Jn. 2:1-2. Jews thought of Moses as a mediator or defense attorney (*defensor*) of Israel before the Lord (Assump. Mos. 11).
[4] Num. 6:24-26.
[5] See Lev. 19:15; Dt. 10:17; 28:50; I Sam. 25:35; Job 22:8; 34:19; 42:8; Prov. 6:35; 18:5; Isa. 3:3.
[6] Mal. 1:8-9.

position as a cup bearer of the king that Jews were able to obtain
the special treatment they were given because of Nehemiah's
intercession before the king.[1] Those who had no bribes or special
intercessors had to make nuisances of themselves in order to obtain
the vindication they desired.[2] Although bribery and favoritism
were well known in Israelite courts, the rabbis noted a problem
of ethics in asking God, who was no respector of persons, to show
special favor to Israel when he judged her.[3] Their concern pointed
up the ancient conflict between the Lord's justice and his favoritism
toward his chosen people, which was basic to the whole doctrine of
election. Together with their belief that they were God's chosen
people was their realistic self-appraisal as a sinful people. Israel
needed more than strict justice; she needed to be given special
consideration or she would never achieve a verdict of "not guilty."
So Israelites prayed for grace in judgment. The author of
II Maccabees paraphrased the priestly benediction as follows: "*And
make peace*—may he pay attention to your supplications and become
reconciled to you (καταλλαγείη ὑμῖν) and not give you up in an
evil time."[4]

SUMMARY

Israel had commandments to fulfill, but it was understood that
she would never keep them all perfectly. Therefore provisions were
made for restitution. Individual Israelites, who had broken commandments and had thus become defiled or sinful, were temporarily
excommunicated from the group and only readmitted after the sin
had been removed. This involved punishment, fines, sin and guilt
offerings, reconciliation with one's neighbor, observance of the
proper baptisms at the proper times, and fulfilling the obligations
related to the Day of Atonement. Those who were restored to the
community had "life," but this was only really possible when the
land was in the possession of the children of Israel. The reason the
Kingdom of God had been withheld was that Israel was still in
her sin. Some defilement had not been cleansed; some members
had not become reconciled to each other. Since the real concern

---

[1] Neh. 1:1-2:10.
[2] Lk. 18:2-8.
[3] Num. R. XI § 7.
[4] II Mac. 1:4-5.

for forgiveness was as a means of acquiring the promised land, the community sin was more important than the individual sin. Individuals were willing to be forfeited for the community. Faithful and zealous Jews were willing to pay any price to win God's favor so that the kingdom could come. Because the delay had been long, there were various solutions offered which prescribed the proper ethics required of God's people to win God's favor. Because the solutions differed, ascetic sects developed within Judaism. These will be considered in the next chapter.

CHAPTER SEVEN

COVENANTAL SECTARIANISM

INTRODUCTION

The nature of sectarianism.—The earliest report of sects is in the works of Josephus. He called the Pharisees, Sadducees, and Essenes "sects" or "heresies" (αἱρέσεις). These were important, respected, religious groups in early Judaism. They were not "heresies" in the later use of the term, meaning the minority groups with unorthodox views from the point of view of those who called themselves "orthodox." Josephus did not describe first century sects in relationship to "mainstream" or "normative" Judaism, nor did he describe a situation in which there was one basic heresy from which the others departed. "Heresies" of the first century A.D. were the main "orthodox" groups in Palestine. They differed from non-sectarians in the extent to which they kept the law. Although "heresy" and "sect" were terms that later were applied depreciatively by *some* sectarians to *other* members of *different* sects, the terms were not originally disparaging.[1] In this chapter, the term "sect" will be used with the same basic meaning intended by Josephus. "Sectarians" and "covenanters" will be considered synonymous and used to describe members of identifiable groups who claimed to be living according to the covenant the Lord made with his chosen people.

OT sectarianism.—The formation of factions has an ancient Israelite history. The Books of Kings and most of the prophets record numerous conflicts that took place among people who worshipped the

---

[1] Josephus, *Vita* 10:12, *BJ* II (119); cf. also *Ant.*XIII (171); XVIII (II). Morton Smith,"Palestinian Judaism in the First Century," *Israel, its Role in Civilization*, ed. M. Davis (New York, c1956), 80, has shown the relationship of Jewish "philosophical schools" (sects) to the contemporary "philosophical schools" in Hellenistic culture. The similarity was close enough to provide Josephus a good basis for using the Hellenistic philosophical schools for comparison, but Jewish sects were not exactly like other philosophical schools. See also Acts 15:5; 24:5 and 26:5 for other non-disparaging uses of the term "heresy" or sect.

same God but differed in their understanding of the way he should be worshipped.[1] Part of the disagreement arose over the practices enjoined in the Pentateuchal holiness rules. The ark of the covenant and the presence of the Lord were in the "camp."[2] Because the Lord was holy, the members of the congregation were required to be holy.[3] Holiness was maintained by contributing the proper offerings,[4] keeping separate from other peoples, observing Sabbaths, feasts, and jubilees,[5] and eating only prescribed (כשר) food.[6] Because different Israelites had different views concerning the importance of various rules and the exact way in which they were to be fulfilled, different religious groups arose in Israel.

Divisions.—An important division took place when Jews were taken into Babylon as slaves. There they lived away from the promised land for many years. When finally some returned, they were oriented differently from the Jews and Samaritans who had remained on the land. Although II Isaiah foretold the reestablishment of the *twelve* tribes and the reunion of *all* Israelites from the corners of heaven,[7] those who returned with Ezra and Nehemiah considered themselves the only good figs and the local people, bad figs.[8] Just as the idolatrous Canaanites, Amorites, and other nationalities whom Joshua overcame were called the peoples of the land (עמי הארץ),[9] so the Jews and Samaritans who had remained on the land were called derisively the "people of the land" by the Jews who returned from captivity in Babylon to replace them.[10]

---

[1] Morton Smith, "The Dead Sea Sect in Relation to Ancient Judaism" *NTS*, 7 (1960/61), 347-360, has shown well the antiquity of sectarianism in Judaism.

[2] See F. C. Fensham, " 'Camp' in the NT and Milḥamah," *RQ* 4 (1964), 557-572.

[3] Lev. 20:7; Num. 5:1-3; Dt. 7:8.

[4] Ex. 25:1-8; 29:38-45; 30:22-38; Lev. 16; 19:23-24; 21:23; Num. 15:18-19; Dt. 26.

[5] Ex. 31:12-17; 35:1-3; 11; Lev. 25; Dt. 15.

[6] Lev. 7:19-37; 17; 22:10-16; Dt. 14.

[7] Isa. 41:8-9; 43:3-9; 49:1-6; 12:21; 56:1-5, 7-8.

[8] Jer. 24:1-10; 29:15-23.

[9] Neh. 9:24.

[10] Neh. 10:31-32. When first written, these views were thought to be original. Later reading showed that R. de Vaux, *Ancient Israel*, tr. J. McHugh (New York, c1961), 70-74, and M. H. Pope, " 'Am Ha'Arez," *ID* (New York, c1962), I, 106-107, both reached the same conclusion with the same assumption. Earlier still, P. Seidensticker, "Die Gemeinschaftsform der

The Jews from Babylon vowed that they would not allow their daughters to marry sons of the "people of the land" or engage in business with them on the Sabbath or on feast days.[1] In this way they separated themselves from the "people of the land" and considered themselves pure and clean in contrast to those whose observance of the law could not be trusted. From then on, sectarians distinguished themselves from those they did not trust to keep laws as they did by calling the non-sectarians "peoples of the land." At that time, in their own judgment, the sectarians were the "orthodox" and the "people of the land," "unorthodox."

Another division occurred during the reign of Antiochus Epiphanes who forced Hellenization upon the Jews and Samaritans. During this crisis, there were those who compromised and gave up the law and others who continued to observe the law even though it caused death to themselves and their children. The Maccabees led an active revolt against Antiochus and the Hellenizers. They gained support from various groups who opposed the lawlessness that then existed in Israel. One of the strong groups to support them called themselves Ḥasidim ('Ασιδαῖοι). They first joined Judas in active rebellion, but withdrew as soon as they were assured of a high priest of the right family.[2]

During the Roman period, especially after Archaelaus had been banished and Roman procurators were introduced,[3] Jews were impatient because their generation did not possess the heritage God had promised the children of Abraham. This evidently meant that they had sinned and would have to change their ways before God would comfort his people by restoring them the land. Different groups had conflicting ideas about God's demands. The Zealots, basing their policy on the story of Phineas [4] and the history of

---

religiösen Gruppen des Spätjudentums und der Urkirche," *Liber Annus* 9 (1959), 120-121, made the same judgment. More recently, E.W. Nicholson, "The Meaning of the Expression עם הארץ in the OT," *JSS* 10 (1965), 59-66, analyzed these articles and other secondary literature on the subject. None of these scholars compared the "people of the land" after the return from Babylon, however, with the "people of the land" before Joshua's conquest.

[1] Neh. 10:30-32.
[2] I Mac. 2:42; 7:13-17.
[3] 6-7 A. D.
[4] Num. 25:1ff.

the Maccabees, took up the sword at every opportunity to attempt to expel the Romans and their collaborators from the land by military force. Pacifists believed Israel had to be punished for her sin.[1] Therefore, Jews were required voluntarily to accept whatever afflictions were placed upon them, believing that this would help cancel the debt and also make the sins of the oppressive nation greater, so that on the day of vengeance God would vindicate the Jews and suppress the Romans.[2] Some, like John the Baptist, came in the way of righteousness, carefully observing all dietary laws and avoiding all defiling contacts. On the other hand, there were many, like the tax collectors, who took advantage of the existing situation, collaborated with the Romans, and made little pretense of observing the Pentateuchal regulations. These were called "sinners" and maybe also "harlots." Those of a more moderate position compromised by mingling with Romans but carefully observed the stipulated tithes, bathed properly before eating, and were careful not to eat with those who were not so careful as they. Monasticism provided some groups a way of avoiding the unclean acts required by marriage. Sects also probably had differences of a nature not directly related to interpretation of the Torah, but reflecting economic, philosophical, or social attitudes. Josephus said that there were three major sects (heresies —αἱρέσεις) in Judaism in his time: the Pharisees, the Sadducees, and the Essenes.[3] By far the most material is available concerning the Essenes. Therefore they will be considered first. After that other sects will be compared with the Essenes, and sectarian practices will be noted even when the name of the sect cannot be determined.

---

[1] II Mac. 6:12-17; 1QS 9:21-23; Ps. Sol. 10:1. See also *Decal.* xviii (95).

[2] See further K. Stendahl, "Hate, Non-retaliation, and Love," *HTR*, 55 (1962), 343-355.

[3] Josephus also told of a fourth sect which fought zealously against Rome. See W. R. Farmer, *The Maccabees, Zealots, and Josephus* (New York, 1956). P. Seidensticker, *Op. cit.*, 126, said Josephus was in error when he classified the Essenes with the Pharisees and Sadducees as a philosophical school. The latter two were philosophical schools, he held, but the Essenes were instead a "Mönchs-und Bruderschaftsbewegung." He did not show, however, that the Pharisees and Sadducees were not also monastic. C. Roth, "Zealots—A Jewish Religious Sect," *Judaism* 8 (1959), 33-40, and G. R. Driver, *The Judaean Scrolls* (Oxford, 1965), accepted Josephus' claim that the zealots constituted a fourth sect and concluded that the Dead Sea Scrolls were written by the zealots.

Essene Economy

The closely-knit structure of the Essene sect effected its whole economic existence in two ways: 1) the common fund of the monastic order, and 2) the hospitality shown to other members of the sect.

1) *The common fund.*—Philo,[1] who evidently described only the monastic Essenes, said that Essenes owned no private property, but that they had pooled all of their resources into a common fund which then was distributed to the individual members as each had need. Members labored daily for wages which were contributed to the common treasury to buy the necessary provisions for the group. Not only was food purchased for the entire group from the common fund but also clothing, which continued to be the property of the group. In addition to the practicality of the economy, this plan permitted strict supervision to see that all foods were *KŠR* and properly tithed and that all Essenes were dressed with garments which did not contain prohibited mixtures of materials.[2] Furthermore those who were ill or aged were treated at the common expense and given the same thoughtful care that parents might expect of children. Hence it was possible for Essenes with no children at all to live to a comfortable and prosperous old age.[3]

The reason for the communistic administration was not given. Bauer, however, showing several other instances in classical literature where people had abandoned their goods because they believed material wealth was the root of all evil, presumed the Essenes had the same motivation for their economy.[4] A more likely possibility seems apparent from the circumstances. In the

---

[1] *Hyp.* XI (4-5). The discussion on Essenes was first written as an article for *The International Standard Bible Encyclopedia*. Part was prepared for an article, "Purity Rules and the Structure of the Essene Community," *RQ* 15 (1963), 397-406.

[2] Lev. 19:19.

[3] *Hyp.* XI (10-13); *Prob.* IX (86-87); see also *Ant.* XVIII (20-22); *BJ* II (122); and Hippolytus IX.iv.19.

[4] W. Bauer, "Essener," *Paulys Realencyclopädie der Classischen Altertumswissenschaft, Supplementband IV* (Stuttgart, 1924), 410-414. Even after the discovery of the Dead Sea Scrolls, Seidensticker, *Op. cit.*, 198, concluded, "Eine Mönchtum in religions-geschichtlichen Sinn hat es in Israel nicht gegeben. Ein solches ist nur möglich in einer Universal-religion . . ." M. H. Deems, "Early Christian Asceticism," *Early Christian Origins* (Chicago, 1961), 91, stated dogmatically, "The Jews were not ascetic. God created the world and it was good and was to be enjoyed." He looked for origins of asceticism in Greek and Roman dualism (p. 99).

ancient Near East there was no social security program or pension plan to care for people in their old age. The principal insurance a person had against neglect and starvation in his old age was the care his children would provide. Therefore children were commanded to honor their parents, which involved provision for old age.[1]

Members of a celibate order, deprived of children, would be neglected in their old age and during periods of illness if some community plan were not provided to fulfill the needs otherwise met by family members. In joining the sect each member was required to give all of his money to the group. This meant that he could not use it to care for his parents in their old age. This undoubtedly worked hardship on some parents, but the children believed that the work for the Kingdom of God was more important than properly honoring their parents.[2] Another important factor in segregated living was the facility whereby all the goods of the community could be kept free from any type of defilement.

2) *Essene hospitality.*—Philo said that no Essene called his house his own in the sense that he was free to exclude other Essenes but that the door was open to visitors from other localities who *shared his convictions.*[3] This means that those who could be trusted to keep the same tithing, heave offering, dietary, and purity regulations could make demands on their hospitality. Josephus said further that Essene customs permitted them to travel without taking any provisions except weapons as protection against brigands, but that in every city an appointed person was responsible for providing visiting Essenes with clothing and other necessities.[4] Hippolytus added that the person assigned to care for traveling Essenes did so from funds provided for that purpose.[5]

The Essene program of hospitality seemed well-planned, efficient, and also necessary for a sect so exclusive in its regulations that its members could not accept the food or other provisions supplied either by Gentiles or other sects within Judaism.

---

[1] Ex. 20:12; Mekilta, *Baḥodesh* 8:1-3; Philo, *Decal.* XXIII (116-118); and *Ant.* IV.viii. 24.

[2] Mt. 8:21-22; 15:1-6.

[3] *Prob.* IX (85).

[4] *BJ* II (125).

[5] Hippolytus, IX.iv.20.

MONASTICISM

Philo,[1] Josephus,[2] and Hippolytus [3] all agreed that the Essenes did not marry. Although Josephus[4] and Hippolytus[5] both conceded that one order of Essenes did permit marriage, they maintained that those who married did so only for the propagation of the race. Hence no more sexual intercourse was permitted than was necessary to produce children. Like others seeking admission, prospective wives were first required to undergo three years of probation and training in sectarian doctrine and could not marry until they had had at least three purification periods to show that they were mature enough to bear children. Furthermore, to avoid unnecessary defilement, Essenes had no intercourse during pregnancy.

The reason given for celibacy was not that the sect objected to children. Indeed, Essenes were willing to raise the children to whom others had given birth. [6] But Hippolytus said that they avoided every deed of concupiscence, distrusting women altogether.[7] Josephus said Essenes thought marriage led to unrighteousness,[8] and that no woman was faithful.[9] Philo expounded at greater length on the wiles of women and the way wives and children could unconsciously divert an Essene's attention from his primary concern.[10]

Pliny said the Essenes had renounced the patterns of ordinary society because they were tired of life and were driven to their accepted way of living by the waves of fortune.[11] Pliny's interpretation has probably led many to associate Essene monasticism with Greek asceticism. Indeed Zeller[12] singled out the Essenes as the sect on Palestinian soil which showed the greatest degree of Hellenistic influence. Marks of Greek philosophy, he said, were to be seen in asceticism which was based on dualism, worship of the

---

[1] *Hyp.* IX (14-17).
[2] *Ant.* XVIII (21); *BJ* II (120-121).
[3] IX.iv.18b.
[4] *BJ* II (160-161).
[5] IX.iv.28a.
[6] *BJ* II (120); Hippolytus, IX.iv.18b.
[7] IX.iv.28a.
[8] *Ant.* XVIII (21).
[9] *BJ* II (121).
[10] *Hyp.* IX (14-17).
[11] *Natural History* V (73).
[12] E. Zeller, *Outlines of the History of Greek Philosophy*, rev. W. Nestle, tr. L. R. Palmer (New York, 1955).

sun, belief in angels, pre-existence of the soul and its survival after death. Bauer said rejection of marriage could be paralleled only in Buddhism.[1] Thomas began his important study on baptist groups because he could not adequately explain either Essene lustrations or celibacy as Hellenistic, Neo-Pythagorean influences.[2] Neither did Thomas think the frequency with which Essenes bathed could be attributed to Jewish practices. The reason he did not notice this was that he did not realize the intensity of the motivation for Jewish asceticism—the reestablishment of the Kingdom of God. Celibacy had the same basis as ablutions—Levitical purity. The motivation for Jewish asceticism has already been considered. Here the Essene sect will be related to the rules observed by Jewish ascetics in general, particularly as they apply to celibacy.

The Essenes and biblical regulations.—Philo said that Essenes observed Sabbaths meticulously. They avoided work and gathered into synagogues to read the books (presumably the OT) and discuss their meaning.[3] Josephus claimed that they were stricter than all other Jews in Sabbath observance, preparing all of their food the day before, refusing to kindle a fire, or even yield to nature's demands for elimination on the Sabbath day.[4] Some Jews of the Graeco-Roman period insisted that elimination take place at least two thousand cubits from the camp.[5] But two thousand cubits was the extreme limit a Jew was permitted to walk on the Sabbath, and some held that the limit was one thousand cubits.[6] Any Jew, then, who refused to defile the camp or break the Sabbath would find it necessary to schedule his consumption so that elimination on the Sabbath was not necessary.[7] Hippolytus maintained

---

[1] Bauer, *Op. cit.*, 428-429.

[2] J. Thomas, *Le Mouvement Baptiste en Palestine et Syrie* (Gembloux, 1935), 22-26, 417, thought the emphasis on ablutions showed Babylonian and Iranian influence. This may be so, but if so, the influence came early enough to have been incorporated into the Pentateuchal purity laws.

[3] *Prob.* IX (81-83).

[4] *BJ* II (147).

[5] 1QM 7:7. The same distance was given the Levites outside levitical cities to pasture their livestock (Num. 35:1-5). It was also the distance Israelites were required to stay from the ark of the Covenant as it was carried into the land (Josh. 3:4).

[6] Sotah 5:3; Erubin 51a; CDC 10:10-21.

[7] The Essene practice of fasting on Friday so that they would not have to defile the Sabbath may have originated from the same motivation as that

that some Essenes would not even get out of bed on the Sabbath.[1]

On other days, Essenes followed the Deuteronomic [2] prescription of taking care of elimination needs in deserted places, modestly covered with cloaks, and carefully covering up the excrement with earth and washing themselves afterwards as if secretion were polluting.[3]

Philo said that the Essenes ate together.[4] Josephus testified that only the initiated were allowed to share the common meals and only after they had bathed and dressed in special linen garments.[5] Hippolytus noted that no one who was of different persuasion was permitted in the house while Essenes were eating.[6] They keep such strict dietary laws that they were not at liberty to eat any other man's food. So rigidly were these rules followed that any member excommunicated from the group was destined to die of starvation.[7] Members would endure tortures or even death rather than eat food offered to idols.[8]

Sectarians believed that oil was defiling, and if they accidently came into contact with any, they would wash themselves to be

which initiated Jewish fasts before feast days (Pes. 10:1). This may also have been the reason for the high priest to have limited his food consumption the day before *Yom Ha-Kippurim*, rather than —as the rabbis said— the effect food would have had on his sleep (Yoma 1:4). The day before the Sabbath or before a feast day was called the day of preparation (*Ant.* XVI [163]; Mt. 27:62; Jn. 19:14). The Essene fast on Friday may have been a forerunner to the Roman Catholic practice of fasting on Friday by abstaining from eating meat. Of course Roman Catholics do not observe the Sabbath on Saturday, nor do they fast to make elimination on Saturday unnecessary. As a matter of fact, they may eat just as much on Friday as any other day. Until recently, however, they have been expected to avoid eating meat on Friday. Hullin 8:1 said that if a man took a vow that he would eat no meat, he would still be permitted to eat fish, eggs, and locusts. The reason these are not classed as meat is that they may be served on the same table with dairy products, since there is no possibility that any of these will be boiled in its mother's milk. Roman Catholics have followed this practice and eaten fish and eggs on Friday. For a discussion of fasts not related to Sabbaths or feast days, see S. Lowy, "The Motivation of Fasting in Talmudic Literature," *JJS* 9 (1958), 19-38.

[1] IX.iv.25.
[2] Dt. 23:12-14.
[3] *BJ* II (148-149); Hippolytus, IX.iv.25; see also Ber. 62a.
[4] *Hyp.* XI (5, 11, 86).
[5] *BJ* II (129).
[6] IX.iv.21.
[7] *BJ* II (143-144); Hippolytus IX.iv.24.
[8] IX.iv.26.

cleansed of this defilement.¹ They were careful not to spit into the
midst of the company or to the right.² Those who wanted to join
the sect were not immediately received into the group but were
given prescribed clothing and equipment and proper food to eat in
separate quarters. Only after two³ or three⁴ years of probation,
if the candidate was observed to be "worthy" (ἄξιος) was he
admitted to the inner circle.⁵ If a senior member accidentally
touched a junior member, he would have had to take a bath to
remove the defilement just the same as if he had touched a gentile
(ἀλλόφυλος).⁶ Hippolytus told of an extremely scrupulous group
of Essenes whose members considered themselves so much different
from the "younger generation" of Essenes that if one of them
happened to touch one of the less rigorous Essenes by mistake,
he would bathe to remove the defilement.⁷ The carefulness with
which Essenes were reported to have kept various regulations
justifies the claim that they were known for their self-control and
respect for the law,⁸ and that they were particularly concerned
for the writings of the ancients that dealt with the welfare of the
soul and body.⁹ Those writings were probably the ancient Pentateuchal rules dealing with cleanness and uncleanness. When these
are carried out explicitly so as to maintain a pure community, the
result would be similar to the military camps where soldiers stayed
away from women and kept themselves and their camps holy.
Holy war soldiers probably observed stringent rules only while on
active duty. When the war or the battle was over they went back
to their wives. During the Roman period, however, the yearning
for freedom was intense, and Jews prayed daily for God to deliver
his people. Since God could save the nation and usher in the
kingdom with only a small remnant of faithful covenanters, the

---

¹ *BJ* II (123); Hippolytus IX.iv.19.
² *BJ* II (147).
³ Hippolytus IX.iv.23.
⁴ *BJ* II (138).
⁵ *BJ* II (138); Hippolytus IX.iv.24.
⁶ *BJ* II (150); H. St. J. Thackeray (ed. and tr.), *Josephus* (London, 1961),
rendered ἀλλόφυλος as "alien," an inclusive term that could mean either a
foreigner or an ʿam haaretz. G. Allon, *Studies in Jewish History* (Hebrew)
(Israel, 1957), I, 126, was more accurate and less ambiguous in rendering
ἀλλόφυλος by נכרי.
⁷ IX.iv.26.
⁸ *Prob.* IX (84); *BJ* II (120).
⁹ *BJ* II (136).

monastic Essenes may have accepted the limitations necessary to
be a holy congregation standing ready for God to act. The marrying
order of the Essenes observed the same rules as well as they possibly
could and still propagate the race.[1] So closely was the Essene
practice of celibacy and avoidance of unnecessary sexual intercourse
in marriage related to purity rules that Josephus, who described
the marriage and celibacy customs of the Essenes, also said *all*
Jews were governed by laws that forbade sexual intercourse except
for the procreation of children.[2] The Essenes differed from the
other Jews by being more careful to fulfill the standard legal
expectations by which they all were expected to live. Some Jews
who were not so observant as the Essenes evidently married girls
too young to bear children. Rabbis called them "those who play
with baby girls" (המשחקין בתנוקות) and said that they, like proselytes, who may also have been careless about purity rules, restrained
the Messiah and hindered his coming.[3] The Essenes, however,
tried not to hinder the Messiah. Further evidence of their observance
of purity rules can be seen in relationship to trustworthiness.

The meaning of "trustworthiness."—Josephus [4] and Hippolytus [5]
referred to the Essenes who were finally accepted into full membership as "worthy" (ἄξιοι). In rabbinic literature, a person who
undertook the responsibility of being "trustworthy" (נאמן) kept
KŠR, fulfilling all the dietary, purity, tithing, and heave offering
regulations that his sect demanded. Although the term generally
meant "trustworthy" in any sense, נאמן also had a technical
meaning that described the person who kept *KŠR*. The "trustworthy" person was to tithe what he ate and what he sold and

---

[1] The marrying Essenes practiced the "rhythm method" of control.
There was no intercourse until the eighth day after a woman's menstrual
period ended. So intercourse began when she would be most likely fertile. As
soon as she became pregnant, there was no more intercourse until another
child was desired. The limitations were made so as to obtain as many children as
possible with as little defilement as possible. The practice has continued in the
Roman Catholic Church until the twentieth century. There have been some
recent relaxations of rules. Now Roman Catholics are permitted to space their
children by reversing the "rhythm method" or employing it just off-beat.

[2] Josephus, *Contra Apion* 2:25.

[3] Nid. 13b. For the relationship between purity and a holy community
see H. Kosmala, *Hebräer-Essener-Christen* (Leiden, 1959), 343-378.

[4] *BJ* II (138).

[5] Hippolytus, IX.iv.24.

bought and was not permitted to be the guest of an outsider
(עם הארץ).[1] The school of Hillel accepted members as "trustworthy" who had observed the regulations without default for
thirty days. The school of Shammai prescribed thirty days for
liquids; for clothing, twelve months.[2]

There is a very close relationship among the terms, "worthy"
(ἄξιος), "worthy" or "ritually permitted" (כשר), and "one who
is worthy of being trusted to stay within the ritually permitted
limits" (נאמן). The contexts show that the use of ἄξιος indicated
by Josephus and Hippolytus is the same sort as the rabbinic use
of נאמן, the differences being only the particular qualifications
required to achieve this standing. The Essenes required a longer
probation period than either the school of Shammai or Hillel.[3]

Josephus and Hippolytus both said that the Essenes believed
no woman could be trusted. It seems unreasonable to believe that
this lack of trust referred to marital loyalty. The text employed by
Josephus and Hippolytus may have intended to say simply that the
Essene sect differed from the group reported in rabbinic literature [4]
in that it did not accept women as persons to be trusted as to
dietary rules, heave offering and tithing rules, and purity regulations. Hippolytus seems to bear out this suggestion when he said
Essenes did not even trust women who wished to devote themselves
to the same polity, such as the wives of marrying Essenes.[5]
Since women of child-bearing age were necessarily unclean about
one-half of the time, it is not surprising that a meticulous, celibate
group would not trust them with matters concerning defilement.

This does not mean that Essenes were misogynists any more
than their common treasury meant that they despised wealth. In
fact they were willing to rear children and *permit these children
to marry* [6]—a strange behavior, indeed, for a group that really had
strong feelings against the character of women. The monastic
order avoided women for purity reasons, and the sect in general
apparently did not accept them as "trustworthy" (נאמנות), but
Philo's description of the Essene understanding of women's wiles

---

[1] Demai 2:2-3.

[2] T. Demai 2:11 (48).

[3] See "The Role of Purity in the Structure of the Essene Sect," 403-404,
fn. 55.

[4] T. Demai 3:9.

[5] Hippolytus IX.iv.18b.

[6] *Hyp.* XI (14-17).

probably reflects his own views as much as that of the Essenes.[1]
The terms τηρεῖν . . . πίστιν, "observing . . . trust," [2] and πιστεύον-
τες, "trusting," [3] may reflect a mistranslation of the Hebrew
נאמנות, "trustworthy." [4]

To be sure, this is only a conjecture, but reason requires some
interpretation other than general hatred for the female sex, and
this suggestion is possible.

SLAVERY

Essene sense of equality.—Of the Essenes, Philo said, "Not a
single slave is to be found among them, but all are free, exchanging
services with each other, and they denounce the owners of slaves,
not merely for their injustice in outraging the law of equality, but
also for their impiety in annulling the statute of Nature, who
mother-like has borne and reared all men alike, and created them
genuine brothers, not in mere name, but in very reality, though
this kinship has been put to confusion by the triumph of malignant
covetousness, which has wrought estrangement instead of affinity
and enmity instead of friendship." [5] One of the ways by which
they show their love of man is "by benevolence and a sense of
equality." [6]

Josephus said, "They neither enter into marriage nor practice
slave holding, considering the latter to lead to unrighteousness and
the former to provide occasion for troublemaking, but they live
by themselves, making use of one another in service." [7]

Although both Philo and Josephus agreed that the Essenes did
not hold slaves, the reasons given for this refusal are quite different.[8]

Philo's reason was that Essenes were convinced of the equality
of all men and for this reason would not treat another human
being in a subordinate fashion. But the egalitarianism Philo
attributed to the Essenes was contrary to their basic outlook on
life. Philo himself noted that in their Sabbath instruction they

---

[1] *Hyp.* XI (14-17).   [2] *BJ* II (121).
[3] Hippolytus IX.iv.18b.
[4] For the Hebrew(?) text used both by Josephus and Hippolytus, see M.
Smith, "The Description of the Essenes in Josephus and Philosophumena,"
HUCA, 29 (1958), 273-313.
[5] *Prob.* IX (70), Loeb. trans.
[6] *Prob.* IX (84), Loeb. trans.
[7] *Ant.* XVIII (21).
[8] Contra P. Geoltrain, "Le Traité de la Vie Contemplative de Philo
d'Alexandrie," *Semitica*, Cahiers X (Paris, 1960).

were ranked "in rows according to their ages, the younger below the older." [1] Josephus said they did nothing without orders from their superiors [2] and were careful to obey their elders.[3] Therefore Philo's pseudo-philosophical explanation of their refusal to have slaves is to be dismissed as a projection of Philo's own views.[4]

Biblical rules.—Jews in Palestine before 70 A.D. might have held Jewish slaves until sabbatical years or Gentile slaves permanently. Both would have been excluded for the Essenes on the basis of ritual purity. If even junior members of the sect could not be touched by senior members, and if their meals could not be eaten while there was a non-Essene in the house, then it would be virtually impossible to keep slaves of any kind. Should a slave have chosen to become an Essene and thereby have been admitted into the community, he would no longer have been a slave. The uncircumcised Gentile had been prohibited by Ezekiel.[5] If hypothetically, Jewish slaves were admitted, it would have taken three years of training before they could have been trusted, and they would have been released on the Sabbath year—at most three more years.

The Levitical rules, then, and not the Essene concern for egalitarianism, prevented the acquisition of slaves among the Essenes. The communistic economy was necessary to provide for those deprived of children, and an organized sharing of each other's work [6] was necessary to meet the needs of those deprived of slaves. The sect gave much more significance to purity rules than Thomas considered reasonable.[7] In fact the rules themselves were not held to be reasonable. They were commanded to be obeyed, not necessarily understood. Also related to obedience to the Torah was the Essene refusal to take oaths.

---

[1] *Prob.* IX.xii (81).
[2] *BJ* II (134).
[3] *BJ* II (146); see also Hippolytus IX.iv.25.
[4] *Deus.* XXXVI (176); *Quis Her.* XXVIII (141)-XXXIV (166); *Mos.* I (35); II (277); *Decal.* ii (5); x (41-43); xxxi (167); *Spec.* I (52); II (72-123); IV (157-159, 231); *Virt.* xix (101); xx (102-103); xxiv (121-124); *Leg.* ii (13); *Ques. Ex.* I.6. Thomas, *Op. cit.*, 8-9, partially concurred with Bauer, *Op. cit.*, col. 393-426, in his belief that Philo's own views were attributed to the Essenes.
[5] *Ant.* XVIII.21. This would be true if the Essenes, like the Rule sect (1QS 9:6) considered their community a "holy of holies" (Ezek. 44:9).
[6] *Ant.* XVIII (21).
[7] Thomas, *Op. cit.*, 22-26.

OATHS

The mishnaic tractate, Shebuoth, deals with oaths. According to the rabbis, a person who swore and broke his oath was obligated to bring an offering,[1] receive stripes,[2] or pay a fine.[3] They thought oath taking was a serious matter, since the curses imposed might prevent the coming of the kingdom.[4] Philo,[5] the author of II Enoch,[6] and some Christians [7] prohibited or seriously limited the use of vows and oaths. Josephus said that any word of the Essenes had more force than an oath. They regarded swearing to be worse than perjury, since any person who was not trustworthy without taking an oath was already condemned.[8] Josephus did not mention the fear they might have had of the curses involved in oath taking, but that certainly was part of the picture. It seems somewhat inconsistent for Essenes to have been forbidden to take oaths, on the one hand, but required to swear tremendous oaths regarding their loyalty to the group and its accepted discipline, on the other. An Essene was expected to accept death rather than break one of the oaths taken on admission.[9] The two attitudes towards oaths were not necessarily inconsistent. The required oaths were necessary to insure the scrupulous self-discipline and prescribed order required of the sect. The refusal to take other oaths was a further mark of carefulness to do nothing that would prevent God from dwelling with a remnant of his people and restoring to them the land promised to the children of Abraham.

DIVISIONS

In addition to the monastic and marrying Essenes, Josephus and Hippolytus both describe other divisions. Josephus said there were four grades, but he described only three: [10] 1) new candidates who remained outside the fraternity for one year; 2) those who

---

[1] Sheb. 3:1-4.
[2] Sheb. 3:7-8, 10-11.
[3] Sheb. 4:6; 5:4.
[4] See further "Some Vow and Oath Formulas in the NT," *HTR* 58 (1965), 319-326.
[5] *Decal.* xviii (84-95).
[6] II Enoch 49:1.
[7] Mt. 5:31-37.
[8] *BJ* II (135); so also Hippolytus IX.iv.22.
[9] *BJ* II (141-144); (152-153); Hippolytus IX.iv.23, 24, 26.
[10] *BJ* II (150).

had successfully completed the first probationary period and were allowed to share the purer kind of water "for sanctification"; 3) those who after two years in the second stage, if found "worthy," were fully admitted into the society.[1] Some have held that the fourth degree was either the children being reared or the officers of the sect, but this is only a conjecture. The four grades may have been degrees of full initiates, divided according to the time of membership. This is also a conjecture.

Hippolytus listed four divisions of Essenes according to the differences of their practice rather than their stages of development, but he also described only three: 1) those who neither carried coins with images nor walked through gates bearing statues; 2) those (called zealots; by others *sicarii*) who killed all uncircumcised who discussed God or the law unless they would accept circumcision; and 3) those who accepted death rather than confess any other Lord but God. Hippolytus added that those Essenes who held to the early rules of order considered themselves defiled if they accidentally touched any later types of Essenes. It is likely that there were grades of membership such as Josephus described, since, though more exacting, these were very similar to the probationary steps necessary for admission into other exclusive groups. It is also likely that there were sects within the sect something like the ones Hippolytus described. There is no probability, however, that the zealots or sicarii described by Josephus were only varieties of the Essene sect. Hippolytus began by misunderstanding his text and expanded his misunderstanding by misinformation. But some elements of his account have historical background. Josephus described the torture Essenes suffered during the war with Rome while holding fast to their convictions.[2]

WORSHIP AND THEOLOGY

Worship.—In addition to their purification, legalistic practices, and sacred meals, the Essenes also sent gifts to the temple but they did not sacrifice at the temple because of its uncleanness (κοινός). Hence they offered their own sacrifices according to the special conditions of purity they observed.[3]

---

[1] *BJ* II (137-138).
[2] *BJ* II (137-138); see also Smith, *HUCA*, 282-283.
[3] *Ant.* XVIII (19).

Essenes also prayed to the sun every morning at dawn, Josephus said, as if entreating the sun to rise.[1] Hippolytus [2] simply mentioned a hymn to God without any reference to possible sun worship. This was consistent with the Jewish practice of reciting the *shema'* and benedictions at dawn.[3]

Theology.—Josephus said Essenes believed in the immortality of the soul.[4] He further explained this doctrine to Romans in terms of Greek theology,[5] but was probably describing the same belief Hippolytus called resurrection of the body and associated with a final judgment.[6] After God, they honored most the name of their lawgiver and punished with death anyone who blasphemed him.[7]

One of the "tremendous oaths" Essenes were required to swear was that they would preserve carefully the books of the sect and the names of the angels.[8] Following the discovery of a text in Qumran dealing with angelology,[9] many scholars are quite willing to accept this passage to refer to a belief in angels among the Essenes.[10]

The Essenes, said Josephus, differed from the Pharisees and Sadducees on the belief in fate, by which he probably meant providence. Essenes believed providence caused all things; Sadducees said providence did not exist; but Pharisees held that some actions were the work of providence and some that of human effort.[11]

---

[1] *BJ* II (123).

[2] Hippolytus, IX.iv.21.

[3] Ber. 1:2, 4. See further W.R. Farmer, "Essenes," *ID* II, 148-149.

[4] *Ant.* XVIII (18).

[5] *BJ* II (154-158).

[6] Hippolytus IX.iv.27.

[7] *BJ* II (143). The lawgiver was probably Moses. The Essenes, like the medieval Samaritans, may have revered Moses much the same way Christians revered Jesus.

[8] *BJ* II (142).

[9] J. Strugnell, "The Angelic Liturgy at Qumran—4Q *Serek Šîrôt 'Olat Haššabbat.*" *Supplements to Vetus Testamentum, Congress Volume, Oxford,* 1959 (Leiden, 1960), 318-345.

[10] For other matters concerning the Essenes, such as sources of information, history, their relationship to Herod, the temple, and more details about individual Essenes, see W. R. Farmer, "Essenes," *ID* II, 143-149.

[11] *Ant.* XIII (171-173); XVIII (18).

Scrolls and Essenes

Among the Dead Sea Scrolls was found a book of regulations for some Jewish sect that has prompted many scholars to presume that the Essenes inhabited the quarters excavated at Qumran and composed all of the documents found in the caves nearby. Strugnell [1] was so confident that this was the case that he suggested the scrolls be considered primary sources by which Josephus, Philo, and others should be corrected. This opinion, though now general, is not universally accepted. Rabin [2] said the community was Pharisaic; Driver [3] and Roth [4] held the group was a zealot community; and Habermann [5] claimed it was Sadducean. Since the name, Essene, has not been found in any of the materials, it is not good scholarship to begin with an assumption as if it were fact. The procedure here will be to examine the unknown sect governed by the Rule of the Community (1QS) and then to compare it with the Essenes already described. Then, without assuming that the Zadokite Document (CDC) was composed by the same community as the one that composed the Rule of the Community, the Zadokite Document will be studied to learn the nature of the sect that followed its rules. This also will be compared with the Essenes to learn the similarities and differences of some of the sectarian movements in Palestine before the fall of Jerusalem.

---

[1] J. Strugnell, "Flavius Josephus and the Essenes: Antiquities XVIII. li, 22," *JBL* 77 (1958), 106-115. The identification of the Dead Sea authors with the Essenes was first made by Sukenik and later defended vigorously by A. Dupont-Sommer. See his *Les Écrits Esséniens découverts près de la Mer Morte* (Paris, 1959), 20-21. Also by F. M. Cross, Jr., *The Ancient Library of Qumran* (Garden City, 1961), 51 ff. C. Daniel, "Une Mention Paulinienne des Esséniens de Qumran," *RQ* 5 (1966), 553-554, not only assumed that the community at Qumran wrote all the scrolls and was Essene, but that, since the members of some sect represented by some of the documents referred to their own group as "Harabbim," therefore Paul meant the Essenes when he spoke of οἱ πολλοί. He observed that no Dead Sea Scroll literature mentioned the name Essene and that the idea that οἱ πολλοί as Paul used it could not refer to Jerusalem Christians (p. 555, fn. 13). He did not consider the possibility that "the many" might be a technical term used by many sects—even Pauline Christians—to describe the whole group of elect.

[2] C. Rabin, *Qumran Studies* (Oxford, 1957).

[3] Driver, *Op. cit.*

[4] Roth, *Op. cit.*

[5] A. M. Habermann, "Benê Çadôk Hêm Haççadôkîm," *Hâ³Âreç* (Mar. 30, 1956), 1-2; see also R. North, "The Qumran Sadducees," *CBQ* 17 (1955), 44-68.

THE COMMUNITY OF THE RULE

Community discipline.—The community governed by 1QS was similar in many ways to the Essenes: those who joined the sect had to contribute all their possessions to the community.[1] Members within the order were ranked according to status[2] and were required to obey superior members. This also was an exclusive sect which required meticulous observance of the law and purity rules.[3] Only those within the sect were considered pure. For all others, ablutions were useless.[4] Those not cleansed might not have contact with pure possessions of the sect, and sectarians were to be kept separate from them.[5] Like the Essenes, members were kept on varying degrees of probation for two years—this rule was more rigorous than those of the schools of Shammai or Hillel.[6] Upon admission to the sect, members were bound by oaths to follow the prescribed order, and failure to keep these oaths would bring upon them the assigned curses of the covenant.[7] In addition, they might be fined or excommunicated. Like the Essenes, the Qumran sect demanded very rigorous self-discipline,[8] agreeing in such specific details as forbidding spitting into the midst of the session or to the right[9] and punishing one who blasphemed the name of God with death.[10]

Love and hate.—Members who belonged to the sect governed by this rule were to love all the sons of light (members of the sect) and hate all the sons of darkness (non-members),[11] just as God loved one spirit and hated the other.[12] Sectarians were not to hate one another.[13] According to a man's spirit, he should either be loved or hated, by which was meant either accepted or rejected from the community "according to the cleanness of his hands."[14]

---

[1] 1QS 1:11-12; 3:2; 5:2-3, 13, 18-23; 9:8-10.
[2] 1QS 2:19-23; 5:23-25; 6:1-6, 8-9.
[3] 1QS 1:12-20; 3:9-11.
[4] 1QS 3:1-12; 4:4-6, 20-21.
[5] 1QS 5:13; 6:16-23; 8:17-18, 24-27; 9:20-21.
[6] 1QS 6:13-24; 8:1-19.
[7] 1QS 5:8-13; 2:5-12; 8:20-9:2.
[8] 1QS 6:24-7:25; 8:20-9:2.
[9] 1QS 7:13; *BJ* II (147); Hippolytus IX.iv.25.
[10] 1QS 6:27; see also *BJ* II (145).
[11] 1QS 1:10.
[12] 1QS 4:1.
[13] 1QS 5:25-26.
[14] 1QS 9:15-16.

The rules in the manual gave direction to the sectarian concerning whom he should love and hate.[1]

Essenes and the Rule sect.—Hippolytus said the Essene was required to vow that he would hate no one who wronged him or was an enemy to him,[2] but this rule may have referred only to members of the sect or hatred may have been given a different meaning, similar to this: "[Let there be] eternal hatred toward the men of the pit in a spirit of secrecy, yielding to them wealth and manual labor as a servant to his master and the submission [fitting] toward one who rules him. But let each be zealous for the decree and its season—for the day of vengeance!"[3]

Although the discipline of the Essenes was not explained in terms of love and hatred, the attitude of acceptance and rejection in terms of willingness to observe prescribed rules was characteristic of both groups. The Rule of the Community described rejection as hatred and acceptance as love.

Like the Essenes, the Rule sect based its existence on the scriptures which were to be read day and night[4] and interpreted. Studying the Torah was the way sectarians prepared in the desert a highway for God.[5] Anyone who consciously transgressed a word from the Torah of Moses was to be banished from the council never to return.[6]

THE ZADOKITES

Community discipline.—Like the Essenes and the Qumran sect, the covenanters called their sect or special group within the sect, "the many."[7] They also ranked people according to status.[8] Like the Essenes, they considered the sanctuary to be defiled,[9] and like the Rule sect, held that there had to be a priest wherever

---

[1] 1QS 9:21.

[2] Hippolytus IX.iv.23.

[3] 1QS 9:22-23.

[4] 1QS 6:6-8.

[5] 1QS 8:15-17.

[6] 1QS 8:20-23. The meaning here dealt with his intent. Whether he did it secretly or boldly, if he broke the law *knowingly*, he was rejected. See also Num. 15:30.

[7] CDC 13:7; 1QS 6:1; 7:3, 10-16, 19-25; 8:19, 26; 9:2; *BJ* II (146); see also Smith *HUCA*, 291.

[8] CDC 14:3.

[9] CDC 20B:23-24.

ten men were present.[1] They meticulously observed ritual purity [2] and the Sabbath,[3] and may have referred to their own group as a "trustworthy house" (בית נאמן).[4] They identified hatred (שנא) with rejection (מאס).[5] They evidently enrolled their members by requiring them to take oaths, which if broken would impose upon the offenders the curses of the covenant.[6] Whenever a person took an oath to turn to the Torah of Moses, the angel Mastemah left him (יסור מלאך המסטמה) if he kept his words.[7] The group did not limit swearing to admission into the sect.[8] Neither did the covenanters prohibit slavery[9] or marriage, but presumed a normal family existence in which members had children.[10] But they did object to bigamy,[11] incest,[12] and sexual intercourse in the holy city.[13] They excommunicated members who violated these rules,[14] and they gave offerings, as did the Essenes.[15] But they had no communistic economy. Instead, each member was taxed for charity,[16] probably to provide for traveling sectarians when they visited.

Sectarian similarities.—It should not be surprising to discover similarities among many of the sects that existed in Palestine before the fall of Jerusalem. Agreements in belief and practice do not by themselves constitute enough evidence to prove identity. The most convincing evidence that the Qumran group was an Essene community was Pliny's statement that the Essenes lived on the west side of the Dead Sea above Engedi. But this does not say whether "above" meant "to the north" or in a position

---

[1] CDC 13:1-2; 1QS 6:3.
[2] CDC 5:6-11; 6:17-18; 7:2-3; 8:7; 10:12-13; 12:43, 46-48, 50-54.
[3] CDC 3:14; 6:18-19; 10:14-11:18; 12:45.
[4] CDC 3:19. See Num. 12:7; I Sam. 2:35; 25:28; I Kgs. 11:38.
[5] CDC 2:15.
[6] CDC 1:17.
[7] CDC 16:5-6.
[8] CDC 15:1-13; 16:1-13.
[9] CDC 12:49.
[10] CDC 15:5-6. Couples were to marry according to the rules of the Torah, however, and train their children to observe the Torah (CDC 7:6-7).
[11] CDC 4:20-21.
[12] CDC 5:8-21.
[13] CDC 12:1-2.
[14] CDC 20B:6-8.
[15] CDC 6:20.
[16] CDC 14:13-17.

that was higher in altitude.[1] Although there are striking similarities between CDC and 1QS, there are important differences: The sect of CDC had no monastic or communistic order and it permitted slavery.[2] It was careful in its attempt to fulfill the law, but not so scrupulous as the Rule sect or the Essenes. The Rule sect was more like the Essene sect than any known Jewish group, and Pliny's description is strongly in favor of identifying the Rule sect with the community of the Essenes, but it is more important to discover the kinds of movements that went on in pre-70 A.D. Palestine than to identify the beliefs of a group with the name of a sect. The ways in which the sect of the Rule and the Zadokite community resemble the Essenes are closely related to the law. The close relationship between the habits of the monastic Essenes and the community of the Rule is noticeable because both groups were extremely meticulous in their observance of the law. The ways in which the marrying Essenes and the Zadokite community differed from the celibate groups was in their modification of the law to make allowances for other practical matters of life. Since they all had the same law and the same ancient tradition and since they all lived in Palestine at the same time in history, similarities were evident. If the sect who composed 1QS had been named "Essene" in 1QS and if the Zadokite sect had referred to itself as an Essene group in CDC, it would then be proper to accept their self-designations and note the variations within the Essene sect. Since this was not done it seems more judicious to note their similarities and differences without forcing conclusions based on inadequate evidence.

THE PHARISEES

Normative Judaism.—Many scholars have assumed that all of the rabbinic literature has been composed and preserved by rabbis who were Pharisees. The strongest evidence for this view is its anti-Sadducean *tendenz*. Josephus and the NT both show Pharisees and Sadducees in conflict, but this does not necessarily mean that the Pharisees were the only people who did not like the Sadducees, even though many scholars have considered no other possibility. Moore has been well received with his hypothesis that "normal" or "normative" Judaism of the first Christian century was best

---

[1] See J.-P. Audet, "Qumran et la Notice de Pline," *RB* 68 (1961), 346-387; C. Burchard, "Pline et les Esséniens," *RB* 69 (1962), 533-569.
[2] CDC 12:49.

represented by rabbinic literature.[1] This was a satisfying conclusion for those who liked the ethics of the rabbis, approved the
Pharisees, and assumed themselves to be the spiritual descendants
of both.[2] But that hypothesis dismissed apocalyptic literature
as of no importance and assumed the Essenes to have comprised
a very minor percentage of Judaism before the fall of Jerusalem.[3]
It also assumed that pacifistic Pharisees made up the majority
party in first century Palestinian Judaism.[4] This construction
has overlooked the war of 66-70 A.D. that was fought to the death
by a great many first century Palestinian Jews. What, then,
happened to the large number of pacifistic Pharisees in the land?
Had they really been pacifistic and the majority party, then they
would have provided such a strong pacifistic religion in Palestine
that the zealots would not have been able to recruit enough soldiers
to fight Rome. Some alternate possibilities are these: 1) The Pharisees were not pacifistic until after the fall of Jerusalem, when they
changed their ethics as a result of the resistance movement. 2) The
Pharisees constituted only a small percentage of Palestinian
residents before 70 A.D. These were pacifistic. After the fall of

---

[1] G. F. Moore *Judaism* (Cambridge, I and II, 1927; III, 1930); I, 83,
126-130; II, 281, *et passim*, was not the first to hold these views on Judaism,
but he made them more popular. See also L. Ginsberg, *The Legends of the
Jews*, tr. H. Szold (Philadelphia, c1901), I, xiii. M. Black, "Pharisees," *ID*
III, 781, also assumes Pharisaism was the immediate ancestor of rabbinic
Judaism, and composed the Psalms of Solomon. He did not claim it to be
quietistic, however. B. Gerhardsson, *Memory and Manuscript* (Uppsala, 1961),
30, basically accepted Moore's thesis with some reservations. J. Aptowitzer,
*Parteipolitik der Hasmonäerzeit im rabbinischen und pseudepigraphischen
Schrifttum* (New York, 1927), xxv-xxviii, whose book is otherwise thought-
provoking, conjectured that some OT books were Sadducean and others,
Pharisaic. If there were Sadducees and Pharisees at the time these books were
written, there is no way of knowing their characteristics at that time.

[2] L. Finkelstein, *The Pharisees* (Philadelphia, 1962), I, 79, also believed
Pharisaism later embraced the whole of Judaism. Justin Martyr, second
century Christian, listed among those sects which orthodox Jews would
not acknowledge: Sadducees, Genistae, Meristae, Galileans, Hellenians,
Pharisees, and Baptists (*Dialogue* 80:4). All of these were apparently existing
sects in Justin's time.

[3] E.g. C. Gordon, *Adventures in the Nearest East* (Fairlawn, 1957), 134-
135, 137-141.

[4] For a portrayal of the Pharisees as a group of democratic, non-mate-
rialistic merchants who were also super-pious pacifists, representing everything good in the Israel-Judah tradition, see Finkelstein, *Op. cit.*, 2 vols.
Another well-known defensive work is R. T. Herford, *The Pharisees* (New
York, 1924), who claimed that the main body of Pharisees remained firmly
attached to a peace policy, "even down to the last war" (p. 51).

Jerusalem, when most of the native population had been killed, the Pharisees became stronger and held more important positions in the diaspora than they had before 70 A.D. 3) They comprised only a small rigorous group of law abiding Jews, very much like the Essenes. They were not always either pacifistic or militaristic, but changed their interpretation of conquest theology depending on the situation. After the fall of Jerusalem, most of the rabbis, most of the time, advised non-resistance against Rome. 4) The remnant that survived the fall of Jerusalem was not just Pharisaic but consisted of different sects whose wisdom is reflected in rabbinic literature. The pacifism of this literature, then, reflects rather a Jewish judgment of the proper way to act *at that time* than the normative views of any sect in Judaism before the fall of Jerusalem.

The Pharisees did not necessarily write all of the rabbinic literature and may not therefore be adequately represented there. Some of the rabbis may have been Pharisees but not necessarily all. Because some of the doctrines in rabbinic literature were similar to those of the Pharisees it has been supposed that they were responsible for the entire body of literature. One of the few to question this possibility was Prof. Guttmann,[1] who called attention to the anti-Pharisaic feelings expressed in the Talmud.[2] It has further been assumed that a group of Jews known as "Associates" (חברים) were Pharisees.[3] Then the question arises: were they all of the Pharisees, or were they only a percentage of a larger group?[4] A still further question is the relationship between the "trustworthy ones" and the "associates."[5] There is no rabbinic

---

[1] A. Guttmann, "Pharisaism in Transition," *Essays in Honor of Solomon B. Freehof* (Pittsburg, 1964), 202-219.

[2] A. Michel and J. LeMayne, "Pharisiens," *Supplément au Dictionnaire de la Bible* (Paris, 1964), fasc. 39-40, cols. 1054-1055, also question the equation of rabbis with descendants of the Pharisees. There is, of course, the remote possibility that anti-Pharisaic statements represented self-criticism, but it seems unlikely.

[3] E. g. K. Kohler, "Pharisees," *JE* IX, 661.

[4] J. Neusner, "The Fellowship (HBWRH) in the Second Commonwealth," *HTR* 53 (1960), 125, first thought that the Pharisees were a large group of which the "association" was only a small fraction. He was evidently convinced of this by A. Büchler, *Der Galiläische Am HaAreṣ des zweiten Jahrhunderts* (Vienna, 1906), but changed his position when he was persuaded that Büchler's thesis had been "demolished by Gedalyahu Allon"—so Neusner, "HBR and NʾMN," *RQ* 5 (1964), 121.

[5] Without noticing a conflict, Finkelstein, I, 66, also said Pharisaic hope for the Kingdom of God was "Part of the every day thought of the

testimony to Pharisees being "associates" or "trustworthy" or those responsible for the composition of rabbinic literature. It is reasonable, then, to admit some ignorance about the relationship of the Pharisees to these and begin an investigation of the Pharisees from some other point, based on more certain information. The earliest sources describing the Pharisees are these: 1) the witness of Paul who had himself been a Pharisee together with the report of the Gospels which were written in opposition to the Pharisees, and 2) the report of Josephus who had also been a Pharisee.[1]

Pharisees in the NT.—The NT consistently reported the Pharisees to have been a careful law-observing group. In the Sermon on the Mount, the Pharisees were chosen as one of the groups whose righteousness Christians must excel if they would be perfect.[2] The Pharisaic community was considered the strictest sect in Judaism.[3] Its members sat on Moses' seat[4] and were known for fasting,[5] washing,[6] and tithing.[7] They were contrasted to tax collectors,[8] and Pharisaic Christians had required circumcision.[9] Paul, before his conversion, was a Pharisee "as to the law"[10] who was extremely zealous for the tradition of his fathers and so persecuted Christians.[11] Pharisees

---

pietists." "Rome might conquer; it could only be for the moment. Ultimately the Lord would prove Himself unique in strength." How did these war-hating Pharisees expect to overthrow Rome peacefully?

[1] Herford, *Op. cit.*, 14, dismissed the NT, Josephus, and the Apocalyptic literature as invalid and Christian scholarship of no importance. In his opinion, "The only true source of information as to the Pharisees, the Rabbinic literature . . . The only real contributions made hitherto to the knowledge of the principles of Pharisaism have been made by Jewish scholars." See further p. 22.

[2] Mt. 5:20.

[3] Acts 26:5. This is all contrary to Finkelstein, *Op. cit.*, I, 10, who pictured the Pharisees as those noted for their "liberalism," "intellectual objectivity," and "tolerance."

[4] Mt. 23:2-3.

[5] Mt. 9:14; Lk. 5:33.

[6] Mt. 23:25; Lk. 11:39.

[7] Lk. 11:42.

[8] Lk. 18:9-13.

[9] Acts 15:5.

[10] Philip. 3:5.

[11] Gal. 1:13-14. In spite of their militaristic record, Finkelstein, I, xiv, in order to show the Pharisees in a good light, said, "So rapidly did Pharisaism spread in the palaces of Rome that the patricians became alarmed . . . The Romans were a tolerant people, but they drew the line at a religion which openly preached *equality of mankind and the futility and wickedness of war*" [italics mine]. After the war of 66-72 A. D. and the Bar Cochba revolt, the Roman alarm was probably not because Pharisees were pacifistic or

criticized Jesus and/or his disciples for eating with tax collectors and sinners,[1] breaking the Sabbath,[2] not washing before eating,[3] and blaspheming.[4] Moreover, there may have been communistic, monastic Pharisees who took vows upon admission the way the Essenes and Rule sect did and turned their possessions over to the group, because they were accused of taking vows that prevented their "honoring" their parents by caring for them in their old age.[5] These Pharisees who lived in Palestine before 70 A.D. appear to have been a very legalistic, activistic sect. Although Josephus' report was written later, he described the Pharisees at a still earlier stage, and his report is consistent with that of the NT.

According to Josephus.—Josephus described the Pharisees as a sect that was already stable when the king, John Hyrcanus, belonged to it. At that time one of the Pharisees, named Eleazar, suggested that Hyrcanus give up the priesthood because there was some question of his mother's having been in captivity in the time of Antiochus Epiphanes. Hyrcanus responded negatively to the suggestion, parted company with the Pharisees, and became a member of the Sadducees.[6] The hostility between the royal power and the Pharisees evidently continued throughout the reign of Alexander Jannaeus. During his reign, he had so much opposition that he had eight hundred Jews crucified, while slaughtering their children and wives before their eyes.[7] Josephus did not say that these people were Pharisees, but he did report that after Alexander's death, his wife, Alexandra, found it necessary to make many concessions to the Pharisees because of the many things they suffered at Alexander's hands.[8] So much favor did she show the Pharisees that Josephus said it was the Pharisees

---

universalistic. The very name, Pharisee—separatist—shows they did *not* believe in equality. That would have been contrary to the doctrine of the chosen people.

[1] Mt. 9:11; Lk. 5:30; 7:36-39; 15:2.
[2] Mt. 12:2; Lk. 2:7; Jn. 9:13-16.
[3] Mt. 15:1-2; Lk. 11:38.
[4] Lk. 5:21.
[5] Mt. 15:1-6.
[6] *Ant.* XIII (288-296).
[7] *Ant.* XII (379-382). For an analysis of the nature of Pharisaic rebellion against Jannaeus, see C. Rabin, "Alexander Jannaeus and the Pharisees," *JJS* 7 (1956), 3-11.
[8] *Ant.* XIII (403).

who really ruled the kingdom while Alexandra was queen. They had so many leading citizens (who had counseled Alexander to crucify the eight hundred?) excecuted that the citizens appealed to Alexandra to put an end to the shedding of Jewish blood.[1] These early accounts disclose the Pharisees as a powerful group but not as a pacifistic body.[2] Further evidence of their power was displayed when they refused to take an oath to Caesar during Herod's reign. In other ways they resisted Herod so much that Herod had many of them put to death.[3] Josephus claimed they were more lenient in matters of punishment than most Jews, but the punishment they inflicted on their enemies in Alexandra's time did not show this to be true.[4] Although this evidence suggests that the Pharisees were a very influential and powerful group, it does not prove that they were the majority party either in the time of John Hyrcanus or Herod.

The only numerical count of the Pharisaic strength said there were more than six thousand Pharisees.[5] This was by no means the majority of Palestinian citizens at that time. In fact, it is only fifty percent larger than the Essene body of four thousand members, which scholars have dismissed as a small sect by contrast to the large Pharisaic party.[6] Josephus nowhere suggested that there were any divisions within the Pharisaic sect, a likely possibility had it been a very large group. Rather he described the Pharisees as a sect which excelled others in accurate knowledge of the laws of their country [7] or of their fathers,[8] and he said that they were very careful in their observance of dietary laws.[9] The more demanding a group was in its legalistic requirements, the smaller it would have been. A moderate interpretation of the law with generous allowances for minor transgressions would have allowed a large group to develop. From Josephus' point of view alone, the Pharisees were considered a small, very influential group of activists that observed the law very rigorously. This seems to describe a

---

[1] *Ant.* XIII (408-415).
[2] See p. 261, fn. 5 and p. 262, fn. 11.
[3] *Ant.* XVIII (41-46).
[4] *Ant.* XIII (294, 410-411).
[5] *Ant.* XVII (42).
[6] Philo, *Hyp.*, XI (75). See Gordon, *Op. cit.*
[7] *Vita* (191-192).
[8] *Ant.* XVII (41).
[9] *Ant.* XVIII (12).

sect that was almost as similar to the Essenes as the Rule sect or the Zadokite sect. Scholars have not called them "Essenes" because Josephus specifically distinguished them by the name "Pharisees." The Pharisaic sect, like the Essene sect, seemed to have been more like a brotherhood or monastic order in the Roman Catholic Church than a major political party in the United States of America. This concurs with what is said of the Pharisees in the NT.

Pharisees and rabbinic literature.—It is very difficult, if not impossible, to learn the character of the Pharisees in the first century of the Christian Era in Palestine from rabbinic literature, which was mostly edited or originally composed in the diaspora sometime between the third and the seventh century A.D., and which seldom mentioned the Pharisees by name.[1] Some early tradition may be preserved in this literature, but it must be demonstrated point by point by comparison with Josephus, Philo, or some other earlier writer. A statement attributed to an early rabbi may have been composed, as well as attributed to him, by a later rabbi. Literature written and preserved by the rabbis may or may not have been written by Pharisaic rabbis, and the date of its composition must still be established by some other criterion than the date at which the rabbi in question lived. Parts of Sifra, for instance, seem to be Pharisaic: Sifra commented on the scriptural passages, "You must be holy (קדשים) for I the Lord your God am holy" (קדוש),[3] by saying, "Just as I am a Pharisee (פרוש), so you be Pharisees" (פרושים).[4] "You must be holy (קדשים); you must be Pharisees" (פרושים).[5] Although the word, Pharisee, also means a separatist,

---

[1] Ignoring chronology, Finkelstein, *Op. cit.*, said, "Josephus simply echoes the statement of the Mishnah." If Hag. 1:8 has any relationship to Ant. XIII.x.6, then the rabbis used Josephus and not vice versa.

[2] Renée Bloch, "Note méthodologique pour l'étude de la littérature rabbinique," *RSR* 43 (1955), 194-227, has successfully demonstrated the accuracy with which it is possible to show materials contained in later literature to have been written much earlier.

[3] Lev. 11:44; 19:1; 20:26.

[4] Sifra 86c.

[5] Although Pharisees seem very much like the Essenes, there is not enough evidence to show that the Essenes could "out-Pharisee the Pharisees" or that the Pharisees composed a democratic political party of modernists as M. Black, "Pharisees," *ID* III 777, holds. Herford, *Op. cit.*, 51, said the Essenes had "practiced an asceticism which was never adopted or even approved by the Pharisees." Herford could have learned more about the Pharisees than he seems to know even from his chosen rabbinic sources.

and therefore might have been used in Sifra only in its general meaning as a synonym for "holy," the ambiguity of the text would have been more likely to appeal to a Pharisee than to any other sectarian. The meticulous care that has been given in commenting on every verse of the Book of Leviticus indicates the work of some person or group very much concerned about purity laws. The Pharisees described by Josephus and the NT indicate that they would have been eligible candidates for this type of scribal work before the fall of Jerusalem, but this kind of confirmation is not everywhere apparent in all rabbinic literature. E.g. there are only five passages in the entire Tosefta and two in the entire Mishnah that mention Pharisees.[1] The discussion between Shammai and Hillel on whether or not a Pharisaic *zab* might eat with an '*am haaretz zab* is consistent with the accounts of Pharisees reported in earlier literature.[2] So also was the report that Pharisees drank no wine and ate no meat after the fall of the temple, because there were no longer sacrifices being offered.[3] R. Joshua said they were being unnecessarily strict. These discussions relating Hillel, Shammai, and R. Joshua to the Pharisees do not prove that these rabbis were themselves Pharisees any more than their discussions with heretics, Sadducees, or Boethusians identify them with those groups. The daily baptizers criticized the Pharisees because they took oaths in the Name when their bodies were not ritually clean.[4] It is not clear, however, whether these criticisms were true of all Pharisees or only a certain group of Pharisees. The accusation that the wounds of the Pharisees would "wear out the world" certainly was not pro-Pharisaic.[5] The quarrels between the Pharisees and Sadducees were reported neither from a pro-Pharisaic nor anti-Pharisaic point of view,[6] so there is little direct evidence that the Pharisees wrote either the Mishnah or the Tosefta.

There are a few references to "associates" (חברים), which

---

[1] T. Ber. 3:25; Shab. 1:15; Hag. 3:25; Sotah 15:11; Yad. 2:20; Sotah 3:4; Yad. 4:6-8. R. Johanan b. Zakkai referred to the Pharisees as if he were not one himself.

[2] T. Shab. 1:15.

[3] T. Sotah 15:11.

[4] T. Yad. 2:20.

[5] Sotah 3:4.

[6] Yad. 4:6-8. R. Johanan ben Zakkai's reference to Pharisees in the third person may mean that he was *not* a Pharisee. So Guttmann, *Op. cit.*, 204.

scholars have identified with the Pharisees,[1] but the rabbis did not make this identification. The "associates," like the "trustworthy ones," were distinguished by the extreme care by which they observed the law.[2] The Pharisees described by Josephus and the NT qualify for the rules ascribed to these groups, but so would the Essenes or any other very law-abiding sect.[3] Samaritans and Sadducees who were observant were called "associates." [4] It would be difficult to conjecture how many sects in Palestine tried to practice every letter of the law. The Dead Sea Scrolls probably reflect the beliefs of more than one sect. The literature that appears most like Essene literature is also most like Pharisaic literature. It is more useful to learn from these the nature of sectarianism in Judaism than to attempt to discern the peculiarities of any one particular sect.

SADDUCEES

Sadducean opposition.—There are no early sources that describe the Sadducees objectively. Josephus said they did not believe in divine providence or intervention or in life after death. They were confident of the freedom of the human will. As people they were contrary, boorish, and even rude, both among themselves and toward other people.[5] The NT concurs that they did not believe in the resurrection; it associated them with the priests; and classified them together with the Pharisees as opponents of John the Baptist and Jesus.[6] In rabbinic literature the Sadducees were shown in discussion with different rabbis. They regularly lost the arguments the rabbis reported, but this was clearly tendential, even though not necessarily Pharisaic.[7] Many arguments were

---

[1] Finkelstein, *Op. cit.*, I, 76; A. Geiger, *Urschrift und Uebersetzungen der Bibel* (Breslau, 1851), 121-125; Neusner, *Op. cit.*, 125-142; C. Rabin, *Qumran Studies* (Oxford, 1957); "The Role of Purity in the Structure of the Essene Sect," *RQ* 4 (1963), 403-404. R. Hummel, *Die Auseinandersetzung zwischen Kirche und Judentum im Mattäusevangelium* (München, 1963), 15, said, "Die meisten Pharisäer dagegen waren einfache Mitglieder einer Pharisäischen Chaburah . . ."

[2] Demai 2:3; T. Demai 2:3-5, 13-3:17; JDemai 23a.

[3] See p. 265, fn. 5.

[4] Nid. 33b.

[5] *BJ* II (164-166); *Ant.* XVIII (16-17).

[6] Mt. 3:7-10; 12:38; 15:1-3; 16:1-6; 16:11-12; 21:15-32; 21:45; 22:15-28; 22:34-41; 23:1-31.

[7] Shab. 108; 152a-152b; Er. 101a; Suk. 43b; Yeb. 63b.

about textual interpretations,[1] laws,[2] or proper calendars.[3] Accepting
all of the insults the rabbis gave the Sadducees as valid, Hölscher
said they did not comprise a sect at all but were instead all scoffers
who made merry over those who stressed rigorous observances of
religious rules,[4] but this contradicts Josephus' report that the
Sadducees, like the Pharisees and the Essenes, were members of
sects. Finkelstein said that the dominant "characteristic of Pharisees was study: that of the Sadducism was contempt for scholarship." [5] Herford observed, "There is no mention so far as I know,
of Sadducean synagogues." [6] If he knew of Pharisaic synagogues,
he did not mention them. He gave one interpretation to the rabbinic
silence on the subject of synagogues for the Pharisees and the
exact opposite interpretation for the Sadducees. The Sadducean
ability to engage some of the most learned rabbis in debate over
technical legal and religious matters, however, contradicts Herford's
and Finkelstein's evaluation of their attitude toward scholarship.
Sadducees were classified together with the Boethusians and heretics as opponents of the Pharisees [7] or rabbis, but some scholars
have attributed to them the composition of the Zadokite Document,
Jubilees, the Testaments of the Twelve Patriarchs, most of Enoch,
and the Assumption of Moses.[8]

Possibilities.—Since there is no certainly identifiable Sadducean
literature or early writings on their behalf, it will be necessary to
deduce their character from the limited evidence available. Josephus
reported that after John Hyrcanus had a conflict with the Pharisees,
he joined the Sadducean party.[9] Since he belonged to a levitic
family, this may confirm the idea that the sect was basically a group
that supported the sons of Zadok as the true priests. If more were

---

[1] Ber. 7a; 10a.
[2] Shab. 108a; Suk. 43b; Hag. 16b; Mak. 5b.
[3] Yoma 53a; Suk. 13b; Men. 65a-65b; Yoma 2a; 22b.
[4] G. Hölscher, *Der Sadducäismus* (Leipzig, 1906).
[5] Finkelstein, *Op. cit.*, I, 97.
[6] Herford, *Op. cit.*, 97-98.
[7] Ber. 3:25; Hag. 22b; T. Hag. 3:25; Men. 65a-65b; Yoma 2a; 19a;
Par. 3:7; Yad. 2:20. Also A. C. Sundberg, "Sadducees," *ID* IV, 160-163.
[8] Black, *Op. cit.*, and Sundberg, *Op. cit.*, for a fuller account of the continued conflicts between Pharisees and Sadducees. Black called much of the
intertestamental literature Pharisaic.
[9] *BJ* II (164-166); *Ant.* XII (295-297); XVIII (16-17).

known of the Hasmonean family tree, the extent to which it adhered to this principle would be better understood.[1] Among the sects that supported the sons of Zadok as priests were those that were represented by CDC and 1QS.[2] Josephus mentioned that the Sadducees accepted no traditional teaching not found in the Pentateuch.[3] The fact that they were often involved in discussion with the rabbis and Jesus indicates that they were more carefully observant of the law than their enemies acknowledged. It is likely that there were scholarly discussions in which the rabbis lost the argument but these were not included in the literature the rabbis themselves collected. In some instances rabbis deferred to Sadducean practice,[4] or noted that the Sadducees were more strict in their interpretation of the law than the rabbis themselves. Some scholars have assumed without evidence that the sect ceased to exist after the fall of Jerusalem. In order to maintain their position, scholars of this persuasion have emended the Talmud wherever a Sadducee was reported in a discussion with a rabbi after 70 A.D.[5] There are too few data to state certainly when the sect began, ended, or the exact nature of the group while it existed.[6]

Members of one group of Jews that belonged to a sect were called "associates" (חברים). Scholars generally identify them with the Pharisees, either as the whole Pharisaic sect or else the strictest observers among the Pharisees, but there is no direct identification of the associates with Pharisees in rabbinic literature.[7] Some scholars who assume that all rabbinic literature is of Pharisaic origin, however, make the further assumption that the members of this group

---

[1] *Ibid.* According to Gen. R. 97 (new version); 99:2, the Hasmoneans were Levites rather than Zadokites by birth.

[2] CDC 3:20-4:5; 1QS 5:2, 9.

[3] See p. 268, fn. 9. Gerhardsson, *Op. cit.*, 24, however, concurred with Lauterbach, *Rabbinic Essays* (Cincinnati, 1951), 27-48, in holding that Sadducees "did not *per se* reject every complement to the Pentateuchal laws, but that they did deny the fully normative standing of such orally transmitted rules."

[4] Par. 3:7.

[5] I. Epstein, *The Babylonian Talmud* (London, c1938), Mo'ed I, 419, fn. 1; 780, fn. 4. But Justin, *Dialogue* 80:4, listed Sadducees among the sects that existed during the second century A.D.

[6] Scholars who assume the sect ended after the temple fell usually identify Sadducees with the temple priesthood.

[7] Some priests were also *Ḥaverim* (T. Damai 3:2-3).

reported in rabbinic literature were also Pharisees. Since this presumes the conclusion before the inquiry, it will be necessary here to proceed from some other position. Instead of using the material describing associates to define the nature of the Pharisaic sect, the first task will be to learn the character of the group or groups that called itself or themselves associates.

Associates were mostly described in contrast to the "people of the land" (עמי הארץ), and their rules given in relationship to the 'amme-haaretz. Associates were not permitted to sell to an 'am-haaretz food that had been moistened so that it was subject to ritual defilement. Neither could they buy from the 'amme-haaretz any kind of foodstuff, either wet or dry. They could not be guests in the homes of 'amme-haaretz.[1] The reason for these limitations was that the associates did not trust the 'amme-haaretz to have kept ritual purity. Therefore both their food and clothing were held under suspicion. Those associates who were suspicious that their fellow associate's food had not been tithed were not allowed to eat it for more than a week, even if they had taken oaths that they would eat. If an 'am-haaretz wished to join the sect and was willing to fulfill all of the requirements except one, he would not be accepted.[2] If he was suspected of breaking only one rule, he was treated as if he had broken them all.[3] The *pater familias* was required to take his vows before the whole society, but his sons and servants could take their vows before him. One of the rabbis mentioned, however, that the associate who took his vows before the whole group and then misbehaved would have committed a more serious offense than his son would have committed by breaking the same rules.[4] An associate's son who spent time with his maternal, 'am-haaretz grandfather was forbidden to eat any pure food offered him by his grandfather, and he was required to consider his grandfather's garments as defiled with *midras* uncleanness.[5] The daughter or ex-wife of an 'am-haaretz who married an associate was required to start at the beginning of initiation into membership.[6] The same was true of a servant of an 'am-haaretz who was

---

[1] Demai 2:3.
[2] T. Demai 2:5.
[3] T. Demai 2:3.
[4] T. Damai 2:14.
[5] T. Demai 2:15.
[6] T. Demai 2:16-24.

sold to an associate. On the other hand, the daughter or ex-wife of
an associate who married an 'am-haaretz or an associate's servant
who was sold to an 'am-haaretz were all treated as associates until
there was an occasion to cause suspicion. The servants or sons of
an associate who studied under the direction of an 'am-haaretz
were treated as associates until their behavior occasioned suspicion,
but the sons or servants of an 'am-haaretz who studied under the
direction of an associate were considered associates so long as they
studied under the associate. As soon as they left, they were considered 'amme-haaretz. Associates were forbidden to send pure objects
to one another by means of a messenger who was an 'am-haaretz,
and associates were not permitted to send to an 'am-haaretz pure objects forbidden to an 'am-haaretz. He could not even grant an 'am-
haaretz' request for food and wine, if it were pure food. Associates
were not permitted to give anyone any product that was forbidden
to them. Furthermore the associate could not accept the word of an
'am-haaretz concerning questions of purity, nor was he permitted to
bless people indiscriminately or offer a table grace or respond with,
"Amen," after the prayers of those who did not follow the correct
doctrines.[2] Associates who mixed dough for baking did not prepare
it as pure food for an 'am-haaretz. Such obligations as giving terumah
or principle and added fifth, which the law required Israel to give to
the priests, were fulfilled by associates by contributing only to priests
who were also associates. A priest who was an associate could eat
or receive a portion in impurity (בטומאה) with a priest who was an
'am-haaretz, but not in purity. An associate who became a tax
collector was excommunicated from the group, but if he gave up
his position as a tax collector he could then be restored and considered trustworthy (נאמן). An associate should not serve either
a drinking party or a banquet for an 'am-haaretz, but if he did, the
food and drink he prepared must be scrupulously prepared so that
all laws were properly obeyed. Should an associate participate in
a drinking party or banquet served by an 'am-haaretz, his society
should not convict him immediately. He might have had his son
tithe for him or he might have mentally vowed to tithe for the
produce he consumed. If a tavern owner who was an associate had
a clerk who was an 'am-haaretz, the owner could go and come and
still be confident that his clerk did not mix the merchandise.[2]

---

[1] T. Demai 2:24.
[2] T. Demai 3:1-9.

In this discussion, the associate was clearly a member of some sect that was very exclusive in its hospitality. He was trustworthy (נאמן) in matters of purity. The group admitted priests to its ranks. The rules that governed the conduct of associates were the rules that governed the Essenes, Pharisees, Community of the Rule, and the Zadokite sect. The associate was a member in full communion with his group, but the name of the group was not given. It is possible that members of all careful sects called their members "associates," but this is just as much of a conjecture as the assumption that all associates were Pharisees. Even though their name is unknown, the nature of the discipline of associates is well-understood against the general sectarian movement in NT times, and the customs of this sort of group can be used to clarify customs of other groups that had been organized for the same purpose in the same period in history on the same geographical territory.

THE SECT OF ST. MATTHEW

Legalism and the land.—In the Gospel of St. Matthew, there is a tradition that is strongly legalistic, Jewish, and sectarian. This is in contrast to the teachings of Jesus found in the *chreias* and parables. The legalistic literature either represents the teachings and practices of one sect or sectarian practices collected and published from more than one source.

The centrality of the land and the Kingdom of God is evident throughout the material. The beatitudes promised blessings that involved the Kingdom of Heaven,[2] "comfort," i.e. restoration of the land,[3] inheriting the land,[4] fulfilling righteousness,[5] receiving

---

[1] Mt. 5:3, 10.

[2] Mt. 5:4.

[3] Mt. 5:5. RSV translated ἡ γῆ, "the earth," but the context deals with OT promises to be fulfilled, and Israel believed she had been promised "the land," meaning the promised land, Palestine. The Latin text of Didache quoted Mt. 5:5 and rendered ἡ γῆ, "*sanctam terram.*" For a basis to consider the Latin text a reliable translation of an early Greek text, see J.-P. Audet, "Affinités littéraires et doctrinales du 'Manuel de Discipline,'" *RB* 59 (1952), 217-238. The likelihood that a late Christian editor would have added the adjective, *sanctam*, is small. This means the land expected was the holy or promised land. 4Qp. Ps. 37:11, 21-22 interpreted the passage, "and the poor will inherit the land" (ארץ), as the Ebionites (האביונים) who would inherit the "high mountain of Israel, the mount of his holiness" (הר מרום ישראל והר[קודשו) (1:8-11).

[4] Mt. 5:6.

mercy,[1] seeing God,[2] and being called God's sons.[3] Contrary to the anti-legalism of the parables and *chreias*, Jesus was here quoted as assuring the disciples that he had no plans for destroying the law, but only for fulfilling it.[4] He would not remove one *yodh* or "horn" from the written law, and he insisted that anyone who would depreciate the law would be given a low rank in the Kingdom of Heaven.[5] The righteousness of this sect of Christianity was more demanding than that of the scribes and the Pharisees:[6] For instance, the law only forbade committing murder, but this sect prohibited anger or name calling to another member of the sect.[7] This was similar to the legalism of the Rule of the Community[8] which punished members severely for becoming angry, disparaging other members unjustly, speaking haughtily, bearing a grudge, speaking folly, interrupting their fellows, or sleeping during a session. The Matthaean sect not only prohibited adultery, but even a glance at a woman so as to desire her.[9] The community was of the same opinion as R. Phineas b. Jair, who said that attentiveness led to cleanliness, cleanliness to purity, purity to abstinence, and abstinence to holiness.[10] The Community of the Rule had similar legislation prohibiting a member from exhibiting his nakedness in the presence of his brother.[11] These rules of propriety were strictly enforced. As with other sects, the group whose ethics was reported in Matthew prohibited any type of oath-taking.[12] In order to build up the treasury of merits, members were forbidden to retaliate, but were instead to return good for evil.[13] Good deeds were to be done to receive God's reward.[14] This was the type of ethics required of those who would be full members of the sect and therefore perfect in law observance.[15]

---

[1] Mt. 5:7.
[2] Mt. 5:8.
[3] Mt. 5:9.
[4] Mt. 5:17.
[5] Mt. 5:18-19.
[6] Mt. 5:20.
[7] Mt. 5:22.
[8] 1QS 6:24-7:25.
[9] Nid. 2:1 gives similar punishment for masturbation.
[10] Sotah 9:15.
[11] 1QS 7:13-14.
[12] Mt. 5:33-38.
[13] Mt. 5:38-47; compare with 1QS 10:16-21.
[14] Mt. 6:1-6; compare with Ps. Sol. 10:1.
[15] Mt. 5:48.

Hospitality.—Like the Essenes, the sect of St. Matthew expected hospitality in every city in the homes of the "worthy" (ἄξιοι). The twelve were sent out without gold, silver, or copper in their belts, no bags, no sandals, and with only one tunic each. They were told: "And whatever town or village you enter, find out one who is worthy (ἄξιος) in it, and stay with him until you depart. As you enter the house, salute it. And if the house is 'worthy' (ἄξια), let your peace come upon it; but if it is not 'worthy' let your peace return to you." [1] The disciples evidently were instructed to come up to a house (εἰσερχόμενοι δὲ εἰς τὴν οἰκίαν), volunteering some greeting, like, "Peace upon you!" [2] The Mishnah gives some of the necessary tests by which a person could learn whether or not the resident was trustworthy.[3] The twelve evidently employed some such means before entering the house. If it was not "worthy," they took their blessings back, perhaps by shaking the dust off their shoes to break the effect of their initial blessing,[4] or else it may have returned automatically if they did not stay. This is similar to the practices of the associates when dealing with *'amme haaretz*: "They do not pronounce blessings over them; they do not say table grace for them; and they do not say, 'Amen!' after their prayers." [5] With exclusive groups there was no fraternizing or sharing blessings with non-sectarians. They were warned not to give "dogs" that which was holy, nor to cast their pearls before "swine." [6] The theology of the group was understood in terms of practices the members knew. It was because of an Essene-like hospitality program that disciples were assured that they could ask, seek, and knock, and be confident that their needs would be met.[7] It was the *traveling* missionaries who depended upon the hospitality of other sectarians who were taught to pray, "Give us today our daily bread." [8] It was the *itinerant* disciples who were told not to treasure up for themselves treasures on earth.[9] They were to travel light so as to have no impediment. They were not to be anxious for

---

[1] Mt. 10:11-13.
[2] Mt. 10:12; also see Lk. 10:5.
[3] Demai 4:6-7.
[4] Mt. 10:13-14.
[5] T. Demai 2:24.
[6] Mt. 7:6. Black's emendation is not necessary.
[7] Mt. 7:7.
[8] Mt. 6:11.
[9] Mt. 6:19.

their material welfare (ψυχή) such as food and clothing. These were cares that the Gentiles had. But covenanters could be assured that God would meet their needs from day to day just as their fellow sectarians did.[2] This was part of the community administration. Travelers who had the same convictions as the residents would always be adequately cared for. They did not need to lay up treasures, but the sectarians, who lived in various cities and were expected to be able to provide for the itinerant members whenever they arrived, would have been obligated to keep a good supply of food and clothing stored up to be prepared for them when they came. Otherwise the whole program would have failed, and the traveling preachers would have been forced to lay up treasures on earth for themselves.

The rigid sinlessness of the sect of St. Matthew was evident in its efforts to have sins forgiven. The member who brought his gift to the altar and then remembered that he had sinned against one of his brothers and had not been reconciled was required to leave his gift and be reconciled first and then offer his gift. His offering would have had no effect unless he had been completely reconciled to all of his fellow sectarians. Furthermore, the sectarian who had been injured was required to forgive his brother, so that the sin against Israel might be removed. God only forgave those who had forgiven others.[2] A sectarian whose brother had asked forgiveness seventy times seven times was required to forgive him.[3] Any covenanter who saw his brother sin was commanded to call his attention to it so that the brother could repent and be forgiven. If the brother refused to repent, even before witnesses and the whole church, he was excommunicated and treated like a Gentile and a tax collector.[4] The community had to be kept sinless, even though small. Only thus could it be the redeeming remnant of Israel. Sects like this believed that they alone were the people of God who had authority to forgive sins or withhold forgiveness. Those not forgiven by the community would not be forgiven by God.[2]

---

[1] Mt. 6:25-34.
[2] Mt. 6:14-15.
[3] Mt. 9:21-22; see further 9:23-35.
[4] Mt. 18:15-17.
[5] Mt. 9:1-8; 16:13-20; 18:15-20.

The Sect of the Johannine Epistles

Belonging.—The epistles of John reflect definite sectarian practices that were similar to those of the Essenes, Pharisees, and the sect of the Rule. The exclusiveness is evident in the description given of the members or brothers, on the one hand, and those excluded, on the other. The faithful members of the sect were those who had life eternal,[1] had fellowship with the Father, Son, and one another,[2] and walked in the light.[3] They knew God,[4] loved him,[5] were born of him,[6] were called his children,[7] remained in him,[8] had confidence in him,[9] and confessed the Father and the Son.[10] They kept God's commandments[11] which also meant doing righteousness;[12] they knew the truth,[13] sanctified themselves,[14] and did not sin.[15] They loved the brothers,[16] gave up their normal existence in the world ($\psi\upsilon\chi\alpha\acute{\iota}$) for them, and continued to care for them in their need.[17] To be this closely bound to a fellowship with God, Jesus, and the brothers meant being divorced from the world, which they did not love[18] but rather overcame.[19] This means they were not now in the world[20] but were instead hated by the world[21] and that for them the lusts of the world for such things as family, property, and social position had passed away.[22]

Outsiders.—Those outside the sect, on the contrary, were in the world, had sensual passions, and earned secular wages.[23] They walked in darkness,[24] sinned,[25] did evil works,[26] did not do righteous-

---

[1] I Jn. 1:2; 2:25; 3:14; 5:11-13, 20-21.
[2] I Jn. 1:3, 6-7.
[3] I Jn. 1:7; 2:6-7.
[4] I Jn. 2:3; 3:6; 4:16.
[5] I Jn. 4:20-21; 5:1.
[6] I Jn. 2:18-27.
[7] I Jn. 3:1-2, 8, 10.
[8] I Jn. 2:18-27; 3:24; 4:13, 15-16.
[9] I Jn. 2:28; 3:21; 4:17; 5:14.
[10] I Jn. 2:23-24; 4:2, 15; 5:1-6, 10.
[11] I Jn. 2:3-5; 3:22-24; 5:2-3.
[12] I Jn. 2:29; 3:2, 10.   [13] I Jn. 2:20-21.
[14] I Jn. 3:3.   [15] I Jn. 3:4-6; 5:18.
[16] I Jn. 2:10; 3:11, 14, 23; 4:7, 11-12, 19-21; 5:2.
[17] I Jn. 3:16-17, 19.   [18] I Jn. 2:15-17.
[19] I Jn. 5:4-5.   [20] I Jn. 3:1.
[21] I Jn. 3:13.   [22] I Jn. 2:17.
[23] I Jn. 2:15-17; 4:4-5.   [24] I Jn. 1:6; 2:11.
[25] I Jn. 3:7-8.   [26] I Jn. 3:12.

ness,[1] and did not belong to the sect.[2] They did not have life [3] but remained in death.[4] They were not of God,[5] did not know God,[6] did not confess that Jesus was of God,[7] but rather said Jesus was not the Messiah,[8] and denied the Father and the Son.[9] They were antichrists [10] and false prophets [11] who were from the devil.[12]

Contrasts.—In this sect, the members were alive, and non-members were dead; the members walked in the light, while the non-members walked in darkness. They loved and were loved by brothers, but hated and were hated by the world. The group distinguished between mortal sins which could not be forgiven and the other sins which could. If the sin was not mortal (i.e. "to death"), a brother might pray for another who had sinned and God would give him "life," which meant retention within the community.[13] The implication is that this would not be true of mortal sins. The Johannine community had at least three degrees of membership: the "children" ($\tau\acute{\epsilon}\kappa\nu\alpha$ or $\pi\alpha\iota\delta\acute{\iota}\alpha$),[14] "young men," [15] and "fathers." [16]

The community had at least two opposing groups: the Jews who did not confess the son, and Christians who did not require circumcision and did not teach salvation through the law. Identification of the first group is apparent.[17] The second requires some deduction. Against that group the author insisted that sin was lawlessness and that the one who was righteous *did* righteous-

---

[1] I Jn. 3:10.
[2] I Jn. 2:18.
[3] I Jn. 3:14; 5:12.
[4] I Jn. 3:14.
[5] I Jn. 4:6.
[6] I Jn. 4:8.
[7] I Jn. 4:3.
[8] I Jn. 2:22.
[9] I Jn. 2:23; 5:10-12.
[10] I Jn. 2:18-22; 4:3.
[11] I Jn. 4:1.
[12] I Jn. 3:8, 10.
[13] I Jn. 5:16-17.
[14] I Jn. 2:12-14, 18, 28.
[15] I Jn. 2:13-14.
[16] *Ibid.* See also I Cor. 2:1-3:3; Heb. 5:11-6:3; and H. D. Owen, "The 'Stages of Ascent' in Hebrews 5:11-6:3," *NTS* 3 (1956-57), 43-53.
[17] I Jn. 2:22-25.

ness.[1] He further argued that Jesus came through the water and the blood—not just the water, as if someone thought that was orthodox. The water has usually been taken to mean baptism and the blood, sacrifice.[2] In support of those who interpret "blood" to mean sacrifice is the assurance that Jesus was the sin offering for Christians' sins,[3] and that his blood cleanses Christians of all sins.[4] But these were not matters to be accepted or rejected. Jesus had been crucified. That was an understood fact, and no doctrine could alter the event. Anyone who accepted Jesus as the Christ at all, accepted him as one who had been crucified. In another context, the author argued that Jesus Christ came through water and the blood—not through water only, with the spirit as a witness. In fact all three are witnesses: water, blood, and the spirit, and the three are one.[5] In the earlier context, the "blood" was not a matter for debate. In the latter the author pressed his case as if some thought Jesus came only through water. Water of baptism was part of the Christian initiation ceremony. The author insisted that the three were one. One what? If sacrifice and baptism form one, it would be one ministry of Jesus. If blood were understood to mean blood of circumcision, then it together with baptism and the gift of the spirit form the three necessary parts of one initiation ceremony. This is true whether circumcision came at eight days or just before adult baptism. Furthermore, there were Christians who did not require circumcision,[6] admitting them by the water and the spirit only. To this the Johannine sect objected. Blood drawn at circumcision was called the "blood of the covenant."[7] Rabbis caused drops of blood to flow from proselytes, because, except for the blood of the covenant heaven and earth would not endure.[8] The passage which said, "In thy blood live"[9] was understood as re-

---

[1] I Jn. 3:4-7; 5:3.

[2] A. E. Brooke, *ICC Johannine Epistles* (Edinburgh, 1912), 137; L. Pirst, *La Sainte Bible* (Paris, 1938), XII, 550; W. Wrede, *Judas, Petros und Johannesbriefe* (Bonn, 1924), 143.

[3] I Jn. 2:2.

[4] I Jn. 1:7. Also before the fall of the temple, proselytes to Judaism were required to sacrifice at the temple which involved throwing blood against the altar (Ker. 2:1).

[5] I Jn. 5:6-8.

[6] Col. 2:11; Gal. 5:2-15; Eph. 2:11-22; also Jewish convictions in Yeb. 46a.

[7] Sifra 58c; Lev. 12:3.

[8] Shab. 137b.

[9] Ezek. 16:6.

ferring to the blood of the covenant.[1] Circumcision was thought by some groups of Jews to be so important that it set aside the Sabbath; not even the merit of Moses could suspend the punishment of neglecting this duty for one hour.[2]

The evidence is not conclusive, but the sectarian nature of I John, the emphasis on righteousness of the law, and the black and white distinctions between non-members and members suggest that this group would also have insisted on circumcision. The argument that insisted on the "blood" seems to refer to circumcision, which together with baptism and the spirit are one.

Hospitality.—It is not certain that II and III John were written by the same author as I John. But it is clear that all three came from a strong sectarian background. It is quite plausible to assume that they belonged to the same sect. The hospitality rules practiced by the group represented in II and III John were probably practiced by the sect of I John, even if they were not all composed by the same sect. They were all sectarian, and sects tended to have similar rules and practices, even though they differed on minor points. III John scolded Diotrephes because he not only turned away strangers who came asking for hospitality, but he prevented others from receiving them as guests.[3] This did not mean that the community was required to accept all guests, but the ones that Diotrephes turned away were those who had been sent out "worthily" ἀξίως of God.[4] They were so careful in their habits that they refused to eat food offered by Gentiles. Therefore sectarian Christians were obligated to meet their needs.[5] The lady (κυρία) addressed in II John was encouraged in the way she should care for her "children." But love was not to be universally extended. They should watch out for those deceivers who did not observe the same teaching. Those who followed other doctrines should not be accepted as guests. In fact, members of the sect were not even to greet these people, because that would be sharing in the evil works of those unbelievers.[6] This is like the sectarian caution not to greet anyone on the way,[7] and the sectarian warning against entering the house of someone who was not "worthy."[8]

---

[1] Mekilta, *Pisḥa* 5:10-11.
[2] Mekilta, *Amalek* 3:109-126.
[3] III Jn. 9-10.   [4] III Jn. 5-6.
[5] III Jn. 7-8.   [6] II Jn. 9-11.
[7] Lk. 10:4.   [8] Demai 2:2; 4:1-7.

The Sect of the Apocalypse

The "worthy."—John of Patmos, who wrote the introduction and conclusion [1] for an apocalypse that he sent to the churches for which he was responsible, disclosed enough views in these few verses to indicate the kind of sect to which he belonged and the kind of religion he considered false. On the one hand, he commended those Christians who hated other groups like the Nicolaitans.[2] He approved of those who had tested others who called themselves apostles so that the members could learn that the others were false.[3] He honored Antipas, the faithful witness, who was killed in behalf of the sect,[4] and was pleased with those in Philadelphia who kept John's word and did not deny his name.[5] He praised those in Sardis who had not defiled their garments, for they were "worthy" (ἄξιοι).[6] and promised that those who washed their garments would enter the gates of the city.[7]

The outsiders.—On the other hand, John condemned those who called themselves apostles but really were not, in John's judgment.[8] They seemed to be associated with the communities of people who called themselves Jews, but were really of the synagogue of Satan.[9] John had no kind words for those who held to the teaching of "Balaam" at Pergamum[10] who put a stumbling block before the Israelites who were committing adultery and eating food offered to idols.[11] By relating the Balaam incident in Num. 22-24 to the Phineas story that followed in Num. 25:1-13, John of Patmos identified the intruder of his own day with the pagan, Balaam. The congregation the intruder taught was compared to the Israelites, like Zimri, who had mingled with the Gentiles. The person he called "Balaam" may have been the same person who called himself an apostle but was not, and the mingling Israelites were probably the same as those who called themselves Jews but belonged to the synagogue of Satan. Either the same leader or another leader of the same general group John called "Jezebel"

---

[1] Rev. 1-3; 22:6-21.
[2] Rev. 2:6.
[3] Rev. 2:2.
[4] Rev. 2:13.
[5] Rev. 3:8, 10.
[6] Rev. 2:4. [7] Rev. 22:14.
[8] Rev. 2:2. [9] Rev. 2:9; 3:9.
[10] Num. 22-24. [11] Num. 25:1-13.

and his congregation was classed as the Israelites whom Jezebel led into the error of committing adultery and eating food offered to idols.[1] These were the "dogs," sorcerers, "harlots," murderers, and idolators [2] against whom John wanted his sect protected. It is possible, but not certain, that these people were also called the Nicolaitans,[3] but the reason why they should have been so labeled is no longer known. The sect that mingled with Gentiles and allowed the members of its churches to eat food offered to idols may have been a liberal group like the Pauline Christians. The "worthy ones" who kept the law and avoided defilement were members of the sect to which John belonged. It was a branch of the Jewish Christian church, which practiced many of the same sectarian observances as did the Essenes, Pharisees, sect of the Rule, Matthean sect, and Johannine sect.

Summary

This chapter is by no means a complete listing of the sects and their origins in Judaism and Christianity. It is rather a few, selected because they could be recognized by sectarian characteristics previously known. Because only one sect was really fully described, only other sects of the same nature could be distinguished. But sectarianism is of ancient origin and has probably numerous other reasons for organization and continuance. The sects discussed here were natural outgrowths of the purity rules when kept very carefully. It is possible that some Jewish groups, like the Essenes and Rule sect, were actually identical; Christian communities, like the sect of St. Matthew and the sect of the Apocalypse, may also have been identical, but the evidence for identification is not without question in either case. The differences between the beliefs and practices of these Christian sects and the Pauline Christians show that Christianity, like Judaism, began with divisions. In neither tradition has there ever been one indivisible community of believers. Sectarianism that began in antiquity continued over into NT times where it was there also related to purity laws. With this many sects of the same nature it will be possible to note three general sectarian practices, namely: initiation, "love," and excommunication. These will be the subjects of the next chapter.

---

[1] Rev. 2:20-21.
[2] Rev. 22:15.
[3] Rev. 2:6.

CHAPTER EIGHT

COVENANTAL PRACTICES

INTRODUCTION

The unknown number of sects that existed in the small land of Palestine over a long period of time must have learned from one another many efficient and approved methods of administration as well as standards of conduct. Those discussed in Chapter VII existed for similar purposes: Their desire for the Kingdom of God made them willing to become extremely ascetic to maintain a pure, sinless community where God would be pleased to dwell. If more were known about the administration and dogma of the sects, more customs could be classified as belonging to all sects. In this chapter only three practices will be considered as traditions which were later quite generally accepted in Judaism and Christianity, with necessary modifications and adaptations. These are: 1) initiation practices, 2) the significance and meaning of love in the exclusive community, and 3) the causes and consequences of excommunication.

INITIATION PRACTICES

Washing and eating.—The practices of baptism and common meals were evidently developed within sectarian groups in their efforts to maintain a ritually clean community. Therefore an associate (חבר) could not receive an ʿam-haaretz as a guest in the ʿam-haaretz's own clothing.[1] The sectarian (חבר) could not admit the non-sectarian (ʿam-haaretz) unless the latter first bathed and changed into the garments of the sectarian. Presumably, once admitted, he was permitted to eat the sectarian food of his host. This would not have been allowed, however, without the necessary precautionary purity measures. This hospitality practice seems to have been transferred to the sectarian communities in relationship to the admission of new members into the communities where they could eat the food restricted to the members of the community. One of the baptizing sects was the Essene community.

---

[1] Demai 2:3.

Essenes.—Candidates for admission to the Essene sect were trained for one year before they were allowed to share the "purer water of purification" (ἀγνείαν).[1] This was not drinking water, but was used for purification (καθαρεῖν). It did not admit the candidate to the common meal. Only full members who were counted worthy (ἄξιοι) of being trusted with the rules of the sect were allowed to eat with other full members. This could not happen earlier than two years after baptism. Even then, full members bathed (ἀπολούονται) in cold water before each meal. "After this sanctification (ἀγνείαν), Essenes congregated in a private dwelling which none of the uninitiated was permitted to enter." [2] From this bathing, they became clean (καθαροί), changed into white garments, and were prepared to eat together food that was approved by dietary laws and completely free from defilement.[3] "Sanctifyting" meant making pure from ritual defilement and usually involved ritual ablutions. E.g. Bathsheba was reported to have been bathing (רחצת) when she was sanctifying herself from her menstrual impurity (מתקדשת מטמאתה). When Moses sanctified the people (ויקדש את העם), they washed (ויכבסו) their garments, probably bathed,[4] and were warned not to touch women. On the Day of Atonement the high priest was required to immerse himself five times, and to "sanctify his hands and his feet" (קדש ידיו ורגליו).[5] The Essenes, then, were not introducing a new custom, but were enforcing in their own community Levitical rules that applied to the temple. Like the associates in their own homes, they treated their community as if it were a holy of holies and their food as if it were sacrificial meat, and they kept themselves as pure as priests serving at the altar. The two steps necessary for admission to this group were: 1) baptism, after one year, and 2) admission to clean garments of the sect and the common meal, after two more years.

The Community of the Rule.—The Community of the Rule kept a candidate on trial for one year before admitting him to touch the purity (יגע בטהרת) of "the many." [6] At that point his property

---

[1] *BJ* II (138-139).　　　[2] *BJ* II (129).

[3] *Ibid.* White garments were worn by priests in their holiness. When Essenes established a priesthood of all believers, they also wore priestly garments.

[4] Ex. 19:14.

[5] Yoma 3:2, 4, 6; 4:5; 7:3, 4.

[6] 1QS 6:14-15.

(הונו) and earnings (מלאכה) were recorded, but he was not yet allowed to touch the liquid (משקה) until the end of his second year in training.[1] At that point, if he met the tests, he was fully admitted "for Torah and legal questions and *purity* [italics mine], and to mingle his wealth; and his counsel will be for the community and its legal questions.

The first step involved admission to touch the pure things, which did not involve the meal. Therefore it probably involved baptism, as was true of the Essenes, which made the candidate pure enough to work in the community and help contribute to its budget.

The second step admitted him to "liquid" (משקה) which may have referred to the use of sectarian immersion pools before changing into clean garments of the sectarian dining hall, or else the drink served at the common meal. Either way, it involved both, since it admitted him to full membership in which his wealth was added to the community treasury, and he was permitted to share in counsel and legal decisions of the full members of the sect. questions." [2]

Shammai and Hillel.—The schools of Shammai and Hillel admitted members to their schools through two steps: 1) liquids (למשקין) and 2) clothing (לכסות). The second step refers to the clean garments given a full member after his bath before each meal. These would not have been given until the person was considered worthy of being entrusted to keep them free from midras uncleanness. Hillel required only thirty days probation before allowing this. Shammai required twelve months.

The first step involved "liquid," which is derived from שקה and means "drink," but it was also used more generally to refer to any of the liquids which, if put on dry produce, would make it subject to defilement. The substances that fell into this classification were seven: 1) dew, 2) water, 3) wine, 4) oil, 5) blood, 6) milk, and 7) bees' honey.[3] Water in an immersion pool was specifically singled out as one of these "liquids" [4] and also the water in a river in which a person stood with water up to his mouth.[5] If a man stood under a water spout to cool or rinse himself, the rule concerning defilement from liquids applies.[6] One of the six cases when Shammai was

---

[1] 1QS 6:19-21.
[2] 1QS 6:22-23.
[3] Mak. 6:4-5; also 2:2.
[4] Mak. 3:8.
[5] Mak. 3:8; 4:1.
[6] Mak. 4:3.

more lenient than Hillel was in allowing initiates to be baptized
(מטבילין) in a rain stream (דורדלית).[1] This means that liquids used for
baptism at the same time had the effect of making a person subject to
defilement. Vessels for which immersion was required (טעונין טבילה) for
purification were washed in liquid (משקין).[2] משקין, then, could apply
to water used for baptism as well as liquid used for drink. Just
as the Essenes were admitted at the first step to share in a purer
water of sanctification, so those admitted by Shammai and Hillel
were allowed to share the משקין of the community, which probably
also referred to the waters of ablution. A person who bathed, both
cleansed himself from impurity and made himself subject to
defilement until he had been thoroughly dried off.[3] Therefore it
was important for Essenes both to bathe and to put on clean
garments. This made certain that the Essenes were free from any
previous defilement and that they did not, before they ate, become
redefiled from contact with contaminated clothing. It was also
important that initiates not be admitted to these rites until they
had been properly trained in their use.

Both Shammaites and Hillelites permitted the first step at
thirty days. Hillel admitted the initiate at once to clothing, whereas
Shammai required twelve months before the second step could be
taken. The steps taken by both were the same as those taken by
the Community of the Rule and the Essenes.

The associates.—Those sectarians who were called associates
(חברים) were first admitted for "wings" (כנפים) and afterwards
for "purities" (טהרות).[4] There has been some dispute among scholars
over the meaning of "wings." Some hold that it means "washing
of hands,"[5] whereas others say it means "clothing."[6] Since the
Essene practice was that of admitting first to baptism and secondly
to clothing, which accompanied further cleansings associated with
the common meal, it is more than likely that here, too, ablutions
preceded "purities." The only occasion at which "purities" preceded

---

[1] Eduyoth 5:2.
[2] JHag. III § 8, 79d.
[3] Mak. 2:1.
[4] T. Demai 2:11; Bek. 30b; JDemai 23a.
[5] The traditional view, followed by J. Neusner, "The Fellowship (HBWRH
in the Second Commonwealth," *HTR* 53 (1960), 132, fn. 18, and 133.
[6] C. Rabin, *Qumran Studies* (Oxford, 1957), followed Luzzatto in accepting
this interpretation.

"liquids" was practiced by the sect of the Rule. There liquid was clearly related to the final step which involved clothing, meal, mingling of wealth, counsel, and legal questions. The term "purities" is so indefinite that it could mean pure objects which the baptized member was entrusted to touch or regulations involving sharing such pure objects as the immersions taken before eating the common meal, food, clothing, and housing. For the associates, "wings" evidently meant ablutions and "purities," clothing, meal, and other responsibilities associated with full membership. For the sect of the Rule, "purities" first meant those objects the initiate could touch after his first step of initiation, and second, sharing the most intimate objects and practices of the sect. The second step was called יגע במשקה which may have been the regular bath before the common meal, the drink served at the common meal, or both.

Christians of the Egyptian Church Order.—The rules for preparation and admission of initiates into Christian communities must have been quite uniform among some groups, because the rules for the Egyptian Church Order have many parallels both to the *Apostolic Constitutions* and the Canons of Hippolytus.[1] In the Egyptian Order the catechumen (κατηχούμενος) normally was trained for three years before baptism. There were exceptions, however, when a person was extraordinarily zealous (σπουδαῖος) and could be allowed to advance more rapidly. The important consideration was character (τρόπος) of the initiate rather than the time (χρόνος) spent in preparation.[2] If, after three full years of training, the initiate was not judged to be well prepared (καλός) or able to maintain ritual purity (καθαρός), he was rejected as one who had heard the word without faith (πίστις).[3] Prior to baptism, candidates bathed every Sabbath for five weeks. If on the day planned for baptism, a woman was defiled from menstrual impurity, she isolated herself and returned for baptism on another day.[4] Baptisms took place in the mornings. Children were baptized first, men, second, and women, last. Candidates removed all

---

[1] All three are placed in parallel columns by H. Achelis, *Die ältesten Quellen des Orientalischen Kirchenrechtes, Erstes Buch; die Canones Hippolyti*, TUGAL VI, 276 (Leipzig, 1891), 76-99.

[2] *ECO* c. 42; also *Apos. Cons.* VIII, c. 31.

[3] *ECO* c. 45.

[4] *Ibid.*

clothing before baptism, including jewelry or any other foreign object (εἶδος ἀλλότριον). The bishop baptized with the assistance of an elder. After the proper prayers, oaths, and confessions, candidates were baptized, clothed, and admitted to the church, where they were served bread and wine and afterwards milk and honey. As with some Jewish sects, this Christian order required a full three year training period. At the end of that period, the initiate was baptized and immediately admitted to full membership which included permission to participate in community table fellowship.[1] Some Christian sects had somewhat different requirements but the relationship between baptism and table fellowship was the same.

Clementine Christians.—The Clementine Christians instructed candidates in the catechism of the sect (*mysteria regni caelorum*) for three months, after which they were permitted to partake of holy things (*possit percipere de sanctis*).[2] When Peter baptized Theon, he immediately broke bread with him and gave thanks to God who had accounted Theon "worthy" (*dignatus*) of his holy ministry.[3] Although the Clementine Christians required a longer probation period than Hillelites, their practices were similar in that both sects admitted members to full membership and dining fellowship immediately after baptism. Other groups, like Shammaites, who required twelve months for full admission, the sect of the Rule, which required one or two more years after baptism, and the Essenes, who required two full years after baptism—all required baptism before full admission to the common meal. The similarity of practices becomes more evident when the two-step program of each sect is diagrammed. [4]

The meal.—The common meal shared only with those who were full members of a group was the type of Passover meal Jesus ate with his disciples before his crucifixion.[5] The insistence that disciples not accept hospitality from any but the "worthy," the warning against receiving any guest who did not believe the accepted doctrine [6] and also against turning away visitors who had

---

[1] *Ibid.* c. 46; see also *CH* c. 135-156.
[2] *Clem. Rec.* III. lxvii.
[3] Acts of Peter 5.
[4] See chart on next page.
[5] Mt. 26:17-35.
[6] II Jn. 9-11.

Two-Step Initiation Program of the Sects

	Essenes	Community of the Rule	Associates	Hillel and Shammai	Egyptian Church Order*	Clementine Christians
Sources	Josephus, *Wars* II (138-139).	Rule of the Community (1QS) 6:13-14.	T. Demai 2:11 Bekoroth 30b and JDemai 23a	T. Demai 2:12 and Bekoroth 30b.	Egyptian Church Order c. 42-103.	Recognitions of Clement III.67.
First Step	One year: "Purer water of sanctification" (ἁγνείαν).	One year: "Touch purity" (יגע בטהרה).	Time not given: "Wings" (לכנפים).	Thirty days: "Liquids" (למשקין).	Three years: "Baptism" (βαπτίζειν).	Three months: "Baptism" *Baptizetur.*
Second Step	Two more years:	One or two years:	Time not given:	Immediately thereafter (H) or eleven more months(S):	Immediately thereafter	Immediately thereafter
	"Touch common food" (κοινῆς ἅψασθαι τροφῆς).	"Touch liquid" (יגע במשקה).	"Purities" (לטהרות).	"Clothing" (לכסות).	"Common meal"	"Common meal" (*percipere de sanctis*).

* *Apos. Cons.* basically the same.

been faithful to the accepted rules,[1] and not eating with Gentiles—all reflect the type of sectarian customs that made baptism and the common meal standard practices of Jewish and Christian exclusive sects. This was also noted in the description of the early church where members were baptized and devoted themselves to teaching, breaking bread, and prayer.[2] They also practiced the sectarian custom of sharing goods.[3] The practice of sharing goods was closely related to brotherly love, which will be considered shortly.

Summary.—The priestly practice of restricting the holy of holies to the priests who were free from any type of defilement and restricting the *terumah* (holy food designated for the priests) to the families of those who served the temple was later extended to laymen when the temple was not functioning or was believed to be defiled. In order to transfer the dwelling place for the Shekinah from the altar to the hearth and the community, individuals and sects kept their homes and community centers free from defilement, limiting hospitality to those who were "worthy" of being in the divine presence. Food was also kept within the restrictively legal limits. The emphasis on freedom from midras defilement and pure food naturally made baptism and community meals important initiation practices of holy sectarian communities. For Christian groups, baptism preceded admission to the common meal. Essenes were also admitted to the purer water of sanctification before being allowed to touch the common food of the community. Other Jewish groups probably practiced the same ceremonies which were called permission to touch "purities" before touching "liquids," use of "liquids" before "clothing," or "wings" before "purities." Because these last terms are not clear in themselves, they have often been misunderstood. When seen together with practices of other sects that existed in the same geographical area, period of history, and religious background, the context seems to require that "wings" refer to ablutions or baptism and that "liquid(s)" refer to the initial baptism or the ablutions before the common meal.

The rules that prompted the early Jews and Christians to live

---

[1] III Jn. 5-10.
[2] Acts 2:38-42, 46; 10:47-11:4.
[3] Acts 2:32-5:14; 6:1-6.

in communities isolated from defiled outsiders required a special
type of existence within the communities themselves. Central to
sectarian life was the brotherly love required of all covenanters.
The nature and extent of covenantal love deserves further examination.

SECTARIAN LOVE

Brotherly love.—Exhortations to love the brothers in sectarian
literature are sufficiently frequent to demand an examination of the
meaning of the love experienced in early Jewish and Christian sects.
Members of the Rule Sect, for instance, were told to love (לאהב)
all the sons of light and to hate (לשנא) all the sons of darkness.[1]
The sons of light were the members of the sect who had brought
into the community all of their knowledge, ability, and wealth
to share in common with other sectarians.[2] The sons of darkness
were all non-members. Sectarians were not to hate one another.[3]
According to a man's spirit, he should either be loved or hated,
by which was meant, either accepted or rejected from the community "according to the cleanness of his hands."[4] The Zadokite
community was told to love (לאהב) each man his brother,[5] and
they were to reject (למאוס) whatever God hated (שנא), indicating
that rejecting and hating were very similar.[6] Among the tremendous
oaths required of Essenes was that they would always hate (μισήσειν)
the unrighteous.[7] From the outset, then, it is apparent that love
had something to do with acceptance and that it could be demanded.
This contradicts the conclusions of many, like Quell,[8] who held
that love was a natural feeling that could not be legally directed,
but there are some impressive usages of love as a command. These
will be considered here. Quell, like others, asumed that he *knew* the
meaning of love. In order to deal fairly with sectarian love, it will be
necessary to avoid such prejudgments, but rather to study the legal
use of the term in biblical and other sectarian literature. From the
numerous examples of love in the Bible only those related to com-

---

[1] 1QS 1:9-10.
[2] 1QS 1:11-12.
[3] 1QS 5:25-26.
[4] 1QS 9:15-16.
[5] CDC 6:20.
[6] CDC 2:15.
[7] *BJ* II (139).
[8] G. Quell, "ἀγαπάω," *TWNT* I, 24.

mandment, providence, or legal contract will be considered here. The term was used in close relationship to emotion, as an emotion itself, or as an expression of feeling.[1] These deserve further study, but not here.[2] The following evidence will show that love was commanded and judged in the Ancient Near East, but it will make no attempt to say that was the only meaning of love known.

The church and the world.—There seems to have been a direct either/or relationship among the sects. Either a person loved the brothers or he hated them. The same division was evident in the early Christian Church. Love (φιλία) for the world meant enmity with God.[3] The ones who loved the world had no love (ἀγάπη) for the Father [4] and had not God as their Father.[5] People chose either

---

[1] Gen. 24:67; 27:4, 9, 14; 29:18, 20, 30, 32; 34:3; Dt. 21:15-16; Jdgs. 14:16; 16:4-5; I Sam. 1:5-17; II Sam. 1:26; 12:24; 13:1, 4, 15; I Kgs. 11:1; II Chron. 11:21; 26:10; Ps. 4:3(2); 11:5, 7; 26:8; 33:5; 34:13(12); 37:28; 40:17(16); 45:8(7); 52:5(4), 6(3); 70:5(4); 78:68; 87:2; 99:4; 109:4-5; 119:47, 48, 97, 113, 119, 127, 140, 159, 163, 165, 167; Prov. 1:22; 4:6; 5:19; 7:18; 8:17, 21, 36; 10:12(11); 12:1; 15:9(10), 12(13); 15:12(13); 16:13; 17:19; 18:21; 20:13; 21:17; 22:11; 27:5-6(4-5); 29:3; Eccles. 3:8; 5:9(10); Song of Songs 2:4, 5, 7; 3:5, 10; 5:8; 8:4, 6, 7; Isa. 1:23; 57:8; 66:10; Hos. 4:18; 9:1, 15; 10:11; 12:8(7); 114:5; Amos 4:5; 5:15; Micah 3:2; 6:8; Zech. 8:19; Mal. 2:11; Mt. 6:5; 23:6; 24:12; Mk. 10:20; Lk. 7:42, 47; 11:42, 43; Jn. 5:42; 10:17; 11:3; 12:43; 13:1, 5, 23; 16:27; 17:23, 24, 26; 19:26; 20:2; 21:20; Rom. 8:28, 37-39; 9:13, 25; I Cor. 2:9; 8:3; 13:1-5; 16:22; II Cor. 5:14; 9:7; 11:11; 12:15; 13:11-14; Eph. 1:5-6; 6:24; Philip. 1:9, 15-16; 2:1-2; I Thes. 1:3; 2:10; 3:5; I Tim. 1:4, 5; 2:15; 4:12; 6:10-11; II Tim. 1:7, 13; 2:22; 3:4, 10; Tit. 2:2, 12; I Peter 1:8, 22; II Peter 1:7; 2:13-15; II Jn. 1; Jude 1; Rev. 2:4, 19; 3:19; 22:15.

[2] C. Spicq, *Agapè dans le Nouveau Testament* (Paris, 1958, 1959), 3 vols., in his extensive work on love in the NT has adequately dealt with the feeling involved in Christian love. He may even have concentrated on the feeling so much that the responsibility involved in terms of material giving was minimized by comparison. For example, his comment on the man who was asked to take all he had and give to the poor, "non seulement la conduite, mais les pensées et les affections sont commandées par le primat de l'ἀγάπη τοῦ θεοῦ!" (Vol. 1, 306). When he noted the Pauline relationship between loving and giving (II Thes. 2:16; Eph. 5:2, 25; Vol. 1, 304-306), he said, "La formulation insiste sur la spontanéité du don et sa générosité en faveur de ceux qui sont aimés." He further noted the pure benevolence, intimacy, spontaneity, generosity, lucidity, and voluntary nature of divine and Christian love (361, 311; see also III, 314, 317, 357). These feelings are all commendable and certainly can accompany giving, but love is possible as the fulfillment of a contract even when these qualities are lacking. The distinctions he accepts between φιλεῖν and ἀγαπᾶν are not valid for the NT (I, 176.).

[3] James 4:4.

[4] I Jn. 2:15.

[5] Jn. 8:42.

to love (ἀγαπᾶν) darkness, and therefore become sons of darkness
or they chose light and became sons of light.[1] It was not possible
to serve two masters. A person who tried, loved (ἀγαπᾶν) one and
hated (μισεῖν) the other. He could not serve God and Mammon.[2]
This was a sectarian viewpoint in which the members loved God,
but hated the world and Mammon.

Those who joined the sect passed from death to life because they
loved the brothers.[3] It was this change of allegiance that caused
the world to hate (μισεῖν) them. [4] The children of God or the
disciples of Jesus could be distinguished from the children of the
devil because the former loved (ἀγαπᾶν) one another as brothers.[5]
Just as the Christian "put on Christ" at baptism, so he also put
on love (ἀγάπη) which bound the community together in love (ἐν
ἀγάπη).[6] Love (ἀγάπη) was of God and those who loved (ἀγαπᾶν)
were born of God and knew God.[7] Those who loved (ἀγαπᾶν)
the brothers had no cause for stumbling.[8] If one did not love
(ἀγαπᾶν) his brothers whom he had seen, he could not love
(ἀγαπᾶν) God whom he had not seen.[9] God loved the Christians
first; therefore Christians were required to love (ἀγαπᾶν) one
another.[10] The earliest message that Christians heard was that
they should love (ἀγαπᾶν) one another.[11]

Love and good works.—Love was not just a feeling that had no
requirements. Those who continued in love (φιλαδελφία) provided
hospitality for traveling sectarians.[12] Their love (ἀγάπη) was shown
by their work and service to the saints.[13] They were urged to stir
each other up in love (ἀγάπη) and good works.[14] Because of Philemon's love, Paul could impose sanctions on him and require him

---

[1] I Jn. 3:19.
[2] Mt. 6:24; Lk. 16:13.
[3] I Jn. 3:14.
[4] I Jn. 3:13.
[5] Jn. 13:35; I Jn. 3:10.
[6] Col. 2:2; 3:14.
[7] I Jn. 4:7-8.
[8] I Jn. 2:10.
[9] I Jn. 4:19-21.
[10] I Jn. 4:10-21.
[11] I Jn. 3:11.
[12] Heb. 13:2.
[13] Heb. 6:10; III Jn. 6.
[14] Heb. 10:24.

to release Onesimus.[1] Philemon and others were commended for
the love (ἀγάπη) which they had toward the saints.[2] Those who
remained in love (ἀγάπη) were freed from fear and punishment on
the day of judgment[3] since love (ἀγάπη) covered a multitude of
sins.[4] Instead they were destined to receive a crown of life and
the kingdom which God promised those who loved him (τοῖς
ἀγαπῶσιν αὐτόν).[5] The commandment to love one's neighbor as
himself was the royal law.[6] Kosmala correctly noted that "'brüder-
liche Liebe' . . . is nicht die Liebe gegen alle Menschen ohne Unter-
schied." [7] Paul exhorted the Galatians to do good to all men, but
especially to the household of faith.[8] This was the group for whom
they held the greatest responsibility and greatest love.

Commanded love.—Sectarians were commanded to love, and told
whom they should love and whom they should hate. This was
not novel for the Jewish sects in NT times. Such commandments
also were made by the ancient Hebrews, but they have puzzled
modern scholars. Quell[9] said that there was an inner paradox of
attempting to apply a non-legal word in a legal direction. Hence
a statement, like, "And you shall love your neighbor as yourself,"
"although couched in a legal style of the usual demand, and containing the legally very closely circumscribed term רֵעַ [neighbor],
is not really a legal statement [italics mine], because the attitude
denoted by the word is one of *natural feeling* [italics mine] which
cannot be legally directed."[10] Quell assumed that "love" referred to a
spontaneous feeling, and therefore concluded that it could not properly be commanded. Because his method was wrong, his conclusions
are erroneous. Note, however, the following texts in which the
commandments *were* made. The beginning point should be to

---

[1] Phil. 9.
[2] Phil. 5:7; Col. 1:4; Eph. 1:15.
[3] I Jn. 4:16-18.
[4] I Peter 4:8.
[5] James 1:12; 2:5.
[6] James 2:8.
[7] H. Kosmala, *Hebräer-Essener-Christen* (Leiden, 1959), 233.
[8] Gal. 6:10.
[9] Quell, *Op. cit.*, 24.
[10] Quell, *Op. Cit.*, 24. Lev. 19:18. S. R. Driver, *ICC Deuteronomy*, 91, 94-95,
without mentioning the problem directly, emphasized both the inward, intense
affection involved and also the duty to render service to Jehovah. He dealt
with fear and service in much the same way.

recognize love as something that *was* commanded. The unknown
quantity is the effect of the commandment when it was obeyed.[1]

Joshua urged the Hebrews to love (לאהב) the Lord their God.[2]
Deuteronomy commanded them to love (אהב) the Lord their God
with all their heart, soul, and might,[3] and further instructed them
to keep the Lord's charge, his statutes, his ordinances, and his
commandments always [4]—which apparently meant the same as
loving God.[5] Israelites were also commanded not to take vengeance
against other Israelites, but rather to love (אהב) the stranger who
sojourned in their territory,[6] remembering that they themselves
once sojourned in Egypt. The Lord commanded Hosea: "Go love
(אהב) a woman . . ." [7] In response Hosea bought the woman for
fifteen shekels of silver and a homer and a lethech of barley and
made her dwell with him under his jurisdiction.[8]

These commandments in the OT are too many and too direct
to be dismissed as mistakes or faulty communication. Furthermore,
in one instance loving had the same meaning as not taking vengeance; in another it meant the proper way to treat a stranger;
in a third it meant buying and providing for another person. These
did not deal primarily either with the Lord's or the Israelites'
feeling but with the way they were expected to behave. To love
the Lord with all one's mind meant with all his mental skills; with
all his soul meant with all his physical existence, being willing to

---

[1] After this chapter was written and in the hands of the editor, I read
W. L. Moran's interesting article, "The Ancient Near Eastern Background
of Love of God in Deuteronomy," *CBQ* 25 (1963), 77-87. Moran independently
held that love could be commanded both in Dt. and non-canonical texts
dealing with covenant or treaty relationships. N. Lohfink, "Hate and Love in
Osee 9:15," *CBQ* 25 (1963), 417, concurred with Moran and said the same
kind of love was meant in Hos. 9:15. J. Coppens, "La doctrine biblique sur
l'amour de Dieu et du prochain," *ETL* 40 (1964), 252-299, objected. Writing
in objection both to Moran and to Robinson, *Honest to God*, Coppens insisted
that in Dt. love meant more than just a covenant relationship. References to
jealousy, election, and fear show that feeling was integrally bound to love.
Coppens did not grasp the main point, however, that performance of a contract could be considered "love" whether or not the feelings of those who
acted were affectionate.

[2] Josh. 23:11.
[3] Dt. 6:5.
[4] Dt. 11:1.
[5] See also Ps. 31:24(23).
[6] Lev. 19:18.
[7] Hos. 3:1.
[8] Hos. 3:2-3.

surrender life in the world for life in the covenant community; with
all his strength meant with all his wealth.[1] Stauffer [2] correctly
said, "The love of God for Israel (Dt. 7:13) is not impulse but will;
the love of God and for the neighbor demanded of the Israelite
(Dt. 6:5; Lv. 19:18) is not intoxication but act." Believers were
to love in deed and in truth—not in speech only.[3] The commandment to love the neighbor as oneself is a summary of other commandments relating to the neighbor. The corner of the field and
part of the fruit crop should be left for him; his property must
not be stolen; and he must not be cheated in business or over-
worked. His wages should be paid day by day. He must not be
abused or injured. He must be judged fairly. His neighbor must not
hate him, cause him to sin, or bear anger against him. All of this
is involved in loving the neighbor.[4]

The commanded love of the OT was continued in the NT.[5]
Paul said that whoever kept these two commandments fulfilled the
whole law.[6] Loving (ἀγαπᾶν) one's neighbor was more approved
by God than burnt offerings.[7] Christians were to love (ἀγαπᾶν)
the brothers just as they feared God and honored the emperor.[8]
John considered the commandment that Christians love (ἀγαπᾶν)
one another to be a new commandment.[9] Christians were told that
they must love one another as Jesus had loved them and were
reminded that the greatest love (ἀγάπη) there was required giving
up one's life (ψυχή) for his friends.[10] Jesus showed his love by
laying down his life for Christians. Christians were therefore told
that they too should lay down their lives (ψυχαί) for their brothers.[11]
Giving up one's life (ψυχή) probably meant leaving the surroundings
in the world where he had earned his living, raised a family, and
participated in usual existence outside the sect, to join a closely-knit
group which required that all contact with the world be forfeited.

---

[1] Sifré Debarim 6:5 § 32 (73a).
[2] E. Stauffer, "ἀγαπάω" (C-F), TWNT I, 38.
[3] I Jn. 3:18.
[4] Lev. 19:9-18.
[5] Mt. 19:19; 22:37, 39; Mk. 12:30, 31, 33; Lk. 10:27; Rom. 13:8-10;
Gal. 5:14.
[6] Rom. 13:8; Gal. 5:14.
[7] Mk. 12:33.
[8] I Peter 2:17.
[9] Jn. 13:24; see also 15:7; I Jn. 3:23; 4:7.
[10] Jn. 15:12-13.
[11] I Jn. 3:16.

By losing his worldly existence (ψυχή) he found his life (ζωή) in the covenant community where he loved the brothers and was loved by them. Christians were told that they must not only love their brothers, but also their enemies against whom they had hateful feelings. This was so that they might gain reward to build up the treasury of merits.[1] Luke interpreted loving (ἀγαπᾶν) one's enemies to mean doing good to those who hated him,[2] a reasonable meaning in a context that required action of a Christian even though his feeling was contrary to that action. In addition to loving neighbors and enemies, Christians were warned not to love the world or the things of the world, because this behavior made it impossible to have the love (ἀγάπη) of the Father in them.[3] Again love could either be for the brothers, saints, and God, on the one hand, or for the world, Mammon, and the things of the world, on the other.

Those who loved (אהבים) the Lord kept his commandments.[4] Keeping commandments meant loving (לאהבה) the Lord, serving him without reservation, walking in his paths, and cleaving to him.[5] Lest scholars think that loving here meant a certain type of feeling, the text clearly said that believers should *serve* with all their heart and soul which meant the same as loving the Lord with all the heart and soul.[6] In one context [7] those who loved the Lord were told to keep his commandments and teach their children to keep them. The other warned them not to pay attention to prophets and dreamers who urged them to serve other gods. Serving[8] the Lord alone meant loving him with all the heart and soul; loving the Lord alone meant serving him with all the heart and soul. Those who loved (אהב) foreign gods went after them and served

---

[1] Mt. 5:32-44, 46; Lk. 6:32-33, 35.

[2] Lk. 6:27. W. C. van Unnik, "Die Motivierung der Feindesliebe in Lukas v. 32-35," *Nov.* 8 (1966), 298, said Luke gave concrete meaning for Greek readers who were uninformed about grace and divine reward.

[3] I Jn. 2:15.

[4] Ex. 20:6; Dt. 5:10; 7:9; 19:9 Neh. 1:5; Dan. 9:4.

[5] Dt. 10:12; 11:13, 22; 19:9; 30:16, 20.

[6] Dt. 10:12; 11:13; Josh. 22:5. B. J. Bamberger, "Fear and Love of God in the OT," *HUCA* 6 (1929), 49, said, "that *love of Jhwh* does not refer to a spontaneous emotional state is indicated by the fact that we are exhorted to love Him (Ps. 31:24) and even *warned* to do so."

[7] Dt. 6:5.

[8] Dt. 13:1-5.

them.[1] Solomon loved (אהב) the Lord, walking in the statute of his father David.[2] Foreigners who became proselytes, loving (לאהבה) the name of the Lord, became the Lord's servants (עבדים), kept the Sabbaths, and held fast to the covenant.[3]

Marital love.—Paul admonished wives to be subject (ὑποτα-χθῆναι) to their husbands and commanded husbands to love (ἀγαπᾶν) their wives.[4] The later Pauline interpreter compared the love a husband had for his wife to the love Christ showed (ἠγάπησεν) toward the church when he gave himself up for her.[5] Giving may have been closely allied with loving. In NT times women had no legal rights and therefore could not own property. That meant that they were dependent upon men, either their husbands or fathers, to provide their needs. In this social structure, wives were instructed to be subject, and their husbands were commanded to love. Since Paul did not require wives to love, love must have had some meaning that was closely related to the task of providing that was the husband's responsibility. The two commands seem to have been counterparts: wives be subject; husbands provide. If the husbands did not provide adequately for wives who were completely subject, wives would have had to suffer. Therefore, it seems that the requirement commanded was more than a feeling; it was also a legal obligation. Quell was right in saying that feelings could not be commanded; but neither could others know when a commandment to feel was broken. Laws have been generally made to be enforced. Therefore all of these commandments to love must have been laws that could have been judged by outsiders who could discern when they had been broken or kept. In the relationship between wives and husbands, it seems that the commandment was that the husband should provide adequately for his wife. In order to check this possibility further, it will be necessary to examine other usages of the expression, love, to see how closely it was related to providing.

---

[1] Jer. 2:25.
[2] I Kgs. 3:3.
[3] Isa. 56:6.
[4] Col. 3:18-19; Eph. 5:25, 28, 33.
[5] Eph. 5:25.

Loving and giving.—In NT times loving was closely associated with giving. God loved (ἠγάπησεν) the world and gave his Son.[1] He loved (ἀγαπᾷ) the Son and gave all things into his hand.[2] He also showed the Son all that he himself was doing.[3] God's love (ἀγάπη) was poured into the hearts of Christians through the Holy Spirit which God gave them.[4] He further showed his love (ἀγάπη) for Christians when Christ died for them.[5] The Son of God loved (ἀγαπήσαντος) Christians and gave himself for them.[6] Together with the gift of his son, God gave the Christians eternal comfort and good hope through grace,[7] freed them from their sins,[8] accepted them as his children,[9] and made them alive together with Christ.[10] All this was a demonstration of God's love. Christ's love for the Philadelphian Christians would be shown by making those of the synagogue of Satan bow before the feet of the Philadelphian Christians.[11]

Christians who had received God's love with his gifts also gave when they loved. The centurion who loved (ἀγαπᾷ) the nation of Israel built the people a synagogue.[12] When Simon Peter confessed his love (ἀγαπᾶν and φιλεῖν) for Jesus, he was commanded to care for his sheep.[13] Corinthians were expected to show the genuineness of their love (ἀγάπη) by making a contribution to the saints in Jerusalem.[14] Knowledge only puffed up, but love (ἀγάπη) built up.[15] Anyone who had material possessions and saw his brother in need but refused to help him was one in whom God's love (ἀγάπη) did not abide.[16] Leaders were expected to be esteemed highly in love (ἐν ἀγάπη) because of their work.[17] It was through love (ἀγάπη) that

---

[1] Jn. 3:16.
[2] Jn. 3:35.
[3] Jn. 5:20.
[4] Rom. 5:5.
[5] Rom. 5:8.
[6] Gal. 2:20; Eph. 5:2.
[7] II Thes. 2:16.
[8] Rev. 1:5.
[9] I Jn. 3:9.
[10] Eph. 2:4-5.
[11] Rev. 3:9.
[12] Lk. 7:5.
[13] Jn. 21:15-17.
[14] II Cor. 8:7-8, 24.
[15] I Cor. 8:1.
[16] I Jn. 3:17.
[17] I Thes. 5:13.

faith became effective;[1] it was the fruit of the Spirit.[2] Love (ἀγάπη) required the Christian to hate the evil and hold fast to the good,[3] refrain from injuring his neighbor, fulfilling the law.[4] Through love (ἀγάπη) Christians were ordered to serve one another.[5] Those who walked in love (ἀγάπη) did not behave in a way that would hurt their neighbors.[6]

The husband, who was the provider, was commanded to love his wife. His wife, who had no material goods to give, was told to be subject. God, who provided for the Christian's needs, both loved and gave to the believer. The Father loved the Son and gave all things into his hands. The Son, in turn, showed the world that he loved (ἀγαπᾶν) the Father by doing that which the Father commanded him.[7] The Christians who loved (ἀγαπᾶν) Jesus kept his commandments[8] or his word.[9] Those who loved (ἀγαπᾶν) God obeyed his commandments.[10] The believer, in his subordinate position, could love God or Jesus only by obeying. The wives, who were in a comparatively subordinate position to their husbands,[11] were told to be subject, but for some reason this subjection was not called love. In NT times, at least, there seems to have been a distinctly masculine quality about sectarian love that required the one who loved to provide. In celibate communistic communities, such as the Essenes, or the Rule sect, the last step of acceptance into full membership required that the initiate surrender all of his possessions to the community. This meant that he loved the brothers. Furthermore, because the communities were structured so that each person was given the material goods he needed from the community treasury, the sectarian loved his neighbor just as much as himself. All the brothers were loved and provided for equally. Brotherly love was obviously a very important part of sectarian life, but it did not originate in NT times. The basis for its existence was firmly set in the OT.

---

[1] Gal. 5:6.
[2] Gal. 5:22.
[3] Rom. 12:9.
[4] Rom. 13:10.
[5] Gal. 5:13.
[6] Rom. 14:15.
[7] Jn. 14:31.
[8] Jn. 14:15.
[9] Jn. 14:23-24; 15:9-10.
[10] I Jn. 5:1-2; II Jn. 6.
[11] Eph. 5:23.

God's love and providence.—The basis for Israel's election was God's love (אהבה) for the patriarchs and their descendants.[1] Because of his love (אהבה), the Lord changed Israel's curse to blessing,[2] multiplied Israel and increased the Israelites' prosperity on the land he promised them.[3] He brought the Hebrews out of bondage from Egypt because of his love (אהבה),[4] and for the same reason promised later to act on Judah's behalf by acting against Babylon.[5] Because of his love for the saints he continued to free the captives, feed the hungry, open the eyes of the blind and lift up those who were bowed down.[6] The Lord loved (אהב) the sojourner, providing him with food and clothing.[7] God made Solomon king over Israel because of his love (אהבה) for Solomon and Israel.[8] Also because of his love (אהבה), he drew Israel to him,[9] but found it necessary to chasten her so that Israel's position of preference might be continued.[10]

Jews after the return of the captives to Palestine refused to believe that the Lord loved (אהב) them, because their lot was not one of happiness and prosperity. The only argument to the contrary was the consideration of Israel's lot in comparison to that of Esau. The Lord hated Esau and laid waste his hill country, leaving all his heritage to the jackels of the wilderness. If Edomites tried to rebuild, the Lord would tear down their construction.[11] God had not given the Israelites much, but he continued to keep them. His love was measured by his provision. According to the Zadokite sect,

> "God loved (אהב) knowledge;
> wisdom and insight he established (הציב) before himself," [12]

suggesting by parallel that establishing wisdom and insight was

---

[1] Dt. 4:37; 10:15; Ps. 47:5(4).
[2] Dt. 23:6(5).
[3] Dt. 7:13.
[4] Dt. 7:8; Hos. 11:1.
[5] Isa. 48:14.
[6] Ps. 146:8.
[7] Dt. 10:17-18.
[8] I Kgs. 10:8; II Chron. 2:10(11); 9:8.
[9] Jer. 31:3.
[10] Prov. 3:12.
[11] Mal. 1:1-5.
[12] CDC 2:3.

the same as loving or providing knowledge. This meaning is consistent with several OT expressions of love.

Parents and children.—The Lord's love (אהב) toward his children was like that of a responsible father to his children.[1] Since fathers were providers, their love was also measured by their giving. When Jacob gave his young son, Joseph, a special coat, this assured the older brothers that Jacob loved (אהב) Joseph more than all his brothers.[2] Isaac loved (אהב) Esau and wanted to give him his blessing, but Rebekah loved (אהב) Jacob and helped him to manipulate the situation so as to receive the blessing himself.[3] Not only were fathers responsible for giving their sons material gifts, but they also showed their love (אהב) by disciplining and instructing their sons.[4] Ruth and Naomi left Moab because they were unloved, since their husbands were not living. When Ruth succeeded in gaining Boaz as a husband, however, then both the needs of Ruth and Naomi were met. Naomi's property was under the supervision and ownership of her son-in-law. When Ruth bore a son, both Naomi and Ruth were given descendants. If it had not been for Ruth, Naomi could not have improved her condition. Therefore, this was an exceptional case in which a daughter-in-law loved (אהבה) her mother-in-law. Her love meant more to Naomi than seven sons.[5] This did not mean that Ruth had more tender feelings for Naomi than her own sons had had before their deaths, but that she provided for Naomi better.

Hebrews who loved the Lord or the name of the Lord expected him to love them.[6] This meant he would preserve them,[7] be gracious to them,[8] hear their pravers,[9] make them dwell in the land,[10] and rise like the sun in his might.[11]

---

[1] Prov. 3:12.

[2] Gen. 37:3-4.

[3] Gen. 25:28; 27.

[4] Prov. 3:12; 13:24.

[5] Ruth 4:15.

[6] D. J. McCarthy, "Notes on the Love of God in Deuteronomy and The Father-Son Relationship Between Yahweh and Israel," *CBQ* 27 (1965), 144-147, agreed with Moran that love in Deuteronomy reflects a contractual relationship, but he also noted a Father-son relationship that presupposed a father's right to chasten and command.

[7] Ps. 145:20.

[8] Ps. 119:132.

[9] Ps. 116:1.

[10] Ps. 5:12(11).

[11] Jdgs. 5:31.

National and international lovers.—The relationship between a master and his slave was very similar to that of a king and his subjects. Saul loved (אהב) David and advanced him to the rank of armor-bearer.[1] He later advised his servants to tell David that because Saul was pleased with (חפץ) David and all the soldiers loved (אהב) him, Saul wished to make David his son-in-law.[2] The soldiers who loved David fought under his leadership. All Israel and Judah loved (אהב) David because he went out and came in before them.[3] Their loving meant fighting battles for him. Even in the advanced position of Saul's son-in-law, David was still the king's servant, and was subject to Saul and Jonathan. His love could be shown in his service to the king. Positions of authority changed when Jonathan made a covenant with David that each would love (אהב) the other as himself, but that Jonathan's love for David would be that of a servant to his master and not vice versa.[4] The subject who loved the king served him; the king who loved the subject provided for the subject well. Because of this, Joab was angry because King David mourned for his son who had tried to overthrow him. Absalom had been David's enemy. Joab had shown his love for David by killing Absalom, who responded by mourning for Absalom. Jaob complained that David had disgraced the soldiers and officers who had rescued him, "because you love those who hate you (לאהבה את שנאיך) and hate those who love you (ולשנא את אהביך). For you have made it clear now that officers and soldiers are nothing to you; for now I understand that if Absalom were alive and all of us were dead today, then you would be pleased."[5] When Jehu, the Seer, went out to meet King Jehoshaphat, he said, "Should you help the wicked (לעזר הרשע) and love those who hate the Lord (ולשנאי יהוה תאהב)?"[6] His criticism was against Jehoshaphat's treaty with the king of Israel to whom Jehoshaphat gave support in battle. The seer Jehu considered the North Israelites to be enemies of the Lord who should have received no support from Judah. Here, support for the wicked meant love for the Lord's enemies. When Solomon

---

[1] I Sam. 16:21.
[2] I Sam. 18:22.
[3] I Sam. 18:15-16.
[4] I Sam. 18:1-4; 20:14-17.
[5] II Sam. 19:5-6(6-7).
[6] II Chron. 19:2.

became king, Hiram, king of Tyre, sent servants to Solomon, because Hiram had loved King David, which meant that Hiram had supported David in international situations. The supporters of Pashur the prophet [1] and the supporters of Haman [2] were called "lovers" (אהבים). Jerusalem's lovers (אהבים) were the countries and political leaders from whom she might have received help before her destruction.[3] Israel's lovers (אהבים) were Assyria and Egypt.[4] The pessimistic wisdom writer noted that the rich man had many who loved (אהבים) him,[5] meaning those who stood by to support him because it was to their own advantage. Not all lovers were alike. Some pretended to be friends, but others would stick closer than a brother, being ready to help in time of need. That was the real friend (אהב) who loved and gave.[6] Jeremiah promised that Judah's friends (אהבים) would fall by the sword and Judah would be taken captive into Babylon.[7] Here, again, Judah's lovers or friends were those who had provided military support for her against Babylon.

In these contexts, love was more closely related to international treaties (in which it was required that one nation support another in time of war or other national crisis) than to any emotional upsurge of feeling. It was also a legal relationship that existed between a slave and his master whereby the slave could expect to have his material needs met by the master who loved him and the master in turn expected work from the slave who loved him. These love relationships had more to do with economic or military advantage than feelings of affection, although one did not necessarily exclude the other. Such love could be required and commanded, regardless of the feelings involved. The covenant relationship that the Lord had with his people had been taken with an oath and therefore the people could expect him to fulfill his bargain no matter how angry he became with them. Those who belonged to the community with whom the Lord had made a covenant were destined to receive the promises of the covenant. They were the ones loved by the Lord and therefore they were called beloved.

---

[1] Jer. 20:6.
[2] Esther 5:10, 14; 6:13.
[3] Lam. 1:2, 19; see also Jer. 22:20; 30:14; Ezek. 16:33; 23:22.
[4] Hos. 7:11; 8:9-13; Ezek. 23:5.
[5] Prov. 14:20.
[6] Prov. 17:17; 18:24.
[7] Jer. 20:4.

The covenant people.—Jesus was identified with the Lord's beloved (ἀγαπητός), the Lord's servant whom he had chosen.[1] ∅ He was the Lord's beloved (ἀγαπητός) Son in whom God was well pleased,[2] and whom the Lord had chosen.[3] Christians who had been delivered were transferred into the kingdom of the Lord's beloved Son (ὁ υἱὸς τῆς ἀγάπης αὐτοῦ).[4] Christians who were slaves of Christian masters were to serve their masters all the more because the masters were both believers (πιστοί) and beloved (ἀγαπητοί).[5] They were brothers whom the slaves were commanded to love. The ones addressed as beloved (ἀγαπητοί) were also children of God,[6] brothers,[7] saints,[8] and fellow workers;[9] they were obligated to render service to the brothers, especially by offering hospitality to those brothers from other geographical locations.[10] They were concerned for each other's well-being.[11] Church leaders referred to other brothers as beloved children (τέκνα . . . ἀγαπητά).[12] Some faithful apostles and Christians were called beloved together with their names, like "our beloved (οἱ ἀγαπητοὶ ἡμῶν) Barnabas and Paul"[13] and "our beloved brother (ὁ ἀγαπητὸς ἡμῶν ἀδελφός) Paul."[14] Those called beloved (ἀγαπητοί) had the promises[15] and expected better things that belonged to salvation.[16] They were admonished to be cleansed from defilement,[17] avoid false prophets,[18] build themselves up in the faith,[19] and love one another.[20] The Israelites were elected as beloved (κατὰ δὲ τὴν ἐκλογὴν ἀγαπητοί)

---

[1] Mt. 12:18.
[2] Mt. 3:17; 17:5; Mk. 1:11; 9:7; Lk. 3:22; II Peter 1:17.
[3] Lk. 9:35.
[4] Col. 1:13.
[5] I Tim. 6:2.
[6] I Jn. 3:2; 5:7.
[7] I Cor. 1:14; 15:58; James 1:16, 19; 2:5; II Peter 3:15; Phil. 16.
[8] Rom. 1:7.
[9] Phil. 1.
[10] III Jn. 5.
[11] III Jn. 2.
[12] I Cor. 4:14, 17: Eph. 5:1; II Tim. 1:27.
[13] Acts 15:25.
[14] Rom. 16:5, 8, 9, 12; Eph. 6:21; Col. 1:7; Phil. 1; II Tim. 1:2; II Peter 3:15; III Jn. 1.
[15] II Cor. 7:1.
[16] Heb. 6:9; see also Jude 3.
[17] II Cor. 7:1.
[18] I Jn. 4:1.
[19] Jude 20.   [20] I Jn. 4:7-11.

for the sake of their forefathers.[1] The beloved, then, were the covenanters who were bound by oath to love God and their fellow covenanters who were also saints. Love in the Song of Songs appears on the surface to be the expression of emotion felt between a groom and his new bride, but it may be an apocalyptic type of literature and the love may be toward the Land of Israel rather than toward a bride.

Those who had been properly initiated into sects were considered "worthy" of being entrusted with rules required for keeping a community pure so that the Lord or the Holy Spirit might dwell there.[2] They were the saints, the faithful, the beloved, the elect. If the community was celibate, they were brothers who had lost their life ($\psi\upsilon\chi\acute{\eta}$) in the world so that they might have life ($\zeta\omega\acute{\eta}$) in the community where all goods were shared in common so that each man loved his neighbor as himself. Life in the sectarian communities was demanding, however, and not all initiates were able to meet the demands. After understood punishments for correction had been administered, these members were excommunicated so that the sect could continue to be pure and sinless. Conditions for dismissal will next receive attention.

EXCOMMUNICATION

New Testament.—Several of the sects studied had careful and rigorous training programs for candidates. Of those who completed their training, only those capable of accepting the required discipline and gaining approval of the group were admitted. Those admitted were among the brothers who loved one another but hated those outside the group. They alone had "life" under the covenant. Those who did not love remained in "death." [3] There was no assurance that a candidate accepted would always continue in love as one who had "life." From the sect of St. John there were some who left the group.[4] There were probably others who were requested to leave. If one of the brothers of the sect saw another

---

[1] Rom. 11:28.
[2] Shepherd of Hermas, Mand. IV. ii; V. i-ii; Sim. V. vi ;VIII. ii; IX. xxviii; X. iii.
[3] I Jn. 3:14-15.
[4] I Jn. 2:19.

sin, he could pray and God would give him "life," which probably meant that his sin would be forgiven and he could be retained within the community.[1] This was only true if it was a sin "not to death" (ἁμαρτία οὐ πρὸς θάνατον). But there were sins "to death" (πρὸς θάνατον). For these prayer would do no good.[2] Since these sins could not be forgiven, this may have meant that the sinners would be excommunicated from the sect where alone there was life. When Paul learned of a member of the Corinthian Church who had improper relations with his father's wife, Paul ordered the church under his authorization to deliver that man over to Satan.[3] The sect of St. Matthew had special rules by which a sinner was invited to repent of his sin, but if he refused even after he was taken before the church, he was to be treated as a Gentile and a tax collector [4]—in other words, he was excommunicated. This was evidently done for any sin of any kind for which one of the saints refused to repent. But not all sins could be forgiven even if the member repented. Like the sect of St. John, the Sect of St. Matthew had a sin unto death. This was committed whenever a person said a word against the Holy Spirit. Such a person could not be forgiven either in this age or in the age to come.[5]

Both the author of Hebrews [6] and the Shepherd of Hermas [7] concur that those who have once been enlightened and initiated into the community having been cleansed of sin by baptism can not be forgiven a second time. For the Gentiles the opportunity for repentance will continue until the last day, but for the saints forgiveness has reached its limit.[8] Those baptized should always thereafter live in purity.[9] If they failed to do this they would be cast out of the society of the righteous and condemned to eternal death.[10]

Unpardonable sins.—It is not certain that the "sin unto death"

---

[1] I Jn. 5:16-17.
[2] I Jn. 5:16-17.
[3] I Cor. 5:1-5.
[4] Mt. 18:15-17.
[5] Mt. 12:31-32; see also the Gospel of Thomas 88:26-30.
[6] Heb. 6:4-6.
[7] Shepherd of Hermas, Vis. II. ii; Mandate IV. iii; Sim. VI. ii.
[8] *Ibid.*, Vis. II. ii; Mandate IV. iii.
[9] *Ibid.*, Mandate IV. iii; XII. iii; Sim. V. vii.
[10] Shepherd of Hermas, Mand. XII. iii; Sim. VI. ii; VII; VIII. vi, viii; IX. xiii, xiv, xvii, xviii.

of the sect of St. John was the same as the unpardonable sin of St. Matthew, but in having *some* unforgivable sin the two sects were similar to several others. Taking the name of the Lord in vain was a very serious offense. The sect of the Rule decreed, "Whoever swears (יזכיר)by the Name which is honored over every name ... either for fear of persecution or for any reason whatever, shall be separated [from the community] and not allowed to return again." [1]

The Zadokites' reasoning was: "[Let him not] swear either by *Aleph* and *Lamed* [El, Elohîm] or by *Aleph* and *Daleth* [Adonai], except for oaths of enrollment [which are taken] with the curses of the covenant ... If he swears by the curses of the covenant before the judges and then transgresses, he is guilty; and [even] if he confesses and repents, they will not forgive him.[2]

Profaning the Name was the same whether done intentionally or unintentionally, in private or public.[3] Other groups had still other sins listed for which there was no forgiveness, such as sinning excessively, sinning in a righteous generation, sinning with the intention of repenting,[4] profaning holy things, despising the set feasts, showing off before his brother in the congregation, nullifying the covenant of Abraham, and revealing secret meanings of the Torah which were not according to the *halakah*.[5] Some of these offenses excluded a member from the age to come and may not have required congregational excommunication in this age, whereas others only entailed separation from the community, never to return, but for many of the sects, exclusion from the community was understood exclusion to mean from the future Kingdom of God as well.

Essenes.—Josephus said that any Essene caught in any grievous sin (ἐπ' ἀξιοχρέοις ἁμαρτήμασαν) would be cast out of the community. Once separated from the community, former Essenes were said to die a horrible death. Since they were bound by oath not to eat food not prepared by Essene supervision, they were forced to eat grass and famish with hunger until death. Sometimes just before death, the group forgave the sinner and readmitted him, but this was not

---

[1] 1QS 6:27-7:2.
[2] CDC 15:1-4.
[3] Aboth 4:4.
[4] ARN 39.
[5] Aboth 3:11; see I Mac. 1:15.

a foregone conclusion.¹ The community was so closely inter-dependent that one who was excommunicated from religious life of the community was also deprived of physical life as well. This may have been an important reason for calling existence within the sect "life" and exclusion, "death."

Vine and branches.—The covenanters were all like so many branches of a vine. If once cut off from the community, they withered and died.² Therefore a person removed from the group was said to be "cut off" (כרת). When Jeremiah's enemies in Judah planned either to exile or kill him, they thought to destroy the tree with the fruit by cutting him off (נכרתנו) from the land of life (ארץ חיים).³ Isaiah said the Lord had cut off (ויכרת) from Israel both head and tail, palm branch and reed.⁴ Some of Eli's posterity was destined to be cut off from the altar.⁵ Any son of Aaron who approached holy things while unclean would be cut off (נכרתה) from the Lord's presence.⁶ A man who no longer wanted his wife in his association gave her a document notifying her that she had been cut off (ספר כריתת).⁷ An entire tractate in the Mishnah, Tosefta, Jerusalem and Babylonian Talmuds dealt with conditions by which a woman could be cut off from her husband.

Social extinction.—Segregation was a basic requirement for covenantal existence. A person who was defiled was required to separate himself from the rest of the community. Sometimes it meant staying outside of camp until he had been purified, after which he could return, but this was not called being "cut off" from the covenant community. Temporary punishment by removal from the purity of the community was usually called separating (הבדיל) the member from the community.⁸ The one who was

---

¹ *BJ* II.viii (143-144).
² Jn. 15:17.
³ Jer. 11:19.
⁴ Isa. 9:13(14).
⁵ I Sam. 2:23.
⁶ Lev. 22:3.
⁷ Dt. 24:1, 3; Isa. 50:1; Jer. 3:8.
⁸ Dt. 29:20; Isa. 59:2; 1QS 2:16; 7:1, 3, 5, 16; 8:24; CDC 9:21-23. A.R.C. Leaney, *The Rule of Qumran and its Meaning* (London, c1966), 197-201, rendered הבדיל as "cutting off." For an examination of the terms *ḥerem* and *anathema* in relationship to excommunication, see D. Macfadyen, "Excommunication," *EB*, VIII, 956-957.

permanently "separated for evil" (ויבדילוהו לרעה) was "cut off" (ונכרת) from the midst of all the sons of light. That did not mean that he was killed but that his lot was to be with those the sect called eternally cursed (ארורי עולמים).[1] Paul, however, spoke of some branches of Israel which, having been cut off (ἐξεκλάσθησαν), would again be grafted into (ἐγκεντρισθήσονται) the chosen community.[2] In the OT, however, "cutting off" was usually final. It sometimes meant a death penalty was inflicted.[3] Some have assumed that this was the basic meaning of cutting off, so English translations have rendered כריתת as "extirpation,"[4] "ceasing to exist,"[5] "extinction,"[6] or "extermination."[7] Aramaic translators in the Mekilta, however, did not give so physical a meaning for the term. הפסק in Aramaic, like כרת in Hebrew, means only "to cut" or "to sever." That did not always mean cutting off one's breath or blood circulation permanently, even when used as a term describing punishment to be inflicted. Jews who were "cut off" from Jerusalem were taken into exile,[8] delivered as captives to the enemy nation,[9] or removed to Egypt to become a curse and a taunt among all the nations,[10] but not killed. Their removal from the land, however, meant social extinction or "death" in a religious sense. Those Gibeonites who were promised that they would not be cut off[11] were allowed to exist on the promised land. Those cut off from Babylon fled each to his own land.[12] When the Lord cut off the inhabitants of Aven, the people of Syria were to be taken into exile.[13] Enemies, horses, sorcerers, soothsayers, mediums, and wizards that were to be cut off were to cease having an existence in the land.[14] They might be killed in the process of being removed,

---

[1] 1QS 2:16-17.

[2] Rom. 11:17-26.

[3] So Ezek. 25:7 and possibly Ex. 31:14-15; see also Mekilta, *Shabbata* 71-75.

[4] So H. Danby (tr.), "Kerithoth," *The Mishnah* (Oxford, 1954), 562-573.

[5] J. Z. Lauterbach (tr.), *Mekilta de Rabbi Ishmael* (Philadelphia, 1949), I, 67, 79; III, 202.

[6] *Ibid.*, II, 250.

[7] *Ibid.*, III, 193-194.

[8] Zech. 14:2.

[9] Obad. 14.

[10] Jer. 44:8.

[11] Josh. 9:23.

[12] Jer. 50:1.

[13] Amos 1:5.

[14] Micah 5:8(9)-12(13); I Sam. 28:9.

but the importance was not that they be killed but that there be
none left in the land, where the covenant community would be
effected by them. They were cut off socially, whether they were
killed physically or not. Not all the prophets Jezebel cut off were
killed, but they were taken out of circulation.[1] When the Lord
cut off the remnant of Baal, he was also to cut off the name of
Baal priesthood.[2] A city or fortress cut off was probably razed to
the ground so that it no longer existed as an administration center.[3]
The same was true of nations that were cut off the face of the earth.[4]
When the Lord promised to cut off man and beast from Edom,
he was to leave it desolate.[5] Frogs were to be cut off from Egypt,
being no longer in houses, where they were not wanted, but only
in the Nile.[6] Kings who were cut off were cut off from leadership
in their communities, which sometimes meant death,[7] but more
important, it meant that their dynasties came to an end;[8] their
leadership was discontinued; and their names blotted out.[9] Those
from the house of David or family of Levi who were promised that
their lineage not be cut off were not only promised that their
posterity could continue to reproduce itself, but that they would
continue to hold their respective offices in the community. They
would not be deprived of their positions.[10] The wicked who were
to be cut off the land would be rooted out (יסחו);[11] they would
never again come against Judah;[12] they would be kept from
entering Jerusalem;[13] their posterity was to be cut off;[14] or their
remembrance was not to be continued.[15] These were contrasted
to the righteous, blessed of the Lord who wait for the Lord to
keep his way, who were destined to possess the land and dwell

---

[1] I Kgs. 18:4-5.
[2] Zeph. 1:4.
[3] Micah 5:9(10); Nah. 3:15.
[4] Jer. 44:4; 48:2; Ezek. 30:15; 35:7; Zeph. 3:6-7.
[5] Ezek. 25:13; see also 14:19-23; 25:16.
[6] Ex. 8:5(4).
[7] Jdgs. 4:24; Dan. 9:26.
[8] I Sam. 20:15(16); 24:50(21); I Kgs. 9:7(8); 14:10, 14; 21:21; II Chron. 21:7.
[9] See Josh. 7:9; Ruth 4:10; Ps. 32:38; 109:13-15.
[10] Num. 4:18; I Kgs. 2:4; 8:25; 9:5; II Chron. 6:16; 7:18; Jer. 33:17-18.
[11] Prov. 2:22.
[12] Nahum 2:1(1:15).
[13] Ps. 101:8.
[14] Ps. 37:28, 38.
[15] Ps. 34:17(16).

there forever,[1] When the Lord cut off Israel's enemies for Joshua
it was because the land the enemy formerly inhabited was allotted
to Israel.[2] These expressions were used in close relationship to
the covenanter's attitude toward community structure, life under
the covenant, and its relationship to the land.

This examination of the expression "cutting off" as it was used
in the OT has shown that it was often associated with physical destruction, but not always. Even when the person, group, or nation
cut off was also killed, the term "cut off" was used rather than "kill"
or "murder" because the emphasis was upon his relationship to the
covenant community rather than his condition of health. This
knowledge will now be applied to compare some conditions in which
the scripture ordered a covenanter who committed an offense to be
"cut off" with the offenses for which later Jewish rules declared a
covenanter would not be forgiven.

Forgiveness and excommunication.—The offense that was most
widely specified as a sin that could not be forgiven was blasphemy
against the Name of Heaven, the Name, the Name honored over
every name, or the Holy Spirit.[3] Since rigorous sects strove for sinlessness, a sinful member who would not repent to be forgiven or
could not be forgiven was excommunicated.[4] The probable basis
of excommunication for blasphemy was the rule that ordered the
person who reviled the Lord or despised the word of the Lord
to be "cut off" from his people.[5] This seems to mean that covenanters understood this law to demand excommunication. Others not
forgiven were those who profaned the holy of holies or despised
set feasts.[6] There are several rules in the Torah to which this
applies: Anyone who ate leavened bread during the Passover
feast was to be cut off from his people.[7] One who was clean and
not on a journey but neglected to observe Passover was to be cut
off from his people.[8] If a covenanter did not afflict himself on the

---

[1] Ps. 37:9, 22, 29, 34.
[2] Josh. 23:4; also Dt. 12:29; 19:1.
[3] T. Yoma 5:6-8(190); 1QS 6:27-7:2; Aboth 4:4; Mt. 18:15-17.
[4] 1QS 6:27-7:2; Mt. 18:15-17.
[5] Num. 15:30-31.
[6] Aboth 3:4.
[7] Ex. 12:15, 19.
[8] Num. 9:13.

Day of Atonement, he should be cut off from his people.[1] A person who did not cleanse himself from his defilement before entering the tabernacle would defile the tabernacle. For this he should be cut off.[2] The Israelite who defiled the sanctuary by offering one of his children to Molech should be killed. If the community failed to do this, the Lord would cut him off from among his people.[3] Later Jews called these offenses profaning holy things.[4] If a man ate the fat of an animal of which an offering by fire was made to the Lord or slaughtered an animal outside the camp and did not bring it to the door of the tent of meeting to offer it as a gift to the Lord, he should be cut off from his people.[5] If a covenanter ate of the peace offerings on the third day after the sacrifice or ate any blood, he should be cut off from his people.[6] A law-abiding sect with this many laws against despising feasts or profaning holy things would be obligated to demand that they be observed. In observing these rules for which the punishment was being cut off from the community, later Jews and Christians enforced the requirements by offering no forgiveness, which meant excommunication. The Torah commanded that the male covenanter who was not circumcised should be cut off from his people.[7] Later Jews understood this to mean that anyone who nullified the covenant of Abraham could not be forgiven.[8] Israelites were forbidden to uncover the nakedness of their fathers' wives.[9] Whoever did such a thing was to be cut off from among the people.[10] It was on this basis that Paul ordered the Corinthian who had done that to be delivered over to Satan.[11] According to the Torah, a person who turned to wizards or mediums,[12] married the daughter of a foreign god,[1] or worshipped idols [14] was to be cut off from the people. Later

---

[1] Lev. 23:29.
[2] Lev. 7:20-21; Num. 19:13, 20. See also Ex. 30:37-38.
[3] Lev. 20:2-5.
[4] Aboth 3:11.
[5] Lev. 7:25; 17:3-4, 8-9.
[6] Lev. 19:8; 7:27; 17:10.
[7] Gen. 17:14.
[8] Aboth 3:11.
[9] Lev. 18:8.
[10] Lev. 18:29.
[11] I Cor. 5:1-5.
[12] Lev. 20:6.
[13] Mal. 2:11-12.
[14] Ezek. 14:6-7(7-8).

sectarians who committed similar offenses in NT times would probably have broken the oath taken with the curses of the covenant and therefore been excommunicated.[1]

Summary.—This examination has shown that Jewish and Christian sects of NT times had rules which required excommunication for certain offenses. Many of these offenses were the very same as those for which the OT rules required "cutting off" from among the covenant community. Although other scholars have generally understood 'cutting off" to mean the physical death penalty, this examination of the expression has shown that the image was that of a vine and the branches which could be cut off, separated from their source of sustenance, and so die. Although many non-technical uses of this term were not considered here, and although the expressions considered frequently involved death for the person "cut off", the basic meaning did not refer to physical death. The person involved was cut off from the land or the community, if he was an Israelite. Many of these were not killed, but rather taken into exile in another land. The Essenes who were cut off from their community were reported to have died of famine because the oaths they took prevented them from eating any food except that provided by the community. This was a very vivid portrayal of the relationship between physical life and religious life for scrupulous sectarian communities. This understanding of excommunication also is coherent with other sectarian practices of initiation and brotherly love and broader concepts of religious life and asceticism in relationship to sectarian faith and social structure and administration.

CONCLUSIONS

In many ways practices and beliefs that were well-established in the OT have been continued into NT times. Many of these can be directly or indirectly traced to the belief in the covenant which had extensive ramifications in the administration, social structures, ethics, and feelings of Jews and Christians of NT times. Without a knowledge of their ancient origin, NT faith and practice may be misunderstood. Both active and passive ethics were found to be national interpretations of ethics motivated by the theology of

---

[1] CDC 15:1-4.

conquest. "Life" was understood at times to mean existence within the covenant community, usually on the promised land free from foreign rule. NT eschatology and Jewish eschatology before and after NT times were found to be based on beliefs related to Sabbath rest and jubilee year release understood in nationalistic terms. The Kingdom of God was identified with the promised land originally and continued in close relationship to the land. The land in question was bounded on the south by Mt. Ḥalak, and to the west or south-west reached either to the brook of Egypt or the Delta on the Nile River. On the north the land was bounded by the Great River, supported by the northern end of the Lebanon mountains. At times the mountains of Galilee and either the Ladder of Tyre (modern Rosh Ha-Nikra) or the Litani River formed the northern limits. The Mediterranean Sea was the western border, and the eastern boundaries consisted of the Sea of Galilee, the Jordan River, and the Dead Sea. More territory was conquered east of the Jordan River, and hopes were expressed to extend the land to the Euphrates, or even north of the mountains that encircle the Fertile Crescent.

Outside the land, particularly in Babylon, there was probably more intense consideration of purity rules, and a rigorous asceticism developed that later was reflected in careful, exclusive, and celibate sects in Judaism and Christianity. They strove to be perfect to pay for the sins of Israel and prepare a clean community in which the Lord might dwell when he chose to comfort his people. The deep consciousness of sin found means of removal by various ablutions prescribed in purity rules and by the Day of Atonement when Israelites hoped all Israel would repent so that the Lord would be gracious to his people and restore the land. The sects that practiced purity rules carefully introduced means of initiation, the requirement of community love, and the practice of excommunication that continued in both Judaism and Christianity. These are not the only consequences of the covenant on Jewish and Christian faith and practice, but they are a few of the results that have been continued without always having been understood.

This study has not attempted to show the changes that developed in the covenantal theology or Weltanschauung of the ancient Near East from the time of Moses to Bar Cochba, or the various new elements that were introduced at different periods by different factions of the community. There were changes, adjustments, and innovations, but they did not change the structure or theology so much that the consequences of the covenant that was introduced by the early Israelites could not be faithfully understood and practiced by later sects in Judaism and Christianity. It was because of the covenant that the practices and beliefs continued as steadily as they did in the face of a changing world.

After these ideas have been carefully considered, refined, and corrected by other scholars, the prophetic task of deciding how Christians and Jews should evaluate these consequences and react to our tradition is still to be undertaken.

THE PRONUNCIATION OF THE TETRAGRAMMATON

Most scholars think the correct pronunciation is Yahweh. Moore has supported the correctness of that pronunciation by observing Theodoret's Greek pronunciation of ἰαβαι or ἰαβε.[1] Further precautions against pronouncing the Name were taken by abbreviations. In some rabbinic literature, for instance, some of the following abbreviations were used: יי, ייי, יוי, or יי׳. It is possible, then, that Theodoret's pronunciation was just as accidental as the ASV, because he may have tranlated into Greek his own pointing of a word which he only saw in abbreviated form, such as ייי. Clement of Alexandria, however, spelled the Tetragrammaton Ἰαουε, Ἰαουαι, and Ἰαο.[2] In early Aramaic papyri, the divine Name was spelled יהו, which Cowley pointed *ya'u* (יְהוּ), but which might also be pointed *yahô* (יְהוֹ).[3] Later magical papyri found in Egypt, often spelled the name ἰαω.[4] This would support the pointing יְהוֹ. In a Leviticus LXX fragment from cave 4, the Tetragrammaton was used and spelled ΙΑΩ, with majuscule letters, whereas the rest of the text was spelled in minuscules. In other LXX fragments, the Name was spelled out in square Hebrew letters, even though the rest of the text was Greek.[5] From the names of OT personages, whose names contained the

---

[1] G. F. Moore, *Judaism* (Cambridge, 1932), 426-427. His reference was to

Quaest. xv in Exodus. The only Samaritan vocalized reference is يهوه (*Yahwah*). Depending on the dialect, this might support the pronunciation, *Yahweh*, if the break were abrupt. If it were more like *Yahewah*, it could be a variant for *Yahuwah* or *Yahowah*. See J. A. Montgomery, "Notes from the Samaritan," *JBL* 25(1906), 49-51.

[2] So G. J. Thierry, "The Pronunciation of the Tetragrammaton," *OS*, (1948), 30-42. See also in the same volume, B. Alfrink, "La Prononciation 'Jehova' du Tétragramme," 43-63; and B.D. Eerdmans, "The Name Yahu," 2.

[3] A. E. Cowley (ed.), *Aramaic Papyri of the Fifth Century B.C.* (Oxford, 1923), 112-114.

[4] K. Preisendanz, *Papyri Graeci Magicae* (Leipzig, Berlin, 1928-31), *passim*.

[5] P. E. Kahle, *The Cairo Geniza* (Oxford, 1959), 223-224. The divine name was pronounced so that people could hear it every Day of Atonement even as far as Jericho (Yoma 6:1; 39b). See also I. Abrahams, *Studies in Pharisaism and the Gospels* (New York, 1967), 26-27.

divine Name, the pronunciation would also be יָהוֹ or יְהוּ. For instance, Jonathan's name was *Yaho-nathan*, "Yaho has given." The name John was *Yaho-chanan*, "Yaho has been kind." Elijah's name was *Eli-Yahu*, "my God is Yahu." The Masoretic text used the vocalizations *hu* and *hi* for words that, according to Arabic or Hebrew of the Dead Sea texts, were followed with an *ah* sound, like הוּא or הִיא for Dead Sea Scroll הואה or היאה; לכם for לכמה; etc. The Masoretes, themselves, may have pronounced these final *ah* sounds, even though they did not write the consonants needed in Dead Sea Scroll Hebrew to indicate the final vowel. As in Arabic, they may have pronounced vowels after the final consonants. Therefore, it seems likely that the divine Name was pronounced יָהֹוָה or יָהֹוָה whenever it was correctly pronounced.[1]

---

[1] S. Mowinckel, "The Name of the God of Moses," *HUCA* 32(1961), 121-133, held that the divine Name originally was "He." In invocation, it became יָ הוּאָה, "Oh He !" He held that the correct pronunciation would be *yà-húwa* (p. 133). The addition of *Ya* in direct address seems likely. This is regularly done in Arabic. See also Pesikta de R. Kaḥana 16:11; E. C. B, MacLaurin, "YHWH, the Origin of the Tetragrammaton," *VT*, 12 (1962). 429-463; A. L. Williams, "The Tetragrammaton-Yahweh, Name or Surrogate ?" *ZAW* 54 (1936), 262-269; and I. Abrahams, *Op. cit.* II, 174-176.

THE MILLENNIUM AFTER THE FALL

CHRISTIANS AFTER CONSTANTINE

The new exodus.—In the fourth century A.D. Maxentius had ordered his subjects to persecute Christians. This continued for seven years until Constantine killed Maxentius.[1] Eusebius, a Christian contemporary of Constantine, interpreted Constantine's victory over Maxentius in terms of conquest theology, claiming that God himself held Maxentius back, and just as he had delivered Israel in the days of Moses, so he delivered Constantine and the Christians in Eusebius' day.[2] In the crucial battle, Maxentius tried to cross a river on a bridge he had built by joining boats. The bridge broke and the soldiers with their heavy armor sank in the river. This recalled to Eusebius' mind the fate of Pharaoh's soldiers at the Reed Sea, so he noted that Maxentius' troops also "went down to the depths like a stone."[3] "They sank like lead in the mighty waters."[4] The deeds of the victors were so much like those of the Israelites rescued from Egypt at the Reed Sea that Eusebius thought the same hymn would be appropriate for both occasions: "Let us sing praise to the Lord for he has been gloriously glorified: horse and rider he has hurled into the sea. My help and shelter is the Lord. That which has happened to me is for salvation."[5] "Who is like you among the gods, O Lord? Who, like you, is glorified among saints, marvelous in glory, doing miracles."[6] Mentioning again and again Constantine's divine guidance and God as the author of the military victory, Eusebius reported that Constantine had his own statue set up in Rome with the Savior's sign in his right hand, at which time he publicly confessed that it was the God of the Christians who had led him in victory.[7] Shortly after Constantine was made emperor, Christian worship was

---

[1] Until 312 A.D.; Eusebius *HE* VIII.xiv-xvii.
[2] *HE* IX.i-ix.
[3] Ex. 14:4-5.
[4] Ex. 15:10.
[5] Ex. 15:1-2.
[6] Ex. 15:11; *HE* IX(3-8).
[7] *HE* IX (9-13).

permitted and church buildings were allowed to be built. The newly built houses of prayer, assembling of bishops, and the congregation of members of Christ's body from far away places, in Eusebius' judgment, were fulfillments of Ezekiel's prophecy that bone would be joined to bone and joint to joint.[1] In the panegyric on the building of new churches, the work was compared to that of Bezalel, the architect of Solomon's temple. Employing Psalms, the author prepared a second hymn of victory: "Just as we have heard, thus we have also seen in the city of our God."[2] The author then commented, "And in what city but that newly constructed and God-erected [city], which is the living church."[3] Still in praise of the church, Eusebius quoted Ps. 87:3, omitting one word, "Zion": "Glorious things have been spoken concerning you . . . city of God."[4] In further praise to Jesus, "the only unique One, the all-good Son of the all-good Father," for whom the Father "saved us, when we were not only sick or afflicted by terrible sores and wounds already decayed, but we were also lying among the dead; . . . [this he did when we] were not just half dead (ἡμιθνῆτας), but even in tombs and graves, completely loathsome and stinking, raising [us] up (ἀναλαβών); as of old, so also now."[5]

It was evident, then, that Christians understood the establishment of the Roman Empire under Christian jurisdiction as a new exodus and restoration of the land. Christians compared the church to Solomon's temple, and the revival of the body of Christ to the resurrection of the dead. The age to come had come; the kingdom was established; the promises had been fulfilled. The God of armies had again proved himself to be faithful to the covenant. The difference was that the kingdom established by this deliverance and conquest was the Roman Empire rather than Palestine. The center of the universe was not Jerusalem, but Constantinople. The change of administration was all that was necessary to transform the Roman Empire from the anti-christ to The Kingdom of God. For most Christians, this was satisfactory, but there were other Christians ("our half-Jews"—*nostri semiiudaei*), probably Jewish Christians, who continued to agree with the Jews (*Iudaei*) in expecting a

---

[1] Ezek. 37:1-14; *HE* X.iii.1-3.
[2] Ps. 48:8; *HE* X.iv.3-6.
[3] *HE* X.iv.7.   [4] *HE* X.iv.7.
[5] *HE* X.iv.11-12; the same Greek word was used to describe the ascension of Elijah (II Kgs. 2:1-10) and Jesus (Acts 1:2).

Jerusalem made of gold and precious stones. This, they confidently
believed, would appear in a future reign of a thousand years, "when all
nations would be subservient to Israel" (*seruiturae sunt Israel*). That
would be a great day when caravans from Midian, Ephah, and Sheba
would come bringing gold, and all the sheep of Kedar as well as
the rams of Nabaioth would be gathered to be sacrificed at the
altar in the temple which would then be rebuilt.[1] From the islands,
Tarsian ships would fly like doves bringing the daughters of
Israel together with their valuable gifts of gold and silver.[2] Aliens
would do the work of rebuilding the wall of Jerusalem, where the
gates would always be open to receive gifts of money and victims
for sacrifice, day or night.[3]

Jerome, himself, thought these Jewish Christians as well as the
Jews of his day were in error. The kingdom they anticipated was
very materialistic, but so was the Roman Empire after Constantine
that Eusebius interpreted as The Kingdom of God. Whether
Christians identified Jerusalem or Rome with the capital of The
Kingdom of Heaven, both based their theology on a belief that
Jehovah was the God of armies. The political organism that later was
called The Holy Roman Empire also arrived at its designation because of the theology of conquest. Because of Christianity's new
status in the Roman Empire, most Christians stopped thinking of
Rome as the anti-christ, but Judaism did not enjoy the same im-
proved status, so it continued to be hostile to Rome and identified
Rome not only with the anti-Messiah, but also with Christianity.

Jews and the millennium.—Medieval Jews continued to write
apocalyptic literature, employing such typically eschatological
terms as "the end" (קץ),[4] "in the end of days" (באחרית הימים),[5]
and the "day of judgment" (יום דין).[6] Furthermore, this literature
was closely related to political events: the end of the Byzantine
rule in the Land of Israel (7th century), the end of the Omayyad
control of the Land of Israel (8th century), the end of the Ab-

---

[1] Isa. 60:6-7.   [2] Isa. 60:8-9.

[3] Isa. 60:10-11; Jerome, *In Esaiam* XVII. lx.1-3, 11.15-28.

[4] See Ibn-Shmuel, *Midreshe Ge'ulāh* (Jerusalem-Tel Aviv, 1953/54), 41,
51, 72, 73, 75, 79, 90, 97, 104, 121, 124, 125, 127, 148, 149, 151, 152, 193,
197, 214, 217, 230, 270, 271, 273, 279, 284, 285, 305, 307, 308, 315, 322,
326, 355, 359, 369.

[5] *Ibid.*, 41, 42, 51, 75, 103, 131, 217, 249, 251, 278, 281.

[6] *Ibn-Shmuel* 226, 227, 322.

basid dynasty that ruled from Baghdad (10th century), the time
when the Khazars were meeting with Jews of the Byzantine
Empire (10th century), and the time of the third crusade in the
Land of Israel (12th century). These were all events which motivated pious Jews to believe that God would soon restore the Land
of Israel to the sons of Abraham.[1] With this belief, Jews were
ready to assist in upsetting the international situation so that the
mighty would fall, and, in the shuffle of powers, Israel would gain
her rightful place on top.

Medieval apocalypses expected two Messiahs: one, the son of
Joseph or Ephraim from Galilee (the Messiah of Israel) who was
expected to lead the Israelites in battle against Armilos and be
killed in behalf of his people. The son of Joseph was to be the
forerunner for the son of David (the Messiah of Judah) who would
succeed in destroying Armilos, claiming his throne at Jerusalem,
punishing all surrounding nations, and ruling the people of Israel
in peace.[2] The arch enemy, Armilos, was probably a deliberate
semitization of Romulus.[3] At times he was identified with Edom,
over which he was King and Messiah,[4] and "Edom" in rabbinic
literature was regularly used as a substitute for "Rome." During
the crusades, at least, he was also identified with the Christian
church. Armilos was a gigantic monster with two heads.[5] He had
a strange origin. There was in Rome a white marble stone created
by the Lord in the image of a beautiful woman. The wicked ones
of the nations of the world, sons of Belial, were excited to passion
and lay with her, and their sperm was kept in the stone. A creature
was formed and the stone burst open and something like a man
came forth. His name was Armilos, the tempter.[6] He called himself

---

[1] *Ibid.*, "General Introduction," 61.

[2] *Ibid.*, 126, 131, 132, 158-160; 195-197; 225-227, 285-286, 302, 304, 307-
308, 312-314, 316-317, 320-323, 328-332, 334, 336, 338, 339, 342-344, 347,
350, 357, 358, 359, 360-361, 362-370.

[3] For the frequency with which a prosthetic *alef* is added before a Latin
or Greek loan word see: אונפיל for φιάλη (T.BB 5:11); אונקולמוס for
κάλαμος (T.BM 9:14; BB3:5); איסקופה for σκάφος (T.BB 4:1); אכסנאי for
ξένος (T. Shebiit 5:21; Erubin 8:4); and אפרון for φορεῖον (T. Yeb. 13:1;
Sotah 15:9)

[4] Ibn-Shmuel, *Op. cit.*, 284, 316, 320.

[5] *Ibid.*, 131, 284, 316, 320. "The Prayer of *R. Shim'on ben Yoḥai*" was
written after the schism of 1054 A.D. After that time the eastern and
western divisions of the church operated under "two heads." See also p.
268-286.

[6] *Ibid.*, 131, 284, 313, 320.

the Messiah and God,[1] but he was really Satan.[2] A variant account said the stone was an image of a virgin, the wife of Belial.[3] Armilos was the one whom the nations (i.e. Christians) call antichrist.[4] He represented to apocalyptic Jews the force that prevented Israel from obtaining national independence. In general this force was the Roman Empire. When Roman Christianity became closely allied with the empire, the church also came to be considered the antichrist, and Armilos evidently personified both the church and the government. Possibly some of the slightly disguised elements of this account may be: Jesus, the Virgin Mary, Gentiles, and the Christian church. In any event this imagery may have symbolized known historical conditions from a patriotic Jewish point of view.

Judaism was not the only branch of the cult of Jehovah that kept alive the ancient conquest theology. Mohammedanism began and developed as an active military religion, and the Christian church took active, religiously motivated, military resistance to it in the crusades. The conditions that irritated the Western church about the holy land had been developing for a number of years before the Council met at Clermont and approved the active military program that followed as the will of God.[5] As the crusades developed, it became evident that the conflict was not only between the eastern and western worlds, the Moslems and the Christians, but also between Christians and Jews. In Europe many Jews were killed by Christians on the way to the holy land, and when swords were crossed in the holy land there were thousands of Jews who fought alongside the Moslems to rid the holy land of the Christians whom they considered the anti-christs. After all, the signs were just right. It was about a millennium since the fall of Jerusalem; Jerusalem was surrounded by armies; surely these were the final oppressions Jews were required to endure before God restored his land to the sons of Abraham. The crusades have been an ethical embarrassment to Christians for many years, but they were based on the same

---

[1] *Ibid.* 284, 313, 320-321.

[2] *Ibid.*, 313, 316.

[3] *Ibid.* 369.

[4] *Ibid.*, 320.

[5] Council of Clermont met Nov. 18-27, 1095. Trouble had begun earlier. 1070 would be exactly the millennium, counting from the fall of Jerusalem. See H. B. Workman, "Crusades," *Encyclopaedia of Religion and Ethics*, ed. J. Hastings (New York, 1912), 345-351 and J. Jacobs, "The Crusades," *JE* IV (New York, 1902), 378-379.

conquest theology that was held by Jews and Moslems at the same time. All three groups believed that they were doing the will of God.

The basis for later Christian theology that spiritualized biblical eschatology may have been strongly influenced by St. Augustine. When the "eternal city" of Rome was sacked by Alaric and the Goths in 410 A.D., St. Augustine was forced to reconsider his whole philosophy of history to take this event into account. This research ended in the composition of *The City of God*. He concluded that there were "earthly cities" and a "heavenly city." Only the latter was eternal, and it was not coterminous with any earthly city. Those who loved themselves even to the contempt of God were citizens of the earthly city, whereas those who loved God even to the contempt of themselves were citizens of the heavenly city. Because Rome had exhibited a degree of justice and virtue and ability to maintain peace, it was allowed to exist for many years, but its fall was caused by its inner deterioration. Later Christians who accepted Augustine's analysis did not find it necessary to identify the church with a nation or with a political theory that bound religion to political success. The new Jerusalem was not identified with geographical Jerusalem restored to political power; the world to come was expected to be in heaven; and the Kingdom of Heaven was not understood in terms of earthly politics. Nonetheless, there continued to be a close relationship between Christianity and political events, based on biblical eschatology.[1]

This brief note only surveyed sketchily two important events in Western history in which the conquest theology of the OT was applied to historical events and one occasion when The Kingdom of God was spiritualized. Medievalists can find many more applications which are important for understanding the relationships between Jews and Christians after the defeat of Bar Cochba.

---

[1] See W. J. Oates, *Basic Writings of Saint Augustine* (New York, c1948), I, xxxiii-xxxvi.

BIBLIOGRAPHY

Abel, F.-M. *Géographie de la Palestine* (Paris, 1933).

Abrahams, I. *Studies in Pharisaism and the Gospels* (New York, 1967).

Achelis, H. *Die ältesten Quellen des Orientalischen Kirchenrechtes, Erstes Buch; die Canones Hippolyti*, TUGAL VI, 276 (Leipzig, 1891).

Aharoni, J. *The Land of the Bible, a Historical Geography*, tr. A. Rainey (London, 1967).

Aland, K. *Did the Early Church Baptize Infants?* tr. G. R. Beasely-Murray (Philadelphia, c. 1963).

—— et al. (eds.) *Studia Evangelica* (Berlin, 1964).

—— and F. L. Cross (eds.) *Studia Patristica* (Berlin, 1957).

Alfrink, B. "La Prononciation 'Jehova' du Tétragramme", *OS*, (1948).

Allegro, J. M. "Fragments of a Qumran Scroll of Eschatological Midrâsîm", *JBL* 77 (1958).

Allon, G. *Studies in Jewish History* (Hebrew) (Israel, 1957).

Alt, A. "Neue Berichte über Feldzüge von Pharaonen", *ZDPV*, 70 (1954).

Aptowitzer, J. *Parteipolitik der Hasmonäerzeit im rabbinischen und pseudepigraphischen Schrifttum* (New York, 1927).

Audet, J.-P. "Affinités littéraires et Doctrinales du 'Manuel de Discipline'", *RB* 59 (1952).

—— "Qumran et la Notice de Pline", *RB* 68 (1961).

Bagatti, B. *L'Église de la Circoncision*, tr. A. Storme (Jerusalem, 1965).

Bamberger, B. J. "Fear and Love of God in the OT", *HUCA* 6 (1929).

Bar-Deroma, H. "The River of Egypt (Naḥal Mizraim)", *PEQ* 92 (1960).

Barrosse, T. "The Death and Sin in Saint Paul's Epistle to the Romans", *CBQ* 15 (1953).

Bauer, W. "Essener", *Paulys Realencyclopädie der Classischen Altertumswissenschaft, Supplementband IV* (Stuttgart, 1924).

Baumgarten, J. M. "1QSa 1:11 — Age of Testimony or Responsibility?" *JQR* 49 (1958).

Beer, G. and O. Holtzmann (eds.) *Die Mischna* (Giessen, 1933).

Bertram, G. "ζωή and βίος in the Septuagint", *TDNT* II, 852.

Betz, O. "Jesu Heiliger Krieg", *Nov.* 2 (1958).

Black, M. "Pharisees", *ID* III.

—— "The Gospel and the Scrolls", *Studia Evangelica*, ed. K. Aland et la. (Berlin, 1964).

Blank, S. H. "Studies in Deutero-Isaiah", *HUCA* 15 (1940).

——, W. M. Roth, and C. R. North. *The Suffering Servant in Deutero-Isaiah* (Oxford, 1956).

Bloch, J. *On the Apocalyptic in Judaism*, *JQR* Monograph No. II (Philadelphia, 1952).

Bloch, R. "Note méthodologique pour l'étude de la littérature rabbinique", *RSR* 43 (1955).

Bonsirven, J. *Le Règne de Dieu* (Aubier, c. 1957).

Borgen, P. "'At the Age of Twenty' in 1QSa", *RQ* 3 (1961).

Bousset, D. W. *Die Jüdische Apokalyptik* (Berlin, 1903).

Bowman, J. "Early Samaritan Eschatology", *JJS* 6 (1955).

Box, B. E. "IV Ezra", *Apocrypha and Pseudepigrapha of the OT* ed. R. H. Charles (Oxford, c. 1913).

Brewer, J. A. *ICC Haggai, Zechariah, Malachi, and Jonah.*
Briggs, C. A. and E. G. *ICC Psalms,* (Edinburgh, c. 1907).
Brockington, L. H. "Septuagint and Targum", *ZATW* 66 (1954).
Brooke, A. E. *ICC Johannine Epistles* (Edinburgh, 1912).
Buber, M. *The Prophetic Faith,* tr. C. Witton-Davies (New York, 1949).
Büchler, A. *Studies in Sin and Atonement* (London, 1928).
—— "The Levitical Impurity of the Gentile", *JQR,* n.s. 17 (1926-27).
—— *Der Galiläische Am HaAreṣ des zweiten Jahrhunderts* (Vienna, 1906).
Bultmann, R. "History and Eschatology in the NT", *NTS* 1 (1954-55).
—— *The Presence of Eternity* (New York, c. 1957).
Burchard, C. "Pline et les Esséniens", *RB* 69 (1962).
Burkitt, F. C. *Jewish and Christian Apocalypses* (London, 1914).
Burrows, M. *More Light on the Dead Sea Scrolls* (New York, 1958).
Cadoux, C. J. *The Historic Mission of Jesus* (New York, n.d.).
Charles, R. H. *Eschatology: the Doctrine of a Future Life in Israel, Judaism and Christianity* (New York, c. 1963²).
—— *The Religious Development Between the Old and New Testaments.*
—— *ICC Revelation* (New York, 1920).
—— (ed.) *Apocrypha and Pseudepigrapha of the OT* (Oxford, c. 1913).
Clavier, H. "Le Drame de la Mort et de la Vie", *Studia Evangelica* III, ed. F. L. Cross (Berlin, 1964).
Cohen, H. *Religion der Vernunft aus den Quellen des Judentums* (Frankfurt, 1929²).
Cohon, S. A. "Original Sin", *HUCA* 21 (1948).
Conway, B. L. *The Question Box* (New York, c. 1929).
Coppens, J. "Les Origines du Messianisme", *L'Attente du Messie,* ed. Cerfaux et al. (Lovanii, 1954).
—— "La doctrine biblique sur l'amour de Dieu et du prochain", *ETL* 40 (1964).
Cowley, A. E. (ed.) *Aramaic Papyri of the Fifth Century B.C.* (Oxford, 1923).
Craig, C. T. "Realized Eschatology", *JBL* 56 (1937).
Cross, Jr., F. M. *The Ancient Library of Qumran* (Garden City, 1961).
Cullmann, O. *Christ and Time,* tr. F. V. Filson (Philadelphia, 1950).
—— *Baptism in the NT* (Chicago, 1950).
Dahl, N. A. "Eschatologie und Geschichte im Lichte der Qumran Texte", *Zeit und Geschichte,* ed. E. Dinkler (Tübingen, 1964).
Dalman, G. *Die Worte Jesu.*
—— *The Words of Jesus,* tr. O. M. Kay (Edinburgh, 1902).
Danby, H. (tr.) "Kerithoth", *The Mishnah* (Oxford, 1954).
Daniel, C. "Une Mention Paulinienne des Esséniens de Qumran", *RQ* 5 (1966).
Daube, D. *The NT and Rabbinic Judaism.*
Davis, M. (ed.) *Israel, its Role in Civilization* (New York, c. 1956).
Deems, M. H. "Early Christian Asceticism", *Early Christian Origins* (Chicago, 1961).
DeVier, W. A. "Water Baptism in the Ancient Church", *BS* 116 (1959)
Dodd, C. H. *The Apostolic Preaching and its Developments* (New York, 1936).
—— *The Interpretation of the Fourth Gospel* (Cambridge, 1954).
—— *Historical Tradition in the Fourth Gospel* (Cambridge, 1963).
Doeve, J. W. *Jewish Hermeneutics in the Synoptic Gospels and Acts* (Assen, 1954).
Donner, H. and W. Röllig. *Kanaanäische und Aramäische Inschriften* (Wiesbaden, 1964) III vols.

Driver, G. R. *The Judaean Scrolls* (Oxford, 1965).
Driver, S. R. *ICC Deuteronomy*.
Drower, E. S. *The Mandaeans of Iraq and Iran* (Leiden, 1962).
Dupont-Sommer, A. *Les Écrits Esséniens découverts près de la Mer Morte* (Paris, 1959).
Dussaud, R. *Topographie Historique de la Syrie Antique et Médiévale* (Paris, 1927).
Eerdmans, B. D. *The Religion of Israel* (Leiden, 1947).
—— "The Name Yahu", *OS* (1948).
Eichrodt, W. *Theology of the OT*, I, tr. J. A. Baker (Philadelphia, c. 1961).
Elliger, K. "Die Nordgrenze des Reiches Davids", *Palästinajahrbuch*, 32 (1936).
—— *Das Buch der zwölf kleinen Propheten* (Göttingen, 1964).
Epstein, I. *The Babylonian Talmud* (London, c. 1938).
Farmer, W. R. "The Patriarch Phineas", *ATR* 34 (1952).
—— "The Geography of Ezekiel's 'River of Life'", *BA* 19 (1956).
—— *The Maccabees, Zealots, and Josephus* (New York, 1956).
—— "Essenes", *ID* II.
Fensham, F. C. "'Camp' in the NT and Milḥama", *RQ* 4 (1964).
Feuillet, A. "Le Discours de Jésus sur la Ruine du Temple" (Suite) *RB* 56 (1949).
Finkelstein, L. *The Pharisees* (Philadelphia, 1962).
—— "Development of the Amidah", *JQR* (n.s.), 16 (1925/26).
Fitzmyer, J. A. "Further Light on Melchizedek from Qumran Cave 11", *JBL*, 86 (1967).
—— "The Bar Cochba Period", *The Bible in Current Catholic Thought*, ed. J. L. McKenzie (New York, c. 1962).
Flusser, D. "Two Notes on the Midrash on II Sam. 7", *IEJ* 9 (1959).
—— "Melchizedek and the Son of Man", *Christian News from Israel* (April, 1966).
Fohrer, V. G. "Die Struktur der alttestamentlichen Eschatologie", *Theologische Literaturzeitung* 85 (1960).
Fritsch, C. T. "TO ANTITUPON", *Studia Biblica et Semitica* dedicated to Th. C. Vriezen (Leiden, 1966).
Frost, S. B. "Eschatology and Myth", *VT* II (1952).
Fuller, R. H. *The Mission and Achievement of Jesus* (Chicago, c. 1954).
Furrer, K. "Antike Städte im Libanongebiete", *ZDPV* 8 (1885).
Gärtner, B. *The Temple and the Community in Qumran and the NT* (Cambridge, 1965).
Galling, K. "Das Deutsche Ev. Institut für Altertumswissenschaft des Heiligen Landes", *ZDPV* 70 (1954).
Geiger, A. *Urschrift und Uebersetzungen der Bibel* (Breslau, 1851).
Geoltrain, P. "Le Traité de la Vie Contemplative de Philo d'Alexandrie", *Semitica*, Cahiers X (Paris, 1960).
Gerhardsson, B. *Memory and Manuscript* (Uppsala, 1961).
Ginsberg, L. *The Legends of the Jews*, tr. H. Szold (Philadelphia, c. 1901).
Glatzer, N. N. "The Attitude Toward Rome in Third-Century Judaism", *Politische Ordnung und menschliche Existenz* (München, 1962).
Gloege, G. *Reiche Gottes und Kirche im Neuen Testament* (Gütersloh, 1929).
Gnilka, J. "Die Essenischen Tauchbäder und die Johannestaufe", *RQ* 3 (1961).
Goodenough, E. R. *The Politics of Philo Judaeus* (New Haven, 1938).
Gordis, R. "The Knowledge of Good and Evil in the OT and the Qumran Scrolls", *JBL* 76 (1957).

Gordon, C. *Adventures in the Nearest East* (Fairlawn, 1957).

Grail, A. "Le Baptême dans l'Épître aux Galates", *RB* 58 (1951).

Greenberg, M. "The Hebrew Oath Partical *Hây/Hê*", *JBL* 76 (1957).

Gressmann, H. *Der Ursprung der israelitisch-jüdischen Eschatologie* (Göttingen, 1905), revised and republished posthumously as *Der Messias* (Göttingen, 1929).

Gunkel, H. *Schöpfung und Chaos in Urzeit und Endzeit* (Göttingen, 1894, 1921²).

Guttmann, A. "Pharisaism in Transition", *Essays in Honor of Solomon B. Freehof* (Pittsburgh, 1964).

Habermann, A. M. "Benê Çadôk Hêm Haççadôkîm", *Hâ᾿Âreç* (Mar. 30, 1956).

Harper, W. R. *ICC Hosea* (Edinburgh, c. 1905).

Harris, J. R. *The Odes and Psalms of Solomon* (Cambridge, 1909).

Hartingsveld, L. van. *Die Eschatologie des Johannesevangeliums* (Assen, 1962).

Herford, R. T. *The Pharisees* (New York, 1924).

Hertz, J. H. (ed.) *The Pentateuch and Haftorahs* (London, 1947).

Hiers, R. H. "Eschatology and Methodology", *JBL* 85 (1966).

Hölscher, G. *Der Sadducäismus* (Leipzig, 1906).

Hoenig, S. B. "The Age of Mature Responsibility in IQSa", *JQR* 48 (1958).

—— "The Age of Twenty in Rabbinic Tradition and IQSa" *JQR* 49 (1958-59).

Hoffmann, D. *Das Buch Leviticus Übersetzt und Erklärt* (Berlin, 1905).

Holtzmann, H. J. *Die synoptischen Evangelien, Ihr Ursprung und geschichtlicher Charakter* (Leipzig, 1863).

Holtzmann, O. "Berakot", *Die Mischna* (Giessen, 1912).

Hummel, R. *Die Auseinandersetzung zwischen Kirche und Judentum im Mattäusevangelium* (München, 1963).

Ibn-Shmu᾿el, Y. *Midreshê Ge᾿ûlâh* (Jerusalem-Tel Aviv, 1953-54).

Jacobs, J. "The Crusades", *JE* IV (New York, 1902).

Jenni, E. "Das Wort 'Olam im Alten Testament", *ZATW* 65 (1953).

Jeremias, J. *Infant Baptism in the First Four Centuries*, tr. D. Cairns (Philadelphia, 1962).

—— *The Origins of Infant Baptism*, tr. D. M. Barton (Naperville, c. 1963).

Jugie, M. "Péché Originel", *Dictionnaire de Théologie Catholique* 12 (Paris, 1933).

Kahle, P. E. *The Cairo Geniza* (Oxford, 1959).

Kasteren, J. P. van. "La Frontière Septentrionale", *RB* 4 (1895).

Kaufmann, Y. *Tôldôt Ha-᾿Emûnâh Ha-Yiśra᾿elît* (Jerusalem, 1954), 4 vols. Originally in eight volumes. Vols. 1-7 have been abridged into one volume and translated by M. Greenberg into English, *The Religion of Israel* (Chicago, 1960).

Kenyon, K. M. *Amorites and Canaanites* (London, 1966).

Kilpatrick, G. D. "The Gentile Mission in Mark and Mark 13 : 9-11", *Studies in the Gospels* (Oxford, 1957).

Klausner, J. *The Messianic Idea in Israel*, tr. W. F. Stinespring (New York, 1955).

Knox, J. "Romans 15 : 14-33 and Paul's Conception of his Apostolic Mission" *JBL* 83 (1964).

Koester, H. "The Purpose of the Polemic of a 'Pauline Fragment'" *NTS* 8 (1961-62).

Kohler, K. "Eschatology" *JE* V.

Kohler, K. "Bar Mizwah" *JE* II.

—— "Pharisees" *JE* IX.

Kosmala, H. *Hebräer-Essener-Christen* (Leiden, 1959).

Kraub, S. "Sanhedren-Makkot", *Die Mischna* ed. G. Beer and O. Holtzmann (Giessen, 1933).

Kraus, H. J. *Psalmen* (Neukirchen, 1961).

Kümmel, W. G. *Promise and Fulfillment*, tr. D. M. Barton (London, c. 1957).

—— "Futurische und präsentische Eschatologie im ältesten Urchristentum", *NTS* 5 (1958).

—— "Die Naherwartung in der Verkündigung Jesu", *Zeit und Geschichte*, ed. E. Dinkler (Tübingen, 1964).

Kuhn, K. G. "βασιλεύς" *TWNT*, I.

Labat, R. *Manuel d'Épigraphie Accadienne* (Paris, 1952).

Ladd, G. E. "Why Not Prophetic-Apocalyptic" *JBL* 76 (1957).

Lambert, W. G. *Babylonian Wisdom Literature* (Oxford, 1960).

Laurin, R. B. "The question of Immortality in the Qumran 'Hodayot'", *JSS* 3 (1938).

Lauterbach, J. Z. *Rabbinic Essays* (Cincinnati, 1951).

—— (tr.) *Mekilta de Rabbi Ishmael* (Philadelphia, 1949).

Leaney, A. R. C. *The Rule of Qumran and its Meaning* (London, c. 1966).

Lewy, H. and J. "The Origin of the Week and the Oldest West Asiatic Calendar" *HUCA* 17 (1942-43).

Licht, J. "Taxo, or the Apocalyptic Doctrine of Vengeance", *JJS* XII (1961).

Liebreich, L. J. "The Compilation of the Book of Isaiah", *JQR* 46 (1955-56), 47 (1956-57).

Lohfink, N. "Hate and Love in Osee 9:15", *CBQ* 25 (1963).

Löw, L. *Das Lebensalter in der Jüdischen Literatur* (Szegedin, 1875).

Lowy, S. "The Motivation of Fasting in Talmudic Literature", *JJS* 9 (1958).

—— "The Confutation of Judaism in the Epistle of Barnabas", *JJS* 11 (1960).

Lundström, G. *The Kingdom of God in the Teaching of Jesus*, tr. J. Bulman (Edinburgh, 1963).

Lyonnet, S. "Le Péché Originel en Rom. 5: 12", *Biblica* 4 (1960).

Macfadyen, D. "Excommunication", *EB* VIII.

MacLaurin, E. C. B. "YHWH, the Origin of the Tetragrammaton", *VT* 12 (1962).

MacNeill, H. L. *The Christology of the Epistle to the Hebrews* (Chicago, 1914).

Manson, W. *The Epistle to the Hebrews* (London, 1951).

May, H. G. "The Righteous Servant in Second Isaiah's Songs", *ZATW* 66 (1954).

Mazar, B. "Canaan and the Canaanites", *BASOR* 102, (1964).

McCarthy, D. J. "Notes on the Love of God in Deuteronomy and the Father-Son Relationship Between Yahweh and Israel", *CBQ* 27 (1965).

McCullough, W. S. "Dog", *ID* (New York, c. 1962), I.

McKenzie, J. L. (ed.) *The Bible in Current Catholic Thought* (New York, c. 1962).

Michel, A. and J. LeMayne. "Pharisiens", *Supplément au Dictionnaire de la Bible* (Paris, 1964), fasc. 39-40.

Milik, J. T. and F. M. Cross, Jr. "Inscribed Javelinheads from the Period of the Judges", *BASOR* 134 (1954).

Minear, P. S. *Eyes of Faith* (Philadelphia, 1946).

Mitchell, H. G., J. M. Powis Smith, and J. A. Brewer, *ICC Haggai, Zechariah, Malachi, and Jonah*.

Montgomery, J. A. "Notes from the Samaritan", *JBL* 25 (1906).

Moore, G. F. *Judaism* (Cambridge, I and II, 1927; III, 1930).

Moran, W. L. "The Ancient Near Eastern Background of Love of God in Deuteronomy", *CBQ* 25 (1963).

Morgenstern, J. "The Suffering Servant — A New Solution", *VT* 11 (1961).

Mowinckel, S. *He That Cometh*, tr. G. H. Anderson (New York, c. 1957).

—— *The Psalms in Israel's Worship*, tr. D. R. Ap-Thomas (New York, c. 1962).

Neusner, J. "The Fellowship (HBWRH) in the Second Commonwealth", *HTR* 53 (1960).

—— (ed.) *Religions in Antiquity. Essays in Memory of Erwin Ramsdell Goodenough* (Leiden, 1968).

—— "HBR and NʾMN", *RQ* 5 (1946).

Nicholson, E. W. "The Meaning of the Expression עם הארץ in the OT", *JSS* 10 (1965).

Noltat, D. "Symbolismes Baptismaux chez Saint Paul", *Lumière et Vie* 26 (1956).

North, R. "The Qumran Sadducees", *CBQ* 17 (1955).

—— *Sociology of the Biblical Jubilee* (Rome, 1954).

Noth, M. *Leviticus*, tr. J. E. Anderson, (London, c. 1965).

Oates, W. J. *Basic Writings of Saint Augustine* (New York, c. 1948).

Otto, R. *Reich Gottes und Menschensohn* (München, 1934).

Owen, H. D. "The 'Stages of Ascent' in Hebrews 5:11-6:3", *NTS* 3 (1956-57).

Perrin, N. *The Kingdom of God in the Teaching of Jesus* (Philadelphia, c. 1963).

—— *Rediscovering the Teaching of Jesus* (New York, c. 1967).

Pirst, L. *La Sainte Bible* (Paris, 1938).

Pool, D. de Sola, *The Oldest Aramaic Prayer the Kaddish* (Leipzig, 1909), reprinted as *The Kaddish* (New York, 1964).

—— (ed.). *The Traditional Prayer Book for Sabbath Festivals* (New York, c. 1960).

Pope, M. H. *Job* (Garden City, c. 1965).

—— "ʿAm HaʿArez", *ID* (New York, c. 1962).

Preisendanz, K. *Papyri Graecae Magicae* (Leipzig, Berlin, 1928-31).

Proksch, O. "ἅγιος . . .", *TDNT* I.

Pryke, J. "Baptism and Communion in the Light of Qumran", *RQ* 5 (1966).

Quell, G. "ἀγαπάω", *TWNT* I.

Rabin, C. *Qumran Studies* (Oxford, 1957).

—— "Alexander Jannaeus and the Pharisees", *JJS* 7 (1956).

Rad, G. von. *Der Heilige Krieg im alten Israel* (Zürich, 1951).

—— *Theologie des Alten Testamentes*, (München, 1960).

—— *OT Theology*, tr. D. M. G. Stalker (Edinburgh, 1965).

—— "Life and Death in the OT", *TDNT* II.

Reimarus, H. S. "Von dem Zwecke Jesu und seiner Jünger", *Fragmente des Wolfenbüttelschen Ungenannten*, ed. G. E. Lessing (Berlin, 1895).

Ritschl. A. *The Christian Doctrine of Justification and Reconciliation*, English tr. and ed. by H. R. Mackintosh and A. B. Macaulay (Edinburgh, 1902).

Roberts, C. H. "The Kingdom of Heaven (Lk. 17: 21)", *HTR* 41 (1948).

Robinson, J. A. T., *Jesus and His Coming* (New York, c. 1957).

—— "The Baptism of John and the Qumran Community", *HTR* 50 (1957).

Rosenberg, R. A. "Jesus, Isaac, and the Suffering Servant", *JBL* 84 (1965).

Roth, C. "Zealots — A Jewish Religious Sect", *Judaism* 8 (1959).

Roth, W. M. "The Anonymity of the Suffering Servant", *JBL* 83 (1964).

Rowley, H. H. "Jewish Proselyte Baptism and the Baptism of John", *HUCA* 15 (1940).

Sabourin, L. *Rédemption Sacrificielle* (Paris, 1961).

Schmidt, K. L., H. Kleinknecht, K. G. Kuhn, and G. von Rad. *Basileia*, *TDNT*, I.

Schweitzer, A. *The Quest of the Historical Jesus, a Critical Study of its Progress from Reimarus to Wrede*, tr. W. Montgomery (London, 1910).

—— *The Mystery of the Kingdom of God*, tr. W. Lowrie (New York, 1901, 1950²).

Seidensticker, P. "Die Gemeinschaftsform der religiösen Gruppen des Spätjudentums und der Urkirche", *LA* 9 (1959).

Sellin, E. "Die Lösung des deuterojesajanischen Gottesknechtsrätsel", *ZATW* 55 (1937).

Shusterman, A. "Sin", *UJE*.

Silberman, Jr., L. H. "Original Sin", *UJE*.

Simons, J. *The Geographical and Topographical Texts of the OT* (Leiden, 1959).

Sjöberg, E. "Wiedergeburt und Neuschöpfung im Palästinensischen Judentum", *ST* 4 (1951).

—— "Neuschöpfung in den Tote-Meer Rollen", *ST* 9 (1956).

Smith, M. "Palestinian Judaism in the First Century", *Israel, its Role in Civilization*, ed. M. Davis (New York, c. 1956).

? —— "The Dead Sea Sect in Relation to Ancient Judaism" *NTS* 7, (1960/61).

—— "The Description of the Essenes in Josephus and Philosophumena", *HUCA* 29 (1958).

Sowers, S. G. *The Hermeneutics of Philo and Hebrews* (Zürich, c. 1965).

Spicq, C. *Agapè dans le Nouveau Testament* (Paris, 1958, 1959), 3 vols.

Staples, X. "Some Aspects of Sin and Atonement", *JNES* 6 (1947).

Stauffer, E. "ἀγαπάω" (C-F), *TWNT* I.

Stendahl, K. "Hate, Non-retaliation, and Love", *HTR*, 55 (1962).

Stern, H. S. "The Knowledge of Good and Evil", *VT* 8 (1958).

Strauss, D. F. *Der Christus des Glaubens und der Jesus der Geschichte* (Berlin, 1865).

—— *A New Life of Jesus* (London, 1865), 2 vols.

Strugnell, J. "The Angelic Literature at Qumran — 4Q *Serek Šîrôt 'Olat Haššabbat*". *Supplements to Vetus Testamentum, Congress Volume, Oxford, 1959* (Leiden, 1960).

—— "Flavius Josephus and the Essenes: Antiquities XVIII, li, 22", *JBL* 77 (1958).

Sundberg, A. C. "Sadducees", *ID* IV.

Taylor, V. *The Gospel According to Mark* (London, 1953).

Thackeray, H. St. J. (ed. and tr.) *Josephus* (London, 1961).

Thierry, G. J. "The Pronunciation of the Tetragrammaton", *OS* (1948).

Thomas, D. W. "*Kelebh* 'dog': its Origin and Some Usages of it in the OT", *VT* 10 (1960).

Thomas, J. *Le Mouvement Baptiste en Palestine et Syrie* (Gembloux, 1935).

Toombs, L. E. "Barcosiba and Qumran", *NTS* 4 (1956-57).

Torrence, T. F. "Proselyte Baptism", *NTS* 1 (1954-55).

Tournay, R. J. "Les Chants du Serviteur dans la Seconde Partise d'Isaïe", *RB* 59 (1912).

Unnik, W. C. van. "Der Ausdruck ἙΩΣ ἘΣΧΑΤΟΥ ΤΗΣ ΓΗΣ (Apostelgeschichte 1:8) und sein Alttestamentlicher Hintergrund", *Studia Biblica et Semitica*.

—— "Die Motivierung der Feindesliebe in Lukas v. 32-35", *Nov.* 8 (1966).

Vaux, R. de. *Ancient Israel*, tr. J. McHugh (New York, c. 1962).

Vermès, G. "Baptism and Jewish Exegesis; New Light from Ancient Sources", *NTS* 4 (1957/58).

Volz, P. *Jüdische Eschatologie von Daniel bis Akiba* (Tübingen und Leipzig, 1903); second edition, *Die Eschatologie der jüdischen Gemeinde im neutestamentlichen Zeitalter* (Tübingen, 1934).

Vries, S. J. de. "Sin, Sinners", *IDB* 4.

—— "The Fall", *ID* II.

Vriezen, Th. C. "Prophecy and Eschatology", *Congress Volume, Supplement to VT* (Leiden, 1953).

Weisenberg, E. "The Jubilee of Jubilees", *RQ* 3 (1961).

Weiss, J. *Die Predigt Jesu vom Reich Gottes* (Göttingen, 1892; 1900²).

Werblowsky, R. J. Z. "On the Baptismal Rite According to St. Hippolytus", *Studia Patristica*, ed. K. Aland and F. L. Cross (Berlin, 1957).

Wieder, N. *The Jedaean Scrolls and Karaism* (London, c. 1962).

Williams, A. L. "The Tetragrammaton-Yahweh, Name or Surrogate?", *ZAW* 54 (1936).

Williams, N. P. *The Ideas of the Fall and of Original Sin* (New York, 1927).

Wilson, R. McL. "The NT in the Gnostic Gospel of Mary", *NTS* 3 (1956/57).

Windisch, H. "Zum Problem der Kindertaufe im Urchristentum", *ZNTW* 28 (1929).

Wolfson, H. A. *Philo* (Cambridge, 1948).

Workman, H. B. "Crusades", *Encyclopaedia of Religion and Ethics*, ed. J. Hastings (New York, 1912).

Worrell, W. H. (ed.). *Fragments from the Cairo Genizah in the Freer Collection* (New York, c. 1927).

Woude, A. S. van der. "Melchizedek als himmlische Erlösergestalt in den neugefundenen eschatologischen Midrashim aus Qumran Höhle XI", *OS* 14 (1965).

Wrede, W. *Judas, Petros und Johannesbriefe* (Bonn, 1924).

Wright, W. *Apocryphal Acts of the Apostles* (London, 1871).

Yadin, Y. "A Midrash on II Sam. 7 and Ps. 1-2 (4Q Florilegium)", *IEJ* 9 (1959).

Zeller, E. *Outlines of the History of Greek Philosophy*, rev. W. Nestle, tr. L. R. Palmer. (New York, 1955).

Zink, J. K. "Uncleanness and Sin, A Survey of Job 14:4 and Psalm 51:7", *VT* 17 (1967).

AUTHOR INDEX

GENERAL INDEX